D1572529

1/30/15
$35.00

THE HUMAN EROS

AMERICAN PHILOSOPHY

Douglas R. Anderson and Jude Jones, series editors

THE HUMAN EROS

Eco-ontology and the Aesthetics of Existence

THOMAS M. ALEXANDER

FORDHAM UNIVERSITY PRESS   NEW WORK   2013

CHABOT COLLEGE LIBRARY

BH
39
.A43
2013

Copyright © 2013 Fordham University Press

All rights reserved. No part of this publication may be reproduced,
stored in a retrieval system, or transmitted in any form or by any
means—electronic, mechanical, photocopy, recording, or any
other—except for brief quotations in printed reviews, without the
prior permission of the publisher.

Fordham University Press has no responsibility for the persistence
or accuracy of URLs for external or third-party Internet websites
referred to in this publication and does not guarantee that any
content on such websites is, or will remain, accurate or appropriate.

Fordham University Press also publishes its books in a variety of
electronic formats. Some content that appears in print may not
be available in electronic books.

Library of Congress Cataloging-in-Publication Data

Alexander, Thomas M., 1952–
The human eros : eco-ontology and the aesthetics of existence /
Thomas Alexander. — 1st ed.
p. cm. — (American philosophy)
Includes bibliographical references and index.
ISBN 978-0-8232-5120-9 (cloth : alk. paper) —
ISBN 978-0-8232-5121-6 (pbk. : alk. paper)
1. Aesthetics. 2. Philosophy, American—20th century.
3. Dewey, John, 1859–1952. 4. Santayana, George, 1863–1952. I. Title.
BH39.A43 2013
191—dc23
2012041923

Printed in the United States of America
15 14 13 5 4 3 2 1
First edition

*For my sons, Adam Hartley Alexander and
Nathan Blake Alexander*

Go in beauty

And for Ka

Contents

PART III: AESTHETICS OF EXISTENCE

PART IV: SPIRIT AND PHILOSOPHY

Acknowledgments

There are a great many people to whom I owe a debt of personal and intellectual gratitude, but several deserve mention here.

First of all I am grateful for the persistence of my colleague (and an editor of the series in which this volume appears) Douglas Anderson, who encouraged me to gather some of my essays in book form. I am also indebted to Helen Tartar of Fordham University Press for her warm support of this project and for her gracious, supportive patience, a bodhisattva for authors.

I have been fortunate in communities of colleagues with whom to discuss and share the life of philosophy, especially those in my department at Southern Illinois University at Carbondale and the members of the Society for the Advancement of American Philosophy. I owe special gratitude to my former colleagues, Mark Johnson, an inspiration from the start, and Genie Gatens-Robinson, whose informed feeling of the natural world has been a touchstone. You opened my eyes. I owe Tao Jiang and Douglas Berger many thanks for their patient help in my efforts to understand Asian thought. I also deeply appreciate the close, insightful, critical discussion of my work by Jim Garrison and Bill Myers. They were especially helpful with the material that went into this book. David Hildebrand and Gregory Pappas also deserve heartfelt thanks for their critical encouragement over the years: *un abrazo*. Words fail in expressing all I owe, intellectually and emotionally, to Felicia E. Kruse, philosopher, editor, and beloved wife.

Thank you all.

Some of these essays, in their original form, appeared in various forums: "Pragmatic Imagination," "The Moral Imagination," "Santayana's Sage," and "The Being of Nature" were published in *The Transactions of the Charles S. Peirce Society*. "Love Calls Us to Things of This World" and "Beauty and the Labyrinth of Evil" appeared in *Overheard in Seville: The Bulletin of the Santayana Society*. "Eros and Spirit" appeared in *The Pluralist*. "Dewey's Denotative-Empirical Method" appeared in *The Journal of Speculative Philosophy*. "The Human Eros" appeared in *Philosophy and the Reconstruction of Culture*, ed. John Stuhr (Albany: State University of New York Press, 1993). "Educating the Democratic Heart" appeared in *The New Scholarship on Dewey*, ed. Jim Garrison (Dordrecht, NL: Kluwer, 1885). "The Aesthetics of Reality" appeared in *Dewey's Logical Theory: New Studies and Interpretations*, ed. Tom Burke et al. (Nashville: Vanderbilt University Press, 2003). "Between Being and Emptiness" appeared in *In Dewey's Wake: Unfinished Work of Pragmatic Reconstruction*, ed. William J. Gavin (Albany: State University of New York Press, 2003). All have been revised.

The standard reference for John Dewey's work is the critical edition, *The Collected Works of John Dewey 1882–1953*, edited by Jo Ann Boydston (Southern Illinois University Press, 1969–91), published as *The Early Works* (EW), *The Middle Works* (MW), and *The Later Works* (LW). References to these works will include volume and page number.

THE HUMAN EROS

INTRODUCTION

The essays gathered here, spanning over two decades, represent my own attempts to explore what may be called an "aesthetics of human existence" in terms of an ecological, humanistic naturalism.[1] They include extensions of my earlier interpretation of the philosophy of John Dewey as well as studies of the thought of Ralph Waldo Emerson and George Santayana. I have also tried to establish connections with Asian philosophy, especially Buddhism, and with Native American wisdom traditions. The overall trajectory of these writings is to contextualize the ideas of "pragmatism" and "naturalism," as popularly understood, within a broader and deeper philosophy of experience. This, too, is a loaded term. "Experience," in the Deweyan sense used here, is *our shared cultural inhabitation of the world.* Art and the aesthetic, instead of being pushed

---

1. I hope to make clear what these terms connote, but I caution that any word ending in "-ism," while sounding intellectual, is usually an excuse for unreflective, vague generalizations that mislead critical reflection.

{ *1* }

to the periphery of philosophy, as is customary, are here seen as central. Insofar as there is now a revival of "pragmatism" under way, the position taken in these essays may provide something of a shock. Many of the new pragmatists are really converts from the analytic tradition that made epistemology Queen of Philosophy. These neopragmatists for the most part are still epistemologists but are now "pragmatic" epistemologists. That is, epistemology is still Queen; it's just pragmatic now. The unsettling news from Dewey (following James) is that epistemology is not what philosophy is primarily about. In fact, Dewey called the tendency of philosophers to interpret everything in light of the problem of knowledge "*the* Philosophic Fallacy."[2] A good deal of what he wrote for his essays in *Studies in Logical Theory* in 1903 and from then on was an effort to contextualize questions of knowing within the larger world of lived experience. For James and Dewey, pragmatism was only part of a much larger, complex philosophy of experience. This is to say that the *meaning* of existence is not limited to, much less coextensive with, *knowledge*, not even knowledge that is "pragmatically" acquired. This is a lesson that still needs to be learned by many now flocking to what glibly passes as "pragmatism." Furthermore, the vistas opened by this larger conception of philosophy are still relatively unexplored. Thus, the essays presented here can be thought of as explorations of a wilderness.

When my book *The Horizons of Feeling* was published, there was just the barest beginning of a revival of interest in Dewey. The lonely struggle by serious scholars like John J. McDermott, H. S. Thayer, James Gouinlock, and others to preserve and advance understanding of the richness of classical American thought had recently been given an unexpected boost from Richard Rorty's *Philosophy and the Mirror of Nature* (1979). Rorty undertook a critique of the whole project of analytic philosophy (which he had confidently once espoused), invoking not only the holy name of Wittgenstein, but the disregarded name of Dewey and the unmentionable name of Heidegger, viewed by many analytic philosophers as "not even a philosopher." Rorty played fast and loose with what he knew of Dewey— he surmised much and missed a great deal, though that did not lessen the confidence with which he made his insouciant pronouncements.

2. See *The Quest for Certainty* (LW, 4:232–33) and *Experience and Nature* (LW, 1:28). Dewey also calls this the "Intellectualist Fallacy."

One result of Rorty's bombshell was a growing reawakening of interest in Dewey beyond the scholars working in classical American philosophy. This was undertaken mostly by people sympathetic to Rorty's deconstructive rebellion. Nevertheless, given the general indifference to the history of philosophy in the dominant Anglophone philosophical movement, it did not rapidly become evident—except to the scholars—that Rorty's Dewey bore only a faint resemblance to the historical John Dewey. Rorty's portrayal of Dewey was similar to a "portrait" by Matisse or Picasso, something done more for the sake of the artistic effects than fidelity to the original. Besides presenting Dewey as an utter relativist, Rorty's Dewey was a deeply bifurcated person; there was a "good Dewey" who engaged in cultural criticism and a "bad Dewey" who frequently succumbed to the siren song of "Hegelian" metaphysics. In this view, Rorty was not alone, for the "two Deweys reading" already had a long history.

The Horizons of Feeling directly challenged the "two Deweys reading" by going back to Dewey's primary concern, the philosophy of experience, and understanding it, as Dewey himself explicitly stated, in terms of aesthetic experience. This approach also challenged the persistent, widespread effort to read Dewey simply as a "scientific naturalist" who espoused a philosophy called "instrumentalism" in which "*the* scientific method" had the last say. Methods of inquiry are legitimate areas of philosophical reflection, but they are not to be confused with the whole of experience. Thus Dewey uses the term "instrumentalism" (or, rarely, "pragmatism") only to refer to a *part* of his general philosophy, which he called "humanistic empiricism" (*Experience and Nature*) and "cultural naturalism" (*Logic: The Theory of Inquiry*). Dewey makes this absolutely clear in a letter to Corliss Lamont: "I have come to think of my own position as cultural or humanistic Naturalism. Naturalism, properly interpreted, seems to me a more adequate term than Humanism. Of course I have always limited my use of 'instrumentalism' to my theory of thinking and knowledge; the word 'pragmatism' I have used very little, and then with reserves."[3]

However much Dewey looked toward science *to illustrate* (but not to define) his view that the sort of thinking we employ in the inquiries we

---

3. Dewey to Corliss Lamont, Sept. 6, 1940, cited in Corliss Lamont, "New Light on Dewey's *Common Faith*," *The Journal of Philosophy* 58, no. 1 (1961): 26.

make in daily life simply gets refined in the procedures of the sciences (and all "arts" or skills), it did not affect his most radical claim: that not all experience is cognitive—that the noncognitive in fact sets the context for the sense of all cognitive inquiries—and that the culmination of experience, the aim of life, was in the embodied, lived experience of consummatory meaning. Philosophy for Dewey was "love of wisdom" in the sense it had for the ancient Greeks: a path to a choice-worthy way of life. Dewey embraced this wholeheartedly. So few philosophers today take this idea seriously that when they read Dewey they miss it by a mile. For them, Dewey, like any good philosopher, *has* to be interested in the problem of knowledge, front and center. Perhaps (as I suggest in the essays) we should change the name of what is now called "philosophy" to "philepistemy." It is more tragic than ironic that Dewey himself has been misread again and again as someone who thought that the natural sciences had the last word on everything. First and foremost, Dewey was concerned with the potential richness of *meaning* experience could have. He valued inquiry because it was capable of rendering our lived experience more meaningful. He called it "experimental" not because all questions were to be referred to the natural sciences but because he thought the habit of mind of open, exploratory, communal approach to problems was more fruitful than the closed-minded, dogmatic, solipsistic approach. Again, Dewey appealed to science as an example, not as the sole authority. It is more accurate to describe Dewey's overall philosophy as a philosophy of meaningful experience, as "humanistic empiricism" or "cultural naturalism," than as a philosophy of scientific method, as "pragmatism" or "instrumentalism."

It was the aim of *The Horizons of Feeling* to bring this fundamental theme to attention, for it affects everything else in understanding Dewey's thought, including his instrumentalism. One recurrent aim of some of these essays is to expand on what I believe is a fairer and more comprehensive reading of a great thinker than that which commonly passes in an ever-swelling tide of secondary literature. More important, I have tried to scout out where these core ideas can take us. It would not be wrong to see these essays as extensions of the philosophy of experience interpreted as "cultural naturalism"—*if* "experience" is understood as *culture*, our shared, embodied, symbolic life, *the meaningful ways we inhabit the world*, and not as sensations, nerve stimulations, or brain events, and *if* "nature" is understood to be manifest most fully in its most complex events (creating a musical composition, raising a child, falling in love, sustaining a friendship, understanding the Pythagorean theorem, or living with the loss of a loved one) rather than primarily physics. Complex events like these, for Dewey, are *more revelatory* of nature than what is discovered in physics, chemistry, or neurology. To know events is one thing and involves methods of inquiry (as in physics, biology, history, etc.); to accord them their full ontological status as being what they are is another. An event is a happening ("*res*," plural "*rēs*," in Dewey's terminology) and its being includes its meaning; it is a disclosure of a potentiality of nature.

The fate of Dewey's philosophy reveals how nearly hopeless it was for him to try to infuse new meanings into old words like "experience" or "nature," words whose philosophical connotations were established in the days of Locke and Newton when the English philosophical vocabulary came of age. I believe it led to Dewey being perhaps the most persistently misread philosopher in history. However much Dewey used examples like geology or farming to illustrate what *he* meant by "experience"— skilled human interactions with environments, the ways we are *in* the world—his readers could hear little more than what Locke meant: "ideas" that somehow separate us *from* the world. Likewise, however much he used "nature" to mean "events of all sorts," his readers heard "whatever physics says." And so Dewey's writings were constantly mistranslated back into the familiar dialect of British empiricism. At the end of his life Dewey was so frustrated by this he proposed changing the title of *Experience and Nature* to *Nature and Culture*. I think that Dewey's attempt to change the semantic focus of established words like "experience," "nature," "means," "end," and a host of others has failed as a rhetorical move. And so the outlook developed here has relied on certain key terms and phrases that I hope are unique enough to draw attention to the ideas, avoiding misassociations, without being so arcane as to be opaque.

Generally, the position that gradually evolved in these essays has three overlapping areas: (1) the urge of the human psyche toward the full experience of meaning and value, "the Human Eros" as I call it, (2) a philosophy of civilization or cultural inhabitation that examines how the Human Eros weaves "spiritual ecologies" for itself through myth, symbol, archetypal tropes, and so on, and (3) an ontology that articulates an ecological sense of the being of nature or "eco-ontology." I hope already it is evident how poorly these areas map onto the current divisions of philosophy, divisions that reflect a particular institutionalized culture of philosophy more than what "Philosophy itself" is. The synoptic term for the position I set forth might be Dewey's own, "cultural naturalism," but perhaps "humanistic naturalism" or "ecological humanism" would be better. These themes developed only gradually, as I said, but a brief retrospective overview of them might be helpful in establishing the continuity of the essays.

The Human Eros

I propose that human beings seek to live with a concrete, embodied experience of meaning and value in the world. We *need* to feel that our own lives are meaningful and have value. This is a biological claim insofar as if this need is denied, we either die or become filled with destructive rage. Long ago, I was impressed by Viktor Frankl's *Man's Search for Meaning*, which recounts his experience as a prisoner in Auschwitz. Frankl, a trained psychiatrist, was confronted with the question: What could he do for his fellow inmates in an environment that was created to strip away any sense of meaning or value from their lives? He tried to help them find something of value in their lives, to create some meaning, even if it is only the attitude one takes toward suffering. Prisoners who despaired inevitably died. Frankl concluded, "Man's search for meaning is the primary motivation in his life and not a 'secondary rationalization' of instinctual drives. This meaning is unique and specific in that it must and can be fulfilled by him alone; only then does it achieve a significance which will satisfy his own *will* to meaning."[4] Frankl is right, though I would say it is more a desire or need—hence "eros"—than a "will."

The Nazi "final solution" is an extreme example of how one group of human beings tries to destroy others by denying them meaning and value, by denying fulfillment to their Human Eros. But we can find plenty of less explicit instances around us of people who are constrained to live in an environment in which others force a sense of worthlessness and insignificance upon them. Growing up not far from the Pueblo and Navajo reservations, I saw many cases of Native Americans who lived in the

---

4. Viktor Frankl, *Man's Search for Meaning*, 3rd ed. (New York: Simon & Schuster, 1984), 105. From his experience, Frankl developed a method of "logotherapy," which formed a part of what is sometimes called the "third force" of "humanistic psychology" (psychoanalysis and behaviorism being the first and second "forces," respectively). Erich Fromm, Ernest Becker, and Rollo May are other examples.

shadowlands of despair. This desperation was not just due to poverty but to the conflict they existentially experienced by living in two cultures with highly dissonant values and with the dominant Anglo culture constantly trying to marginalize the indigenous one.[5] When we see an individual case in which a parent abuses a child or one partner in a marriage gains self-worth by devaluing the other, we see the relationship as "sick" and often urge intervention. Why we cannot so easily notice this when it is between groups of people is puzzling, though repressed guilt and result-ant denial are no doubt partly responsible. The point is that we *do* recog-nize the removal of meaning and value from someone's life as a way of destroying that individual. Conversely, we recognize that when human beings do have a strong sense of meaning and value in their lives they seem filled with an affirmation of life (an affirmation that can be expressed as self-sacrifice for a person, cause, or ideal). What we need is a world that makes sense and sustains values that present us with meaningful choices so that we may lead lives that are experienced as fulfilling. *This* is where "the problem of meaning" begins. A great deal of what we do both indi-vidually and collectively is striving to sustain the Human Eros, either through energetic creativity or through negation of those things that are seen to be threatening to it. (It may be that the problem of fundamental-ism in many religions comes from the sense of fear and anger its adher-ents feel in reaction to what they perceive as the destruction of the very world that gives meaning to their lives.) One "demonstration" of the Human Eros as a central feature of human existence lies simply in asking what happens to a person's life when all sense of meaning and value is stripped away.

Connected with the thesis of the Human Eros are some auxiliary claims. First of all, I believe with Dewey that our engagement with the world, our undergone or felt way of "being in the world," is primarily qualitative, not cognitive. Our unconscious as well as conscious attunement is a condi-tion upon which thought and inquiry depend. Consciousness is simply the focused part of this wide field, and it is fundamentally concerned with

---

5. This is the theme of Leslie Marmon Silko's fine novel *Ceremony*. The Diné (Navajo) idea of a "skinwalker," or witch, is someone who (1) tries to stop the flow of life and remain perpetually youthful, (2) keeps wealth for himself alone, and (3) lives as an individual with no connection to a community. The white culture surrounding Diné on all sides of their reservation could be said from the Diné point of view to be a culture of witches, for it is characterized by (1) obsession with per-petual youth, (2) materialism, and (3) individualism.

temporal transition. The qualitative field is often neglected, and yet it is constantly, pervasively present. One reason why Dewey finds the aesthetic experience of philosophical importance is that in such experiences this dimension is not only brought to consciousness but is acutely felt as the guiding "sense" of the experience.[6]

Also, temporality—"temporal quality" in Dewey's words, not "temporal order"—pervades our existence.[7] Our sense of temporality involves not only dimensions of past and future, but all sorts of complex modalities of attitude that are better exhibited in the tenses, aspects, and moods of inflected languages than in formal logic.[8] William James was right in describing our personal experience as a "flow" or "stream" that cannot be captured dynamically by concepts. Concepts are "graspings" or "cuts" made in the flow to help us have coordinated responses to the world.[9] They help us organize the world so we may act in it. But when concepts are used to understand experience itself a problem emerges. Bergson called our effort to understand this dynamic experience by means of concepts the "cinematographical mechanism of thought"; the flow of inherently temporal experience is now read as being "really" like a series of fixed photographic frames. This, Bergson argued, essentially obliterates temporality, reducing it to a spatialized mathematical linear succession.[10] Bergson's criticism of philosophers trying to approach the question of temporality through basically spatialized concepts is as relevant today as when he made the claim in 1907. Dewey argued that time was most fully understood in terms of personal history, the unfolding of a life.[11]

There is something to Martin Heidegger's rather sweeping charge that ever since Parmenides fixed *the* meaning of Being as the indicative present tense, third person singular, "It-Is" (*esti*), Western thought has been toiling in the wake of this fateful turn. For me this is most evident in the fixation upon the primacy of identity over continuity—even to the point of trying to understand continuity in terms of identity. While I do not see

6. See Dewey's essay "Qualitative Thought" in LW, 5:243–62.

7. See *Experience and Nature* (LW, 1:91–92).

8. See Joan Bybee, Revere Perkins, and William Pagliuca, *The Evolution of Grammar: Tense, Aspect and Modality in the Languages of the World* (Chicago: University of Chicago Press, 1994).

9. As the Latin root of "concept," *concipio*, "to lay hold of," reveals. Compare German *Begriff.*

10. See William James, *The Principles of Psychology*, ch. 9, "The Stream of Thought," and Henri Bergson, *Creative Evolution*, ch. 4.

11. See Dewey's essay "Time and Individuality" in LW, 14:98–114.

this, as Heidegger does, as a fundamental "forgetfulness of Being," I do think this fixation on identity has had significant consequences for Western thought. It is inherently linked to Dewey's point about the "Philosophic Fallacy," philosophers' assumptions that all experiences are *also* instances of knowing. One key theme of these essays, then, is the effort to put transformation and continuity in the place of identity. Each moment is an instance of transformation, not a bare identity. Continuity invokes ideas of process, probability, and degree (for which Peirce coined the term "synechism").[12] The idea of transformation, marginalized in Western philosophy, is a central theme in Native American traditions, epitomized in the figure of the Trickster (Coyote, Inktomi, Raven, Nanabozho, etc.). It is also a central theme in the Buddhist idea of "emptiness" or "inter-being" (*śūnyatā*).

Imagination, therefore, also plays an important role in the position developed here. I agree with Mark Johnson (the influence of whose work can be seen throughout) when he says, "Without imagination, nothing in the world could be meaningful. Without imagination, we could never make sense of experience. Without imagination, we could never reason toward knowledge of reality."[13] Imagination is temporal and modal. I describe imagination as "the ability to see the actual in light of the possible." This includes the fund of historical experience that exhibits the play of possibility in the past and constitutes the funded background of actuality in the present. Our possibilities grow out of the actuality of the present and the past. Also with Johnson, I think imagination is "bodily." That is, it is not a mental faculty, a "picture-making" power, but is a dynamic structuring of experience that arises from our lived embodiment; initially it gives us patterns of possible actions that are rooted in our own vital human form but gives us these possibilities *as* possibilities, and so open to consideration apart from immediate action.[14] Our lived body provides many basic projective schematic structure patterns that guide action and thought, which then become the ways through which we come to conceptualize the possible. One prominent example of

---

12. See especially Peirce's essays "The Law of Mind" and "Evolutionary Love," both in *Collected Papers*, Vol. VI, ed. Charles Hartshorne and Paul Weiss, (Harvard University Press, 1935), paragraph 202 f. and 272 f., and in *The Essential Peirce*, Vol. 1, ed. Nathan Houser and Christian Kloesel (Indiana University Press, 1992), p. 312 f. and p. 352 f.

13. Mark Johnson, *The Body in the Mind* (Chicago: University of Chicago Press, 1987), ix.

14. There is also a deep affinity in this view with the thought of Maurice Merleau-Ponty.

this, as Johnson shows, is the important (if unnoticed) role of metaphor in reasoning.

I would like to add to Johnson's view that beyond physical bodily structures there are social ones. In other words, "the body" (the root of our metaphors by which we make sense of the world) must be understood socially and not just organically. "The body" would include structures of interaction between people (e.g., friend-enemy, mother-child) as well as our crucial imaginative ability of "taking the role of the other" in order to help regulate the meaning of our behavior. This view was generally framed by Dewey in *Experience and Nature* and developed in more detail in the lectures of George Herbert Mead, posthumously published as *Mind, Self and Society*. Through this mutual imaginative ability, symbolic action and symbols themselves become possible, as does the establishment of a world of shared experience, in which "you" and "I" become a "we." The creation of symbols transformed our mode of existence; we could expand the range of the possible in the present, changing the meaning of situations. The establishment of symbolic life allowed for the creation of culture as something passed from generation to generation. In other words, the life of symbols in all their interrelations and transformations is part of our "embodiment." Culture as a form of life is the condition of human experience and so of human existence as human.

Human temporality is also constituted by the organic form of a "lifetime." The pattern of human life, or Vita Humana, is not a succession of events, a chronology; it is an organic structure of existence, a *life*, and its events constitute a *lifetime*. A lifetime is not just a personal or individual narrative going from birth to death; it can also be a social and historical narrative. Narrative incorporates its parts in terms of a growing, organic whole. A human lifetime is an event in a social and historical place and time. Our temporality is engaged from the beginning through coexistence—at the very start in the womb. As children we experience growth and learning. Indeed, education is a crucial aspect of human existence, for without it the new generations would lose the civilizing contact with the culture of the past and that culture itself would die. Education is the vital transition of culture from one generation to the next, an ongoing dialogue between death and life. Insofar as society focuses on the isolated individual and makes the individual a series of momentary, transient feelings and desires, the idea of the Vita Humana gets lost. One strange instance of this in philosophy is the now venerable approach to ethics as simply a question of rules and actions with no concept of a human *life* or a *lifetime* entering in.[15]

The Human Eros and the idea of the Vita Humana constitute a continuum for an aesthetics of human existence, "aesthetics" here being used more in the sense of an "existential phenomenology" or even "philosophical anthropology" of existence than "philosophy of art and 'aesthetic' experience" in the customary contemporary usage. It is more than bizarre that there is no central "subject" in the standard subdivisions of contemporary Anglophone philosophy that is focused on human nature itself. "Philosophy of mind" is a thin, poor shadow. Our full existence as human beings, with lives that are lived through, is addressed either in terms of our being either knowing machines or faceless "agents" invoking moral rules. The idea of the Vita Humana is meant to designate the idea of the human life, driven by the need for experiencing meaning and value, as a more fundamental philosophical framework than either epistemology or ethics.

Spiritual Ecology

As an extension of the Human Eros, we might designate culture as constituting the "environment of meaning and value" that the Human Eros weaves for itself in its inhabitation of the earth. We are *in* nature *through* culture. Human beings need to live meaningful lives and cultural environments are conditions for that possibility. They are, so to speak, "ecologies of the spirit." They transform a biophysical environment into a "world." Different cultures establish different forms, but the forms are not "artificial" in the sense that is used in the dismissive comment that implies "cultures are relative." Cultures grow in specific regions and are creative responses to those regions. They bear the mark of their homes even when transplanted. They usually contain a set of symbols that help render the environment meaningful, not simply in a cognitive sense, but in the sense of bearing deep value and importance.

---

15. Of course, this is also the concern of Alasdair MacIntyre's *After Virtue*. But originally I encountered the idea long before in my grandfather's study of the Native American worldview; see Hartley Burr Alexander, *The World's Rim* (Lincoln: University of Nebraska Press, 1953). The term "Vita Humana" is taken from him. The idea is developed in a projected book, *Living Mind*, the draft for which was published in *The Pluralist* (vol. 3, no. 1, 2008).

"Rain" for the Pueblo peoples is not a name for a meteorological event: It is life, it is a gift of the ancestors, it comes from a feathered sky serpent, Avanyu, a god who floats above the desert, clothed in clouds, with a tongue of lightning and great beards of falling water; it purifies and gives life to the world. The symbol is not a false representation, something that could be summarized in propositions. It is an expression of a whole way of life and the reverence a native dweller of the dry Southwest feels toward precious rain. Some time ago, when the ruin of a thirteenth-century sacred *kiva* (an underground ceremonial chamber) was excavated near Albuquerque, it was found to have strange but beautiful frescoes of parrots spitting water, flying rattlesnakes, and lightning coming from pots. The Pueblo Indian workers helping excavate the site immediately knew what they meant. Indeed, the very structure of the kiva itself was expressive of a whole orientation to the world. A kiva is dug into the earth, for it was from the earth that the first people emerged. The sacred orientation is *earthward*. Contrast this with the Western orientation of the sacred as *skyward*, an idea powerfully expressed in medieval cathedrals. Heaven is "up" and God is "outside" of the universe altogether. Western culture is challenged in trying to develop a sacred connection to the environment. I once saw a film of a Hopi singing to a small seedling of corn with great tenderness—how else would you address the Corn Mother? I see one of the major problems facing our environmental crisis as the basic anesthetic relationship members of industrial cultures have to their environments.

If we are to care for the planet, we must feel that care existentially, that is, aesthetically. How can we genuinely take care of something we don't "care" for? Of course, the Anglo-American business culture relates itself to the world in a different way—as economic resource and exchange. The metaphors drawn from this life pervade our thought more and more. Take as an example the schema "education is a business."[16] Our administrators tell us that a university is a corporation that sells a commodity to consumers. Teachers are manufacturers of "student credit hours" and are measured by productivity standards. Even in the rarefied atmosphere of philosophy, we say that we "buy" or "don't buy" an idea. My point is that

---

16. The pervasive way metaphors guide thinking has been compellingly analyzed in the work of Mark Johnson and George Lakoff. See especially their *Metaphors We Live By* (Chicago: University of Chicago Press, 1980) and *Philosophy in the Flesh* (New York: Basic Books, 1999).

cultures are as much "creative responses to the world" as the actions of single organisms; they are situated and situating. Some cultures may be richer in serving the Human Eros than others, just as some ecologies promote biodiversity and others reduce it. In this sense, then, our forms of cultural inhabitation are "ecologies" for the Human Eros and can be studied in terms of a general philosophical ecology or "eco-ontology."

The philosophical study of cultures as ecologies of the human spirit is another important area that has by and large remained ignored by contemporary philosophy. It is something completely missed by "ethics" or "political theory." Cultural anthropologists, especially "symbolic anthropologists" such as Clifford Geertz, Victor Turner, and Mary Douglas, should be resources for philosophers, perhaps more than neuroscientists or artificial intelligence experts. Of course, when most Anglophone philosophers think of "real science" they think of physics and not of something like anthropology. But our prioritization of physics is itself the function of a deep cultural narrative—a Mythos, in my terminology—of which we are only subliminally aware, one that has been unfolding for the past five hundred years of the "modernist" revolution. Nevertheless, I believe philosophy needs to pay great attention to the sorts of environments various cultures weave to serve the Human Eros, and anthropology is of far more use for this than physics. A cultural concept of philosophy calls for a wide literacy in world civilizations and the development of nuanced semiotic skills rather than just the highly formalized abstractive transformations of symbolic logic. In a sense, I agree with Ernst Cassirer and Susanne K. Langer that philosophy is (or should be) in part the study of "symbolic forms."

Thus, I have undertaken some cultural explorations in the following essays, in the areas of both Asian thought and Native American wisdom traditions.[17] I have also employed a set of ideas that are perhaps best set forth in the final essay of this book, "Eros and Spirit." The most important of these ideas is that of "Mythos." (Not "myth"; I leave the word "myth" to its colloquial English usage, a "false story"; there is no hope of rescuing it.) A Mythos is an important story that helps establish the

17. Just as I distinguish philosophy as "love of wisdom" from philepistemy, "love of knowledge," recognizing that the two have overlapping common areas, so I distinguish inherited cultural "wisdom traditions" from philosophy per se. Insofar as philosophy is concerned with wisdom, it should study and listen to wisdom traditions.

meaning of the self, a people, and the world. Mythos is crucial to the Human Eros. Let us begin with a personal example: Each of us has a set of stories about ourselves that lie "ready to hand" to convey the sense of who we are, where we are, and what we are doing. Some of these may be fairly simple, like telling someone where one grew up or what we do for a living. But in that story there will be certain places that have deep meaning: the place by the creek where the bright orange eastern newts or "red efts" lived; the ever-present, looming mountain of constantly changing light that overshadowed one's hometown; the sight and smell of endless cornfields all around the little Iowa town; the bluffs above the Mississippi; and the great river itself. In telling stories of such places that are special to us—that have come to constitute part of our very identity to the extent that if memories of them were lost we would be changed—we devote care in describing them that goes beyond a feeling of fondness. Such places and the stories we tell about them can be sacred to us, and sacred things must be handled with care. Such things are part of who we are and speak of how we came to be who we are, what we care about, what "home" means.

There are also Mythoi that lie at our deep core, stories or events that are so important and so personal that they are not carelessly shared—and sometimes they are suppressed from our consciousness but are determinative structures nonetheless, perhaps more so as a result. Growing up constantly needing a father's approval that rarely came or living with a neurotic mother who was unceasingly and sharply critical, losing a close friend to death, having to kill another human being on a distant battlefield—these are core Mythoi. Insofar as we approach them when they are ours, it is with the terror and fascination (*tremendum et fascinans*) that Rudolf Otto said characterized (in part) the experience of the holy. There are also Mythoi that project what might be called "life narratives" for ourselves. They account for what we think we are doing with our lives: following my true love of music rather than making money, sacrificing myself to care for a dying spouse, achieving fame, power and wealth or setting it all aside.

Cultures have ongoing Mythoi just as individuals do, ranging from grand, over-arching "meta-narratives" (America's "we are the story of freedom" Mythos for example) to the Mythoi of religions, professions, or one's ethnic group or tribe, including the fate of one's people, such as the inherited legacy of slavery or the holocaust. Although Mythoi *can* take on a narrative form, I do not mean for them to be thought of as just articulated narratives—indeed, articulated narratives of Mythoi are often attempts to express the deeper Mythoi of a culture or oneself. Most Mythoi exist as symbols, many on a semiconscious or subconscious level. Mythoi may be embodied in a variety of ways, such as rituals, customs, political institutions, works of art, even inherited memories. There is, for example, the Mythos of Philosophy as it functions in the Western tradition. We philosophers tell a story to ourselves as well as to our beginning students, "How Philosophy Came to Be." Its overarching narrative is the liberation of reason from myth (our Mythos wants us to think we have escaped Mythos!). The Greeks dismissed the gods and their own curiosity about the cosmos led to science. Then, after succumbing to superstition for a thousand years (when people argued over how many angels could dance on a pinhead), about five hundred years ago, thanks to philosophy, science revived and gave birth to our mastery of nature as well as to liberty and "The Rights of Man." And here we are today! And so we see colleagues toiling away on their articles that concern hardly anyone, fighting Lilliputian wars that will be forgotten in a few years; but they, consciously or not, are ritualistically embodying a Mythos, so much so that if one challenges this Mythos to the one holding it (arguing, for instance, that the six orthodox Hindu systems are philosophy), the person will get quite defensive and irate and declare something to the effect that "*That* is not philosophy!" (Our Anglophone philosophers are really quite tribal.) Of course, there are different Mythoi of the Origin of Philosophy in India and China. Indian philosophy arose in the Upanishads with claims by the various sages to have a wisdom (concerning the ultimate reality of Brahman and the truth of reincarnation) that went beyond the Vedas, and the subsequent development involved responding to the question whether the Vedas were ultimately to be rejected (as with Buddhism) or integrated (as with Vedanta). Philosophy in China begins with a concern in recovering the "Way" (*Dao*) of living in harmony. My point is that philosophical traditions narrate their own Mythoi about what philosophy is and how it came to be, and most Western philosophers are quite oblivious to their own mythic self-understanding, nowhere more apparent than in their rejection of "myth."

In discussing Mythos, I distinguish tropes, types or tropic symbols, avatars, and constellations. This terminology need not detain us much now. Tropes are the deep, constitutive meanings and values of a culture: Freedom for Americans, Obedience to the Law for Judaism, Logos for the Greeks. Tropes are embodied in a variety of types or tropic symbols. Think of the many ways in which "Freedom" gets represented in American culture, from the stock characters of The Cowboy or The Rugged Individual to Fourth of July celebrations to elections to American foreign policy. Avatars are the concrete, specific embodiments of types: John Wayne as Tom Doniphon in *The Man Who Shot Liberty Valance* or Harrison Ford as Han Solo. The hapless war in Vietnam was for us an attempt to embody an avatar of this trope of Freedom through the type of "defending democracy." We were reenacting the Mythos of our own Revolution oblivious to its being transplanted into a context in which we had become the colonial power. Finally, some cultural tropes are so closely and dynamically connected (not always harmoniously) that they form what I call "Constellations." Freedom is a Trope closely connected to Individualism for Americans. But it is also closely connected to the trope of "Law," so that we must tell stories about when being a nonconformist is good—Cool Hand Luke—and when it means one is simply an outlaw—Liberty Valance. A great deal of a culture's thought and art deals with exploring these close relationships and their tensions. The Greek tragedies or writings of the Hebrew prophets are prime examples of exploring core cultural ideas and their tensive relationships, but so is Thoreau's *Walden*.

Thus I believe that philosophy should incorporate the study of civilizations, examining the various ecologies of the spirit that give us forms of inhabitation, that give us *worlds*. A culture is a "home," an *oikos*. Cultures can be studied in terms of being responses to the Human Eros, providing it with the ecologies of meaning it needs to thrive. The study of cultural ecologies leads to the more general question of nature and the being of nature, which might be designated as "eco-ontology."

Eco-ontology

As a theme in the following essays, the topic of "eco-ontology" is most explicitly developed in two of the more metaphysically oriented discussions, "Between Being and Emptiness" and "The Being of Nature." Since it is crucial as a reconstruction of naturalism, these essays are presented in the first section along with thematically related essays on Dewey. Besides suggesting the idea of "nature" as inter-related, evolving "natural histories" environmentally situated, the term designates the attempt to

rethink Western ontology, the philosophy of being, in terms of nature—
this in contrast to the traditional attempt to think of nature in terms of
being. I am tempted, like Dewey, to use the familiar—too familiar—term
"naturalism," except that it, too, has probably been poisoned beyond
redemption. As noted, it commonly is taken to mean that nature is
whatever "science" says it is—"science" here being understood to be
whatever is most reductionistic: physics, neurology, or whatever. Those
who proclaim some sort of naturalism tend to exhibit what John Herman
Randall Jr. once called "nothing-but-er" philosophies, for example,
Hobbes's claim that nature is "nothing but" matter in motion. In terms
of our self-understanding, this temperament was represented several
decades ago by the behaviorists who flocked around B. F. Skinner; today
we have the reductive and eliminative materialists who turn toward
neurology and artificial intelligence. Such types of naturalism contrast
sharply with nonreductive versions, including the Deweyan view that
nature is not just what science, especially a "hard" science, says. For
Dewey, *nature is what nature does.* Events, *rēs*, are the manifest varieties
of existences of all types, *natura naturata,* but are seen as arising from
"Nature" understood as a creative matrix or potentiality, *natura naturans,*
for "nature" must include the possible and the potential, not just the
existent and actual. In other words, whatever legitimate causal conditions
one may discover for a given type of event, a full account of the event in
terms of its manifest ontological realization acknowledges that its "being"
is most completely found in its "doing." It is what we ask about when we
say "What happened?" or "What is going on?" And this tells us something about the nature of nature: an event discloses a genuine possibility
of existence, born from the womb of nature as it were.[18] If a poet com-
poses a poem or someone breaks a solemn promise, it tells us something
about *nature* and not only about ourselves. Coleridge's writing of "Kubla
Khan" cannot be understood simply as a brain event; "writing poetry" is
understood on the human level, and this tells us something about nature
in addition to humans being poetical creatures. (One wonders what an
eliminative materialist thinks is "really going on" when he presents a
paper!) Among the many events manifested in existence, the writing of

---

18. Both Greek *phusis* and Latin *natura* connote "that which is born" or "that which has arisen as
it is by nature." The correlated verbs *phuō* and *nascor* mean "to bring forth, give birth, grow, arise,
come to be."

poetry is one, and so shows us a real potentiality of nature as such. Nature is such that both poets and eliminative materialists are genuine possibilities. Thus one key theme in the understanding of nature put forth here is a recognition of "emergentism," the capacity of nature to generate new modes of existence and, with them, new sorts of events.

If the term "naturalism" could be rescued from its reductionist associations, it could be used. But I think it may be easier to experiment with a term like "eco-ontology" to counteract the gravitational weight of meaning in what is generally understood as "naturalism." The term "eco-ontology" also has the advantage of recognizing that philosophy itself must overcome its own habits of mind in order to rethink nature along genuinely ecological lines. We have theories of ecology that have not yet asked what ecological thinking is. Most of Western philosophy has posed the "question of being" in terms that resist an ecological outlook. Aristotle, great biologist as he was, thought of nature in terms of species, not in terms of relations of species and environments. Dewey's naturalism, by contrast, is one of the most impressive efforts to think along ecological lines, emphasizing the fundamental dynamism of the organism-environment interaction and the interrelated, temporal webs of events that have bearing on each other; i.e., situations. Though Dewey did not use the term "ecology" (which itself was hardly in use at the time), his position is thoroughly committed to what today would be recognized as an ecological way of thinking.[19] Thus the term "eco-ontology" refers to the endeavor to think of nature in terms of interactive systems, natural histories, diversity, process, change, and transformation.

It is crucial that philosophy endeavor to establish new conceptual pathways insofar as we must, as a species, develop ecologically sound modes of inhabitation of the earth. One of the persistent troublesome legacies from the Western tradition has been its obsession with identity as the mark of "Being." As noted, this begins with Parmenides, but it marks all the major ontologies in Western philosophy, from Democritus' atoms, Plato's self-identical Forms, and Aristotle's substances to the Cartesian

19. "Ecology" (or *oecologie*) was coined in 1866 by Ernst Haeckel, though, obviously, its meaning has grown as it has come to describe a genuine science. Ecology as a science was pioneered in the 1950s by Eugene Odum's path-breaking work. See Donald Worster, *Nature's Economy: A History of Ecological Ideas*, 2nd ed. (New York: Cambridge University Press, 1994) for a history of the ideas, and Eugene P. Odum and Gary W. Barrett, *Fundamentals of Ecology*, 5th ed. (Independence, KY: Brooks/ Cole, a Division of Cengage Learning, 2005) for an introduction to the field.

ego cogito, Kant's *ich denke*, and Russell's logical atoms. An eco-ontological approach would stress the idea of continuity over identity (with "identity" itself being understood through continuity), just as it would stress the importance of relation, process, transformation and inter-being over substance, essence, and "states." Plurality and complexity are emphasized over unity and simplicity. Understanding things in terms of their "natural histories" is an *ecological virtue* not a "genetic fallacy." Eco-ontology embraces polymodality, and it does so in a more complex manner than the constrained parameters of modal logic. To reiterate, languages in their nuances of voice, mood, and tense indicate more completely the ranges of our ways of orienting ourselves to the events of nature.

Then there is the issue of being itself. One of the guiding themes of eco-ontology is the primacy of nature over being. This goes against the grain of the Western tradition (but not all of it). Some exceptions are the early Greek philosophers, who began with the question of nature (or *phusis*) and only later encountered the problem of being. While Plato and Aristotle prioritized being, nevertheless the Stoics (and then, following them, Spinoza) affirmed "God or nature"—*Deus sive natura*. John Scottus Eriugena, in his *Periphyseon*, saw "nature" as wider than "being" insofar as it included "what was not" as well as "what is." In the eleventh century, Solomon ibn Gabirol argued for creative matter as coequal with form in his *Fons Vitae*. Nicholas Cusanus and then Giordano Bruno had God as the "enfolded" (*complicans*) potential infinite who "contracted" or "unfolded" (*explicans*) into the actual infinite universe. F. W. J. Schelling, though beginning with an identity philosophy, balanced it with a *Naturphilosophie* that made nature the way in which Spirit comes to create and so know itself. Whitehead kept God as part of a more inclusive natural order. The American tradition embraces a spectrum of "naturalisms" from Santayana to Dewey. One of the most important is the neglected figure of Justus Buchler, who proposed that "nature" must be the inclusive category, since it is nothing but orders of relations, and whatever is unrelated to nature is simply unrelated; if by the term "supernatural" we mean something that is unrelated to nature, then it is simply meaningless.[20]

---

20. See Justus Buchler, *The Metaphysics of Natural Complexes*, 2nd ed., ed. Kathleen Wallace et al. (Albany: State University of New York Press, 1989). In all fairness, Plato raises the problem of "the unrelated" in the *Parmenides* and tentatively proceeds to propose a solution in the *Sophist*, 246ff.

In trying to rethink the tradition, it is not only crucial to explore the work of radical thinkers like Buchler, who struggle to overcome it from within, but it is also important to look at non-Western philosophies as well as at the worldviews of other peoples as embodied in their wisdom traditions. Insofar as our thinking is guided by metaphors, whether we are aware of them or not, it is immensely helpful to see the constellations of metaphors another culture uses to make sense of the world. Here I have found the wisdom traditions of Native Americans refreshingly instructive. The metaphors that appear in origination stories (what we would call "creation myths") are those of cooperative action and experimental discovery. In terms of non-Western philosophical traditions, I find Buddhism a useful contrast. It had a complex and sophisticated philosophical tradition of its own (reaching back, like ours, for 2,500 years) based on a rejection of the idea of anything being substantially self-sufficient, purely actual, and absolute. What is problematic in Buddhism, at least as far as an ecologically oriented philosophy is concerned, is its ultimate concern with liberation from *samsāra* and the suffering it brings. Thus eco-ontology tries to steer a middle course between Western substance and essence identity-based metaphysics and the relational, process, renunciatory view of Buddhism.

Indeed, I think it is possible to have a pluralistic (or "polyphonic") approach to the question of nature reflecting the different voices we may use to invoke or speak of it. Four such voices, for example, are the scientific voice, the humanistic voice, the ontological voice, and the transcendental voice. Each of these invokes nature in its own way. But each voice has the capacity to try to claim that it and it alone should be the proper mode of address and that the others should remain silent. The scientific voice at its most extreme becomes scientism, which seeks to repress all other voices, despising humanistic concerns, ontological concepts, and above all claims of transcendental self-realization, spiritual self-knowledge or *gnōsis*. Likewise, a radical humanistic outlook, such as we find with Socrates or Sartre, focuses exclusively upon the human world. The ontological voice, at its extreme, becomes a skeletal world, such as we find in Wittgenstein's *Tractatus*, where "to be" means "to be a fact, the subject of a true or false proposition." The transcendental voice at its extreme easily loses all the others as it becomes pure mysticism. My point, however, is that these (and other) voices can be co-present to each other for the sake of polyphonic understanding. This involves the difficult art of listening.[21] Thus part of the eco-ontological approach is the cultivation of polyphonic listening as well as speaking.

Conclusion

I have grouped these essays into four main headings. The first section, "Nature and Experience," initially presents two essays dealing with what I consider to be two of Dewey's most important claims. The first, "The Aesthetics of Reality: The Development of Dewey's Ecological Theory of Experience," shows Dewey's explicit awareness of the need to contextualize the problem of knowing within the larger domain of life that is not engaged in inquiry. I see Dewey's 1905 article "The Postulate of Immediate Empiricism" as a definite turning point in his development. The second, "Dewey's Denotative-Empirical Method: A Thread through the Labyrinth," discusses his poorly understood first chapter in *Experience and Nature*—one he felt the need to rewrite completely for the second edition—on the nature of his "denotative empirical method." I argue here that in trying to make this chapter clearer, Dewey actually obscured the radical nature of his approach (consonant with "The Postulate of Immediate Empiricism"). By appealing to scientific method as an *example* of the denotative method, he led generations of readers to assume that "the" scientific method *was* the denotative method. I have appended a point-by-point comparison of the two versions.

This section also includes two essays discussing the "eco-ontological" position outlined above, putting Dewey into conversation with the Madhyamika Buddhism of Nāgārjuna in one ("Between Being and Emptiness: Toward an Eco-ontology of Inhabitation") and with Justus Buchler in the other ("The Being of Nature: Dewey, Buchler, and the Prospect for an Eco-ontology"). The former contrasts the Western tradition's "ontology of identity" with Buddhism's "ontology of emptiness" and argues that an ecologically oriented ontology must find a middle path. The latter essay grapples with two powerful conceptions of naturalistic ontology, Dewey's and Buchler's, the issue coming down to an ontology

---

21. It is telling that a century of analyzing the meaning of meaning simply in terms of propositional form and reference had nothing to say about the necessary dimension of meaning: reception, *listening*. John Dewey, Hans-Georg Gadamer, and Martin Buber are notable exceptions.

that ultimately does make a commitment to a plurivocity of "being"—
being, said in many ways—or to one that insists, as Buchler's "ordinal
naturalism" does, upon a univocity of being, "to be is to be a natural
complex."

The second section, "Eros and Imagination," includes essays largely
bearing on the Human Eros and the related themes of imagination and
education. The first essay ("The Human Eros") is a statement of the thesis
of the Human Eros itself against the relativism of Rorty and the constructivism of Stanley Fish. Though somewhat dated by its involvement in
"the culture wars" of the early 1990s, it is included because of its clear
articulation of a main theme through all my essays. This is followed by
two studies on the role of imagination in pragmatism, one ("Pragmatic
Imagination") a survey of the topic in the figures of Peirce, James, and
Dewey, the second ("Moral Imagination: Beyond Putnam and Rorty toward
an Ethics of Meaning") a more focused discussion of the role of imagination in the moral thinking of Dewey, R. M. Hare, and Hilary Putnam. It
argues that Dewey has the most fully developed position, one that opens
up a prospect of an "ethics of meaning" based on the Human Eros rather
than the familiar schools of rule-bound ethics (utilitarianism and deon-
tology) and "virtue ethics." The final essay in this section ("Educating the
Democratic Heart: Education, Pluralism, and the Humanities") addresses
the question of what education must seek in providing the basis of a
genuinely democratic culture, arguing against Alasdair MacIntyre's
attack on liberalism and stressing the importance of educating the moral
imagination through the humanities.

The third section, "Aesthetics of Existence," takes up themes dealing
with the role of the aesthetic as the fulfillment of the Human Eros in life,
not just in Dewey's thought but in the thought of George Santayana,
Ralph Waldo Emerson, and Native American culture. The opening
essay ("'Love Calls Us to Things of This World': Santayana's Incredible
Lightness of Being") contrasts Dewey's embodied aesthetics with George
Santayana's starkly contemplative or "spiritual" concept of the aesthetic
life. Both thinkers find the aesthetic as central to existence, but they
pursue quite different ways of realizing it. This is followed by an essay
("Mountains and Rivers without End: The Intertwining of Nature and
Spirit in Emerson's Aesthetics") that compares the aesthetic as self-
realization in nature as found in Emerson's transcendentalist view of
human existence in nature with classical Chinese philosophy. The final

two essays are dialogical explorations in Native American thought. One ("Creating with Coyote: Toward a Native American Aesthetics") looks at the dominant metaphors for "creation" found in Native American origin stories that reveal surprisingly "pragmatic" themes of social cooperation and experimentation. The last ("Tricksters and Shamans: Aesthetics and the Archaic Imagination") attempts to contrast our common concept of "the aesthetic" (as in "the aesthetic attitude") with the shaman's experience of entering into an alternative, existentially powerful and transformational reality for the sake of healing in this world. This may be a more genuine way to approach art and itself be something of a cure for our "postmodern" predicament.

The final section, "Spirit and Philosophy," presents essays that deal with the question of "spirit": that is, the general orientation of human existence to nature. Again, Santayana provides a fascinating contrast to Dewey as well as presents a concept of philosophy that has its own merits. The first essay ("Santayana's Sage: The Disciplines of Aesthetic Enlightenment") explores Santayana's conception of philosophy as a discipline of "aesthetic enlightenment," a way of life that leads toward an ideal of "the sage" much in the manner of Hellenistic systems. The second ("Beauty and the Labyrinth of Evil: Santayana and the Possibility of Naturalistic Mysticism") takes up the problem of how an aesthetic philosophy may respond to the problem of evil by exploring Santayana's own interesting analysis of Plotinus' position. Santayana's aesthetic ideal is one of disengagement. I argue that this is not the only possible attitude, given the assumptions, and that in the Buddhist practice of "insight meditation" (or *vipassanā*) there is the same attentiveness to experience but with the aim of compassionate insight and conduct as a result. The third essay in this part is an extended reflection on the role of spirituality in John Dewey and focuses on the significance of *A Common Faith* in the Deweyan corpus. I argue for the importance of this text in interpreting Dewey's overall thought and maintain that he presents us with an alternative form of spirituality, "the spirituality of the possible," over against the traditional "spirituality of the actual" that has marked the Western tradition. Life is not just a piecemeal adjustment of going from one situation to another, but involves a general orientation of "existence as such." Dewey himself understood his own mystical experience in this way. The concluding essay, "Eros and Spirit: Toward a Humanistic Philosophy of Culture," presents my own approach to a general philosophy of culture and civilization, looking at culture in terms of the idea of "spiritual ecology" discussed above.

Philosophy in the Anglophone world has been largely presented in the twentieth century in terms of seeing itself as a "scientific" project (understanding "science" in terms first of mathematical physics, then as a "science" of the use of language, and now as connected to "brain science"). Continental thought has largely been a reaction to the scientific project, seeking some alternative "science of consciousness" (as in phenomenology), a reflective methodology of the human studies (hermeneutics), or as a social praxis of deconstructive criticism (i.e., Marxism without consequences). I believe philosophy has a genuinely humanistic mission that addresses the most fundamental issues of meaning in existence on a range of levels, from the individual to the cultural. This cannot be a humanism that abstracts the human from the natural world. It must firmly see our existence as being-in-nature, and so philosophy has an obligation to articulate as rich a conception of nature as possible. Our reductionisms are ultimately part of that grand Mythos of the modern era, the "mastery of nature." This has not been a path to wise living. I hope that philosophy may become part of our struggle toward a new form of inhabitation.

PART ONE

NATURE AND EXPERIENCE

ONE

THE AESTHETICS OF REALITY

The Development of Dewey's Ecological Theory of Experience

The Transcendence of Epistemology

The period between Dewey's emergence as a major philosophical voice and his becoming the leading figure in the movement that became known as "pragmatism" is not well understood. That it was something of a mystery to Dewey himself is evident by the prominence it has in his intellectual autobiography, "From Absolutism to Experimentalism." In 1887, with the publication of his *Psychology*, Dewey, rather than Royce, could well have been called the crown prince of American idealism. In 1903, with the appearance of *Studies in Logical Theory*, Dewey was recognized as the head of the Chicago School, which was understood as presenting a platform of radical, "pragmatic" idealism that was taking an affirmative, indeed enthusiastic, approach to contemporary sciences, unlike the defensive, theologically driven idealism dominant in Germany and England and represented in America by Royce, among others. Yet Dewey had already been strangely silent on the topic of "idealism" as such for some time. He left Chicago in 1904, hotly resigning his position in the controversy over his wife's dismissal from heading the Laboratory School. By 1905 he was at Columbia, and that was the year his article "The Postulate of Immediate Empiricism" appeared. This article is, I believe, one of the most radical and revolutionary pieces Dewey wrote, though it is also far from being a clear, accessible statement of the nature or implications of those crucial ideas that indicate a sea change in Dewey's philosophy. It quite explicitly is a response to James's articles on radical empiricism, which had begun to appear in 1903, though the relationship of radical empiricism to "pragmatism" was still nebulous. It was in 1916 that the collection of articles known as *Essays in Experimental Logic* appeared, containing in its lengthy introduction perhaps the most sophisticated explanation to date of Dewey's theory of experience. And it would be almost another decade until the appearance of Dewey's most systematic exploration of the idea in *Experience and Nature*.

As one looks at the developmental dynamics of Dewey's early period, there seems to be a variety of issues that demand his attention: ethics, logic, psychology, pedagogy, and so on. It is less clear whether there is a basic, underlying issue that drives Dewey from one formulation of his thought to the next. If one looks, however, at the trajectory of his thought, especially from the *Psychology* to the introduction of *Essays in Experimental Logic* (and beyond to *Experience and Nature*), the importance of Dewey's "Postulate of Immediate Empiricism" becomes evident, summing up not only his discontent with idealism, but also realism, and it anticipates the most profound issues that would characterize Dewey's mature philosophy. This involves, I believe, a transformation of a major commitment of the Western tradition from its very inception in the pre-Socratic period on: the correlation of the object of knowledge with the nature of reality. Though articulated by Parmenides, it is perhaps most clearly exhibited in Plato's famous "Divided Line," with its gradations of the diverse cognitive powers of the soul on one side and their appropriate cognitive objects, ontologically graded, on the other.

Dewey's radical shift is to question this equation, and it is first explicitly manifest in "The Postulate of Immediate Empiricism." Knowing for him becomes merely one aspect of the ways in which reality manifests itself, a contextualized and mediating way, but certainly not final or ultimate. Rather, experience in its noncognitive forms indicates a qualitatively rich and aesthetically diversified field of meaning, conscious and unconscious, that supports and renders intelligible the cognitive enterprise itself. This is one reason why Dewey's own thought is poorly described by the term "Instrumentalism," which refers specifically to the theory of inquiry, of knowing. Dewey had difficulty in finding a fitting name for his complete philosophy of experience. The list of terms introducing the subject in the revised first chapter of *Experience and Nature*, "naturalistic empiricism" and "naturalistic humanism," left Dewey unsatisfied, so that by 1938, in *Logic: The Theory of Inquiry*, he used the phrase "cultural naturalism." Dewey's frustrations reflected both the depth of his insight and the inability of his opponents—as well as many of his followers—to grasp the nature of his revolution, an inability echoed in the work of many neopragmatists, who still hold on to the correlation of natural objects and the objects of knowledge, of metaphysics and epistemology. It was one of Dewey's major claims that while nature manifests itself in a variety of ways, in one sense it exhibits itself most in its fullest and most complex actualizations, which for Dewey were expressed in the artistic-aesthetic mode of experience that is the subject of *Art as Experience*. Knowing, inquiry, science do not have the final word on nature.

The purpose of this essay is to sketch out some of the major steps that led Dewey to his radical break with this fundamental commitment of the Western tradition. It asks that we look at Dewey's philosophy as setting the stage for a more developed exploration of the idea of an ontology of environed or ecologically situated being, an "eco-ontology," to use my own term. In this way, then, the introduction to *Essays in Experimental Logic* has a crucial place in the Deweyan corpus, not only in its resolutions of the tensions that had driven Dewey's philosophical development from the arms of idealism, or in its anticipations of the position laid out in *Experience and Nature*, but in terms of being an "introduction" to one of the most forceful statements of Dewey's instrumentalism. Questions of inquiry must be contextualized within the fundamentally noncognitive enterprise of experience. Attempts, moreover, to read Dewey as somehow contributing to "epistemology" must be questioned. To understand Dewey's revolution is to grasp fully that what has occupied the role of "an epistemology of *knowledge*" in the West for Dewey must be replaced with the nature of an aesthetics of *learning*.

The outcome of understanding this revolution is highly significant. The world of the twenty-first century faces the double problem of confronting an emerging global civilization that is already significantly engaged in the process of environmental degradation of the planet and the widespread destruction of biodiversity. A philosophy that engages us in ways of environmentally and ecologically conceptualizing our interactions with the world and is oriented toward an aesthetically deep, ongoing experience of life is one that may help us negotiate successfully the daunting challenges ahead.

Dewey's Chicago Years

As the University of Chicago emerged from the marshes in 1892, it was clear that President Harper intended to make three departments the center jewels in the crown: Semitics, classics, and philosophy.[1] Rockefeller was funneling millions of dollars into the project, as were Chicagoans. Harper needed builders of departments and he could afford them: he would have Paul Shorey in Greek and, soon, James Henry Breasted in Egyptology along with a large portion of Yale's Department of Semitic Languages. But who would build the philosophy department? He sent feelers out to "established, solidly respectable men" like George Herbert Palmer of Harvard (Rucker, 11). William James discreetly suggested his old friend, Charles Sanders Peirce. Harper was cautious—wasn't there some "problem" with Peirce back at Hopkins years ago? Harper decided to write Palmer. Palmer was shocked: "I am astonished at James's recommendation of Peirce," he gasped; after admitting that he "had no personal acquaintance with Peirce," Palmer went on to "advise" Harper to make "careful inquiries" into the reports of Peirce's "broken and dissolute character." "I am sure it is suspicions of this sort which have prevented his appointment here, and I suppose the same causes procured his dismissal from Johns Hopkins" (Rucker, 10). Peirce, in fact, was not "safe"—the fundamental flaw in his character revealed itself to his fellow Victorians, as Joseph Brent has shown, in actually daring to marry his mistress after finally getting a divorce from his estranged wife.[2] Though the theme of this essay is Dewey, we might pause for a moment to reflect on the very different department Peirce might have built. Whatever its

1. See Darnell Rucker's *The Chicago Pragmatists* (New Haven, CT: Yale University Press, 1969). See esp. the introduction. The letter by Palmer is also quoted in Brent's biography of Peirce. See the following footnote.
2. See Joseph Brent, *Charles Sanders Peirce: A Life* (Bloomington: Indiana University Press, 1993), esp. 151–60. There were of course other factors—Peirce's arrogance, his carrying on a double career between Johns Hopkins and the Geodetic Survey, and the attack on his standing as a mathematician by Simon Newcomb, a respected colleague in the field.

character, there might have been a laboratory, but I doubt there would have been a laboratory school.

It was then that James Tufts suggested a young professor at Michigan, John Dewey, who, said Tufts, "is a man of a religious nature, is a church member and believes in working with churches" (Rucker, 10). The comment, true at the time, was about to become dramatically inaccurate—such are the vagaries of academic appointments! As Robert Westbrook has pointed out, when Dewey left the church in moving from Ann Arbor to Chicago, he never affiliated with any other denomination again.[3] The offer was made and accepted, and the remarkable decade of Dewey's years in Chicago began.

When Dewey arrived, he was recognized as one of the foremost exponents of absolute idealism in the United States (George Sylvester Morris, Dewey's mentor, had died in 1889 and Royce had only published two philosophical books: *The Religious Aspect of Philosophy* in 1885 and *The Spirit of Modern Philosophy* in 1892). Dewey also was the author of two books, a study of Leibniz and the *Psychology*, a sophisticated attempt to wed empirical psychology with idealist metaphysics, while junking Hegel's cumbersome a priori dialectic. He had published an impressive monograph in ethics, the *Outlines of a Critical Theory of Ethics* (1891). This work astutely critiqued the classical panorama of ethical theories and restlessly argued for a dynamic character-based ethics of self-realization. In 1894, it was superseded by Dewey's first schematic analysis of moral psychology, *The Study of Ethics: A Syllabus*, which advocated what Dewey briefly dubbed "experimental idealism" (EW, 4:264).[4] The influence of James's *Principles of Psychology* was everywhere.

When he left the University of Chicago in 1904, he was no longer a contender with Royce as the leading defender of absolute idealism. Dewey had been moot on the whole question of idealism. In fact, there had been

---

3. Robert Westbrook, *John Dewey and American Democracy* (Ithaca, NY: Cornell University Press, 1991), 79.

4. Robert Westbrook rejects the connection of this term with any metaphysical position and sees it referring simply to "the role of ideals in moral idealism" (Robert Westbrook, *John Dewey and American Democracy*, 6 1n.4). But the whole point of the sort of idealism Dewey had advocated was precisely the connection of these two subjects. Dewey's continuing struggles in this area can be examined in the three series of lectures on psychological ethics edited by Donald Koch: *Lectures on Psychological and Political Ethics: 1898* (New York: Hafner Press, 1976), *Lectures on Ethics: 1900–1901* (Carbondale: Southern Illinois University Press, 1991), and *Principles of Instrumental Logic: John Dewey's Lectures in Ethics and Political Ethics, 1895–1896* (Carbondale: Southern Illinois University Press, 1998). It would be only in 1908 that Dewey would, in collaboration with Tufts, publish the *Ethics*, the profound outcome of two decades of wrestling with the subject.

pointed criticisms of Green, Bosanquet, Lötze, and Royce, but these could still be interpreted as family squabbles. Now he was the recognized leader of educational psychology; his own contributions to the science not only were aligned with James's functional empiricism, but stood on a par with it and, in fact, had advanced it on certain key points, especially in such breakthrough pieces as "The Theory of Emotions" (1894) and "The Reflex Arc Concept in Psychology" (1896). Though Dewey continued to give important lectures on moral psychology, his major books and monographs dealt with education—*Interest in Relation to Training of the Will* (1899), *The School and Society* (1900), and *The Child and the Curriculum* (1902). More and more Dewey had been absorbed in the problem of knowledge viewed in terms of an active process of inquiry rather than an elaborate epistemological system of elements and laws providing a background for justifying beliefs. In his contributions to the *Studies in Logical Theory* (1903), Dewey had trained his guns on the formalistic system of Herman Lötze as a case study exemplifying the futility of metaphysical epistemology. Dewey was now so insistent on treating logic in terms of a functional or genetic process that an exasperated Charles Sanders Peirce savagely reviewed the book. Unlike the British logicians, whose work, Peirce said, "may be expected to lead to results of high value for the positive sciences," Dewey's work must be classified with that of the German logicians, like Husserl (briefly mentioned), which makes truth "a matter of linguistic expression" rather than as a "matter of fact." "The Chicago school or group are manifestly in radical opposition to the exact logicians, and are not making any studies which anybody in his senses can expect, directly or indirectly, in any considerable degree, to influence twentieth century science." Indeed, the new century would see the hegemonic dominion of a mathematical logic utterly contemptuous of "psychological questions" and "the genetic fallacy." Peirce added that though Dewey claimed to be opposed to the German school, "had he not put so much emphasis upon it, we should hardly have deemed the point of difference so important." Peirce found the whole thesis perplexing: "He seems to regard what he calls 'logic' as a natural history of thought." Exactly so.[5]

---

5. See Charles Sanders Peirce, *Collected Papers*, 8 vols. (Cambridge, MA: Harvard University Press, 1931–58), 8:190–91.

Years later, when Dewey roughly sketched out his intellectual autobiography, he referred to this period as one of "drifting" away from
Hegelianism, though—a point that is often missed here—remaining
deeply impressed by *Hegel*, if not by his followers (LW, 5:154). Indeed,
looking back, we can see in this period Dewey moving in some ways
closer to the concrete "spirit" of Hegel's own philosophy and away
from the more dualistic renditions of T. H. Green and the other British
idealists, as well as those of George Sylvester Morris and Josiah Royce.
Dewey adds a tantalizing detail in the coauthored semi-autobiography
for the Library of Living Philosophers volume devoted to him: "There
was a period extending into my early years at Chicago when, in connection with a seminar in Hegel's Logic I tried reinterpreting his categories
in terms of 'readjustment' and 'reconstruction.' Gradually I came to
realize that what the principles actually stood for could be better
understood and stated when completely emancipated from Hegelian
garb."[6] A common interpretation of what happened during Dewey's
Chicago years is that as he became dissatisfied with religion, even liberal
Christianity, and more engaged in experimental work, he went through
an antimetaphysical period. Upon arriving at Columbia and falling under
the influence of people like Woodbridge, Bush, and Montague, Dewey
once again began to tinker with metaphysics, the culmination appearing
some twenty years later in *Experience and Nature* (1925), a book that can
pretty much stand as the antithesis of Dewey's old *Psychology* of 1887.

Though there is some truth to this assessment (Dewey has sharp words
about metaphysics in his letters of the period), I would like to raise three
issues concerning it. First, such a view really does not answer for us *why*

6. *The Philosophy of John Dewey*, edited by Paul Arthur Schilpp (Boston, MA: Tudor Press, 1951;
originally 1939), 18. The biography is attributed to "Dewey's daughters," with Jane Dewey appearing
as editor. The words, however, are quoted as directly from Dewey in the text. Notes and stenographic
typescripts of some of Dewey's lectures from this period exist, though it is still difficult to pinpoint
the course or year when he makes this shift. A transcript from 1897 on Hegel's *Philosophy of Mind*
stays close to Hegel's own terminology while notes taken by H. H. Bawden (no earlier than 1902)
from a course Dewey taught on Hegel's logic begin with the phrase: "Restating Hegel's meaning in
psychology terms, he is asking here, What is initiative, momentum, [of] that process?... Interpret bg
[being], non-bg, & becoming in terms of focus & background [&] attention" (John Dewey Papers,
Southern Illinois University at Carbondale). The 1897 lecture has recently been published as *John
Dewey's Philosophy of Spirit*, ed. John R. Shook and James A. Good (New York: Fordham University
Press, 2010). The autobiography goes on to add with regard to the publication of the four essays by
Dewey that this was "a final and complete break with his early Hegelian idealism" and the launching
of "his instrumental theory of reflective thought" (p. 33).

Dewey became disappointed with "experimental idealism," for such a doctrine could have worked very well as a theoretical underpinning to Dewey's psychological and political vision. Second, merely to label such a period of fundamental change "drifting" does little more than provide us an excuse for not looking for the details that culminated in what was a radical transformation. Worse, it provides ammunition to those critics of Dewey's mature philosophy who see it as a confused mishmash of later naturalism and empiricism added on to an unchanged, early, fuzzy idealism that crops out here and there in such places as his metaphysics, aesthetics, ethics, and so on.[7] Third and finally, we are presented with the mysterious, pivotal essay of 1905, the year of Dewey's appointment to Columbia, "The Postulate of Immediate Empiricism." I believe this essay is one of the most crucial in Dewey's career because it formulates, albeit in a fumbling and annoyingly condensed manner, what I take to be the guiding insight of his mature philosophy: that reality is not synonymous with the object of knowledge. The range of experience and the realms of meaning and value extend far beyond the cognitive and, in fact, provide the supporting conditions within which inquiry makes sense. Such a thesis challenges the twenty-five hundred years of Western philosophy stemming from Parmenides's identification of Being and the known: "For it is the same thing, To-Be and To-Know."[8] Dewey's rejection of this is a *metaphysical* thesis, a profound one I believe, and it seems a strange bolt from the blue from someone who had "given up" metaphysics for educational psychology.

In the rest of this essay I will explore the development of Dewey's reconstruction of the thesis that knowledge is the measure of reality. My central claim is that by stressing the dynamic side of idealism while rejecting Hegel's dialectical logic for experimental psychology, Dewey was driven to contextualize the activity of knowing within a larger and richer view of experience. His work in educational psychology reinforced the importance of a theory of learning over the traditional philosophical emphasis upon "epistemology," the theory of knowledge. This is an insight

---

7. This problem has been explored, at least with respect to Dewey's metaphysics and aesthetics, in my book, *John Dewey's Theory of Art, Experience, and Nature: The Horizons of Feeling* (Albany: State University of New York Press, 1987). But also see the studies by Stephen Rockefeller and Jennifer Welchman for somewhat different analyses of Dewey's early development. Robert Westbrook's treatment also makes some interesting points.

8. See Parmenides, DK, 3 and 8.

we would do well to consider today. I will then look at the culmination of the transformation of Dewey's philosophical outlook in an article published just after his arrival at Columbia, "The Postulate of Immediate Empiricism." This piece not only well exemplifies the profound change that had occurred during Dewey's Chicago period, but anticipates most of the major metaphysical developments of his later thought. After examining the argument presented in "The Postulate of Immediate Empiricism" I will show why I think it has radical implications even for today, especially for constructing a metaphysics that takes ecology seriously. (I cannot discuss here other intertwined threads contributing to the change in Dewey's philosophy during the Chicago years, such as his theory of ethical conduct and his theory of democratic life.) But I conclude by reflecting on the contemporary importance both of a theory of learning over epistemology and an ecological ontology over the ontology of perfection that has dominated Western philosophy.

The Absolute Goes to School

Justice can hardly be done here to the philosophical depth of Dewey's early period. The surprising thing is that while Dewey was an idealist, he was a remarkably original and powerful one. His early thought, in my view, far exceeds anything else done under the banner of idealism in America until we get to the later thought of Josiah Royce or even the thought of John William Miller.[9] From his earliest writings it is evident that Dewey rebelled against anything that smacked of the abstract, formal, and lifeless. He had been drawn to idealism for the reason that it promised to be able to treat experience in all its richness and organic wholeness. British empiricism, with its atomic mental particles governed by mechanical "laws of association," and Neo-Kantianism, with its Prussian bureaucracy of faculties automatically executing their judgments, never held any appeal for him. Thus he quickly adhered to the dynamic idealism of Hegel, filtered through the inspiring teachings of his beloved professor, George Sylvester Morris, and backed up by the liberal

---

9. I have undertaken a partial study of this period in my book, *John Dewey's Theory of Art, Experience, and Nature: The Horizons of Feeling* (Albany: State University of New York Press, 1987). For Miller, see the study by Stephen Tyman, *Descrying the Ideal* (Carbondale: Southern Illinois University Press, 1993).

interpretation of the British Thomas Hill Green. But the Hegel of the 19th century was the Hegel of the *The Science of Logic*, not *The Phenomenology of Spirit*. The West was going through pervasive, deep changes, social, political, and cultural, and clutched at anything that seemed to discern order and reason at work, from Swedenborgianism to dialectical materialism to social Darwinism. But for Dewey, Hegel's dialectic presented yet another formalistic a priori system removed in the end from the concrete in all but name. Even if Hegel's concepts moved in a ghostly ballet, it was no substitute for life. Dewey wanted life.

Dewey had thus embraced only one side of Hegel (and so he never was an "Hegelian"—what is Hegel without the *Logic*?) and was casting about for something to replace the very engine of Hegel's metaphysical dynamo; he found this also at Johns Hopkins in the teaching of G. Stanley Hall, one of the first experimental psychologists in the United States. Psychology presented itself as the scientific study of individual consciousness. Idealism presented itself as the claim that self-consciousness could establish that it was the constituting origin and ground of everything else. Dewey put two and two together: psychology must be the science that gives us access to ultimate reality. Only in his mid-twenties, Dewey, ever prolific, presented the arguments for his "psychological idealism" from 1884 on, culminating in his first original book, the *Psychology* (1887).[10]

This book is one of the weirdest small masterpieces in the history of idealism. It rigorously presents itself as a textbook in psychology and appeals to the latest empirical research coming from Germany, while holding down the references to idealist metaphysicians to a discreet, well-hidden few. Hegel is not mentioned, but the beginning is well laid out—every instance of consciousness is also an instance of self-consciousness, and thus of knowledge (EW, 2:7–8). Ranging over the three cardinal faculties of Knowing, Willing and Feeling, with careful and often insightful discussions of memory, imagination, intellectual feeling, aesthetic perception, and the formation of a moral identity, Dewey architectonically leads the reader from the most immediate analyses of personal experience onward and upward to the necessary postulate

---

10. Among the important articles indicating Dewey's earliest position are "The New Psychology" (1884), "The Psychological Standpoint" (1886), "Psychology as Philosophic Method" (1886), and "Knowledge as Idealization" (1887). All are in EW, 1.

of Absolute self-consciousness as the underpinning Reality of everything. We are thus presented with the "scientific" conclusion:

> We find the unity of the psychical process already studied, and therefore their ultimate explanation, in the fact that man is a self; that the essence of the self is the self-determining activity of will; that this will is an objectifying activity, and that, in objectifying itself, it renders itself universal. The result of this activity is *knowledge*. . . . The objective universal result is at one and the same time existent in the medium of the individual's consciousness. This subjective activity is *feeling*. (EW, 2:362)

Dewey concludes asserting that moral will is the realization that the real and the ideal *ought* to be one and the "Religious will is the realization that they are one because man is a self-determining power. It is the realization that a perfect will is reality" (EW, 2:362). Dewey flirts with heresy: Freedom is achieved "through the realization of the union of finite and the infinite Personality"—does God *need* us to be free just as we need Him? (EW, 2:362–63). He finishes off by listing all the "contradictions" that follow if this conclusion is rejected: Knowledge cannot be universal, only subjective, feeling can never be fully satisfied, for the ideal will never be real, and the will likewise will be frustrated and arbitrary, never becoming a rational desire. All psychical life is "the progressive realization by the will of its ideal self" achieved by the "idealization of the actual," ending in the insight that "real and ideal are one" and that "truth, happiness, and rightness are united in one Personality" (EW, 2:363).

G. Stanley Hall, Dewey's former teacher, and William James had both had their work cited in support of this thesis; they were not pleased, Hall saying that it was like using geology to account for the six days of Creation, James merely clucking over how bloodless and abstract this ideal "Personality" seemed to be compared with real life.[11] What was remarkable for Dewey, even in this early work, was how well he integrated willing and feeling together with knowing. The aesthetic was no doormat to the temple of the Absolute, as it was for Hegel (with religion being the door and philosophy the edifice). But for our purposes, I want to notice how well this book falls into the fundamental commitments of what

11. See George Dykhuizen, *The Life and Mind of John Dewey* (Carbondale: Southern Illinois University Press, 1973), 55.

might be termed "the ontology of perfection," the legacy of the Greeks, the medievals, and, in their own way, the moderns. The basic claim is that Being is complete or perfect, needing nothing beyond itself to be. The fundamental access to this truth is through an act of intellectual insight. Being, as object, is realized in a timeless moment of knowing; Reason realizes its fullest power in achieving this insight. At the most fundamental level, Being is the known; the self is the knower, and both are mutually implicated, at the very least through a common ground, at most by being identified.[12] Thus Being is the object of contemplative insight, absolute knowledge, and apodictic insight is the essence of consciousness and the self. Being is self-identical, autonomous, atemporal. To the degree the self is assimilated to its prime object, it, too, is self-identical, autonomous, and atemporal.[13] It is the Parmenidean turn of Western philosophy at work.

When the *Psychology* appeared in 1887, Dewey was not thirty; it would go through two revisions by 1891. But 1890 was the year marked by the publication of William James's *Principles of Psychology*. Not only did this instantly eclipse any pretense Dewey's book could have as being the American answer to German or British psychology, it struck at the roots of the idealist philosophy itself and in the name of all that had committed Dewey to idealism in the first place: fidelity to the organic richness of experience and moving flow of life. The fundamental assumption was that for subject and object to be united in an act of knowledge (or self-knowledge, for idealism), some active synthesizing power was needed, be it the Form of the Good, the Active Intellect, God's illumination, the Transcendental Ego, or the Absolute. James asked why experience needed "synthesizing" when it didn't come in pieces to begin with. Distinctions and concepts emerged out of the ongoing process of life as functional refinements, useful in directing and responding to the course of the world. Life didn't need "saving" by reason to be made whole; all along it

12. In the *Republic*, Plato's analogy of the Sun makes it clear that the Soul as knower and the Forms as objects of *noēsis* are caused and connected by the Form of the Good (508ff.). Aristotle's divine principle, the Unmoved Mover, is both knower and known without requiring any further transcendental ground. When Augustine collapses the hypostatic One of Plotinus (which is identified with Plato's Form of the Good) into the Christian God, the ultimate Being, the same move is accomplished. God is the self-caused all-knower eternally beholding the history of creation from beyond time.

13. This, of course, is one of the theses of the *Phaedo* and is found again in Aristotle's cloudy remarks on the active intellect and again in Books X and XI of the *Confessions*.

was "reason" that had depended on life. Dewey must have been stunned. His greatest effort in defense of the vitality of experience had to appear now as an elaborate, useless machinery. Dewey could, of course, have written a feisty defense of idealism and souped up his psychology. This is what Royce would have done and what, no doubt, Morris, Dewey's spiritual father, would have urged. But Morris had died the year before. In May of 1891, Dewey wrote James, nominally to thank him for some kind remarks on Dewey's syllabus, *Outlines of a Critical Theory of Ethics.* The letter is candidly revealing about Dewey's own struggles:

> But unless a man is already living in the gospel and not under the law, as you express it words thrown at him are idle wind. . . . The hope seems to be with the rising generation. . . . Many of my students, I find, are fairly hungering. They almost jump at any opportunity to get out from under the load and believe in their own lives. Pardon the confessional character of this note, but the man who has seen the point arouses the confessional attitude.

Dewey then added a postscript:

> I don't know that I told you that I have had a class of four graduates going through your psychology this year, and how much we have all enjoyed it. I'm sure you would be greatly gratified if you could see what a stimulus to mental freedom, as well as what a purveyor of methods and materials your book has been to us.[14]

Dewey had work to do.

During the course of his stay at Chicago, Dewey would tackle the problem of knowledge again and again. I cannot detail this progress, but three important milestones were reached respectively with "The Superstition of Necessity" (1893), "The Theory of Emotions" (1893–94) and, above all, in "The Reflex Arc Concept in Psychology" (1896). I will only summarize the central thesis of the first. "The Superstition of Necessity" analyzed the idea of necessary judgments in terms of how they functioned in inquiry. They did not grant access to an a priori world of perfection; rather, they were moments or phases in which previously disconnected judgments were united into one new fact. Dewey still believes that gradually this will lead us toward the ultimate fact of the

---

14. Ralph Barton Perry, *The Thought and Character of William James* (Boston: Little, Brown, 1935), 2:517.

Absolute, but now the Absolute itself will lack "necessity." During this discussion, Dewey hits upon an entirely new conception of what the "object of knowledge" is, not a fixed "fact" out there waiting to be discovered, but a transformative focus in a broader field of inquiry, which "has its origin in the practical needs of our nature" (EW, 4:24). Necessity and contingency get their meaning teleologically, i.e., functionally: "Necessary means *needed*; contingency means no longer required—because already enjoyed" (EW, 4:29). Logical necessity is simply practical, teleological necessity "read backward" (EW, 4:33). (No wonder history had appeared so "necessary" to Hegel! No wonder his "science" could not predict the future. Wasn't it Kierkegaard who pointed out "we live forwards but understand backwards"?) Dewey was trying to show *how* we could also *understand* forward, that is, that knowledge is inherently temporal, even in its "formal" logical relations.[15]

While "The Theory of Emotion" and "The Reflex Arc Concept in Psychology" provided Dewey's basic models of affective, interactional, developmental learning behavior, the *Studies in Logical Theory* (1903) carried out a sustained criticism of the whole "epistemological" approach to philosophy in favor of seeing experience in terms of its "natural history"; that is, its "ecology." From the start, Dewey is emphatic in refusing to privilege knowledge:

> Reflection busies itself alike with physical nature, the record of social achievement, and the endeavors of social aspiration. It is with reference to *such* affairs thought is derivative; it is with reference to them that it intervenes or mediates. Taking some part of the universe of action, of affection, of social construction, under its special charge, and having busied itself therewith sufficiently to meet the special difficulty presented, thought releases that topic and enters into more direct experience. (MW, 2:299; EEL, 76)

The antecedents of reflection and its consequents are not cognitive; they are what call thinking forth and that into which it passes, and this, says Dewey, has great implications for "the relation of truth to reality" (MW, 2:298; EEL, 75). "Thinking is a kind of activity which we perform at specific need, just as at other need we engage in other sorts of activity: as

---

15. James makes this reference to Kierkegaard in *Pragmatism*. The Harvard edition points to *The Journals of Søren Kierkegaard* (see sec. 465) as a locus but does not say how James became acquainted with it.

converse with a friend; draw a plan for a house; take a walk; eat a dinner; purchase a suit of clothes, etc." (MW 2:299; EEL, 77). The basis is laid for placing learning as more significant than knowing, of placing the process of growth above static insight, a method of discovery above a method of justification. The rest of the essays critique not Hegel but Lötze, whose reputation was already fading, and do not directly raise again the question of the relation of truth and reality. This would not happen until Dewey's move to Columbia.

Emersonian Interlude?

In looking over Dewey's publications from the mid-1890s to the year of his departure from Chicago in 1903, there is not much that would indicate the sort of revolution that his thought was undergoing. The various papers and monographs, as noted, concern themselves with psychology, ethics, and pedagogy, such as *The School and Society* (1900) and *The Child and the Curriculum* (1902). In 1903, however, Dewey was asked to deliver a paper commemorating the centennial of the birth of Ralph Waldo Emerson. This neglected essay is worth close attention, not least for the way in which Dewey, characterizing Emerson as "the philosopher of democracy," in many ways presents an outline of the philosopher *he* would become, that is, "John Dewey, the philosopher of democracy." To prepare for the talk, Dewey read through Emerson's *Essays*. After he had delivered the paper, he wrote late in the summer to one Warring Wilkinson that he was "rereading some of his [Emerson's] essays this summer" and "could not but be struck by the extent to which he has anticipated various points to which modern psychology has already come, or in the direction in which it is rapidly moving" (August 3, 1903). In the essay itself, Dewey has high praise indeed for Emerson "as the one citizen of the New World fit to have his name uttered in the same breath with that of Plato" (MW, 3:191). This was not just hyperbole; Dewey meant it: Emerson was an *American* embodiment of philosophy.

The essay begins by attacking the notion that Emerson is not a philosopher at all but a "string of pearls loosely strung." Such a view, Dewey observes, says more about the limits of the person who holds it than it does about Emerson, who, Dewey maintains, presents us with "a logic that is finely wrought," one that is present but not obvious (MW, 3:184). He quotes from Emerson's essay "Intellect": "We want in every man a long logic; we cannot pardon the absence of it, but it must not be spoken.

Logic is the procession or proportionate unfolding of the intuition; but its virtue is as silent method; the moment it would appear as propositions and have separate value, it is worthless" (MW, 3:184). This, I believe, is the anticipation of an idea that would only really be fully developed in 1930 in one of Dewey's most important essays, "Qualitative Thought." The central claim of that article is that our conscious or cognitive processes, our instrumental reasonings, depend on a vast, submerged sense of our whole embodied comportment in a situation. That is, logic presupposes a precognitive, felt or "had" sense of a situation. Dewey goes on to say, "To Emerson, perception was more potent than reasoning; the deliverances of intercourse more to be desired than the chains of discourse; the surprise of reception more demonstrative than the conclusions of intentional proof" (MW, 3:185). Dewey then quotes from Emerson's "Circles": "Good as is discourse, silence is better and shames it." While philosophy desires to render thought explicit, there must be a depth of intuition that is not explicit; the philosophical analysis presupposes the prerational insight—the poet and philosopher cannot be neatly divided one from the other. This intuition does not direct us to some "higher faculty," but points instead to the richness of common life. Emerson sees "idealism" in the pregnant richness of ordinary experience and believes philosophy must render that experience more luminous instead of transcending it. Emerson, says Dewey, "finds truth in the highway, in the untaught endeavor, the unexpected idea, and this removes him from their remoteness. His ideas are not fixed upon any Reality that is beyond or behind him or in any way apart. . . . They are versions of the Here and Now, and flow freely" (MW, 3:189). For Emerson, "spiritual democracy" is in "the possession of the unquestionable Present" (MW, 3:190). In other words, Emerson would restore to "the common man" the primacy of human experience and its capacity to embody ideals concretely. Emerson respected our "common nature" that shall issue "in their due season propositions, systems and logical expositions of the world" (MW, 3:191). These are ideas that would find expression as Dewey's own in the speech given to those honoring his eightieth birthday, "Creative Democracy— the Task Before Us."

Of course there is a danger in making too much out of what might be dismissed as a piece of rhetoric. But there is also a danger in ignoring the genuine nature of Dewey's *encounter* with Emerson. Emerson opened up for Dewey the possibility of a democratic philosophy of experience. What Dewey appropriates from Emerson is the significance of the prereflective but tacitly intelligent context out of which thought itself arises, upon which it depends and which it serves to illumine. That is, Emerson taught *faith* in ordinary experience, in its possibilities and capacities, and the *duty* of thought to reveal and actualize those possibilities; thought follows from experience, not the other way. Dewey fixes on Emerson's challenging insight: that philosophy should not try to escape the fact it is grounded in that "silent logic." Indeed, one might contrast the portrait Dewey drew of Emerson point for point with the one he drew the following year of Herbert Spencer, who stands as a sort of antithesis of everything Dewey praised in Emerson: Spencer is the epitome of someone for whom abstractions, not experience, constituted the substance of philosophy. As noted, Dewey eerily described Emerson in terms that eventually would be applied to Dewey. I believe that Dewey had a presentiment of himself, the philosopher he would become, in his encounter with Emerson. In Emerson, Dewey found a thinker who could put faith in experience over reason and see in the hidden, intuitive parts of experience the very conditions of what becomes the explicit, luminous portion in conscious reasoning. In addition to the Jamesian view of experience as a flow out of which practical reason arises, Dewey now had another piece to the puzzle: The rational develops out of the prerational, and the poet is at the heart of the philosopher. If so, this would be part of the catalyst that ultimately led to his rejection of the equation of reality and the object of knowledge and disposed him to embrace the rapidly developing pragmatist movement in 1905.

The Postulate of Immediate Empiricism

As one of the first of Dewey's articles to appear after his appointment to Columbia, "The Postulate of Immediate Empiricism" may well have caused some colleagues to wonder whether they had made a mistake—three eminent philosophers, including Columbia's own F. J. E. Woodbridge, wrote sharp criticisms appearing in the newborn *Journal of Philosophy* where the article had been published, eliciting equally sharp responses from Dewey.[16] Dewey thought well enough of the article to include it in his 1910 anthology, *The Influence of Darwin on Philosophy*,

---

16. The article, responses by Bakewell, Bode, and Woodbridge, and Dewey's responses are in MW, 390–404.

though he added a disgruntled note stating he had been "unreasonably sanguine" that his careful description of empiricism at the beginning "would forefend misapprehension" (MW, 3:166). This, at least, would prepare Dewey for another forty years of critical misunderstanding regarding the central ideas in his philosophy.

Dewey began his essay firmly allying himself with "that vital but still unformed movement variously termed radical empiricism, pragmatism, humanism, functionalism"—something he had not directly done so far (MW, 3:158). He proposed to state the fundamental but tacit presupposition that marked this movement off from any other, "a presupposition as to what experience is and means" (MW, 3:158). He wanted to reject any baggage imported into the sense of the term "experience" by associations with "sensationalistic empiricism" or transcendentalism (i.e., idealism), both of which "fall back on something which is defined in non-directly-experienced terms in order to justify that which is directly experienced" (MW, 3:158, n. 2). Dewey presumably means such second order conceptual entities as Lockean ideas, "laws of association," manifolds, forms of intuition, transcendental egos, Absolute Spirit, or whatnot. Dewey refers the reader to two places where such assumptions have been criticized, *Studies in Logical Theory* and his 1902 two-part essay "The Evolutionary Method as Applied to Morality." Both approaches are driven, Dewey adds, by setting up "certain methodological checks and cues for attaining *certainty*" (MW, 3:159, n. 2). The latter essay contrasted British empiricism with Dewey's appeal to experience; experience allowed for genetic or historical method, examining how ideas and value judgments arise from and function in practical situations. In the *Studies* Dewey had put it more bluntly: "It is not metaphysics, it is biology which enforces the idea that actual sensation is not only determined as an event in the world of events, but is an occurrence occurring at a certain period in the control and use of stimuli" (MW, 2:244).

With these warnings in mind Dewey was prepared to introduce his radical postulate: "Immediate empiricism postulates that things—anything, everything, in the ordinary or non-technical use of the term 'thing'—are what they are experienced as" (MW, 3:158). Had Dewey wanted his readers to be reassured that radical empiricism or pragmatism amounted to little more than a return to Protagorean relativism, he could not have done better, except perhaps add an example that would confirm the fear, which is what he did. When a horse trader, a timid family man, a jockey, and a zoologist look at a horse, he said, each one sees something different: a "good buy," a "safe ride," a "winner," or a specimen of "*equus* descended from *Eohippus*." Dewey does not come right out and assert that there is no "horse in itself," but he does say that none of the accounts given by these different people will turn out to be "less real" than others, and so be judged to be "merely phenomenal." The same is true, adds Dewey, of "the psychologist's horse, the logician's horse or the metaphysician's horse." "In each case," he says, "the nub of the question is, *what sort of experience* is denoted or indicated . . . so that we have a contrast not between Reality, and various approximations to, or phenomenal representations of Reality, but between different reals of experience" (MW, 3:159). If we slip back into the mentalistic understanding of "experience," then Dewey would seem to be advocating a Berkeleyan world where God has dozed off.

Dewey tried to avoid such a reading in the next paragraph, but only seemed to get himself in deeper trouble. This postulate, he argued, is usually thought to be equivalent to saying that "things (or, ultimately, Reality, Being) are only and just what they are *known* to be or that things are, or Reality *is*, what it is for a conscious knower—whether the knower be conceived primarily as a perceiver or as a thinker being a further and secondary question." Dewey dismisses this as "the root paralogism of all idealisms" of whatever stripe and "if not the root of all philosophic evil, one of its main roots"—and it would be hard to see, given this thesis, what doctrine in the history of the West did not automatically fall under this rubric (MW, 3:159–60). Even Hobbes would be classified as an "idealist" here. Dewey explains:

> By our postulate, things are what they are experienced to be; and, unless knowing is the sole and only genuine mode of experiencing, it is fallacious to say that Reality is just and exclusively what it is or would be to an all-competent all-knower; or even that it *is*, relatively and piecemeal, what it is to a finite and partial knower. Or, put more positively, knowing is one mode of experiencing, and the primary philosophical demand (from the standpoint of immediatism) is to find out *what* sort of an experience knowing is—or, concretely how things are experienced when they are experienced *as* known things. (MW, 3:159–60)

This paragraph stands as a marvelous example of Dewey's classic involuted, stammering, murky style. He comments in "From Absolutism to

Experimentalism" that when his early "schematic interest" was predominant "writing was comparatively easy," but since then "thinking and writing have been hard work" (LW, 5:151).[17]

The problem with the traditional assumption that Reality "really" is only as it appears to a knower is that it "leaves out of account what the knowledge standpoint itself is *experienced as*" (MW, 3:160). When "the knowledge standpoint" is placed within its natural context, Dewey finds that it arises from a prereflective, qualitatively felt situation and passes into an aesthetic one, serving a mediating and transformative role between them. Dewey rejects "grounding" knowledge upon a transcendental or dialectical analysis of the "possibility of knowledge"—the move that had inaugurated idealism and had led to the thesis that to be able to grasp its own conditions, the human mind had a self-transcending power to apprehend itself as the Absolute; i.e., the view Dewey had originally adopted. But when looked at as "experience," taken in Dewey's sense of "natural history," knowledge does not "ground" other types of experience; it is "grounded" by them. The process of knowing has its whence and its wither in events that are not instances of "knowing" at all.

The "root of most philosophic evil" had been to regard such experiences as either tacit instances of knowledge secretly employing vast, hidden epistemological machinery or to dismiss noncognitive experience as irrelevant, deceptive, or meaningless with respect to the nature of Reality. In the first camp we might find as paradigmatic instances those who believe that any experience of whatever stripe is also implicitly an instance of knowledge and forming cognitive judgments: the Stoics, Thomas Reid, Leibniz, Kant, Hegel, Husserl, Ryle, Sellars, Chisholm, Dennett. In the second camp we would find those who acknowledge that some experience is non-cognitive but either utterly dismiss it as having ontological significance (for example, Descartes, Hume, Carnap, Stevenson, Rorty) or take its nonepistemic character as pointing toward degraded orders of Being (Plato, Aristotle, Plotinus, Augustine, Aquinas,

---

17. Dewey actually makes a revealing insight: "My development has been controlled largely by a struggle between a native inclination toward the schematic and formally logical, and those incidents of personal experience that compelled me to take account of actual material.... Anyway, a case might be made out for the proposition that the emphasis upon the concrete, empirical, and practical in my later writings is...a reaction to what is more natural, and it served as a protest and protection against something in myself which, in the pressure and weight of actual experiences, I knew to be a weakness" (LW, 5:150–51).

Hegel, Peirce). The only tradition that seems to stand as an exception to the rule would be those thinkers who have implicitly accepted the argument that what is noncognitive is incomprehensible. Here we find what might be termed philosophers who advocate a "metaphysics of the will" in which the arbitrary ("free") nature of the will is asserted over against the authority of reason, thereby giving it creative access to Reality or even creating it (Schopenhauer, Nietzsche, Kierkegaard, James, Bergson, Sartre). In his early period Dewey had followed the Hegelian approach of seeing all "phenomenal" or personal experience as fragmentary and incomplete instances implicated on the order of Reality in the infinite self-knowledge of the Absolute. Now, in "The Postulate of Immediate Empiricism," Dewey followed the lead James had given in his *Principles of Psychology* of taking the phases of experience functionally, seeing how they operated together in the fulfillment of life activity. Knowing was in the service of life, not life in the service of knowing.

Dewey tried to illustrate this complex thought with a mundane example. When I am preoccupied and am startled by a noise, the noise is immediately imbued with the qualities of alarm. It is a frightful thing though it is not yet known. Upon discovering the cause to be the wind making the window shade tap, the fearsome quality is transformed into a sense of security and the situation, being resolved, contains within it an object which may truly be said to be "known," the shade, because a judgment about it has been made as a result of inquiry. The experience may fade off into a sense of mingled relief and humor, with a residual habit to check the window shade first should any similar noise be heard. The brute shock of alarm and the lingering amused relief are not instances of *knowing* because they are not, in themselves, inquiries guided by some method or plan of action. In Dewey's later terminology, they are "had" or "undergone." Instead of seeing them as involving tacit cognitive judgments, Dewey sees the phase of inquiry presupposing the noncognitive in order to make sense. Without the startling noise, no inquiry would have been initiated; without the sense of resolution or "closure" (as Dewey would call it), the inquiry would not have ended—there would have been no "object" that would have been the focus of a judgment. In the experience, there has been a process of transformation that integrated different aspects of experience so that sense or meaning was made. As Dewey rather awkwardly put it, "The experience has changed; that is, the thing experienced has changed—not that an unreality has given place to a reality, nor that some transcendental (unexperienced) Reality has changed, not that truth has changed, but just and only the concrete reality has changed" (MW, 3:160). In other words, the process is one of *learning* rather than *knowing*.

Dewey's whole thesis rides on the claim that neither the moment of fright nor the moment of relief after the identification of the cause has been made are *experienced as* moments of *knowing fright* or *knowing relief*. An experience of "knowing fear" would be to submit oneself to tests of courage or to undertake a psychological inquiry into what things cause fear under which circumstances. Likewise, "knowing relief" could range from simple personal techniques in dealing with frustration to studying conditions under which people tend to achieve satisfaction by responding to disturbing circumstances in an effective manner. Should anyone object that to have the feeling of fear or relief was also an instance of "knowing," Dewey's response is simply that this is not empirical but involves instead a hypothesis about experience, a hypothesis, moreover, that assumes its own truth in arguing for the thesis.

But we can still frame the obvious question: "Wasn't it *really* the window shade all along? The search didn't change *it*; what happened was that my confused state of mind was replaced by a well justified belief." Isn't Dewey still caught in the Protagorean nightmare where "objects" out there change all the time as people perceive them? Dewey's analysis is still entirely from the viewpoint of the experiencing subject, not the objective world, and thus can still be criticized as exhibiting the "Hegelian Bacillus." Such is the case of the "realists" who responded to Dewey throughout his career; e.g., Woodbridge (in the case of this very essay), Lovejoy, and Santayana later on. What can Dewey say to this? It is my claim that it was Dewey's attempt to respond to this problem that led him to develop the naturalistic metaphysics that began to take shape with such essays as "The Practical Character of Reality" (1908), "The Subject-Matter of Metaphysical Inquiry" (1915), the important introduction to *Essays in Experimental Logic* (1916), and on to *Experience and Nature*. Dewey had to frame a metaphysical outlook in which the whole idea of "objective reality" was exposed for the historical construct that it was and replace it with something other than Protagorean subjectivism or a metaphysical voluntarism. This was by no means an easy task (some would say: of course, since it is impossible).

The next year, in 1906, Dewey made his divorce from idealism explicit in his presidential address to the American Philosophical Association, "Beliefs and Existences." This was made more evident the following year in a direct attack on idealism, "Experience and Objective Idealism." The central claim in both pieces was his rejection of any school of philosophy that committed the "intellectualist fallacy" of equating the real with the known. In identifying the ideal with the real, idealism simply made ideals ineffective in ordinary experience. An effective ideal was a *possibility* of the world and as such might help direct action to make it an embodied actuality. In separating the real from the known, Dewey had also broken with the commitment of regarding it as absolutely actual. A new metaphysics would be needed.

The Essays in Experimental Logic

The introduction to Dewey's 1916 anthology *Essays in Experimental Logic* is more than seventy pages long. Were it read together with Dewey's other famous, lengthy article that appeared the next year, "The Need for a Recovery of Philosophy," we would see the combined use of creative speculation in the former with trenchant criticism of the history of philosophy in the latter that characterizes *Experience and Nature*. Dewey had to try to formulate the general theory of experience that underlay his work from the early 1900s on; the most important element he notes immediately is the placing of logical functions "in their temporal context" (EEL, 1; MW, 10:320). Dewey has rejected firmly and clearly any appeal to a transcendental condition for logical judgments and is fully conscious that any logic, no matter how formal, must ultimately be understood as embedded in temporality, which for Dewey means both contextually and transformationally.

A second key theme is the recognition that logic, so understood, is not a "foundation" for a fundamentally cognitive relationship between an "epistemic knower" and a "world" whose nature is likewise summed up in its status as a "known object." Knowledge—and so logic—exists within a noncognitive temporal framework, arising from experiences that are noncognitive and passing into experiences that are also noncognitive. However one may positively characterize the experience out of which inquiry arises, says Dewey, be it "social, affectional, technological, aesthetic, etc.," it "cannot be called a knowledge experience without doing violence to the term 'knowledge' and to experience" (EEL, 2; MW, 10:320). The history of philosophy is filled with pervasive abuse of this key point, because when we *think* about experience, it takes on the quality of *thinking* and so appears naturally to the philosopher as primarily an affair of knowing. What is needed is to remember that knowing occurs within the qualitatively richer spectrum of life itself: "[T]he intellectual element is set in a context which is non-cognitive, and which holds within it in suspense a vast complex of other qualities and things that in the experience itself are objects of esteem or aversion, of decision, of use, of suffering, of endeavor and revolt, not of knowledge" (EEL, 4; MW, 10:322). Thus, the primary step in philosophical reflection for Dewey must be a firm and vivid remembrance by the philosopher of life itself, which also is a recognition of the temporality of experience and the functionality of distinctions that emerge from it—what Dewey will characterize in *Experience and Nature* as "the empirical-denotative method."

The primary feature of this larger "nonreflectional" type of experience (as Dewey called it) is that in spite of the diversity and complexity it may have, all parts of it are "saturated with a pervasive quality" (EEL, 5; MW, 10:322). Indeed, if the word "thing" is taken in its Latin sense of *res* (or, in Greek, *pragma*)—that is, as "affair" or "event"—we can understand how this quality takes on the salient trait: the qualitative character of a political campaign, a romance, or of being sick (to give Dewey's examples). To see "things" in terms of being *rēs* also confirms that they are articulated wholes with focus and context: "brilliancy and obscurity, conspicuousness or apparency, and concealment or reserve, with a constant movement of redistribution" (EEL, 6; MW, 10:323). The "axis" of the event remains, though what is in focus is changing, and this focus is consciousness. The term Dewey selects for this "immense and operative world of diverse and interacting elements" is "experience" (EEL, 7; MW, 10:323). He argues that this term is preferable to words like "environment" or "world" precisely because it implies a "focus of immediate shining apparency" (EEL, 7; MW, 10:324).

To root "logic" in a temporal, contextualized, experimental activity of inquiry means that this qualitative, noncognitive background must also be recognized and its conditioning presence acknowledged in the process of thinking. Looking back over the period in which the essays making up *Essays in Experimental Logic* were written, Dewey at last is able to articulate fairly clearly this radical view of experience which had been working itself out ever since, I think, his first, shattering encounter with James's *Principles of Psychology*. By 1916, Dewey was able to see just how deep a gulf separated his philosophy from the majority of other philosophical positions which maintained the crucial equation between reality and the object of knowledge. Dewey was still sanguine, however, that in spelling out his disagreement over this issue and by putting forth his alternative situational view of experience that at least his critics would comprehend what he had done. Deep habits die hard, as Dewey would discover. *Experience and Nature* devoted its original first chapter to this thesis—but in light of the pervasive misunderstandings the book provoked, he felt compelled to rewrite the first chapter for the second edition and then return again and again to writing a long critical introduction reviewing the history of philosophy that would remain unfinished at the time of his death.[18] This idea still remains perhaps the most significant—and unrecognized—contribution of Dewey's philosophy.

Dewey struggled the rest of his career to formulate an alternative outlook, one that was not only more faithful to experience as it is experienced, but one that could also be the basis of enlightened, intelligent living; i.e., wisdom. His greatest effort in this direction, *Experience and Nature*, has been repeatedly misread and abused by generations of scholars from Santayana and Morris Cohen to Bernstein and Rorty as being infected with idealism because of its emphasis on the issue of experience and the process-oriented, situational nature of knowing. At ninety, a frustrated Dewey even toyed with junking the term "experience" for "culture," in the title of the book, as if that would do any good. To get these ideas across, he and his odd friend Arthur Bentley tinkered on a fancy new terminology, pedantic enough to be attractive even to the new wave of scientistic philosophy in the 1940s, but without success—except, perhaps, for one term. The older term "natural history" had recently come to be replaced by another: "ecology." In *Knowing and the Known*, Dewey and Bentley briefly appropriated it as an example of their broader term "transaction." The "descriptive spade-work of the ecologies" has shown that environments evolve just as organisms do: "Ecology is full of illustrations

---

18. Drafts of this introduction were edited by Joseph Ratner for the edition of *Experience and Nature* published in *Later Works*. The manuscripts published as *Unmodern Philosophy and Modern Philosophy* (Carbondale: Southern Illinois University Press, 2012) are part of this critique.

of the interactional . . . and it is still fuller of illustrations of the transactional" (LW, 16:117, 120). Rather than fighting the ghosts of idealism in Dewey's thought, we do far better to see his work presenting the rudiments of an evolutionary metaphysics that replaces the Greek ideal knower with a creative ecosystem in which change, plurality, possibility, and mutual interdependence replace the canonical concepts of substance: timelessness, logical identity, self-sufficiency, and completion. Such a position might be called "ecological emergentism" and its metaphysics in particular "eco-ontology."

Conclusion

In this essay I have tried to sketch two sides of the revolution Dewey accomplished, the crucial years of which were spent at the University of Chicago. By abandoning the ontology of perfection and its presupposition of the privileged ideal knower, Dewey at once created the possibility for replacing the traditional philosophical project of epistemology, analyzing how we know or upon what foundations knowledge is possible, with a theory of learning. It is, after all, learning in which imagination, not merely reason, transforms our past into a meaningful future. Learning allows us to adapt to new circumstances and communicate with those different from us rather than force us to defend the old and familiar and demand others adapt themselves to our ways of thinking. In its broader conceptions, Dewey points toward an ecological conception of metaphysics in which certain "generic traits" are used to keep the diverse areas of inquiry constantly in touch with each other, not allowing them to lapse into disconnected self-contained disciplines. Metaphysics thus becomes the intelligence of intelligence and provides the basis for intelligence applied to the most fulfilling ideals of human conduct, which Dewey calls wisdom.

A contemporary Deweyan would point out how much the equation of reality with the object of knowledge still permeates our philosophical assumptions. We may have abandoned Plato's view of reality as constituted of ideal Forms along with Aristotle's conception of *ousia* as a formed individual, a member of a known species. But we largely follow the early modern view of the real as a physical substance known through mathematical physics and we still try to identify mental states with propositional attitudes. There is still the tacit assumption that the objective world in and of itself, apart from our experience, is essentially determinate and complete. There are formal laws governing fixed identities and *that's it*. Dewey's philosophy offers us the opportunity to step back and question that assumption and perhaps adopt a more ecological approach to philosophical wisdom. The world of the twenty-first century has two central problems: preserving the planetary ecosystem and creating the basis for mutual understanding between diverse peoples in a world verging toward overpopulation. Given these looming concerns and the barrenness of contemporary philosophy, we might do worse than reconsider the advances begun by Dewey almost a century ago to formulate an ecological ontology and with it an ecological view of experience in which the aesthetic context of inquiry is acknowledged.

TWO

DEWEY'S DENOTATIVE-EMPIRICAL METHOD
A Thread through the Labyrinth

In teaching *Experience and Nature*, I once had my students do a one-page writing assignment after having read both versions of Dewey's first chapter, "Experience and Philosophic Method." The question was, "What is Dewey's Denotative-Empirical Method?" They were forewarned—did not Dewey himself feel compelled to rewrite the whole first chapter for the second edition?[1] But in reviewing their responses I was reminded of the old story (told in Rumi's *Masnavi*) of the blind men and the elephant: the elephant is like a tree trunk, like a snake, like a rope, like a large flat leaf, like a smooth piece of wood, like a wall.[2] The exercise achieved my immediate purpose, which was of course to shake the assurance of anyone who approached this book with the false confidence that the terms "experience," "method," or "denote" (or any of the other key terms) were easily understood. We found that Dewey, instead of "clarifying" the

---

1. See Dewey's own admission of "failure" in the preface added in the 1929 edition, LW. 1:3ff.
2. See A. J. Arberry, trans., *Tales from the Masnavi* (London: Routledge, 1994), 208.

{ 54 }

method to be used in the rest of the undertaking, made it a question that haunted us throughout the reading of the book. It only seemed fair I should make the attempt as well.

I will present what I consider to be the central features of Dewey's "denotative-empirical method"—which he presents as *philosophical method*—and expand somewhat upon them. The result is not merely to have a more complete articulation of Dewey's "method" but also to imagine where the ultimate goals of the rich "way" of experience that Dewey opened up can lead us.[3] This also permits going beyond merely seeing Dewey as an "instrumentalist" and to contextualize "instrumentalism" within a broader and deeper philosophical methodology. Instrumentalism is Dewey's theory of inquiry; i.e., his theory of knowing. The "denotative method," on the other hand, is *philosophical* method; i.e., a way of preventing philosophy from succumbing to "intellectualism"; it is a way of putting "knowing" in context and making "experience" serviceable for the real philosophical project: wisdom. Here I find aesthetics a particularly significant, though neglected, aspect of Deweyan philosophy. I will give a careful synopsis of what Dewey himself says about the denotative-empirical method in both versions of the introductory chapter, focusing on the less well known (but, I maintain, more successful) draft of 1925. Both take up the "problem of philosophy" and present "the denotative-empirical method" as a corrective. I believe that so few of Dewey's interpreters have understood the real nature of this method and its implications for how we *do* philosophy that it holds some revealing lessons for us, which many, including those who profess to be "pragmatists," may find surprising and even troubling.

Dewey asks the reader to discern between "experience" as a philosophical concept and *experience* as it is lived, as "had" or "undergone" and as "done." This is accomplished within the context of a highly refined philosophical work that presents its own "theory" about experience. Dewey wants to theorize about experience, but not in a way that allows the theory to hide experience on its pretheoretical level. The "denotative-empirical method" is given as a method of "disclosing" experience without transforming it into a mere theoretical object. A good deal of Dewey's so-called murkiness comes from this difficult endeavor.

---

3. I say "way" to avoid the false dichotomies introduced by the terms "theory" or "method."

The concern for a "thick" view of experience is evident even in Dewey's *Psychology* (1887) and it was the reason he was susceptible to the influence of James's *Principles of Psychology*. By 1905 Dewey had made a revolutionary move with his "The Postulate of Immediate Empiricism" to reject the equation of "Reality" with "the Known." Reality was not primarily encountered in moments of knowing. This break with twenty-five hundred years of Western philosophy governs the subsequent development of Dewey's thought, achieving its first coherent statement in the 1916 introduction to the *Essays in Experimental Logic* and then in *Experience and Nature*. It is this turn that makes, I believe, *Art as Experience* more of a key in understanding Dewey's philosophy than has been generally recognized.

Philosophy, Dewey says, has been highly successful in substituting its own secondary, refined, theorized concepts of experience for experience "in the raw," and so it has generated its history of dualisms. The initial problem, then, is to get highly theoretically oriented and conceptually clever thinkers to *remember* what it is to be alive. This cannot be accomplished by substituting yet another concept. Nor can it be done by setting forth some highly schematized "method" that claims to offer a content-free procedure, like Descartes' *Regulae* or even Locke's "plain historical method." The method cannot *be* formal, not even like the six stages of the "pattern of inquiry."[4] It must be intuitive, circumspect, involved with its content, humble, and receptive and thereby "open" to surprises, and it must recognize it comes from the lived world. It must be crafty in discerning its own "selective emphasis" and prejudices. Beyond that, it must be "wise" rather than clever: it must "know itself" without making itself an object of knowledge. (The Greek injunction *Gnōthi Seauton* meant more "Remember who you are"—i.e., a mortal; *gnōsis* is an intimate bringing of oneself back to one's existence rather than a formalized, teachable knowledge like *epistēmē*.) Humility is needed more than cleverness to accomplish this. In this sense, Dewey's method is Delphic *gnōsis*.

The 1925 version begins by noting that "experience" is "a weasel word" that can mean a repudiation of the a priori or a concern with what is, ultimately, "subjective," the former alluding to the "empirical" methodology of science, the latter to introspective psychological theories of the

---

4. See *Logic: The Theory of Inquiry* (LW, 12), ch. 6.

nineteenth century. Dewey rejects the latter view completely. We begin, then, with either the "experience in gross . . . in its primary and crude forms" and note features of the world in which it arises while also bearing in mind the refined objects in which it may terminate, or we may begin with "refined selective products and work from them back to the primary facts of life" (LW, 1:366).[5] The danger with the latter approach is that philosophy builds on what it considers to be scientific "facts" that are but historical objects capable of undergoing further transformation. A more serious danger is that the "immediate facts of gross experience" are discounted, in which case, Dewey says, "philosophy itself commits suicide" (LW, 1:367). The method that begins with those gross objects, however, "requires unusual candor and patience" because "coarse experience is Protean, a thing of moods and tenses." The artist gives us reports of it as much as the "informed technician." Too often have empiricists substituted "dialectical notions" for "experience as humanly lived" (LW, 1:367). "Not safely can an 'ism' be made out of experience." A philosopher like Bertrand Russell "sees" a chair as a theoretical object of color and shape that is the subject of true and false propositions. But, for Dewey, the one who sits in the chair experiences it more fully, especially if the chair has contextual and historical meanings. Getting caught up in theoretical objects may "convince many a student that the nearer he gets to the reality of experience, the further away he gets from all the experience he ever had" (LW, 1:368). Better to take the "behavior of Odysseus' dog upon his master's return," says Dewey.[6] To begin with gross, or "macroscopic," experience does not discount science; it simply rejects its privilege. Science (or knowledge) is a "phase of human experience" like magic, myth, or poetry: "imagination is to be noted as much as refined observation" (LW, 1:369). As Dewey puts it in 1929, "the very meaning and purport of empirical method is that things are to be studied on their own account, so as to find out what is revealed when they are experienced"

5. In the 1929 version Dewey begins by appealing to the scientific method as evidence that "experience" and "nature" can get along (digressing into the paradox of how a late, "small" part of nature can "reach down into it")—with the result that it seems that the method he himself employs is the scientific method rather than a much broader "method of experience." The 1929 version begins with an attack on dualism whereas the 1925 version labors to present the reader at the outset with the difference between primary and secondary experience. In the 1929 version Dewey only gets to the primary-secondary experience distinction much later (LW, 1:15ff.).

6. See *Odyssey*, Book 17, l:290ff. The old dog *recognizes* (*enoēsen*, 301) Odysseus after twenty years and dies.

(LW, 1:13–14). This method goes beyond secondary objects of knowing to objects of "gross" experience to "study" its subject matters to see what they "reveal" *in* experience. How it goes about "showing" what is "revealed" is not clear. How does one approach primary experience without making it secondary experience? We have only been given a negative directive: don't begin with knowing or its objects.[7]

Dewey's next major point is that "experience" is not limited to consciousness, much less "knowledge." Ignorance, skillful habits, and "fatal implication in the remote"—the very stuff of tragedy—are aspects of experience as well. The clear and distinct may exist in special circumstances, but "twilight, the vague, dark and mysterious flourish" (LW, 1:369; compare 1:27). The subconscious has been almost as much presented as a refined, theoretical object as "experience," but such "crimes" should not prevent us from "refusing to admit that what is not explicitly present makes up a vastly greater part of experience than does the conscious field to which thinkers have so devoted themselves" (LW, 1:369–70). Knowledge is one type of experience, but so are "disease or religion or love," and in all of these there are "forces and potential consequences" that are *in* the experience whether they are objects of consciousness or rational inference or not.[8] Death itself, says Dewey, is one of the great "matters of experience" that is surely *in* experience. "Experience," as Dewey uses the term, means something "at least as wide and deep and full as all history on this earth" (LW 1:370). It includes the "whole wide universe" of fact and dream, actuality and possibility, truth and falsehood, consistency and inconsistency. This is quite a claim, and I wonder how many of us "instrumentalists" have come to terms with it.

Here Dewey believes that the "value of experience as method in philosophy" stands revealed: "*denotation* comes first and last, so that to settle any discussion, to still any doubt, to answer any question, we must go to some thing pointed to, denoted, and find our answer in that thing" (LW, 1:372). This statement may be one of the most frustrating and

7. Dewey's concerns over "intellectualism," or equating the real with the known, come relatively late in the 1929 version (LW, 1:28ff) making it easier to assume "science" as a paradigm. His interest in science is that it gives others a "map" of its conclusions and "points back" to primary experience (LW, 1:16–17).

8. In the 1929 version Dewey says, "If experience actually presents esthetic and moral traits, then these traits may also be supposed to reach down into nature, and to testify to something that belongs to nature as truly as does the mechanical structure attributed to it in physical science" (LW, 1:13).

obscure that Dewey ever uttered. Experience means the universe, and to solve any problem we just "denote" some "thing" and "find our answer" there! Dewey tries to illuminate this dark saying by contrasting the "denotative method," as the method of "showing," with rationalism. The value of the idea of "experience" for philosophy is none other than "the finality and comprehensiveness of the method of pointing, finding, showing" (LW, 1:372). "Were the denotative method universally followed by philosophers, then the word and the notion of experience might be discarded" (LW, 1:372).[9] But it is necessary as long as philosophers seek to define reality "according to esthetic, moral or logical canons"; i.e., defining reality in terms of some selected features and not in terms of everything found in experience. "Experience" pragmatically functions as a "cautionary and directive word . . . to remind us that the world which is lived, suffered and enjoyed as well as logically thought of, has the last word in all human inquiries and surmises" (LW, 1:372). "This is a doctrine of humility," Dewey adds, "but it is also a doctrine of direction. For it tells us to open the eyes and ears of the mind, to be sensitive to all the varied phases of life and history." Above all, Dewey stresses, it acts to prevent philosophy from identifying the "real" with "the known."

This is a remarkable aspect of the method that is obscured in the 1929 version. Here the method takes on a moral and aesthetic character: we are *cautioned* to remember experience in its noncognitive richness and variety—we are asked to think about what it is like to *have* or *live through* various experiences like love, grief, bravery, or fear of death. The doctrine "makes us *humble*." But it also "opens the eyes and ears" of the mind. It makes us sensitive, aware, and receptive to what the world has to tell us. We do not merely remember superficially, but we engage the world with "mindfulness."[10] We are also open to learning from experience, *hearing* what it has to say, not interposing the ego and its presuppositions. The denotative method is a method for aesthetic receptivity and openness.

9. Compare 1929: "If the empirical method were universally or even generally adopted in philosophizing, there would be no need of referring to experience" (LW, 1:14ff.). Again, in this version Dewey confuses matters by using science as an example, thereby seemingly giving it the privilege he is at pains to discount.

10. I believe that the Buddhist term *Sati* is quite appropriate here. It is attentive but nongrasping awareness so that the true nature (*Dharma*) of experience can be realized without distortions of the ego. Dewey's notion also involves the kind of careful listening attention that opens us outward toward something or someone.

In the 1925 version of the chapter, Dewey stresses the *noncognitive* aspects of experience and sees the denotative method as a way of bringing them into view. In 1929, in the effort to make himself better understood, Dewey uses the *scientific method* as an *example* of how experience and nature "get along." Dewey appeals to science at the very start and continues to do so at critical junctures.[11] Readers who had been troubled about his earlier appeal to myth, magic, and dreams revealing nature would be reassured, Dewey must have reasoned, by seeing that his main point could be illustrated by science and the experimental method. This not only made him deemphasize the richer description, it also obscured his basic point and made it sound as if it were *science—knowing*—that "really" disclosed nature. The result was that Dewey was read as privileging science—a common and persistent misreading. In the revised chapter he discusses how science, beginning with the gross objects of primary experience, refines them and then *returns* to the primary world so that its objects are now *understood* and seen as *continuous* with other phenomena.[12] The term "denotative method" as meaning "empirical method" is introduced at this point (LW, 1:16). When Dewey said "empirical" he meant to refer to the range of types of experience. But his readers heard "empirical method" as "scientific method"; i.e., a process in which knowledge, truth, and verification are primary concerns. Thus readers came to understand the denotative method itself *as* scientific rather than as *illustrated* in science.

The implication is also different: now we understand and control events. In both versions, he stresses that "denotation" comes "first and last." It goes back to the roots of reflective experience and returns reflection to the life world. His use of scientific examples in 1929 makes him sound as if the denotative method were the same as the "theory of inquiry." Whole interpretations of Dewey have been based on this confusion. The scientific method reveals something about the denotative method: that it

---

11. A parallel synopsis of the two versions of chapter 1 is appended to the end of this essay.

12. "That the subject-matter of primary experience sets the problems and furnishes the first data of the reflection which constructs the secondary objects is evident; it is also obvious that test and verification of the latter is secured by return to things of crude, macroscopic experience—the sun, earth, plants, and animals of common, everyday life. But just what role do the objects attained in reflection play? Where do they come in? They *explain* the primary objects, they enable us to grasp them with *understanding* instead of just having sense-contact with them" (LW, 1:16). The whole stress on the role of *knowing* undercuts much of what Dewey has tried to say about limiting the usually privileged status of knowledge and makes him sound as though his is just another sort of cognitivist project, which it is not.

begins and ends with primary experience. The scientific method is not identical with the denotative method, but is rather something illuminated *by* it. The denotative method attempts to make us fully *aware* of the world *beyond* our "ideas" of it.[13] This method "is the only method which can do justice to this inclusive integrity of experience" (LW, 1:19). The denotative method is meant to contextualize the *cognitive* interests of philosophy within the *noncognitive* scope of life. It is a method *for philosophy* that aims at *reminding* it of its *origins* in a prereflective world as well as of its *obligations* to make life more meaningful and value-rich.[14] This does not mean rejection of cognitive objects or rational methods, but it does involve understanding them as developments out of a precognitive, prerational world and leading back into it. The "tangled and complex" aspects of the world, its vagueness, mystery, and obscurity, are not "appearances" beyond which a rational structure exists that is made manifest in the moment of knowing the truth. Rational truth exists *because of* this primary world (LW, 1: 374). The world is not primarily an object of knowledge, nor is the mind essentially an amalgam of "beliefs," and the fact that philosophers have made it so is why Dewey sets forth this "method" as a corrective for philosophy. The denotative method asks philosophical reflection to remember the world in humility and with attentiveness and then to direct our thought back toward that world. "Denotation" is not any specific "pointing" but rather an art of remembering the world.[15] Denotation "points" not only to the world but also to its past and its possibilities.

13. Dewey has only one previous discussion of "denotation," a comment from the "syllabus" (or synopsis) of a course taught in 1922–23 called *Types of Philosophic Thought* (MW, 13)—fairly close to the time he gave the Carus Lectures, which became *Experience and Nature*. He contrasts signs as denotative with those that are "signifying—connotative": "To point, indicate, is ambiguous; may mean a direct *act* or the function of evidence. Denotation is the former; is non-logical. With reference to connotation, pointing means selecting the things which determine the meaning-content, 'intension' and the things to which meanings apply—extension. Denotation as direction of inquiry and experiment, search, is the essence of the empirical method. When search stops without detecting connecting links of things found, it is traditional empiricism. To follow up the search till connections are found is scientific, experimental empiricism" (MW, 13:389). Denotation here means "search," the creative side of science, not the "identification" of predetermined and recognizable objects or settled definitions. Compare this with the discussion from *Logic: The Theory of Inquiry* (LW, 12:352ff.)

14. "Thus there is here supplied, I think, a first-rate test of the value of any philosophy which is offered us: Does it end in conclusions which, when they are referred back to ordinary life-experiences and their predicaments, render them more significant, more luminous to us, and make our dealings with them more fruitful?" (LW, 1:18).

15. For Dewey's rather insightful discussion of ostensive definition (anticipating the later Wittgenstein), see *Logic: The Theory of Inquiry* (LW, 12:59ff.).

This is not to claim that the prereflective world has no structure—that it is merely pure *apeiron* (another criticism often made of Dewey). Life exists because the world *does* have structure; life is a response to some of those structures. But they exist in a general and flexible way, and these features are expressed in language by the various adjectives used to describe experience: as religious, political, esthetic, intellectual, etc. (LW, 1:375). In other words, Dewey limits the role of knowledge to make room for the ontological significance of meaning. The world is such that it gives rise to joy, grief, love, hate, dreams, and clearheaded judgments. These are not "in us" but are "in the world." They are *events*: "*being* and *having* things in ways other than knowing them . . . exist and are conditions for reflection and knowledge" (LW, 1:377). The having of experience, in fact, is ultimately "indescribable." That is why it must ultimately be "pointed to" or "shown." The qualitative aspect of experience is ultimate. "All cognitive experience must start from and terminate in being and having things in just such unique, irreparable, and compelling ways. And until this fact is a commonplace in philosophy, the notion of experience will not be a truism for philosophers" (LW, 1:378).

Dewey illuminates "denotation" with two subsequent points. First "experience" denotes "the world" in a "double-barreled" way: "the field, the sun and clouds, and rain, seeds and harvest, and the man who labors, who plans, invents, uses, suffers, enjoys" (LW, 1:384; compare 18–19). "Denotation" means understanding how "Nature" is in human existence and human existence is in Nature.[16] We can call this the "denotation of events within situations and of situations within events." The double movement is important: We go from something of focal interest, like human existence, to understanding how it is implicated in the world and also from the world to the ways it is embedded in and transmuted by human existence.

The second point is that "the denotations that constitute experience point to history, to temporal process" (LW, 1:384). Our inquiries have erroneously focused on trying to make things "wholly or completely present" and so "exclude movement and change." Thus to grasp "things" as "phases" of events makes us comprehend anything present in terms of its histories and possibilities. The denotative method breaks down

16. "Life" and "history" are terms that are equally "double-barreled," says Dewey (LW, 1:19).

the "isolated individual" fact in terms of putting it in its situation; it also follows it back through time as well as projects it against its immanent future potentialities and more indefinite possibilities. "Experience is history," states Dewey, even when we are caught up in the immediacy of the present (LW, 1:385). Denotation includes the grasping of temporality in even apparently "timeless" objects. "But in fact anything denoted is found to have temporal quality and reference" (LW, 1:385).[17]

Dewey describes the denotative-empirical method largely in negative terms, as warnings for philosophers: It warns us against making experience a "stuff"; it prevents us from accepting traditional distinctions, like mind and body, as ultimate; it tells us that intellectual distinctions are the result of selection and that the distinctions of reason are embedded in a prerational world. It seeks to "relive" the processes whereby various interpretations come about "with eyes constantly upon the things to which they refer" (LW, 1:386). It reflects on the "groupings" objects fall into by way of general adjectival or qualitative marks, not privileging those that are "cognitive." It teaches us to "experience" knowledge *as it is undergone or had* rather than simply to "know" it. It asks us to begin with the world in its complexity rather than with simplifications of it.

A final aspect of the denotative method emerges: Although it warns philosophers not to privilege any one quality of experience over another as more "real," this does not change Dewey's belief that philosophy is the "pursuit of wisdom," which is to say "a branch of morals" (LW, 1:387). Wisdom means living wisely, not knowing a lot of "facts." And so the denotative method is appealed to because it is part of the "art of experience" that philosophy aims toward, that is, wisdom.

What then is the "denotative-empirical method"? Negatively it says: Do not begin to philosophize by thinking upon the objects of secondary, cognitive experience. Do not equate the Real with the Known—even inquiry instrumentally conceived is not all there is in life. Do not cut off an individual event of being from its context or environment. Positively it enjoins: Begin and end all reflections with an awareness of the world that

---

17. Temporal quality presents a particularly difficult concept in Dewey's account of experience, one deserving its own extended treatment. Suffice it to say that "temporal *quality*" is not the same as the phenomenon of temporal succession but refers to the structure of "doing and undergoing," the transformation of potential into actual, and the way in which a "history" is "consummated" at any given moment (see LW, 1:82–92). The fullest account of the nature of temporal quality is in the third chapter of *Art as Experience*. But see Dewey's astute account at LW, 1:387.

transcends thought. Approach that world with humility and with an open mind: Have a receptive awe of and curiosity in the world. Strive to see the world in the individual and the individual in the world. This is a double process: To see how the world is transmuted by an individual event is different from discerning how that event affects the world. It discerns the structures of the world in the varied responses human beings have— responses symbolized and expressed in religion, myth, art, and culture. It teaches us to see "events" rather than fixed identities or essences. Events are not bare happenings but rather the outcomes of natural histories. The method teaches us to think in terms of evolutionary histories. Nor do we cut off the horizon of the creative future from the being of an event but instead remain mindful of the open-ended possibilities that anything carries within it here and now. The nature of process is transformation and individuality is the mark of a history not of a substantial identity. The goal of our attentive receptivity and awareness of the world is the enrichment of human existence. It asks that philosophy be a love of wisdom, not a love of knowledge.

I think we have evidence for the peculiar importance Dewey came to attach to art and aesthetic experience, for art engages just such abilities as these to deal with "experience" in the primary sense of the word and to exhibit or show the presence of the world, temporally as well as situationally, in the consummatory objects it creates. The aesthetic consciousness aligns itself so closely to the "denotative method" that I am willing to say that the latter is really Dewey's effort to get philosophers to start thinking like artists. We cannot "prove," only "disclose" (LW, 1:10).[18] Of course, at its best, science does this as well and art, at its worst, does not.

But how might an actual use of the "denotative method" work in philosophy? It is somewhat bizarre that a now venerable pragmatic tradition has hardly addressed this topic. One clear reason is that it might involve a transformation of philosophy to the extent that those of us engaged in the new way might not even "look" like philosophers to our colleagues. It would direct us toward teaching students to see ideas in context and to see why ideas from various times and places were ways in which human beings struggled with their existential conditions: the earth and heavens,

18. For example, Dewey does not "refute" subjectivism but instead shows how it results from the rise of individualism and the value of "property" in the seventeenth century (LW, 1:23ff. and 367ff.).

birth, life, sex, death, hunger, fear, love, and so on. It would require us to put the critical mind in abeyance in order to hear what ancient myths and rituals have to say. We would have to have an insatiable curiosity about the sheer diversity of culture and life, and so we would have to know a lot more about other cultures and the histories of our own. The texts that we turn to might have to be those of religion or literature more than "philosophy," which, as Dewey says, more often than not reflects the lack of the denotative method. Finally, we might have to think about what wisdom for the twenty-first century might actually mean.

Comparison of 1925 and 1929 Versions of Experience and Nature: *Chapter 1, "Experience and Philosophic Method"*

First Edition (1925)	Second Edition (1929)
1. Empirical method and problems with the term "experience" (365).	1. Terms proposed for Dewey's philosophy: empirical naturalism, naturalistic empiricism, naturalistic humanism (10).
2. Two approaches: Gross-to-refined vs. refined-to-"primary facts of life"; dangers of latter; "candor and patience" needed for former; role of *artist* as example (366–67).	2. Instead of experience and nature being opposed with experience as a veil hiding nature, here it is a method for penetrating nature *as in science* (10–11). Experience reaches down into nature and piles the goods high like a miner (11).
3. Seventeenth-century empiricism as warning of dangers of latter approach; example of sitting in a chair vs. Bertrand Russell's description of a "chair" as "patches of color"; Dewey takes approach of "the dog of Odysseus" who recognized his master (367–68).	3. Experience is latecomer in evolution; *science* shows it does enter into possession of nature; example of *geologist* (11–12).

(Continued)

First Edition (1925)	Second Edition (1929)
4. The primary world *no more* *scientific* than it is magical, political, artistic, etc. (369).	4. Experience is of as well as in nature: Things are "hows" of experience. Experience also has stretch; i.e., inference (12–13). Just because it is late in evolution doesn't mean it isn't capable—as *science* shows (13). In *science* we begin with experience (13).
5. Experience is not consciousness; consciousness is only the "focus of experience." There are also habit, ignorance, and that "twilight" where "the vague, dark and mysterious flourish" (369). Death is in experience. Experience is the banks as well as stream; this includes "all history on this earth"; Compare James: Experience is double-barreled (370); it includes potential as well as actual (371). "Experience for philosophy is method, not subject matter": It includes "dreams, insanity, illness, death, labor, war, confusion, ambiguity, lies and error" (370).	5. Experience is not materialistic: "Ideal" aspects also in experience (13–14).

First Edition (1925)	Second Edition (1929)
6. Denotation as method: "denotation comes first and last" as "pointing" or "showing" (371–72); contrast with rationalism as method. It is a method for philosophers (372). When the precarious, uncertain, irrational are acknowledged along with the good and the beautiful and true, we may dispense with the term "experience." This is a "doctrine of humility" (373).	6. The aim of the book: to discover some general features of experience for a philosophical theory of the universe; empirical method for philosophy liberates *as it does for science* (14).
7. Philosophy begins with refined premises: Empiricists as well as Rationalists and Skeptics, all philosophers need to be reminded where refined objects come from (374). Most things are not matters of "belief" at all (374).	7. *Science* does have to talk about experience because it is used (14); Roger and Francis Bacon had to argue for it (14).
8. There is prephilosophic selectivity in the order of the world: Men respond to the "pressures of natural events" via art, religion, politics, industry, thought, etc. (375); Philosophy as intellectual tends to begin with intellectual objects, e.g., statements (375); we need things that make us labor, surprise us with beauty, or "compel obedience under penalty" (376).	8. Gross vs. refined experience; example of *science*: It explains the primary objects, e.g., the use of an eclipse in testing Einstein on light (15–16).

(Continued)

First Edition (1925)	Second Edition (1929)
9. Even mystical philosophers make the mystical a form of knowledge (376). Others make moral or religious experience the canon. The world may be mystical or moral, but when we make knowledge claims, inquiry is needed to warrant them (376–77).	9. The denotative method: It is pointing, showing (16–17); lack of it implies no *verification*, no enlargement of meaning; philosophy then becomes abstract. Traditional philosophical objects as constituting what is supremely real vs. the denotative method, which opens further inquiry (17). The test of philosophy: Does it illuminate the world? (18).
10. Being and having vs. knowing (377–78); "all cognitive experience must start from and terminate in being and having things . . ." (377). Modern and ancient philosophy equate reality with the known (377); this renders impossible the distinction between knowing vs. being and having (377).	10. Empirical vs. nonempirical philosophies: James on "double- barreled" aspect of "experience"—the planted field, the harvest, the farmer, etc. (18). "Life" and "history" are similar (18–19). Empirical method the only one that does justice to this (19).
11. The "problem of knowledge" is not a problem: This removes the need to solve the relation of sensory knowledge and intellectual (377–78). Knowledge is something we have (378); the "given" is a selection made in a larger context of inquiry (379).	11. Naturalistic empiricism avoids dualism. Naturalistic empiricism leads to *tools and technologies* (20). The history of *science* is one of liberation (20). Problems with seventeenth-century concept of experience.

First Edition (1925)	Second Edition (1929)
12. The denotative method is realistic: "Real" means "things done and suffered" (380); this is prior to any "subjective-objective" distinction that is practically drawn; theoretically a continuum is prior (380–81). The things men fight for are not "subjective"; the aesthetic is in the world (381–82).	12. Subject and object: Mental and physical objects are discriminated out of ordinary experience (21). Our natural bias is to the objective (22); subjectivism as advance and coexistent with rise of individualism (23). Example of Russell's chair (24–25).
13. Experience as experiencing is a modern notion. Its importance lies in discerning the role of the body in experience, but this must be taken as active performance and not as "states" of mind (382). We experience meanings (383).	13. Philosophical objects: Philosophy tends to treat them as primarily real (26); but desire and reverie are real too (27). What is in experience extends further than what is known (27); it is important to note the dark and twilight (27–28).
14. Memory: Culture is the primary memory (383); the potential is experienced when we act in the world; intellectualists minimize it (383). Modern philosophy made experience the known instead of essences (384).	14. The vice of philosophy is intellectualism (28–29); knowledge is a way of control (29). Intellectualism results in the subjective nature of the mental (30).

(Continued)

First Edition (1925)	Second Edition (1929)
15. The method's use: denotes the field, the sun, the clouds, rains, seeds, harvest and farmer" (384). Man in nature is man subjected; nature in man is intelligence and art (384); the philosopher needs to be reminded of the prior integration (384).	15. This is due to selective emphasis (31); value of certainty (31), elements, the eternal (32); choice is useful in action (34). Do not commit the "Philosophic Fallacy" (34).
16. Denotation as historical and temporal: "Experience is history . . ." (385); there are no timeless objects.	16. No Guarantees: method points out where and when, like *science* (34); the value of experiments (35).
17. Experience not a stuff but a method (385–86). It is a cautionary method (386); we are "on guard" not to treat distinctions, like mental and physical, as primary. We are "reminded" that prephilosophical experience groups objects into other categories than "known"— indeed knowledge itself is had before it is known (386). It "cautions" us to begin with complex entanglements rather than simplifications (387). Temporal quality is not a reversal of process or stability (387).	17. Three fallacies (36).

First Edition (1925)	Second Edition (1929)
18. Philosophy and "the moral fallacy": Most philosophical simplifications are due to moral interests so "all philosophy is a branch of morals" (387). Philosophers have been thinkers of leisured class—they turn things that are the result of processes into eternal and prior meanings (388). The empirical method reveals the role of choice in focusing on what is taken as primary (389); "protects" us from making the consequent antecedent.	18. Primary experience of little value (37): Philosophy tends to borrow from intellectual objects of the science of the day (37); but this is not how science operates (38).
19. Empirical method as map: It shows how things are arrived at (389). The idea is not to eliminate choice but to acknowledge it and make it more intelligent (390).	19. What empirical method requires: Trace things back to primary experience, and bring secondary objects back to primary experience (39).
20. All philosophies employ empirical subject matter (391). We need "respect" for experience (392).	20. Empirical philosophy: It will study life experience (40); it is intellectual disrobing (40).

THREE

BETWEEN BEING AND EMPTINESS
Toward an Eco-ontology of Inhabitation

Philosophy and Wisdom

Philosophy today stands in a problematic relationship to wisdom. Introductory texts still relish defining *philosophia* as "the love of wisdom."[1] But, as anyone reading on discovers, the ideal of wisdom itself is long gone. In its place is the view that philosophy provides exceedingly clever and conflicting answers to puzzles that do not particularly relate to the conduct of life or the discovery of its profoundest meanings. Most of those puzzles have to do with the problems of the justification of beliefs, putting philosophy in an auxiliary relationship to the project of knowledge. The inquiry into the nature of rational justification and the implications of holding beliefs is not something to be condemned. But it

---

1. Though "the friend of wisdom" might be more accurate. Being a *philos* in ancient Greece, however, meant you would be ready to die for the honor of your friend and do nothing to disgrace it in your own deeds. To be a "friend" of wisdom in this sense meant a life of commitment to that which is noble.

is very different to see this project as a part of the more complex whole of wisdom than as the sole end that everything else serves.[2] Philosophy today is practiced very differently from the way it traditionally was. (Perhaps we should call this modern discipline "philepistemy" rather than "philosophy.")[3] In spite of what the introductory textbooks say, most members of the established profession are not interested in the question of "wisdom." The modern practice of philosophy, like the university itself, appropriated a quasi-scientific model in which rigorous technical analysis of discrete problems, isolated and concentrated upon for their own sake, is believed to lead to the increase in "knowledge." A further development is the assimilation by universities and their components of models of science in service to international corporations.[4]

The search for wisdom examines what it means to live a human life that exemplifies an art of existence, a life that reflects a qualitative, emotionally nuanced insight into the human condition as it exists in the world, which requires an equally extensive and sensitive awareness of the world itself. This ideal defined the nature of philosophical discipline as understood by the ancient Greeks as well as by John Dewey. It meant living well in such a way that a distinctly human excellence is achieved through our capacity for intelligent action, that is, action that consciously realizes ends that fund existence with reflective meaning and value.[5] This goal transcends the endeavor to satisfy a given desire by negotiating the complexities and dangers of life; it involves a realization of humanity in

2. The thought of John Dewey is thus exceptional in that it explicitly attempts to relocate the quest for knowledge back within the context of the general issue of wisdom. See *Experience and Nature* (LW, 1: 50, 305–6) as well as section 4 of *Human Nature and Conduct* (MW, 14).

3. Likewise, we should distinguish the collective cultural wisdom that is uncritically passed along from one generation to the next as "wisdom traditions" rather than "philosophy" per se, which must have a degree of critical reflectiveness and individual responsibility in thinking. But there is no reason why philosophy, as I have described it, should ignore wisdom traditions; indeed, it should pay great attention to them. Thus I designate three partially overlapping areas: wisdom traditions, philosophy, and philepistemy. Philosophy overlaps both, though neither of them overlaps with each other. Thus philosophy involves critical self-reflection, as wisdom traditions do not, though it is concerned with wisdom, and it shares with philepistemy concern over criteria for knowledge, belief, truth, meaning, etc., but not as self-contained subjects.

4. See William Reading's *The University in Ruins* (Cambridge, MA: Harvard University Press, 1995).

5. It could be argued that the earliest Greek thinkers, the Milesians, did not exemplify this ideal (though Heraclitus and Pythagoras certainly did), undertaking speculative inquiry for its own sake. I would argue that the Milesian revolution had political overtones, challenging as it did the very basis of aristocratic government; i.e., its legitimation by mythology. Philosophy began as a democratic critique.

oneself through harmony with nature. Desire is educated in accordance with a deep meaning of human existence seen in terms of nature itself. A wise human life is one that necessarily illustrates awareness of what is important in life and is lived in awareness of the world. Wisdom is manifested in the relation of life to the world in which it is lived. This requires being aware of the possible meanings of the situations in which we find ourselves in spite of their complexity. To understand a situation is to grasp it in terms of the possibilities it has as well as its immediate actualities, their contexts and histories. In order to interpret the actual in light of the possible, we need to see the potentialities of the present in terms of their abilities to realize a meaningful human life. Such a life realizes ideals that fulfill us and that exhibit responsibility and care for our environment— for it is the environment, cultural as well as natural, that is the ground of those ideals. In order to do this we need to be able to approach the present with a range of possible ideals of conduct. It is paramount to recognize that any endeavor to think in a Deweyan mode is to engage in the practice of philosophy as the love of wisdom, and this involves a fundamental recontextualization of the contemporary practice of philepistemy.[6]

Though the conscious goal of inquiry into wisdom was first articulated by philosophy, all cultures have cherished some ideal of wisdom. One need only compare the characters of Odysseus, Aeneas, Moses, Jesus, Confucius, the Buddha, or Coyote, to grasp how diverse the ideals of wisdom have been. While all cultures stress the centrality of wisdom in human existence, it is equally clear that wisdom is capable of a plurality of idealizations. Philosophy is the conscious, critical inquiry into the idea of wisdom, but it includes an exploration of the range of prereflective or precritical cultural ideals of wisdom. This is especially important from a pragmatic point of view insofar as cultures have successfully realized meaningful human lives. The practice of philosophy, then, requires investigations into the pragmatic implementation of the desire for wisdom

---

6. Philosophy, as it was understood in the ancient world and in medieval times, aimed at wisdom in this practical as well as theoretical sense. Moreover, it was thought impossible, then, to be able to embark upon the strictly cognitive tasks of philosophy without adopting a way of life that sought to embody an ideal of wisdom. Even Aristotle, who separated the theoretical sciences from the practical arts, accepted that a person could not be called wise who was not *eudaimon*, or "doing well." *Theoria* was undertaken because it was for him the realization of a genuine human excellence, our natural zest in understanding the universe.

in the diversity of human cultures past and present. Philosophy needs *experience* not just method.

The abandonment of the ideal of wisdom in modern times is one of the key events in the history of philosophy, though it passes largely unrecognized. The story of how this happened is important, having its origin in the crisis of the modern period, though it cannot be told here. The modern age, beginning with Bacon, Galileo, and Descartes, rejected the teleological cosmology of the Middle Ages and put in its place the idea that the task of knowledge was to discover the facts of nature in order to make ourselves "masters and possessors of nature."[7] This is what ultimately drives the debates concerning a "true method."[8] The problem of how these facts would be used was left to desire. The life of the philosopher-scientist was thus not tied to an ideal of "wisdom." Descartes' *Discourse on Method* is a revolutionary document also in the way it separates the quest for knowledge from that of the good life. The code of ethics it advocates is rational self-discipline combined with the art of living "like a man who walks alone and in the shadows."[9] The primary rule is to obey the customs of the country (including religious ones)— quite a contrast to the figure that speaks to us in the pages of Plato's *Apology*.[10] The culmination of this bifurcation can be found in Kant's utter separation of knowledge from morality and aesthetics.

To think *philosophically* means to critique and reconstruct these modernist assumptions in light of the question of wisdom. In contrast to philepistemy, philosophy begins with a humanist imperative: it inquires into the meanings of human existence for the sake of wisdom; that is, it puts human experience in relation to a deep existential meaning of

7. Descartes, *Discourse on Method* VI, 62.

8. Francis Bacon's Aphorisms in the *Novum Organum* express this eloquently: "Human knowledge and human power meet in one, for where the cause is not known the effect cannot be produced. Nature to be commanded must be obeyed, and that which in contemplation is as the cause is in operation as the rule" (Aphorisms I:ii). The rendering of the formal cause as an operational rule is prophetic of the course of modern philosophy.

9. *Discourse on Method* II, 17. The Renaissance archetype of the modern scientist-philosopher is the "magus," one who aims at mastery of nature's powers, not contemplation of its causes. See Francis A. Yates, *Giordano Bruno and the Hermetic Tradition* (Chicago: University of Chicago Press, 1964). Besides Bruno, Paracelsus likewise becomes a key figure.

10. Descartes' *Discourse on Method* becomes a key text scripting the "code of ethics" for the modernist intellectual. *The Meditations*, likewise, is a book in ethics; truth is obtained by disciplining the will. But it is an ethics for knowledge, which itself is undertaken for power, not for realizing a better life.

the world. Philosophy alone does not seek wisdom: human beings every-where do. The variety of cultures may be regarded as creative adaptations within different circumstances, but all seek to frame the possibility of a meaningful, value-rich existence. Thus philosophical method begins with inquiry into cultures and their wisdom traditions in order to discern the "shapes of wisdom." Philosophers must acquire deep and broad experience of embodied wisdom. These ideals are expressed symbolically, in social institutions, religion, mythology, and art. In contrast, then, to the modernist quest for "pure" methods that are value neutral and aspire to mathematical formalization, philosophy must seek a broad, global literacy of human cultures. It must become aesthetically and spiritually attuned to the "shapes of wisdom" expressed in diverse cultures. This requires a flexible plurality of methods that gain their meaning in connection with their content, not apart from it. In short, philosophy primarily exists as a humanistic discipline, though it also looks beyond the human condition into the nature of nature.[11] While philepistemy will follow the fads generated by the succession of various "pure" methodolo-gies seeking to be analogs of "the" scientific method, philosophy's first goal is cultural literacy in the worlds of human existence, past and pre-sent. Qualitative, deep aesthetic experience rather than epistemological certainty is the first goal of philosophical inquiry. In short, philosophy must begin with broad experience of the complexity of the human and natural world. There is no method that can substitute for experience.[12] In situating human experience, nature itself must be understood. Wisdom is an art of inhabiting the world by attending to the world. Nature is the environment of our desire for wisdom, and wisdom discloses the ecology of environments.

Beyond the inquiry into the ideals of wisdom and the ecology of nature, philosophy has a critical, reconstructive role in the present. It must diagnose the deeper underlying problems of civilization so that

---

11. It must be explicitly emphasized here that Dewey's frequent—and frequently misunder-stood—appeals to scientific method (itself but one type of inquiry) were further contextualized for him within this larger enterprise of constructing a democratic culture that genuinely fulfilled human beings in their collective and individual lives. In other words, Dewey's "instrumentalism" refers to a *part* of his thought. See his essay "Philosophy and Civilization" (LW, 5). The plurality of methods is sound Aristotelianism and can be successfully applied to a nonreductionistic study of nature.

12. As Mill said critically of Bentham, "Bentham's knowledge of human nature is bounded. It is wholly empirical, and the empiricism of one who had little experience." "Bentham," in *The Philosophy of John Stuart Mill*, ed. Marshall Cohen (New York: Modern Library, 1961), 23.

these problems may be intelligently overcome. The world of the twenty-first century faces what may be the ultimate challenge in the survival of many species (including our own). In addition, we face the explosion of the human population, possibly beyond sustainable numbers, and the development of an intimate worldwide electronic culture of corporate consumerism. The civilization of modernity, now exported around the globe, carries with it its inherited dichotomies. These must be critiqued. Not only does this require an exploration of the negative consequences of certain assumptions, but an historical understanding of how those assumptions were generated and how they evolved. To critique the present, we must understand its historical genesis, especially in terms of the interplay of metaphysical commitments and social legitimation. Worldviews are narratives that empower.[13]

But we must go beyond critique and also articulate ideals that can successfully help reconstruct the problems of the present.[14] The ideal of wisdom we need must endeavor to comprehend and respond to the ecological aspect of nature and to facilitate communication among the diversity of the world's cultures that must cooperate and live together now as close neighbors rather than as exotically distant lands. In this context, the conflation of the idea of "philepistemy" with philosophy becomes an extravagant luxury. Wisdom, as noted, involves a deep awareness of human life and the world in which it exists so that the way of life is a realization of human existence as an expression of nature. The present moment calls for reconstruction at the ontological level. Philosophy is concerned with the basic ways human experience and nature interexist. What sort of wisdom is called forth by the crisis of modernity? One that facilitates awareness of how human existence is interconnected. The quest for wisdom needs an eco-ontology.

Of all twentieth-century philosophies the thought of John Dewey offers the most promise for an ecologically wise naturalism that also addresses the plurality of cultures. Dewey's own thought, however, was enmeshed in a number of assumptions that prevented these aspects of his

13. Here the thought of Marx, the Critical Theorists, and Foucault are extremely helpful—as is that of Dewey—in seeing how theory makes "reasonable" a certain type of social system of empowerment.

14. Thus the purely negative work of people like Adorno or Rorty must be regarded as abandoning the philosophical project in the end, leaving us with aimlessness, not wisdom.

thought from developing as far as they might.[15] It is not my purpose to criticize Dewey here, but to use his thought as a background, especially in sketching out the features of an ecological ontology. I attempt to develop themes so that they might contribute toward a humanistic as well as ecological wisdom. What I present here in particular is the outline of an ontological framework that serves as a counterpart to the humanistic views I have developed under the term, "the Human Eros." I relocate philosophical reflection as an engagement with the possibility of wisdom, searching for those ideas and ideals that might negotiate the impending crises we face. Ontology must be undertaken consciously within that general problematic. Contemporary wisdom must find ways of living and understanding that put us in a moral and aesthetic, as well as cognitive, balance with our environment, its inhabitants, and the global human communities that must share this planet forevermore as neighbors and fellow citizens rather than as exotic strangers.

Having already stated my conception of the philosophical enterprise, one so at variance with the way it is now predominantly practiced, I will proceed to address the "human" side of the relationship, seeing how the quest for wisdom arises from the deep impulse toward living meaningfully, which I have called "the Human Eros." Then I move toward the ontological side, outlining the aim of ontology as compassionate intelligence. In trying to articulate an eco-ontology, it is necessary to engage in a historical critique of the major ideas in the Western tradition that inhibit this development, in particular the idea of Being as identity. A possible contrast to this idea, one which at first promises to be more ecologically relevant, is located in the Buddhist doctrine of emptiness, especially as refined by Nāgārjuna (ca. 200 CE). But this also reveals difficulties for an eco-ontological wisdom in terms of retaining an ideal of world-renunciation. I conclude by describing the elements of an intermediary position that develops the idea of natural histories as creative continuities, including some reflections on the "home," or *oikos*, of philosophy as a wisdom

15. While I do not accept the shallow criticisms of Dewey as an uncritical advocate of science, much less as an unthinking "optimist" or "liberal," his critique of modernism could have been stronger, his development of his ideas on civilization more extended, and his confrontation with Western metaphysics more systematic. Thus I find his aesthetics, ethics, social philosophy, and metaphysics of most use.

of *in*-habitation. This attempt toward an "ecology of being" or "eco-
ontology" is thus presented as a directive for wisdom.

THE HUMAN EROS

Before undertaking this investigation, I need to summarize the central
ideas that have constituted my own efforts to think "beyond Dewey"
under the humanistic thematic of what I call "The Human Eros."[16] This
is primarily a claim that human beings by nature seek to experience the
world as a fulfillment of meaning and value.[17] "Meaning" and "value,"
terms of extensive analysis and refinement in twentieth-century philosophical discussion, should be taken here in their Deweyan senses.[18]
For example, these terms should be understood as they might be used
in ordinary circumstances when people ask if their lives have any
"meaning" or "value." Meaning and value initially belong to a continuous domain of interaction that is aesthetically undergone prior to
any cognitive mediation, though this material may be mediated and
refined instrumentally.[19] That is, human beings experience the world as
filled with meaning or value not primarily as the result of consciously
deliberative or instrumental inquiry, but as a qualitative whole of continuous interaction that has the promise of consummatory experience. It
is within this whole that instrumental inquiry itself takes on significance.
When human beings have experiences that give them a sense of the
depth of the meaning and value of their lives, they are fulfilled.[20] Both
meanings and values are directly embodied in the existential components
of their experiences. Not only do these meanings and values exhibit
a wide and differentiated spectrum, language can at best only crudely
designate various generic parts of that continuum, which manifest
themselves in the upsurge of the present in radical individuality and

---

16. For a presentation of this view, see my essay "The Human Eros" in this volume, chapter 5.

17. See Dewey's acknowledgement of this key idea in *Experience and Nature* (LW, 1:272).

18. My own effort to spell this out is undertaken in my book *John Dewey's Theory of Art, Experience, and Nature: The Horizons of Feeling* (Albany: State University of New York Press, 1987). Valuing is an integral ongoing phase of organizing situations and helps discern what features are to function as "facts" within inquiry.

19. See chapter 3 of *Experience and Nature* and Dewey's seminal essay "Qualitative Thought" (LW, 5).

20. Fulfillment need not be "happiness" in the sense of feeling good; it is a *realization* of a deep meaning *of* the world *in* human existence.

incommensurable freshness. One reason the arts have such power is their ability to lead us toward these experiences that are above and beyond the uses of strictly cognitive language.

To comprehend what "meaning and value" further signify, we need only think about what is involved in eradicating human life of those features so that existence itself is experienced as a negation: degradation, loss of empowerment, destruction of identity, reduction of existence toward pure instrumentality—in short, everything a human being can experience that conveys "You are not human" or "Your life is meaning-less and without value." History provides horrific examples of consciously undertaken endeavors whereby one group seeks to destroy the humanity of another: the Nazi and Japanese holocausts of the Second World War; the slave trade; the near genocide of Native peoples in the Americas and elsewhere; and so on.[21] But often this negation can be unobtrusively present in the ordinariness of everyday experience. One need not even think of the ghettos of Europe or America, the "homelands" of Africa, or barrios of the poor everywhere. One of the key features of degradation is invisibility. One is simply not seen; one's suffering is not noted.[22] Most societies require immense amounts of suffering to perpetuate their own structures, and many aspects of their codes of ethics involve training privileged members to avoid noticing suffering, or if it is noticed to interpret it as a "natural state" or "the will of God" or "the law of karma." [23] Jesus was a revolutionary in that he forced a society to notice those whom it preferred not to see; one forceful way he did this was merely by having people of different classes *eat* together.[24] The negation of the world can also be apparent in the destruction of meaningful environments for commercialized exploitation of mindless human sprawl.[25] When civilization

---

21. Elie Wiesel's writings explore this idea; Viktor Frankl (see *Man's Search for Meaning*) developed his "logotherapy" in reaction to it. The thought of Ernest Becker (e.g., *The Denial of Death*) is also in touch with this issue.

22. Ralph Ellison's *Invisible Man* is an eloquent testimony to this aspect of the negation of human existence.

23. The repression that civilizations—at least some civilizations—require is not the repression of the id, as Freud thought, but of compassion.

24. See John Dominic Crossan's major study, *The Historical Jesus: The Life of a Mediterranean Jewish Peasant* (New York: HarperCollins, 1991) and his shorter (and somewhat clearer) *Jesus: A Revolutionary Biography* (New York: HarperCollins, 1994).

25. E.g., the destruction of environments essential for a species' existence, the destruction of species themselves, and the thoughtless appropriation of land for the sake of human suburban expansion.

does not creatively and wisely serve the Human Eros, but frustrates it instead, alienation, nihilism, and destructive rage are the consequences.[26] Correlated with this primary claim about the Human Eros, that all human beings desire to experience the world with meaning and value, are several other theses. One is that human experience is pervaded by "temporal quality."[27] Temporal quality is an aspect of *all* experience; it is a way human beings are *in* situations. The present is the outcome *of* a history and is oriented tensively *toward* a future.[28] The "present" is not a static "now" but rather a dramatic reconfiguration of a process that has a narrative order. In other words, the structure of time as it enters into human experience of the world is creative and dramatic. It is not a steady mathematical flow nor a sequence of self-identical moments, timeless in themselves.[29] The present is an act of reconstruction.

In addition to the priority of aesthetic wholeness in situations and the narrative form of temporal quality, the Human Eros points to the conditioning and conditioned role of community in the experience of meaning. First, communities reflect the temporal nature of care in human existence. Biologically, we need other people, and that is a fact of our existence as fundamental as the need for water or oxygen. As newborns, we enter a world of preverbal care; we learn language within that world and come to care for others as a result.[30] Meaning arises in the process of communication, and the consciousness of self and world is made possible by the imaginative extension of experience into the roles of others so that

26. The loss of meaningful environments and ideals of wisdom may partially explain the upsurge in random acts of impulsive violence in a society that is technologically advanced and economically thriving.

27. See *Experience and Nature* (LW, 1:72, 82–92). Dewey distinguishes temporal quality from seriality. Temporal quality is the dialectic of undergoing and doing in every event that gives that event a horizon of past and future, of actuality and potentiality, in short, that marks it as a phase of process and lends it the capacity for growth. Temporal quality is a feature of *everything*, including formalized abstractions like numbers.

28. The term "tensive," originally used by Dewey, is preferable to his subsequent term "problematic."

29. In this sense, a Deweyan philosophy must acknowledge the similarity of Heidegger's analysis of *Dasein*, though significant differences remain.

30. Thus one major difference between Heidegger and Dewey is that Heidegger sees the horizon of human finitude in death whereas Dewey supplements it with the indefinite horizon of love. Though death may individualize, the ability to love and give to others (including, indeed especially, future generations) reconstitutes the individual back within both the social and the natural. Love transcends death.

we may interpret ourselves to ourselves.[31] Human experience is a temporal flow—conditioned by care, narratively structured, pervaded by a noncognitive qualitative sense of situations; furthermore, it is a dialogical
process of communication in which imagination is absolutely crucial.[32]
And formal methods do not lend themselves well to these issues.

Constructively, the Human Eros seeks to mediate the world in terms of
building symbolic worlds that validate human existence. The Eros, unless
frustrated, is essentially creative. Religions, political systems, cultural
traditions articulate homes for human beings to live in; these "homes"
are as vital to our existence as the environmental conditions of oxygen,
food, and water. Culture is part of our human environmental being.[33]
Civilizations, as noted above, are experiments of the Human Eros. They
articulate worlds out of symbols that help human beings experience their
world as a place for defining what a meaningful, value-rich human life
is by orienting the Human Eros toward an ideal of wisdom. Cultures
provide existential environments as homes for the human spirit.[34] Most
cultures concentrate on celebrating and articulating what it is to live a
meaningful human life, in spite of what oppression this may require. [35]

To study these cultures philosophically, then, involves seeing them as
striving to meet a deep need to experience human life in the world
as a meaningful and value-rich event. Acknowledging the Human Eros
allows us to look at all cultural practices (including philosophy itself) as
symbolic experiments in life. This approach requires investigations into
historical context and development. It also points to the importance of
aesthetic experience and imagination as constitutive grounds of human
reasoning. Our reasoning occurs within situations, which have a pervasive,

31. The social-communicative genesis of the self and of consciousness is the theme of chs. 5 and 6
of *Experience and Nature* as well as of George Herbert Mead's *Mind, Self, and Society*. This claim
contrasts strongly with Heidegger's limited focus on the problem of individuation over against the
"social" characterized as *das Man*.

32. Thus, in the face of the "cognitive science" movement, I find studies such as those done
by Robert Coles of much more significance for obtaining insight into the human situation. See
especially *The Spiritual Life of Children* and *The Moral Life of Children*. Cultural anthropology, not
physics, should be our ideal.

33. It should be recalled that Dewey proposed changing the title of his major work from *Experience
and Nature* to *Culture and Nature*, thereby avoiding, he hoped, the subjectivist connotations of
"experience."

34. See my essay "The Technology of Desire," in *Philosophy and Technology: Philosophical
Perspectives*, vol. 8, ed. Paul Durbin (Dordrecht, NL: Kluwer, 1991).

35. After all, at dinner we comment on the taste of the food rather than the suffering of the animal
that made it possible.

qualitative aspect that unifies them as frames of reference. Objects, things, actions, events—all have their being by being situated within a context. The qualitative unity of the context may be subliminal or, as in the experience of art, heightened into conscious experience. The transformative nature of situations, part of their reconstructive temporality, involves the constant use of imagination, conceived here as the ability to employ and play with alternative interpretive schemata. Intelligence is precisely this ability to see the actual in light of the possible as well as to grasp it as an outcome of a history. In other words, imagination is a requirement of pragmatic intelligence as well as wisdom.[36]

ONTOLOGY AS COMPASSIONATE INTELLIGENCE

The investigation into the Human Eros marks, as I said, the humanistic side of my position: Human beings have a need to experience the world with meaning and value. But this is also an ontological question, not merely because it is a feature of human "being" but because it is the *world* that can be meaningful and rich in value. It is through interpretations of being that we inhabit the world and appropriate the world in terms of its possible meanings. We need now to inhabit the world with an ecological wisdom. This wisdom must grapple with ecological issues and communicate across the diversities of cultures. The question arises *for us* historically as a question of achieving eco-ontology, since this is conducive to the sort of wisdom we need. Ontology as an inquiry is situated within the problematic of existence, and this is always historical. It seeks to understand the ways in which it means to be. Because it is undertaken in terms of the search for wisdom, it acknowledges its origin in the historical needs of the Human Eros. We undertake ontological inquiry because human beings are involved in the world.

The question of the world arises from the Human Eros, but it is addressed to the world. Reflection must be undertaken with a sense of acknowledgment of and responsibility to that which is investigated. Ontology thus begins in an attitude of genuine *caring* about the world. To look at the world merely in terms of a value-neutral epistemic field

---

36. See my discussion of this in "Pragmatic Imagination," in this volume, chapter 6. Also see Mark L. Johnson's *The Body in the Mind* (Chicago: University of Chicago Press, 1987) for a technical discussion of the nature of imagination and its employment of schemata.

requires forcing the modernist dualism—the repression of wisdom as an end and a lack of acknowledgment of the erotic origins of thought from the start. Ontological care is concern for the being of the world. Thus care has the aspects of compassion and intelligence. Because thought emerges from and operates within an affective, emotional horizon of feeling, we can designate care as compassion. Compassion aims at clarity of insight into the world in terms of seeing the present as the outcome of a process, comprehending how it is *to be affected*. The suffering of the present is discerned by clear-headed sympathy. Care also aims at clarity of insight into the possibilities of the present, and this is intelligence. Ontology may therefore be designated as a discipline of compassionate intelligence concerning the undergoing and doing of the world.

An eco-ontology, functioning reflectively within the general quest for wisdom, must think of the ends to which its concepts and distinctions aim. Ontology asks the question of the meaning of being in service to the Human Eros with care for the world. It aims at establishing a house of wisdom. In our current context, this requires the critical investigation of the historically important ideas of being and how they have successfully or unsuccessfully connected us to the world. It discerns the ways in which we suffer and act in the world. It asks, pragmatically, what are the ecological consequences of the various meanings of Being? Thus, we must undertake an inquiry into the meanings of Being in the West that may have led toward the ecological ignorance that characterizes modernity. In particular, we must look at what in the history of Western ontology has prevented looking at the world *primarily* in terms of interactive relationships, contextual reciprocities, temporal continuities, and, not least, compassion. As suggested above, we must focus in particular on the ideas of identity, form, completion, and power.

But an eco-ontological approach also seeks to investigate and articulate concepts that make us more intelligent inhabitants of the planet who are more capable of communicating with each other. One important aspect of this would be developing concepts that facilitate understanding the world in terms of environmental interactions.[37]

---

37. John Dewey dominates the twentieth century as the only thinker to articulate an ecological concept of philosophy; Heidegger did so only to some extent and Wittgenstein not at all, unless the interactive descriptions of the language games of the later period could be extended as a descriptive ecology of practices. But the lack of a critical role for philosophy even in his later period makes this problematic.

In addition to developing ideas out of our own traditions (however resistant they may be to that end), we must investigate the ontologies of other cultures' philosophies that may be more amenable. That we look at the ideals of wisdom that have characterized civilizations or cultures very different from the West and have manifested respect for the world and compassion for other beings is critical. In other words, are there non-European ontologies that facilitate an ecological wisdom? Though several examples are available (such as Chinese and Native American cultures), the Buddhist tradition offers the strongest contrast to the West. Buddhism developed a rigorous philosophical literature while criticizing the very ideas central to the Western ontologies of identity. A strong commitment to ontological identity was not conducive to wisdom, according to Buddhism, and was, in fact, harmful. In articulating this view, the idea of the interrelational existence of everything (*pratītyasamutpāda*), or "emptiness" (*śūnyatā*), became central. Also, the Buddhist emphasis on compassion (*karuṇā*) as a practical result of discernment or insight (*prajña*) into the fundamentals (*dharmas*) is highly important. If we are compassionate beings, capable of an affective insight into the nature of others, especially in terms of their suffering, we are more disposed toward perceiving problems and generating solutions that transcend our individual, national, and species versions of egocentrism. Thus Buddhism may be of service as an alternative in seeking an eco-ontological wisdom. In the following sections, I will contrast the Western idea of Being as perfection of form and self-identity with the Buddhist analysis of emptiness or "inter-being" in light of their service to an eco-ontological ideal of wisdom.

Being as Identity, Process as Emptiness

There are three major transformations of the idea of Being in the history of the West: the Greek identification of Being with perfection of form, the medieval identification of Being (in the primary sense) with God (infinite perfection), and the modern identification of Being with matter and physical power. These all have problems for an eco-ontology: the reification of identity as a characteristic of substance, the real as transcendent, or the real as reduced to the mechanistic relations of matter and force, with the status of mind left ambiguous at best. Obviously a detailed historical analysis would be needed to do justice to this topic, and what follows here can only be a sketch.

In the Greek tradition that goes from Pythagoras and Parmenides to Plato and Aristotle, we find the coalescence of several powerful ideas defining what it means "to be": form, perfection, identity, the subject of predication.[38] The Pythagorean positing of "number" (*arithmos*) as the *archē* of nature led to the idea that it is by seeing into the mathematical harmonies of the universe that one attains purification as well as truth. Number combined limit and void, expressed as harmony, and the knowledge of nature's harmonies purified the soul. But number was mainly form, and form was limit, measure. Form gave the basis for truth; i.e., it perfectly accommodated rational speech, *logos*. Parmenides, seeing that the Pythagorean account of the void (*to kenon*) failed such criteria, eliminated it altogether as "What Is Not," since it could neither be nor be coherently thought or expressed. This left the primal monad, without generative duality, and this he called Being, "It Is" (*esti*), an absolute identity that alone could be the subject of true propositions.[39] In contrast to the senses, it was intellect, or *nous*, alone that could achieve the insight into this truth. In listing the various "signs" of Being, Parmenides states that it is one, whole, perfect, unchanging, never not itself; it never "was" nor "will be" but always "is," a timeless present. Thus "to be" means to be timelessly self-identical, the object of a logical intuition that makes possible an absolute, necessary truth claim. *Nous* is precisely this insight into the true identity of something.[40] Moreover, Being is "full," without degree, one part not being "more" or "less" than another. An absolute unity has no parts. Plato and Aristotle wrestled with the extreme conclusions of this position. Plato attempted to retain the Parmenidean view of Being as the self-identical (*autos*), the source of true insight, along with the

---

38. That we are looking at a tradition is important to keep in mind: Parmenides developed his ideas from Pythagoras as Plato did from both Pythagoras and "Papa Parmenides" and Aristotle from Plato.

39. See Parmenides, Fragment DK 8. It is my belief that Parmenides began as a Pythagorean (as stated by Diogenes Laertius) and encountered the paradox of asserting nonbeing in initially working out a cosmogony, the account of which he still gives us as the "deceitful *logos*" in the last part of his poem. The Pythagorean monad, the "seed" from which all other numbers "grew" by "inhaling" the void, could *not* grow because there was no "void" to "inhale." Thus Parmenides' One is the original Monad regarded as complete and incapable of change. The consequences of this view were fundamental for the West.

40. In Homer, *nous* explicitly is the power to see through disguises. In *Iliad* III.396 Helen perceives the true identity of Aphrodite and in *Odyssey* XIX.301 Odysseus' dog recognizes his master; i.e., has direct insight into the true identity in spite of outward appearances; i.e., the transformations of nineteen years of war and hardship as well as further temporary magical disguising by Athena. To "know" in the sense of *noein* is to recognize true identity behind the appearance.

Pythagorean view of form as the basis for cosmic measure. He introduced an intermediary domain that was caught perpetually in time between Being and not-Being, an analogical realm in which nothing was ever really itself, but "like" an ideal paradigm.[41] Aristotle rejected this attempt to save nature as a kinetic mimesis of Being, and so he had to defend the idea that there were logically identical subjects for predication in the world itself, rather than in Plato's world of the Forms, identifying them with the species and their constitutive individuals.

What is important here is to note that what dominates throughout is the notion that a self-same identity, akin to that of numbers, constitutes that nature of a "being." The nature of process is understood in terms of achieving "fullness" or completion and definition. To be is to be perfected, formed, brought to closure, and so the subject of true identification. The implications for the West have been not only an emphasis on formal definitions in order to understand something but also the corresponding belief that "what there is"—be it Platonic Form, Aristotelian *ousia*, essence, atom, soul, mind, sense datum, monad, or atomic fact—is fundamentally a self-contained, individual entity. The universe is built out of these individuals and their logical relationships. [42]

Medieval thinkers, in stressing the supremacy of an all-powerful Creator, had to relegate finitude to the derivative created world. Being in its primary sense was infinite. The ambiguity in the idea of "power" (as passive potentiality or active force) allowed the medievals to make God infinitely powerful without making Him thereby absolutely "potential."[43] One of the revolutions achieved in the Modern period is that God's infinity was gradually ascribed to the universe itself.[44] Advances in mathematics, culminating in the calculus, made it possible to imagine

41. These problems persisted in the ideal world of the Forms, and Plato's later philosophy tries to show how "nonbeing" must be introduced even there, if only in the manner of negative predication (as in the *Sophist*). But beyond that he is forced to posit a "matter" for the Forms in terms of "the Greater and the Lesser" that allows for infinite numbers, series, and all articulations of continua. See *Philebus* and Aristotle's cryptic remarks in *Metaphysics I* on Plato's later thought.

42. I do not think it is merely accidental that the civilization of the West has been characterized by intense formalism, intellectualism, and individualism.

43. The key figure here is Plotinus, whose One transcends the Forms and so is "beyond" Form, and so limitless. Because actuality was equated with form, he ascribed *dunamis*, "power," to the One.

44. This was one of the central ideas of Giordano Bruno, a heresy that cost him his life. See Alexandre Koyré's *From the Closed World to the Infinite Universe* (Baltimore: Johns Hopkins University Press, 1957).

a physical world capable of infinitely precise mathematical description.[45] Thus each physical body could be as perfect, absolute, and self-identical as a Platonic Form. What mathematics could not do was provide the momentum for the material bodies, and this came to be the "power"—as inscrutable as God—that was given by God to the universe at the creation.[46] As theism diminished in the rise of modern science, what was left was the idea of a universe constituted at once of an aggregate of individuals, each logically and ontologically independent, endowed with an irrational "power." Both Nietzsche's metaphysics of "the Will to Power" and the logical universe of Wittgenstein's *Tractatus* are consequences of this position.[47]

It is clear that such commitments inhibit achieving an ecological interpretation of the world or aspiring toward an ecological wisdom. First, nature itself is understood as constituted of substantial individuals, internally absolute and contingently externally related. Interactive systems are derivative. Because modernism lost the passive sense of potentiality for the active sense of power, process is understood as a function of a quantity of force subsumed under formal laws of transformation. Individuals behave in accordance with the laws of their own beings, a *conatus sese conservare*, which, on the human level, leads to the view that individuals naturally act only out of self-interest determined by desire. The best hope is that this self-interest can be enlightened so that a social machine can be constructed in which these potentially conflicting desires are harmonized.[48] In short: Nature is a machine, individuals are absolute, and reason exists to serve desire. When Dewey set out to articulate a genuinely ecological philosophy of nature and society, he realized that this involved a critique of the philosophical heritage of the West.[49] It is not surprising he was misunderstood at every step.

---

45. Once Galileo eliminated the Euclidean belief that there were "perfect" solids, he realized that *all* bodies were capable of "perfect" geometrical expression.

46. See Newton's General Scholium in the *Principia*. Motion is introduced externally to the atoms.

47. Nietzsche, rejecting rationality, sees the task of power as culminating in creative individuality; Wittgenstein, assuming the givenness of individuals as logical subjects, makes time a mystery.

48. The insight into the essential relationship between modern material atomism and the political state is due to Hobbes; it is still fundamentally embodied in the work of John Rawls.

49. That Dewey himself realized this is made clear in the unfinished drafts for the new introduction to *Experience and Nature*. See LW, 1, appendix 1.

One difficulty Western philosophies have is that deep assumptions that run through the whole tradition, such as those I have characterized, are the most difficult to discern if one does not step out of that tradition from time to time. In reflecting on the possibility of an ecological wisdom, the Buddhist worldview certainly presents itself as an impressive alternative. Buddhism has developed cultural traditions of great sustaining power (and so in their own right worthy responses to the Human Eros) and has maintained a sophisticated intellectual development for twenty-five hundred years. Its appeal as a resource for an ecological wisdom lies in its emphasis on the ideal of compassion, its ideal of moderation as a "Middle Way," and its refusal to draw any sharp distinction between human beings and other living creatures. Its resourcefulness in dealing with the problems of psychology (especially moral psychopathology), and, perhaps most important, its rejection of "self-being" (*svabhāva*—what we would call a doctrine of substance) as a desirable metaphysical possibility also recommend it.

Again, I can only briefly describe some key points very generally. The teachings of the Buddha are deeply critical of the metaphysical ideas that had been articulated by the thinkers whose views are represented in the Upanishads, in particular, the view that at the heart of one's inmost being (*ātman*) there was nothing other than the absolute and ultimate truth (*Brahman*).[50] The position of the Upanishads is somewhat different from the Parmenidean insight that there is only one ultimate, absolute Being. The goal was not logical insight, but "liberation" (*mokṣa*) from reincarnation.[51] The world is reduced to illusion and "magic" (*māyā*), so that the ethical implication is the duty to "play one's part" selflessly as an actor.[52] The Buddha disagreed with this view. The mystical search for the absolute Self was, in the end, just an extension on a higher level of the everyday grasping after the empirical ego. It was grasping that manufactured

50. See David Kalupahana's *A History of Buddhist Philosophy* (Honolulu: University of Hawaii Press, 1992) and Edward Conze's specialized study *Buddhist Thought in India* (Ann Arbor: University of Michigan Press, 1967).

51. A major difference between the doctrine of *Brahman* and Parmenides' Being is that *Brahman* is totally beyond any conceptual or logical formulation, being boundless. It transcends any direct insight into the identity of something that *nous* obtains, being realized in the state of nondual, unintentional consciousness.

52. Such is the advice given to the hero Arjuna by the god Krishna in the Bhagavad Gita. The result is that Arjuna does pick up his bow and fight his relatives, friends, and teachers. Had the Buddha been his charioteer rather than Krishna, very different advice would have been given.

the self, and this gave rise to suffering because the world itself was inherently an interconnected process. He thus rejected any inner absolute self (*ātman*) as well as any metaphysical appeals to an Absolute (*Brahman*), and showed an intense concern for developing an ethics of daily kindness and compassion, at variance with extreme asceticism or selfless performance of karmic duty. While he retained the ideal of "liberation," it seems to mean absolute selfless peace in which one no longer suffers the "turmoil" of the world, which he called *dukkha*.[53] The Buddha articulated his "Eightfold Path" as a "Middle Way" for navigating the stream of life so that one "made it through" to *nirvāna*, the selfless peace achieved by the extinction of cravings based upon illusory and indeed harmful ideas (such as being an absolute individual or self).[54]

While the ideal of compassion (or *karuṇā*) as well as benevolence (*mettā*) was cultivated, this was not done so in a way that any idea of "self" became involved. The source of most of the turmoil and struggle in the world arose precisely because people thought of their "selves" as "real" in the sense of being substantial when, in fact, they were about as self-sufficient and permanent as soap bubbles. The "self" could be analyzed into its various momentary, transitional components (or *dharmas*).[55] The empirical ego was a function of the relational process of the world, dependent on conditions and giving rise to consequences (*karma*). When the idea of the substantial self vanished into these transitory relationships, the source of *dukkha* itself vanished. To achieve this end, the nature of the world was characterized in such a way as to emphasize its

53. While often rendered as "suffering," this word embraces a broad spectrum of meanings that include "impermanence," "instability," and "lack of self-sufficiency." Thus all of the things that we would call "happy," "good," or "pleasant" are equally instances of *dukkha*, not because they are "illusory" and in fact are "painful," but because they are temporary and depend on circumstances to be realized. Thus they are not absolute. This is not a cause for pessimism; it is simply how things are.

54. The Eightfold Path was a pragmatic approach to the fact of *dukkha* and was aimed at reducing it as a causal factor as much as possible. It consists of Right Understanding, Right Thought (or compassion), Right Conduct, Right Speech, Right Livelihood, Right Effort, Right Mindfulness, and Right Concentration. See Walpola Ruhala's excellent introduction, *What the Buddha Taught* (New York: Grove Press, 1974).

55. The term *dharma* meant initially "that which upholds" in the sense of "duties." From that it came to mean the "parts," or "elements," that constitute the whole, the "law" or custom governing them, and so the "teaching" of the Buddha and the Buddhist "way." The *dharmas* of the self are the "Five Heaps" or elements in continuous flux: matter, sensations (including "mind" as the faculty of thoughts), perceptions, "mental formations" (like acts of will that generate karma), and consciousness or awareness of objects.

interdependency by the technical term *pratītyasamutpāda* or "dependent co-arising."[56] The world is constituted as a process of interconnected relationships. There is no "self" above and beyond this process. Our identity is similar to the identity of a river, and the names given to people are basically like the names given to rivers. The famous formula for "interdependence" is, "When that is present, this comes to be; on the arising of that, this arises. When that is absent, this does not come to be; on the cessation of that, this ceases."[57] What is articulated by this expression is a "middle principle" of genetic relativity, not some absolute, underlying "cause." In other words, it is a principle of descriptive, pragmatic value. It helps us pay attention to the way we are in the world. The early Buddhist tradition, then, developed a nonsubstantialist, interrelational view of the self and world for therapeutic ends. Not only were the ideas of "self," "identity," and "substance" critiqued, they were seen as positively harmful.

Five centuries after the Buddha's death, at the apex of Buddhism in India, a series of texts as written developing this idea, which is now called "emptiness."[58] The texts, written as secret discourses of the Buddha to his most advanced disciples, laid the basis for what became the Mahayana traditions of East Asia, especially the philosophically important Madhyamika or "Middle School." "Emptiness" was the term used instead of *pratītyasamutpāda* because the older schools of Buddhism had come

---

56. See Kalupahana, *A History of Buddhist Philosophy*, ch. 4. Kalupahana notes that *pratītyasamutpāda* (Pali: *paticcasamuppāda*) is formed from the past participle, stressing the present as the outcome of the past. This makes it closer to a radical empiricist view of causality than a substance-attribute or radical atomistic view of existence; i.e., the present is its relations, including temporal relations, not a "thing" that "has" relations or an unrelated atomistic present moment. The present includes what Kalupahana calls "the obvious past and the obvious future." In contrast to an appeal to any sort of transcendent abstract principle, the Buddhist view of causality remains focused on a lucid awareness of the world as experienced. Kaluphana is aware of the deep affinity of this view with pragmatism.

57. Kalupahana, *The History of Buddhist Philosophy*, 56. See *Majjhima Nikāya*, I.263. As Kalupahana notes, the use in Pali here of the "locative absolute" retains the "radical empiricism" of the temporality of the relations which would be lost in formalizing the expression into a conditional or hypothetical inference. Likewise the uses of "this" and "that" are experientially denotative rather than inferential logical subjects (i.e., individuals). And so the fallacy of denying the antecedent is not committed. See pp. 56–57.

58. These are collectively described as the *Prajñāpāramitā* sutras or "Perfection of Wisdom" texts. The term *sunya*, as Edward Conze notes, comes from the Sanskrit root *SVI*, "to swell." In a world-view governed by contrariety, what can be considered to be "swollen" from the outside is also "hollow" on the inside. Likewise it may be "swollen" due to something foreign filling it up and bloating it. See Edward Conze, *Buddhism: Its Essence and Development* (New York: Harper and Row, 1975), 130–31.

to a set of dogmatic convictions, especially about the ultimate reality of the fundamental components of the empirical self, or *dharmas*.[59] To grasp after such theoretical constructions as if *they* were the "really real things" was no better than grasping after the idea of the self, be it empirical ego or *ātman*, as an absolute, for this led to the same sort of egotistical action that produced and involved oneself in *dukkha*.[60]

Especially as developed by the philosopher Nāgārjuna (ca. 200 CE), the idea of emptiness was introduced not simply as a metacategory to interpret the ontological status of the *dharmas* but also for use in deflecting the tendency to reify the objects of one's theories.[61] Its purpose was to direct attention back to the practical issues of living daily in a mindful manner. In other words, it safeguarded that theory was undertaken for the sake of compassionate existence and not as a further development of the ego. The Buddha, in his advice to Kaccāyana, had advocated a "middle view" between extreme metaphysical theses such as "Everything exists" and "Nothing exists."[62] Explicitly building on this, Nāgārjuna argued that just as one should avoid ideas of absolute identity, so should one avoid ideas of absolute otherness.[63] A provisional, practical sense of "identity" can be used as long as one does not fall into positing some sort of self-same substance. This is also true of "motion" or "element." These terms designate parts of the continuum of becoming. They are webs of relations rather than fixed essential identities. Hence, to see into their true nature is to see them as "empty," that is, as dynamic, relational, and vague,

59. This was rather like reductionistic tendencies in the West to resolve physical objects into ultimate bodies or minds into "ideas," "sense data," "brain states," "propositional attitudes," or whatever.

60. The sort of suffering, anger, and abuse one sees in academic departments in debates over "ideas" is an example of the sort of problem these texts addressed.

61. Nāgārjuna is an extremely important and difficult thinker, the subject of widely conflicting interpretations, some of which, like Radhakrishnan's, strive to assimilate him into mainstream Indian Vedantist monism. See the brief discussion in Kalupahana's *A History of Buddhist Philosophy*, ch. 16, and the essay on the Mādhyamika by Douglas Daye in *Buddhism: A Modern Perspective*, ed. Charles S. Prebish (University Park: Pennsylvania State University Press, 1975). See the more extended studies by Frederick Streng, K. Venkata Ramanan, Jay L. Garfield, Kenneth Inanda, and David Kalupahana. The study by Garfield is especially clear.

62. This is of course a perfect refusal to get caught on the horns of the Parmenidean dilemma. See Kalupahana, *A History of Buddhist Philosophy*, 162 and also 158–59. The Discourse to Kaccayana is in the *Samutta Nikāya* (2:16–17).

63. As Kalupahana notes, "This is a rejection of the rationalist solution to the problem of causality.... Hence Nagarjuna turns to the pragmatic definition of an event as fruit (*artha*), arguing against the rationalist that the fruit is dependently arisen, neither pre-existing as a substance nor something absolutely different, without at the same time arguing for an essentialist explanation that the fruit itself is a unique event." *A History of Buddhist Philosophy*, 162.

discerned by our practical orientation to and involvement with the world.[64] The function of the doctrine of emptiness, then, is not to present a "higher" metaphysical principle into which explanatory factors, like *dharmas*, are resolved. Its function is to help us use all conceptual distinctions practically, seeing how they contextually and dynamically apply to the process of the world, especially with reference to the issue of suffering.[65] One of the main claims made by Nāgārjuna about emptiness is that it, too, is "empty."

Buddhist philosophy was useful in overcoming ordinary beliefs and the attachments they generate, but one must overcome the philosophical concepts themselves. To achieve *prajñā*, or insight into the fundamental truth of something, is to see it as "empty," as a contextualized, transitory process. Unlike *nous*, which was logical insight, *prajñā* involves the compassionate disillusion of identity, for there is no self-identical subject to be "recognized," though the suffering is real enough. The "thing" is revealed in its utter clarity as both "this," "such," and "empty." The idea of emptiness was applied to all forms of dichotomized thought, including the tendency of older Buddhism to contrast the world of attachment (*saṃsāra*) with the world of bliss (*nirvana*). Under this analysis, the old niruāna dualism collapsed: *Nirvāna* is nothing other than *saṃsāra*. This does not mean that the Buddha's Third Noble Truth is rejected, that there is no *nirvāna*. Rather, it is how we "handle" the world that makes the difference, especially if we see it in terms of being a *process of transformations and in relationships*. The individual being is not seen as a "substance" with a "self-identical" logical unity, but as a phase or moment of mutually interdependent relationships. The individual is seen in the intensity of its temporary uniqueness or *tathatā*, "suchness." (Zen art expresses this idea very clearly.) By seeing into its emptiness one can respond to it with more compassion as well as understanding. *Prajñā*, or

64. See Kalupahana's *A History of Buddhist Philosophy*, 163–66 and Nāgārjuna's major work *Mūlamādhyamakakārikā*, especially ch. 15. Nagarjuna, like Zeno, offered reductios, dialectical analyses of all substantialist claims, showing that they were internally self-contradictory. "Substance" (or "self-being") cannot be conceived without "other-being," and so is not substantial, likewise "other being derives from "self-being." See translations in studies mentioned in note 54. It is important to understand that Nāgārjuna did not believe he had another thesis to set over against these. Kalupahana's interpretation is noteworthy in stressing the moderate, "middle" position of Nāgārjuna as well as bringing out his similarities to American pragmatism.
65. One is reminded of William James's statement that "Pragmatism unstiffens all our theories, limbers them up and sets each one at work." *Pragmatism*, Lecture II (Cambridge, MA: Harvard University Press, 1974), 32.

the deep insight into circumstances, was supposed to give one "skillful means" (*upāya*) to alleviate the suffering of specific individuals and motivate them toward enlightenment.

The Buddhist teaching on emptiness may be contrasted at every point with the West's emphasis on substance and identity. The Buddhist ethics of egoless compassion may also be contrasted with modernism's glorification of the atomic individual driven by self-interested desire. But has it succeeded in providing the alternative basis for a genuinely ecological wisdom? In many respects, Buddhism retains the marks of its birth in India: the aim of the individual to find liberation from the cycle of existence, or *saṃsāra*, even where *nirvāna* and *saṃsāra* are realized to be the same. While the Buddha himself advocated a "middle way" between asceticism and indulgence, in the end his was the path of renunciation. The Mahāyāna tradition accommodated itself further to the needs of the world (or else it would not have survived in the Confucian cultures of East Asia), but one can still see that it does not necessarily lead toward more ecologically intelligent action. To see *all* beings as suffering, not just human beings, as "Buddhas in the making," may not stimulate one to take an urgent, active role in maintaining the health or welfare of *particular* species or ecosystems as a whole. To renounce the world is not a call to engage it. The arts of the haiku, brush painting, and the tea ceremony may make one more sensitive to aspects of the world, but have not noticeably affected Japan's whaling industry. Buddhism has had difficulty articulating itself as a political philosophy.[66] In other words, while the Buddhist doctrine of emptiness offers an important and deep alternative to the Western ideas of identity, substance and power, an eco-ontological philosophy needs to go further.

Eco-ontology

The goal of wisdom is to guide the Human Eros toward fulfillment; that is, to secure a world that provides the conditions for an experience of a meaningful, value-rich existence. The sort of ecological wisdom proposed here includes both the ideal of living well as human beings upon the earth and the ideal of responsible, intelligent, compassionate insight

---

66. The twentieth century has seen an effort to make Buddhism more political. See Christopher Queen and Sallie King, *Engaged Buddhism* (Albany: State University of New York Press, 1996).

as conditions for ontological reflection. We saw that the ideal of wisdom has faded in the West, while retaining its deep metaphysical commitment to an ontology of identity. In the modern period this has meant a world-view in which individuals are to be seen in external relationship to the world and each other. The existential disposition toward the world has become the control of nature's power for the sake of subjective goods determined by desire. The Buddhist tradition, by contrast, offers a challenge to this approach. Identity is due to "ignorance" and is the source of suffering. By adopting a view of the world as a conditioned and conditioning process, "things" (including selves) are seen as "empty," giving rise to an ethics of compassion and nonattachment. The danger here, in spite of the pragmatic middle path Buddhism takes, is an overemphasis on the goal of renunciation, ending up with what Dewey called an "art of acceptance" in contrast to the West's emphasis on the "art of control."[67] An ecological wisdom must be able to integrate both of these types of arts and regulate them in light of an ideal of a responsible, caring, compassionate, and creative ideal of existence. What is needed, then, is a philosophical ontology that has a view of nature as interactive, evolutionary, and nonreductionistically emergent and a view of human intelligence as aesthetic and moral as well as cognitive. The basis for such a philosophy is provided in Dewey's thought and can be further adapted and developed toward that end.

Dewey himself advocated a humanistic or "cultural naturalism" that took a nonreductionistic, process-oriented view of the world in which various aspects of nature were understood in terms of interactive fields or situations that received various conceptual articulations by the diversity of inquiries human beings make. Human beings are involved in this process in terms of "undergoing and doing," which is both qualitatively immediate and relationally mediated. Situations are the funded outcomes of histories and contain potentialities for further development. Experience is pervaded by a qualitative aesthetic horizon and aims toward an ideal of conduct by means of an imaginative and practical reconstruction of the present. Human intelligence understands the present in terms of its actualized, historical past and discerns those potentialities in it so that

---

67. See *The Quest for Certainty* (LW, 4), chs. 1 and 4. Dewey himself saw the history of the West as generating more "arts of acceptance" than "arts of control," which was a genuinely positive contribution, in his view, of the modern period.

an evaluation may result in conduct that experimentally seeks to realize an ideal of the good, which, on its realization may be continually critically reevaluated. Metaphysics has a crucial role in this enterprise as a descriptive account of the "generic traits" nature manifests in experience. These traits allow us to connect different aspects of the world so that we can identify functional continuities and avoid setting up dysfunctional dichotomies. Metaphysics, in other words, keeps intelligence functioning for the sake of wisdom. It lays the basis for extensive, deep communication across disciplines.

Like the Buddhist doctrine of emptiness, this approach avoids reification of identity or the positing of substances. Individuals or entities exist within situations as relational, interactive phases of events. In other words, they are synchronically and diachronically situated in environments as constitutive of their being. To be is to be environed. Since events are marked by temporal quality and so have histories, they are susceptible of being characterized with an evolutionary account of their genesis. We grasp their "whatness" not in an atemporal, identity-based essence formulable in a definitional *logos*, but in terms of an environmental-historical narrative. While the West has continually sought a core self-sameness to capture the "essence" of "things" and the Buddhist tradition has dissolved both "essences" and "things" in the arising and disappearing concatenations of the *dharmas*, an eco-ontological account will search for the "natural history" of the subject at hand. An event will be understood—always provisionally—in terms of the situational interactions that constitute its history and its contemporary potentialities. "Natural history" designates the account of how a thing comes to be within its situated contexts. This is an environmental concept, since it locates any individual within its ambit and understands it in terms of interacting with the actualities and potentialities of that ambit. To be is to be the product of a history.

History necessarily includes a narrative of how various potentialities are actualized and come to constitute the factical history of that being. We understand "what" the thing is in terms of seeing the world it comes from and how it functioned within it.[68] The event is dramatically understood in

---

68. This is the practice obscurely indicated by Dewey in both versions of the first chapter of *Experience and Nature* as the "empirical-denotative method." It is the method of Natural History.

terms of actions that have reconstructive or transformative power. This is a more integrated concept than the Buddhist view of the intrinsic "emptiness" of the *dharmas*, though, like that view, it refuses to posit a substantial underlying "selfsame identity." Identity is not a useful idea when dealing with a creative process, unless it is understood in terms of the function of "identify*ing*," in which case the realities of difference, development, and transformation are taken into account. The boundaries of the history are vague, not absolutely finite, and one may extend or limit them in various ways as one tries to understand the narrative at hand. Nevertheless the parts are (or can be) connected together with degrees of meaningfulness. (This is why multiple biographies of the same individual are not only possible but desirable.) Instead of the act of dissolution of the illusory identity into the webs of relations sanctioned by Buddhism, a natural history asks for a detailed and intimate inquiry into the evolutionary ecology of the subject, and the "subject" is the creative process of transformations of potentialities into actualities. To be is to be transformative.

The idea of natural history also is helpful in dealing with the problem of teleology. Aristotle was able to pull Plato's Forms down to earth at the cost of making the species fixed.[69] Though Aristotle's doctrine of essence succumbed to the problems of the ontology of identity described above, he did describe natural organisms in terms of temporal development, using his ideas of form, matter, actuality, potentiality, and entelechy. Had this aspect of Aristotle's philosophy dominated over the theology of the Unmoved Mover, the history of Western ontology might have been different.[70] The loss of Aristotelian teleology in the modern period also had devastating consequences for the project of virtue ethics, so that one sees today struggles to overcome both Galileo and Darwin to retrieve it.[71]

---

69. The problem was that of Parmenides: Being cannot become. Plato identified Form with Being and so put it beyond the domain of Becoming. To bring Form into the world, then, meant a compromise: Individuals come to be and die, but the species retain the eternal character of Being.

70. Indeed, his key term for *ousia*, misleadingly rendered as "essence" (*essentia*), is *to ti ên einai*, "the what it *was* going to be." The verb *ên* is significantly the imperfect tense of *einai*. *Essentia*, derived from the Latin verb "to be," *esse*, should have been the rendition of Aristotle's *ousia*. This term was misleadingly rendered as *sub-stantia*, "that which stands underneath."

71. The works of Alasdair MacIntyre and Martha Nussbaum are cases in point; it is of considerable note that neither really confronts how an Aristotelian ethics is possible without Aristotle's metaphysics. It is also of note that neither seems in the least cognizant of Dewey's overcoming of this problem.

To understand events in terms of natural history, however, retains the Aristotelian distinctions of actuality/form and potentiality/matter without leading to either the idea of the fixity of species or that of the identity of the individual.[72]

Actualities and potentialities are features of situations and processes. The actualities realized as the outcome of the past carry their own range of potentialities for the future. These potentialities are indeterminately articulated in radiating webs. Only a certain range of potentialities is immanent in a given situation, and from the realization of any of those, others may become immanently realizable. There is a large sedimented history that forms the predominant tendencies in the present. But the present is not entirely limited by them. There is always a degree of random variation and creative individualization. The transformative reconstruction of the present realizes some of the situation's potentialities and not others, and so a history grows. One might compare this sort of radial evolutionary teleology with that of a conversation, whereas Aristotle's view of teleology is more like that of a linear recitation (or *mimēsis*) of a previously written work. At any given moment in a conversation there is a constituting context within which remarks make sense or not; over time the conversation may range considerably, so that a remark at one time would not have been expected some time earlier. Yet, if one follows the conversation, it can be understood in terms of its history. This "conversational" or radial teleology is the pattern of evolutionary change. Natural history, rather than logical analysis (or Abhidharma techniques) helps us discern it.[73] To be is to have radial teleology.

If natural history indicates the facility with which eco-ontology interprets the present in terms of the past, the present must also be interpreted in terms of its future potentialities and immanent creative transformations. The dynamic fusion of the historical past and the open future in the creative present is designated by the term "continuity." Continuity is the temporal establishment of natural history. Thus eco-ontology replaces the idea of identity with that of continuity, dynamically understood.

---

72. Raymond Boisvert's *Dewey's Metaphysics* (New York: Fordham University Press, 1988) argues for a limited retention of the Aristotelian idea of form in Dewey, as my own book argues for a limited retention of the idea of potentiality.

73. In Buddhism, Abhidharma was the disciplined analysis of the complex momentary existence of the self and world into its component *dharmas*.

First, continuity is temporal; it is not a formal series. Second, it is creative; it is not algorithmic. Subsequent parts are not reduced to expressions of formal functions. Continuity realizes individuality-within-environment. In particular, it is exhibited in the idea of growth. It engages the present out of a past for the sake of a future. The present is the moment of transformation, and so of individuation. Creative individuation is historically temporal. This is what it means to be "present."[74] To be is to be continuous.

It is through acts of historical individuation that continuity is established. Continuity thus involves the ideas of spontaneity, creativity, and individuality. Each moment presents unique novelty and freshness as a fusion of past potentialities into a new actuality. Though it arises from the past, the present cannot be reduced to it. It exists as a fulfillment of the past, and so exists as its current meaning. The present itself, though, is a complex modality that intertwines the actualization of the past in the present as the fulfillment of those potentialities immediately in the past with the potentialities of the immanent future that it may become. Beyond the immanence of these potentialities is the continuum of possibilities extending toward the horizon of the future and the factical necessity of the determining past.[75] The complex intertwining of these modes in the present is existentiality, the *agōn* or moment in its dyadic push and pull and in the limited freedom of creative selection.[76] Continuity, then, is the tendency of natural process toward the establishment of a consummatory history.[77] In the context of human beings, time is the drama of the Human Eros. While emphasizing the environment and history of events, eco-ontology equally stresses the role of creativity in the present as integral to temporal continuity.[78] Individuality is the synthesis of the situation

---

74. This saves eco-ontology from the deconstructionist dismissal of being an ontology of "presence." If "presence" is understood as factical being-at-hand, it falls into the ontology of identity criticized above. But presence as pragmatically understood is creatively engaged, and so not completely formed or actualized. The present is not only "vague," but dramatically significant, penetrated by imagination as well as reason.

75. The continuum of pure possibility I designate by the Greek term *apeiron* and the delimiting frame of the necessity of the factical past by the Greek *anankē*. The present is the "struggle" (*agōn*) between them.

76. The dyadic nature of existence is discussed by C. S. Peirce in his category of Secondness. Its selective freedom is discussed by William James, most famously in "The Will to Believe."

77. This is why Dewey presents his primary example of it in terms of the aesthetic; see *Art as Experience* (LW, 10), ch. 3.

78. See Dewey's highly important discussion of this in "Time and Individuality" (LW, 14).

through action guided by imaginative insight into the potentialities at hand. It requires an understanding of the present as the outcome of a history in which there are tensive elements constituting the phase of undergoing. The insight into potentialities involves interpreting the present in terms of its possible meanings. The idealization of one or more of those possibilities sets an end-in-view that makes reconstructive or transformative action a way of mediating the open tensiveness toward qualitative closure. The basis for a genuine individualism, then, is all one with deeply informed knowledge of the world and its history as well as creative imagination and moral courage. When profoundly realized, this environmental individualism fulfills the Human Eros. To be is to be individual as dramatically achieved.

In achieving its history, the Human Eros must care for the world. Care is intentional: it is care *of*. To care is to understand the history and possibilities of a subject so that the subject is manifest in its meaning as beautiful. The beautiful here is not the "well-formed" or pretty. It is that which manifests the Light of suchness. The transient clarity of the world is grasped in all its affective and moral as well as intellectual complexity. The Buddhist term *prajñā* is appropriate here, for this is insight into the world in its clarity motivated by compassionate awareness that in turn enables one to select the "skillful means" (*upāya*) to respond to the world. To grasp the world in its unstable mode of undergoing (*dukkha*) is to have compassionate insight; to grasp it in terms of guiding it toward a consummatory history is to respond with intelligent eros. One seeks to eliminate ignorance and meaningless suffering for fulfillment and the creative establishment of individuality or "creative mindfulness."

Being oriented to the world, one's own existence becomes an opening for concern. "Concern" here is understood in its Quaker sense, as that which leads one forth from the innermost depths of one's being toward that which needs one in the world.[79] The human community, the animal kingdom, the biosphere, and the geosphere itself can be grasped as objects of concern as insight discerns them. Concern may therefore be experienced for fellow human beings, animals, ecosystems. We must avoid the reification of identities but discern interactive histories of continuities. Creative transformation involves integration of the future into the

79. See Alfred North Whitehead, *Adventures of Ideas*, ch. 9, sec. 3.

meaning of the present through individuation that becomes open to the world by insight, care and concern. Because individuality is environmental, we are called upon to care for the world by the Human Eros itself.

The Home (Oikos) of Philosophy—Inhabitation

Philosophy reflects our human embeddedness in the world. It offers the possibility of responsible inhabitation in pursuit of ecological wisdom. To *in*habit is to have the habits that make one at home, the wisdom of the environment. Wisdom must inhabit this world, not another. Disembodied philosophy tries to live without environment. It is a disservice to its origins and is possible only through a primal act of forgetting. The initiating moment of philosophy is not just separation in reflective thought but also acknowledgment of the sources of existence. Philosophy arises in response to the tensive nature of the world within which human beings find themselves. To undertake thought without acknowledging its origin in need is to repress its own motives and to refuse acknowledgment of its grounding. Criticism is moral, involving the active disposition of curiosity and receptivity to discovery, a generosity toward the play of free possibility the world can offer. To inhabit the world is not to dominate or renounce it, but to play in it, learn from it, care for it, and realize the beauty of its meanings. "Ecology is the wisdom of being at home in the world."[80]

In the twenty-first century, philosophy is morally compelled to acknowledge its origins in the life of our species on the planet. The act of forgetfulness that allows us to drive the living systems of the planet toward extinction can no longer be accepted, even—perhaps especially— when presented at face value as "professional philosophy." Nor, in its new horizon of global existence, can North Atlantic philosophy maintain its traditional narcissism. Thought must call out to thought on a global level. Philosophy must accept the place where it lives and dwells, its home, or *oikos,* which it has a responsibility to manage as well as within which it draws its life. The possibilities of an eco-ontology to fulfill this end are numerous. It relocates the task of philosophy with the traditional project of wisdom. It engages the wisdom traditions and philosophies

---

80. Eugenie Gatens-Robinson in conversation.

of other cultures. It demands that philosophy be a humanistic as well as naturalistic discipline that has a complex literacy about the cultural dimensions of human experience as well as an ecological scientific literacy about the natural world. It distrusts pure methodologies. It recognizes the origin of philosophy in the Human Eros and turns that Eros toward the problem of formulating wisdom for an ecological global community. It believes the purpose of thought is to save the world.

FOUR

THE BEING OF NATURE

Dewey and Buchler and the Prospect for an Eco-ontology

Nature and Naturalism

American philosophy has been dominated by the theme of "Nature."[1] From Edwards to Emerson to Dewey to Dennett, American thought has variously invoked Nature. But to articulate a philosophy of Nature is not thereby to espouse a form of "naturalism." In fact, philosophies undertaken in the name of "naturalism" seem to have a different temperament than those that begin with the *thought* of Nature as such. As a theme, "Nature" invites an expansive mood for reflection, while "naturalism" sounds constrictive and combative. "Nature" disposes the mind to musement, "pondering," *theoria, Denken*—to becoming

---

1. In order to emphasize Nature as the object of thought, wonder, and mystery *as well as* scientific inquiry, I have capitalized it. I am sympathetic with Frederick J. E. Woodbridge's remark on "Nature" as a proper name rather than as a mere denotative noun: "I am afflicted with a sense of indecency whenever I refer to Nature as 'it,'" *Essay on Nature* (New York: Columbia University Press, 1940), 4. This is also in keeping with John Herman Randall Jr.'s usage.

Emerson's "transparent eyeball." "Naturalism" has something of a doctrinal, even dogmatic, flavor, since every "ism" draws a line in the sand. The initiating mood of philosophical thinking is important: To begin by being *against* something rather than *wondering about* something has pragmatic consequences. Anger and fear (for good Darwinian reasons) are modes of constricting attention and readying extreme "fight or flight" responses. Like most other "isms," "naturalism" mainly designates what its adherents are *against*. The usual definition of "naturalism" gives it a negative formulation: "Naturalism is a rejection of the supernatural." This begs the question, since what counts as "supernatural" rather depends on what Nature is. The Greek gods were as "natural," as much the children of φύσις, as mortals and represented important natural forces: the earth's gift of grain, the tempestuous sea, procreative desire, and so on. Thus naturalism as "antisupernaturalism" turns to "science" (always the hard sciences: physics, chemistry, neurology) to determine not so much "what there is," but "what there isn't."[2] This sort of thinking, driven by a rejection of what it regards as "supernatural" and turning toward some *idea* of science, is usually (though not always) pulled in the direction of materialism. With this comes a dominant, even exclusive, focus on epistemology conceived as scientific knowledge, so that Nature comes to mean "what is known by the (hard) sciences." Let us call this ideology "scientism." Thomas Hobbes offers a paradigm example, but Daniel Dennett is a good contemporary instance.

There are humanistic naturalists who try to pull naturalism away from the powerful gravitational field of scientism, such as many of the contributors (including John Dewey) in Yervant Krikorian's *Naturalism and*

---

2. Thus Sidney Hook: "Naturalism is opposed to all known forms of supernaturalism, not because it rules out a priori what may or may not exist, but because no plausible evidence has been found to warrant belief in the entities and powers to which supernatural status has been attributed. The existence of God, immortality, disembodied spirits, cosmic purpose and design...are denied by naturalists for the same generic reasons that they deny the existence of fairies, elves, and leprechauns." "Naturalism and Democracy," in *Naturalism and the Human Spirit*, ed. Yervant Krikorian (New York: Columbia University Press, 1944),45. The positive formulation stresses the connection to experimental inquiry. James Gouinlock says that "naturalism grew out of the emerging intellectual temper that demanded that any cognitive claim, including those of philosophy, be testable in publicly experimental conditions." "Naturalism," in *American Philosophy: An Encyclopedia*, ed. John Lachs and Robert Talisse (London: Routledge, 2008), 531. See also Randall's "Epilogue: The Nature of Naturalism," in Krikorian, 354f., and William M. Shea, *The Naturalists and the Supernatural* (Mercer Island, WA: Mercer, 1984), esp. 63ff.

the Human Spirit.[3] But even while Dewey himself escaped scientism, many of his readers—beginners, trained philosophers and not a few Dewey scholars, too—read *him* in a scientistic way. At the beginning of "Ontological Relativity," Quine acknowledges his debt to Dewey regarding the connection of meaning with behavior. Soon it becomes pretty clear that he thinks Dewey is a "behaviorist," that "behavior" is "observable behavior," and *that is all there is to meaning.*[4] Thus, if Nature philosophers are to use the term "naturalism"—and I think we must—we need to prevent it from being confused with its scientistic avatar. "Naturalism" best resists the narrowing power of scientism by remaining deeply and broadly focused upon the *question* of Nature, *including,* but not limited to, what is revealed through *all* the sciences. Instead of beginning by determining what we are *against,* let us be open to the various ways "Nature" may be *invoked* for thinking. Invocational thinking begins in the mood of wonder and tries to be "polyphonic"; that is, to hear the various voices in which Nature may be articulated or housed in human utterance. Of these, the ontological voice, which asks about the being of Nature, offers a powerful counter to scientism.

Besides wonder, another crucial mood is care. Here the ordinary sense of the term "naturalist" helps, designating anyone who has an abiding, informed, concrete interest in and care for Nature. (It is rather strange how many philosophical naturalists really don't *care* that much about Nature!) A *naturalist* not only begins in wonder at the spectacle of cosmic process but also develops thoughtful care regarding it. The naturalist engages in θεωρία—that passionate speculative curiosity that gave birth to the Greek mind itself. A naturalist sees Nature as "κόσμος": not just the "universe," but something orderly and fair to behold. Many naturalists are fine scientists—scientists who do not succumb to "scientism."[5] But Emerson's transformative response to the exhibit of the vast, organized spectrum of life in the *Jardin des Plantes* was also that of a naturalist: "Not

3. Dewey's contribution, "Antinaturalism in Extremis," can be found in LW, 15:46–62.

4. "When with Dewey we turn thus toward a naturalistic view of language and behavioral meaning...we recognize that there are no meanings, nor likenesses nor distinctions of meaning, beyond what are implicit in people's dispositions to overt behavior." *Ontological Relativity,* 28–29. Contrast Dewey's rich meaning of "experience" with Quine's "impacts at our nerve endings" (*Word and Object,* 20).

5. E.g., Stephen Jay Gould. The polemics between Gould and Dennett on the subject of Darwinism vividly illustrate the distinction between a genuine naturalist and a scientistic ideologue.

a form so grotesque, so savage, nor so beautiful but is an expression of some property inherent in man the observer—an occult relation between the very scorpions and man. I feel the centipede in me—cayman, carp, eagle, & fox. I am moved by strange sympathies, I say continually, 'I will be a naturalist.'"[6] It is hard to imagine such a story told of Rudolf Carnap.

Philosophy delves deeper and wider than the spectacle of Nature as cosmos when it raises the question of the *being* of Nature. Now this inquiry may remain focused on "what there is," the nature of beings rather than the being of Nature, and pursue an ontology focused solely upon existent actualities, ignoring the being of potentials, possibles, and the unmanifest depth of Nature. Recall Quine's scorn for the metaphysician who over-populates his ontology with a "slum of possibles," preferring instead his own "desert landscape" ontology, where to be an entity "is, purely and simply, to be reckoned as the value of a variable."[7] The result is a meta-physics of "things" thought of as an aggregate of determinate objects of cognition. Or, with Spinoza, "what there is" may be the whole unified system of Nature, but still a thing, a *factum*, writ large. Alternatively, besides recognizing actualities, an ontology can include the being of potentials (e.g., Aristotle), possibles (e.g., Whitehead), or "powers" (e.g., Schelling). Heidegger took a radical approach, positing a fundamental "ontological difference" between beings and being, where being is not a "ground" for beings but an "Abyss" (*Abgrund*), not a thing but an "event of appropriation" (*Ereignis*), permeated by "no-thingness."[8] An ontology of Nature must be open to the variety of modalities and the mysterious depths of Nature lest it lose itself in a "thing-metaphysics." But it should also worry about radical dichotomies. As Plato's Eleatic Stranger recom-mends, when presented with a sharp "either-or," the philosopher should give the child's answer of "both."[9] So the naturalist asks about the being of Nature without reducing it to an aggregate or totality of "things" or setting up some division between Nature and being. Ontology must be undertaken *within* Nature.

---

6. *Journals*, July 13, 1833.
7. See Quine's "On What There Is," in *From a Logical Point of View* (Cambridge, MA: Harvard, 1953), 1–19, esp. 3–4, 13.
8. On Heidegger's ontological difference, see *Being and Time*, 6ff.; *The Basic Problems of Phenomenology*, 28, 317; "What Is Metaphysics?" *Identity and Difference*; and *Contributions to Philosophy*.
9. *Sophist*, 249d.

Two Ontologies of Nature: Dewey and Buchler

I wish to explore two such ontologies: those of John Dewey and Justus Buchler. Each presents us with a nonscientistic naturalism, and both have relevance for how an ecologically oriented ontology, an "eco-ontology," might be developed. Dewey's thought is relatively well known, whereas Buchler's highly original work remains comparatively neglected, and so will be the focus here.[10] The similarities of themes in their thought can be contrasted with their radically different approaches. Buchler is a precise, systematic thinker who explicitly formulated a categorial natural ontology, an "ordinal naturalism," in his *Metaphysics of Natural Complexes*.[11] His naturalism is articulated in the context of his "metaphysics of the human process," which itself develops a theory of meaning or "human utterance" as "judgment," broadly conceived so as to include "doing, making, and saying."[12] Dewey, like Heidegger, is an exploratory thinker for whom thought is always *unterwegs*. His metaphysics is an open-ended, experiential description of the "generic traits of existence," of "existence as existence," as well as a descriptive "natural history" of the emergent continuities between Nature and culture (LW, 1:50, 52, 308; MW, 8:6–7). Existence is Nature: fields of events of "doing and undergoing" revealed through culture or "experience." Like Buchler, Dewey raises the question of Nature in connection with a theory of culture. While defensibly coherent, Dewey's work could not easily be called "systematic." Dewey is more comprehensive in vision than Buchler, whose books are

---

10. Justus Buchler (1914–91) was an original thinker working in the American naturalist tradition as it was being eclipsed by the rise of analytic philosophy. He obtained a degree from Columbia (writing on Peirce with Ernest Nagel, resulting in *Charles Peirce's Empiricism*) and eventually was appointed to the faculty where he was a friend and colleague of John Herman Randall Jr. In 1971, he joined the faculty at State University of New York at Stony Brook, where he taught until 1981. His thought engages a variety of thinkers, especially Dewey, Santayana, and Whitehead. His major works are *Toward a General Theory of Judgment* (1951, rev. 2nd ed., 1979), *Nature and Judgment* (1955), *The Concept of Method* (1961), *Metaphysics of Natural Complexes* (1966, 2nd ed., 1991), and *The Main of Light* (1974). See the entry on him by Kathleen Wallace in *The Blackwell Guide to American Philosophy*, ed. Armen Marsoobian and John Ryder (Malden, MA: Blackwell, 2004), 271–86. Two important studies of his thought are Beth J. Singer, *Ordinal Naturalism* (New York: Columbia University Press, 1983) and *Nature's Perspectives: Prospects for Ordinal Metaphysics*, ed. Armen Marsoobian, Kathleen Wallace, and Robert S. Corrington (Albany: State University of New York Press, 1991). This last title has a fine memoir of Buchler by Sidney Gelber.

11. *Metaphysics of Natural Complexes*, 2nd expanded ed., ed. Kathleen Wallace and Armen Marsoobian, with Robert S. Corrington (Albany: State University of New York Press, 1991), hereafter cited in the text as MNC. Buchler's metaphysics is consciously active throughout his other books.

12. The three modes of judgment are technically called "active, exhibitive, and assertive"; see especially *Nature and Judgment*, 20ff., and *Toward a General Theory of Judgment*, 48ff.

compact in explanations and parsimonious with examples. Both treat Nature as pluralistic, nonreductive, dynamic, relational, and polymodal, and so they are supportive of developing an ecological ontology. Both replace the substance-attribute metaphysics of the Aristotelian-Scholastic traditions with dynamic relations and functional categories. Both reject "ultimate atomic substances" as well as atemporal first causes. Both are conducive to developing ecological habits of philosophical reflection, which the various traditional "metaphysics of identity" are not.

It will be instructive to examine the central ideas in both Dewey's and Buchler's ontologies insofar as they seem rather complementary and yet operate with such different approaches. Dewey's experiential and existential approach stresses an interactionist, transactional, or ecological view of Nature as an "affair of affairs," evolving new, "emergent" levels of interaction with an open-ended creative teleology. Experience, as the cultural ways humans inhabit the earth, not only "reaches down" into Nature, exploring its possibilities, but is "a growing progressive self-disclosure of nature itself" (LW, 1:5). By describing the "generic traits of existence" that turn up in all the specific modes of experience and discourse, metaphysics is a tool of criticism, finding continuities where others find sharp divisions.[13] Metaphysics helps prevent the isolation of domains of experience that give rise to absolute dichotomies or "dualisms"; for example, what is described as "selectivity" at the level of physical behavior is continuous with responsiveness at the biological and individuality at the human level.[14] To see these levels in terms of the natural history of evolution prevents the dichotomy of "mind" and "matter." This experiential approach acknowledges the pre- and postcognitive contexts necessary for any cognitive inquiry—not all experience is a form of "knowing." This is one reason for the notorious impression of "vagueness" in Dewey's metaphysics, which is not due to a lapse of philosophical acumen, but due to a penetrating realization that "existence" is revealed through more than just "knowing-experiences." Metaphysics deals with how Nature reveals itself throughout the range of human existence.

---

13. Dewey nowhere gives a list of these traits, but they include continuity, situation, stable-and-precarious, quality or immediacy, relation or means, interaction/transaction, potentiality, existence, selectivity, emergence, end or closure, individuality, community, novelty, temporality, natural history, value. A comparison can be made with Plato's "greatest kinds" of the *Sophist* (249bff.), which are an "interweaving of forms" throughout Being; i.e., pervasive features of all other forms.
14. See LW, 1:195ff.

Buchler's approach is categorial and "ordinal." It is concerned with developing precise, general categorial concepts that allow us to think of Nature rigorously but relationally; it interprets relations in terms of sets of orders, hence "ordinal naturalism."[15] Buchler presents a systematic philosophy that works against entrenched tendencies toward atomism, essentialism, or monism. As often happens in systematic philosophy, Buchler simply sets forth axiomatically key ideas whose ramifications are then laid out. Dewey "discovers" his generic traits along the way in his involved endeavor to describe a world of creative continuities in dialogue with the history of philosophy. Metaphysics for him is a prolonged meditation on how human history has engaged Nature so that its pervasive, diverse features, its "ways," can be gradually discerned, articulated, and become recognized in the array of our experiences. Metaphysics reveals continuities. These different approaches are reflected in their philosophical terminology. Dewey invests ordinary words with his own philosophical meanings, a strategy that often backfires (e.g., the persistent misreading of Dewey's use of "experience"— i.e., "culture"—as "perception"). Buchler employs a novel, quirky set of terms that has unfortunately left his thought confined to a small circle of those fluent in the dialect.

Alternatives to "Substance": Situations and Natural Complexes

Let us begin by comparing Dewey's and Buchler's alternatives to the classical idea of substance: Dewey's "transaction" or "situation" and Buchler's "natural complex."[16] Dewey's "situation" defies simple definition—even description—since it is not wholly definite. Situations are what "things,"

---

15. Beth Singer coined the term "ordinal naturalism" while working with Buchler, who accepted it. See her *Ordinal Naturalism* (1984), 21. Buchler states, "Every complex is an order and belongs to an order of complexes. Thus orders are inclusive and belong to more inclusive orders" (MNC, 92). "Order" for Buchler is not to be contrasted with "disorder" but with "what is not and cannot be related," a concept he finds incoherent. See "Probing the Idea of Nature," in MNC, 265ff. Thus everything is some sort of order, i.e., is "natural," since "order" is synonymous with "nature" and "real" for him.

16. "*Substantia*" (Latin for "what stands beneath") was already a poor translation for Aristotle's *ousia* ("being"), derived from the verb "to be" (*einai*) via the feminine participle (*ousa*). *Ousiai* are not "underneath" or "behind" experience; they display their whatness in their *doing* (*energeia*): The rabbit shows its rabbitness *in* rabbiting, not by "standing under" the "phenomena." Thus, with enough "experience" (*empeiria*, "hands-on" experience, not sensation), one grasps the "essence" (another badly translated term: *to ti ēn einai* is the "what it *was going* to be"; *ēn* is in the *imperfect* tense). One might say that Kant's noumena/phenomena dualism, where "experience" *hides* substance, is the outcome of a lousy translation.

or discriminated objects, are *in* and *of* (LW, 12:72ff.) They are ways in which events, *res*, are mutually and dynamically embedded in the world with all the inherited complexity of their histories and indeterminacy of their possibilities.[17] Objects only exist within situations; i.e., situations are ontological "environments." Situations are integrated and organized by a pervasive quality (in human experience) or undergone immediacy that is not cognized but which makes cognition possible; it is the tacit, mutual involvement of conditions of undergoing.[18] In human existence, it is our established, prereflective, qualitatively "had" world that gives sense to specific actions, including inquiry, speech, thought, affection. Because it is prereflective and not cognized, philosophers tend to ignore it, thereby committing the "intellectualist fallacy" of turning everything into an object of cognition: hence the ontologies of "substances." Situations have an indefinite "horizon" with a defining pervasive quality; they also have a "focus," a vortex of transformation which manifests itself in human experience as the "tensive" or "problematic." Around this focus is the "context" that includes variously discriminated objects, functions and values that can be denoted or which "exist," i.e., "arise, stand forth" (Latin "*ex-sisto*"), as "things." This is the interface of past and future, of actual and possible, undergoing and doing, that constitutes each *res* as a center of creative individuation. *Transformation*, not *identity*, is at the heart of each pulse of existence.[19] The inherently nebulous descriptions Dewey gives of "situation" have been a constant source of criticism, especially from "intellectualists" (who completely miss the point of Dewey's utter rejection of their starting point). Pragmatically, Dewey's approach undercuts seeing the world as ultimately constituted by individual "things," independent substances, atomic facts, or whatever, conceived as complete actualities inherently definite in logical as well as extensional space and time and only "externally related." Dewey reminds us of the "whence and whither" as well as the interconnectedness of events, their transitory belonging and "suchness." Thus "being"

17. For Dewey's use of *res* see *Essays in Experimental Logic*, Introduction (MW, 10:322–23) and LW, 1:83–84. On "situation," see Dewey's letters to Arthur Bentley, July 15, July 19, and August 31, 1943, in *John Dewey and Arthur Bentley: A Philosophical Correspondence*, ed. Sidney Ratner and Jules Altman (New Brunswick, NJ: Rutgers University Press, 1964).

18. See "Qualitative Thought" (1930), LW, 5:243–63. Dewey's focus on the "qualitative" manifestation in human experience is not meant to limit situations to human ones. The qualitative is the immediacy of existence which *may* embody an inherited history or process.

19. See "Time and Individuality" (1940, LW, 14:98–114).

(or "existence," for Dewey) is not grounded in *fixed identity* but in *dynamic continuity*: It involves temporal relation and temporal quality, the "had" rhythmic "undergoing-and-doing" of immediate existence, and the emergent, abiding, and evolving natural histories of events.[20]

Buchler's idea of "natural complex" was likewise meant to supplant the traditional idea of substance with one conducive to a relational ontology. Unlike Dewey, Buchler provides a clear definitional principle: "Whatever is, in whatever way, is a natural complex" (MNC, 1). But he begins with a different concern. While Dewey begins with a vast horizon of "experience" (i.e., interaction), Buchler begins with the act of "judgment" (doing, making or saying). A natural complex is anything that is "discriminated," a "discriminandum," that is, "anything identified or discovered or imagined or discerned or sensed or posited or encountered or apprehended or made or acted upon . . ." or "whatever we talk about" (MNC, 1, 233). This includes literally anything that can serve as the object of attention: objects of perception, logical abstractions, imaginary characters, historical events, and immanent possibilities. Buchler complains that Dewey's use of "existence" is not wide enough to do justice to the "reality"— Buchler's preferred term—of such natural complexes (MNC, 8–9). Buchler acknowledges there are natural complexes beyond the range of human discrimination, but for us they are disclosed through what judgments are *about* (MNC, 23, 233–34). As such, a natural complex does not include the pervasive, tacit, penumbral "horizon" or quality of the noncognitive aspects of Dewey's situation. Buchler acknowledges "contexts" as potential *objects* of future *judgments* that can "locate" the natural complex at hand (MNC, 5). Buchler did not care for Dewey's insistence that "immediacy of existence is ineffable" (LW, 1:74). Nor did he like the idea of a pervasive but indefinite unifying quality to a situation.[21] While Buchler

20. Temporal quality is a precognitive existential "pulse" of time prior to any instrumental or "timed" relation to the world. Temporality is as fundamental for Dewey as for Heidegger; see LW, 1:82ff., 119–20, 194ff., 202, 210ff.

21. Buchler mistakenly thinks this means that there is something in principle ultimately "unanalyzable" for Dewey (MNC, 29; see LW 1:74, 89). What Dewey says is as *had* or *undergone*, quality marks a "terminus" of existence, sheer "thatness." This is a generic trait that pervades experience. But it can be felt and be constitutive of meaning, as in art. Any particular quality may be inquired into or made an object of thought, but then it occupies the status of an object in *another* situation with its own ineffable features. See LW, 12:74. Buchler himself denies on principle that any natural complex can be "completely" analyzed, since there are no simples or absolute termini. But he lacks anything like Dewey's sense of the "pervasive quality" of a situation that becomes so important in Dewey's theory of aesthetic experience. Instead, Buchler speaks of the "contour" of natural complexes, the continuity, totality and integration of its locations (MNC, 22).

does not commit Dewey's "intellectualist fallacy" of equating the real with the known, access to the real as actual or possible subject of judgment is through "doing, making or saying."

From a Deweyan perspective, a "natural complex" as an *object of attention* is simply part of a situation, the "focus" under reconstruction and its relevant context. For Dewey, any complex would be *existentially*, not just "ordinally," embedded in the fields of interactions and possibilities unfolding in process. A situation as unfolding history is what makes any judgment possible and so cannot itself be the "object of judgment." But it does give sense to the context. This is why moods and feelings are important ways in which human beings are aware of Nature not only in noncognitional experiences but also in cognitional ones. It is not clear how far any situation extends for Dewey. Some critics, like Russell, believe Dewey could think of Nature as "one big situation," a claim that usually precedes labeling him a closet absolute idealist. This is manifestly wrong and Dewey directly rejected the charge.[22] Dewey always speaks of situations in the plural; there are at least as many situations as histories undergoing transformation. To think of situations as discretely individuated, sharply delimited "things" capable of being quantified lapses back into the metaphysical outlook Dewey is avoiding. Knowing gives us "objects" to focus upon, but experience simply is more than knowing. Knowing must be situated. Thus Nature reveals itself in many ways—the whole range of "experience."

While Dewey's concept of situation is greater in scope than Buchler's natural complex, there is no question Dewey could have better articulated this idea by far. Buchler, to his credit, tries to be more specific, emphasizing the *potentially* determinate location of any complex. By definition a natural complex can and must be always located in another. By this principle Buchler consequently infers there can be no final or ultimate natural complex, no "totality," for it could not be "in" anything; it could not be "located."[23] We cannot therefore speak of "Nature" as a whole, as a "complex of complexes" or even "an order of orders" (MNC, 100, 26off.).

---

22. See Bertrand Russell's "Dewey's New *Logic*" and Dewey's reply in *The Philosophy of John Dewey*, revised ed., ed. Paul Arthur Schilpp (Greensboro, NC: Tudor Publishing, 1951), esp. 544 f.

23. "In" denotes "relevance" for Buchler, or, with Locke, "pertinence" (MNC, 16; see *Essay* IV.vi.11). Buchler is sensitive to the nonspatial senses whereby one thing can be said to be "in" another, but the spatial metaphors dominate his language.

And so it is not some sort of totality; there is no one "ultimate fact," no "Absolute"; it is not an "it." Nature is radically pluralistic. Likewise there are no ultimate simples; a complex always locates further complexes within it and so on. An ultimate simple, if it is truly *simple,* cannot be *related* and so cannot be located or even be an object of judgment.[24] Although Nature is pluralistic, it is not atomic but radically complex. Complexity is due to having "traits," some of which constitute the "integrity" or prevailing character of a natural complex. But traits, like everything, are *also* natural complexes and so not simple. Further, any natural complex can be a trait of some other. For any natural complex to be discriminated, it must be located; it is "real" only in terms of its relations in a given order. (One peculiar example is Buchler's claim that the house receding from view *really does get smaller* in the "order" of vision, if not in the order of physics.) While aiming for conceptual rigor, Buchler rejects as incoherent any idea of ultimacy, whether that of an all-embracing whole or ultimate atomic simples. Such termini simply reflect where judgment has come to a stop (MNC, 11). To be a natural complex is to be *thoroughly* relational without any "totality" of relations or any final *relata* making any relation a *tertium quid.*

What, then, is "Nature"? Just the various orders of natural complexes? Aside from the orders that actually are, Buchler includes possibilities as natural complexes, as long as they can be "located." Buchler wishes to prevent natural ontology from limiting itself to "what there is," i.e., being an ontology of "things." But he also wants to draw attention to Nature as a *source* of natural complexes. This goes beyond simply designating "possibles" as types of natural complexes. Buchler reintroduces and reformulates Spinoza's distinction between *natura naturans* and *natura naturata.*[25]

---

24. "Whatever can be discriminated . . . is related to that within which or from which it is discriminated. . . . [A] perfectly simple, homogeneous trait . . . would also have to be single, unrelated and inaccessible. . . . A simple would not only lack the possibility of being described; it would lack all possibilities" (MNC, 17–18). Complexity is irreducible for Buchler; any "simple" is just the terminus of current analysis: ". . .every discriminandum whatever offers a prospect for query. . . . A complex, if it is accessible at all, is analyzable and interpretable without end" (MNC, 5–6; see 11ff.). Buchler quotes the maxim of Anaxagoras: "Neither is there a least of what is small, but always there is a less. . . But there is always a greater of what is great" (MNC, 14). Buchler does not want to say that judgment *creates* the natural complex, thereby making Nature some sort of construct—though at times it is difficult to see how he avoids this.

25. These terms have a tangled history anterior to and subsequent to Spinoza's famous usage. For Spinoza *natura naturans* is infinite substance "conceived through itself" and *natura naturata* designates the infinite and finite modes conceivable only through it (*Ethics* I. XXIX. Schol., *Short Treatise* I. viii–ix). See the appendix for a discussion of the terms and ideas behind them.

For Buchler, these terms distinguish Nature as *generative of order* from the *actual or possible orders* of Nature constituting natural complexes. Nature as *natura naturans* "is the presence and availability of complexes. It is the provision and determination of traits—of providingness . . . It provides man, for instance, with the possibilities, the circumstances and the substance of judgment" (MNC, 3). It is evident in the "fertility" of any complex, its constant "arising," change, and novelty, its ability to admit new traits or come into new relations, or, in Buchler's terminology, its "alescence" (MNC, 100).[26] *Natura naturata*, by contrast, denotes "what obtains" or "what does prevail and what has arisen" (MNC, 53, 100). Nature as *natura naturans* is not "orders of possibility" so much as "possibility of orders," possibility for new relations to "obtain" and "prevail." Nature as *natura naturata* signifies the related, determinate, prevailing orders, *possible and actual,* that *do* obtain, which Buchler terms "the World." *Natura naturans* is not "*an order* of orders," something determinate, but "the order which permeates them all . . . by which new orders are discriminable and explorable" (MNC, 100). Even to call it "the order" may go too far. As Buchler clarifies in a later essay, it is, rather, the "*ordinality*" of Nature.

> When nature is defined baldly as "orders of whatever variety and number," too little is suggested of a difference in emphasis between the concepts of nature and the World. The focus is on *natura naturata*: we are given the crop, but not the seeding, not the productive principle. The definition in terms of ordinality corrects this. Some years ago I defined nature as providingness, the provision of traits. The intent was to abstract from the partly eulogistic common suggestion of purposive or planned accumulation, as well as of agency, and to amplify the suggestion of sheer putting forth, or bringing forth sheer geniture, for better and for worse. The conceptions of nature as providingness and as ordinality are continuous with one another and with the conception of nature as "orders." This continuity can be conveyed by utilizing both members of the twin *natura naturans* and

---

26. Alescence (from Latin *alescere*, "to grow up, increase") "is that dimension of nature in which the specific integrities of complexes *initially* are what they are and how they are, whether in time, whether within an organization of traits or within an order of encounter. It suggests origination or nascence or incipience, the incipience of growth, of irrelevance, or of oddity, or of deterioration; the incipience of ordinal relocation or difference within an order. Variation is difference insofar as it is initial" (MNC, 56).

natura naturata. Nature as ordinality is *natura naturans*; it is the providing, the engendering condition. Nature as "orders" is *natura naturata*; it is the provided, the ordinal manifestation, the World's complexes. ("Probing the Idea of Nature," MNC, Appendix 4, 276.)

"Nature" is both *naturans* and *naturata*: "Nature is ordinality and relationality, prevalence and alescence, possibility and actuality" (MNC, 200). This development is an important aspect of Buchler's ontology, one that I think introduces something above and beyond the idea that "whatever is, is a natural complex."

Buchler's Paradoxes of Natural Complexes

Buchler introduces this modal distinction between *natura naturans* and *natura naturata* so that we do not think of Nature as some aggregate of "facts." But it leads to problems that can be called "Buchler's paradoxes of natural complexes":

1. If any subject of judgment or discrimination is ipso facto a natural complex, then insofar as "Nature" *itself* is such a subject, it *is* a natural complex. More specifically, is *natura naturans* a complex? If not, Buchler cannot even talk about it or the "ordinality" of Nature—and yet he does. Or does *natura naturans* go beyond the limits of natural complexes? Is it "real" in some other way? Call this "the paradox of the universality of natural complexes."

2. A "natural complex" is an ultimate *univocal* categorial concept: *whatever* "is," in "whatever way," *is* a natural complex. Everything is not only referred to the category of natural complex, but everything *is* a natural complex. Aristotle refers all categories to *ousia*, but does not *make* relations, qualities, quantities, etc. *ousiai*. Thus, "natural complex" functions as an ontological "simple" more ultimate than Aristotle's category of substance. Can a pluralistic ontology be grounded on a doctrine of the "univocity of being"? If "natural complex" can be applied indifferently to anything and everything, how does it support a pluralist metaphysics? Can fundamental complexity and polymodality be expressed by univocity? Call this "the paradox of the univocity of natural complexes."

With regard to the first paradox, one aim of the idea of natural complex is to keep open the possibility of further "query" and analysis. In this respect it is akin to Dewey's situation encompassing objects of knowledge. Both Dewey and Buchler are trying to avoid an ontology of things, but Buchler (unlike Dewey and somewhat like Kant) has tied his substitute for substance to the function of judgment, however broadly construed. Dewey's situations are not *objects* of judgment but are *conditions* for inquiry; if a situation becomes denoted, it thereby becomes an object *within another situation*. Situations enable instrumental thinking and often for that very reason are submerged and not in our awareness. But it is otherwise in those experiences Dewey calls consummatory and religious. In them, the pervasive nature of the situation is felt as constitutive of the meaning of the experience. Such "had" feelings or moods are not direct objects of judgment or cognition. As noted before, Buchler's natural complex could be understood as objects and their contexts within a Deweyan situation. This may help solve the particular problem of whether or not Nature (or *natura naturans*) is a natural complex.

Buchler uses "*natura naturans*" to indicate the *possibility* whereby natural complexes may be determined at all, the "source" of order that is not itself *an* order: "the providing, engendering condition," an ἀρχή, something like the old Greek ἄπειρον. Thus, strictly speaking, *natura naturans* is not a natural complex. But it must have some ontological status if only to prevent ontology from limiting itself to *natura naturata*, to "what there is." I think the *natura naturans–natura naturata* distinction challenges the claim that everything is a natural complex. And it is the sort of idea that might lend further articulation to Dewey's existential-empirical concept of Nature. Buchler's *natura naturans–natura naturata* distinction, a problem in his system, works better in Dewey's existential-empirical approach to Nature and adds something important to it, just as Buchler's idea of natural complexes needs Dewey's idea of situations while lending further articulation to the concept of "context."

The resolution of the previous paradox has bearing on that of univocity. Not everything can be said to be a natural complex or be an object of judgment. What should be emphasized is plurivocity, "of being said in many ways." And Buchler undertakes just such an analysis of the modalities of possibility (especially qua potentiality) and actuality and their interrelationship in the last chapter of *Metaphysics of Natural Complexes*, which I think is the crowning achievement of the work and a fitting rebuttal to Quine's "desert landscape" ontology.[27] And it is from just such a modal ontological analysis that Dewey's metaphysics of situations could most benefit. If we drop the universal applicability of the term "natural complex," the paradox of univocity disappears. "To be," consequently, is *variously* said, and not just as "to be a natural complex." Nature is the intertwining creative temporal continuum of *natura naturans* and *natura naturata*. Nature is not necessarily arrived at by "judgment," but also via moods of wonder and mystery—by the full range of what Dewey's "denotative-empirical method" includes in the task of the *philosophical* recollection of the experience of existence.[28] This is part of what I earlier called the "invocational" or "polyphonic" approach to thinking about Nature.

Pluralism, Relations, and Guiding Ontological Principles

In comparing Dewey's and Buchler's core metaphysical ideas, we have seen how the difference in approaches led to very different, though mutually supportive, conclusions. It would be beneficial to look briefly at three more comparisons: (1) their concepts of pluralism, (2) their concepts of relations, and (3) their concepts of basic guiding ontological principles (Dewey's "principle of continuity" and Buchler's "principle of ontological parity"). Both Dewey and Buchler make pluralism and complexity fundamental. Dewey's pluralism is experiential; because each situation is transformative, it is inherently unique. Individuality is understood as the creative response to existence. That is, for Dewey, pluralism is bound up with the idea of process as temporal quality, as *transformation*. Dewey asks us to understand this in terms of our embodied experience; our individuality gives us insight into the nature of time itself.[29] Buchler defends the irreducibility of plurality on categorial grounds in terms of the function

27. See Justus Buchler's explicit response to Quine on this point in MNC, 189n18.

28. See my "Dewey's Denotative-Empirical Method: A Thread through the Labyrinth," chapter 2 in this volume. In an interview, when pressed on the question whether naturalism could accept something beyond judgment, Buchler said, "I don't want to introduce a notion of naturalism which would accept mystery in some sense." *Journal of Speculative Philosophy* 3, no. 4 (1989): 262. For him this included Dewey's idea of "God" in *A Common Faith*. This marks a deep division between Buchler's and Dewey's naturalism. As Carlyle said to Emerson in disagreement, drawing a line with his finger on the table between them, "Then, sir, there is a line of separation between you and me as wide as that and as deep as the pit." See Gay Wilson Allen, *Waldo Emerson* (New York: Viking, 1981), 497.

29. Again, see Dewey's "Time and Individuality," LW, 14:98–114.

of judgment. We have already seen his use of "natural complex" as a way of preventing the positing of ultimate wholes or atomic elements. It is *ordinality*, the possibility of *further judgments* of "location," that makes complexity irreducible. So here again is the difference between an experiential-existential and an ordinal-categorial approach. Dewey's approach looks toward existence as a basis for insight; Buchler articulates a formal condition.

Let us consider relations. Again, Dewey thinks of relations primarily in terms of *temporality*, as existential or experiential events of "interaction" with rhythmic phases of "doing and undergoing" (LW, 1:207). Biologically, relations come with the structures, affordances, and habituations of the organism toward its environment. In human existence relations emerge through action mediated by instrumentalities beginning with the body, but culminating in arts, symbols, and language (LW, 1:105). Relations are first and foremost *temporal* functions within situations; they deal with the situation in terms of its history and possibilities. "Tools" (especially language) engage the world in terms of possibilities and so expand a situation beyond its present qualitative immediacy. To be shut in a room is to be confined; to see part of the wall as a door is to have the choice to leave. This is why inquiry is so important for Dewey—it enlarges the meaning of the world; it opens up possibilities. But relations can also be "funded" or qualitatively embody histories. Anybody can look at my mother's old grand piano and see a big black thing. But I see it full of my mother's love of music, her playing it daily, her teaching pupils. Whereas anybody would just see the object, I feel its resonant past life and its present overwhelming solitude and silence. Relations for Dewey are ways we engage the world in time—including the most formal abstractions of mathematics or logic.

Buchler's approach to relations is categorial and ordinal. "To be" is "to be related." "Nature" comes to mean "what is related" or "is capable of being related." "All natural complexes are relational, though not only relational. . . . Whatever is, is in some relation" (MNC, 24). As we have seen, this means to be located within one or more natural complexes and to locate other natural complexes. Since this is what it means to be "natural," the meaning of the supernatural signifies "that which is unrelated." If "natural" means "discriminated" or "discriminable," the "non-natural" or "supernatural," conversely, would mean that incapable of being discriminated, that is, located in some order or locating other orders. If there is a God, it would have to be a natural complex. And as we saw, there can be no ultimate simples for they cannot be related. They, too, cannot be objects of judgment. The unrelated (the unnatural) is beyond discourse; it "is not." Buchler analyzes relations in terms of the "integrity" and "scope" of a complex. "Integrity" refers to the finitude of the complex "having just the relations . . . that it has" in whatever order it is located (MNC, 21–22). "Scope" defines the inclusiveness of a complex, which can be comprehensive and generic, or pervasive and recurrent (MNC, 35–36, 103ff.). If two complexes are related, "each is at least a condition for the scope of the other" (MNC, 104ff.). General Lee at Gettysburg is part of the scope of President Lincoln; Gettysburg is relevant to Lincoln in his struggle to preserve the Union. Lincoln is relevant to the scope of Lee at Gettysburg in Lee's hope that a victory would finally result in granting the Confederacy its independence. Each of these men is part of the "integrity" of the other; that is, each is strongly relevant to the other in the way that Colonel Joshua Chamberlin's mustache is not. Buchler's concern is to have a nuanced way of articulating relevance. But temporality is not pervasively fundamental for Buchler, who says "Some prevalences have a temporal aspect, others do not" (MNC, 68). He does not find time "relevant" to a Euclidian demonstration even if it takes time to do it. Of course we *can* focus on the problem-solving process, but then we are dealing with a new complex. So here, too, we see a marked difference between an existential-experiential approach, which is radically temporal, and an ordinal one, which is not.

Finally, let us contrast two guiding principles, Dewey's principle of continuity and Buchler's principle of ontological parity. Dewey and Buchler are both antihierarchical as well as antireductionist thinkers. The principle of continuity challenges the dichotomies and "either-ors" the intellect likes to set up. It is not to be thought of as some static, actualized continuum in a spatialized way, but as temporal process. Once again, time is central for Dewey. Continuity is dynamic. Dewey addresses Nature from an emergent or evolutionary perspective, as an unfolding of processes that generate new forms of organization that are genuinely novel, new "plateaus of existence" (LW, 1:208). His "principle of continuity" asks us to understand what things are not only by what they do and can do but in terms of their development, their "natural histories," and

their possibilities.[30] This is "emergentism": While human existence
certainly emerges out of biochemical events, it is not reduced to them;
human existence realizes some potentialities of biochemistry just as life
reveals potentialities of matter. [31] The more complex realities give more
insight into the possibilities of Nature. But "more complex" does not
mean "more real" in the sense of denying some degree of existence to
the less complex. Nevertheless, it is more revelatory. Dewey is firm in
saying that whatever Nature "is," *it is what it does*. And if the event is
making poetry or agonizing over a moral dilemma, then Nature is, in
those ways, poetic and moral. For Dewey, the more something manifests
the creative potentiality of Nature, the more it reveals about Nature.
Creativity is at the heart of Dewey's concept of Nature. The principle of
continuity asks us on the one hand to discover natural histories but on
the other to see some events as more revelatory, more "epiphantic," of
Nature than others.[32]

   Buchler also rejects any idea of reductionism or ontological hierarchy,
but does so in a more radically neutral way that does not ask us *actively* to
look for continuities and natural histories. Nature is an equally open field
of any type of judgment or query. Buchler is critical of how metaphysics
has privileged some types of natural complexes over others as "really
real," culminating in the idea of "degrees of being" (MNC, 4). In response
to the confusing relationships among "being," "existence" and "reality,"
Buchler proposes what he calls "the principle of ontological parity."
Everything is a natural complex, but "no complex is more 'real,' more
'natural,' more 'genuine,' or more 'ultimate' than any other" (MNC, 31).
Every natural complex is *de facto* "real." The corollary is that no discrimi-
nanda can be consigned to "nonbeing." This does not mean various *kinds*
of degrees are not discriminable within a given order, just no degrees of
reality. "The principle of parity obliges us to receive and accept all discri-
minanda" (MNC, 33). Poetry is as real as physics; Titania and Bottom are

30. See *Logic: The Theory of Inquiry* (LW, 12:26–31) and my analysis in *John Dewey's Theory of
Art, Experience and Nature: The Horizons of Feeling* (Albany: State University of New York Press,
1987), 94ff.
   31. Dewey's best explanation of this principle is in *Logic: The Theory of Inquiry* (LW, 12:26ff.).
   32. "For it is reasonable to believe that the most adequate definition of the basic traits of natural
existence can be had only when its properties are most fully displayed—a condition which is met in
the degree of the scope and intimacy of interactions realized" (LW, 1:201). Chapter 7 as a whole
should be consulted.

as real as Shakespeare; the Ptolemaic system is as real as the Copernican. Thus the principle of ontological parity avoids hierarchical as well as reductionistic ontologies. But what does it accomplish?

Here, too, a paradox arises. The principle of ontological parity is the feature of Buchler's metaphysics that is perhaps most commonly accepted by his advocates.[33] It has a nice democratic ring to it—this is its real punch—and it preserves metaphysics as something other than the search for the "highest being" that provokes so many critics. The principle is defended by a critique of "the principle of ontological priority" (MNC, 33).[34] Buchler is careful to say nothing is "more or less real" than anything else. This is converted by most of his advocates into saying everything is "*equally* real." [35] If there are no *degrees* of reality nothing can be "*equally*" real to anything else and the meanings of "no more" and "no less" are left vague at best. I think this problem also arises from Buchler's univocal sense of what is real, namely, "to be a natural complex." Insofar as this means "to be a (possible) subject of judgment," I worry that "reality" simply becomes empty of ontological articulation. Kathleen Wallace, one of the foremost Buchler scholars, tells us that "in a metaphysics of natural complexes such as Buchler's, there is no *ontological* distinction between the real and the unreal."[36] Elsewhere, Buchler actually rejects the significance of the term "reality" altogether, leaving the whole matter of anything's *ontological* status in limbo.[37] This was what Kant aimed to accomplish, handing the natural realm over to an ontologically neutral, purely phenomenal, realm where "existence" was denied to be a concept and so not a predicate. Just as "real" ends up having no other special

33. For example, simply see the index in the anthology, *Nature's Perspectives: Prospects for Ordinal Metaphysics*, ed. Kathleen Wallace et al. (Albany: State University of New York Press, 1991), under "Ontological Parity." See also Beth Singer's *Ordinal Naturalism* (Lewisburg, PA: Bucknell University Press, 1983), 168–71, and Stephen David Ross's *Transition to an Ordinal Metaphysics* (Albany: State University of New York Press, 1980), 8, 108ff, who sums up the idea: "the principle of ontological parity takes metaphysics off its pedestal" (110).

34. This is extensively discussed in *The Main of Light*, ch. 4, as a defense of artistic reality.

35. Buchler is careful to frame the principle in negative terms: Nothing is more real than anything else. But his advocates readily put it in the positive form that "everything is equally real." For example, Sidney Gelber and Kathleen Wallace: "Ontological parity...is a commitment to the equal reality of all beings" (*Nature's Perspectives*, 52; see the index for "ontological parity" for many other examples.). Again: "Affirming the equal reality of whatever is[,] Buchler's ontology is guided by a principle of ontological parity." Kathleen Wallace, "Justus Buchler," in Marsoobian and Ryder, op. cit., 274.

36. Kathleen Wallace, "Justus Buchler," in Marsoobian and Ryder, 272.

37. "The notion of 'reality' has never been helpful to theoretical understanding and has often impaired it" ("On the Concept of the World," MNC, Appendix 3, 259).

significance, neither does "Nature," since it simply means "reality." The principle of ontological parity allows Nature to vanish like the Cheshire cat. Buchler's interest in avoiding any sort of "principle of ontological priority" like the "Great Chain of Being" has gone to an opposite and, I believe, unnecessary extreme.

We have seen how the "univocity of natural complexes" generated paradoxes. Here the principle of ontological parity empties the idea of natural ontology of meaning. In discussing this principle, Buchler approvingly quotes John Herman Randall Jr., who said, "The significant question is not whether anything is 'real' or not, but how and in what sense it is real, and how it is related to and functions among other reals."[38] Randall, following Aristotle, is concerned with "how many ways being is said," not with making being said to be in *one* sense or be said "equally" of everything. In keeping with this sensible goal, it is better to attend to the different ways we articulate polymodal dimensions of Nature. Call this "the principle of ontological plurivocity." Peirce's modal distinctions among his categories constitute an example of ontological plurivocity. The nuanced modalities articulated in human languages and symbol systems would provide other indications of how "the being of Nature" is variously understood.[39] As Heidegger said, it was a fateful day when Parmenides seized upon "*esti*," "It Is," the third person present active indicative, as the *only* way Being can truly be spoken. Buchler's analysis of the interrelationship of actuality and possibility is a better indication for the prospects of a polymodal natural ontology than his "principle of ontological parity." Again, this would involve locating Buchler's ordinal ontology within Dewey's experiential-existential one, adding to it Buchler's sensitive analysis of actuality and possibility.

Buchler devotes the last chapter of *Metaphysics of Natural Complexes* to this topic. According to the principle of ontological parity, possibility is "as real" as actuality. "The encounter of men with possibilities is at least as important and extensive as their encounter with actualities"

38. MNC, 30, quote from *Nature and Historical Judgment* (New York: Columbia University Press, 1961), 131.

39. Anthropology and linguistics may be of more help here than modal logic. See the famous study of the Hopi concept of time by Benjamin Lee Whorf, "An American Indian Model of the Universe," reprinted in *Teachings from the American Earth*, ed. Dennis Tedlock and Barbara Tedlock (New York: Liveright, 1975), 121–29.

(MNC, 149). In keeping with the requirement of ordinality, there are no "pure" or completely unrelated possibilities. "Possibilities . . . are always possibilities *of* and *for*; a natural complex has certain possibilities—not any whatever" (MNC, 130). There is no "realm of the possible"; possibilities do not "always exist." They may arise and prevail or cease to obtain. But possibilities cannot prevail unrelated to actualities; actualities cannot prevail unrelated to possibilities. "Possibility is the reach of actuality, actuality the ballast of possibility" (148). Possibilities are extensions of the "contour" of a natural complex—a projection of a set of relevant traits. For such projection, Buchler coins the term "prefinition." "Prefinition embraces both extension or continuation and rooted conditions of that which is to constitute the extension" (MNC, 165). Prefinition does not so much predict the future of a complex, as it finds "*relative* limits, the limits immanent in its prevalence" (MNC, 165–66). Buchler also provides a nuanced discussion of the relation of potentiality and power as types of possibility. Potentiality reflects noted similarity between complexes; e.g., the "sort" of thing that "kind" of creature might do. Power, on the other hand, refers to a potentiality that has been realized in a complex and may be again. Buchler is dismissive of "logical possibilities" taken as meaning mere "absence of contradiction." What happens is that we tacitly transpose traits from one order into another. Here on earth it *is* contradictory to say a player can hit a baseball into orbit; it might be possible on some asteroid. Logical possibility is contextual. But Buchler's analysis stops short of discussing in what sense *natura naturans* is a "principle" of possibility.

Prospects for an Eco-ontology

William James said, "Metaphysics is nothing but an unusually obstinate effort to think clearly."[40] I have argued that it is important to maintain a philosophical concern with the subject of "Nature" that does not succumb to the narrowness of what has passed as "naturalism." The question of the being of Nature is one way to maintain an open, nuanced approach insofar as listening to the ontological voice helps keep the

---

40. *Principles of Psychology*, vol. 1, 145.

scientistic version of naturalism at bay. Both John Dewey and Justus Buchler have presented important ontologies of Nature, similar in aim, but quite different in method and focus. The Buchlerian approach deserves to be better known and carefully reflected upon though it requires, I believe, the existential-experiential context of Dewey's metaphysics. Be that as it may, naturalists who originate thought about Nature in terms of genuine care about it can explore the prospects for an eco-ontology drawing upon these ideas.

Buchler's revival of the old *natura naturans–natura naturata* distinction may offer a better route than the "ordinal" theory of natural complexes. We do not need to adopt Buchler's (or Spinoza's) *specific* understandings of this distinction. Let us say that *natura naturans* designates Nature approached as the polymodal *being* of Nature and that *natura naturata* designates the specific "ways" or determinate *existential* orders of Nature. While this distinction may be described as an "ontological difference," it should not be conceived as some radical dichotomy, a dualism between beings and being. Rather it should be thought of as a continuum. The empirical concerns of the naturalist exist at the end that is *natura naturata*, but the task of exploring "what there is" extends to the more general orders of nature and the evolution of the universe itself, where it begins to engage ontological questions. At the other end we find the concerns of *natura naturans*, ranging from the question of the being of entities to that of generic traits, modal dimensions, being itself, and the noncognitive encounter of mystery.[41] Together, as the dynamic intertwining of the unmanifest and manifest, they constitute *natura*, φύσις, Nature. Thus, the use of these terms not only reflects thought originating from the *care* for Nature that motivates *naturalist* philosophical thinking, but it serves to distinguish objects of different ontological concerns and questions. The concern with *natura naturata* can be described as *existential*; i.e., a concern with the being of what exists, "what there is," the determinate or manifest. The concern with *natura naturans* can be designated

---

41. Here I wish simply to acknowledge that orientation to Nature that involves other forms of experience than that of cognitive analysis. Heidegger's later philosophy is testimony to the philosophical significance of this, but I also intend to include transcognitive experiences of the holy, east and west.

ontological; i.e., a concern for the being of Nature as such.[42] The former asks "What are the orders of Nature? How are they related? How did they evolve?" The latter asks, "What is the polymodal being of Nature, manifest and unmanifest?"[43] For example, Dewey's concerns to articulate the "generic traits" of Nature, the "principle of continuity," or his view of "time as individuality" are questions addressing *natura naturans*, whereas his concerns to discuss the various emergent existential plateaus exhibited in cosmic evolution and specific cosmic histories (including human ones) would address *natura naturata*. (Situations would be the nexus or interface of *natura naturata* and *natura naturans*.) The distinction between these two, as noted, is not rigid. But it serves to keep us from solely thinking about "facts" and "things" in the order of existence or about abstractions like "being" in ontology proper.

While this makes the question of the being of Nature more fundamental, in a sense, than the existential question, this is not to be understood as another attempt to privilege "Being" over Nature. Quite the contrary. Not only is being understood as the being *of* Nature, but Nature is understood as more fundamentally inclusive than being. Buchler briefly refers to thinkers besides Spinoza who make Nature the "inclusive category," with Eriugena providing a fascinating medieval example.[44] This thesis may seem odd, given the long tradition in Western philosophy of regarding Nature as a temporal order derivative from or dependent upon eternal being, whether as an emanation (in Neoplatonism), as creation

42. This is not exactly the same as Heidegger's "ontological-ontical" distinction, where the ontical deals with beings as beings in terms of ready-to-hand and present-to-hand and the ontological deals with the question of the "Being of beings." I intend the "existential" to refer not just to "beings" but to the evolutionary order of Nature as cosmos. Nor do I see an "abyss" *between* the existential and the ontological modes of reflection. The existential and ontological domains are permeable. They lead into and out of each other. But I do include the sorts of inquiries Heidegger undertakes as "ontological."

43. By "unmanifest," I mean to indicate ontologies that do not simply articulate generic categories but which engage "the mystery of being," as in Marcel and Heidegger—not to mention Emerson and Thoreau.

44. See "Probing the Idea of Nature" in MNC, 262–63, 267–68. Buchler only mentions Eriugena and Aquinas besides Spinoza, but one could easily add the Presocratics, the Stoics and Epicureans, Bruno, Schelling and others. At the beginning of Eriugena's *Periphyseon* (more commonly known as *The Division of Nature*), the Teacher says, "Often I investigate as carefully as I can and reflect that of all things which can either be perceived by the mind or surpass its concentrated efforts the first and highest division is into what has and what does not have being. At such times the general designation of them all occurs to me, *physis* in Greek and *natura* in Latin. . . .'[N]ature' is a general name for all things, whether or not they have being," *Periphyseon: On the Division of Nature*, vol. 1, trans. Myra L. Uhlfelder (Indianapolis, IN: Bobbs-Merrill, 1976), 1:1.

(in medieval thought), or as a function of "substance" (in modern philosophy). But this way allows ontology to be understood as inquiry into the *being of Nature*, into *natura naturans*, not simply the *being of being*. To make ontology at home *within* Nature helps counter the Platonic tendency in Western thought to set being *above* Nature as well as the Aristotelian tendency to treat being as an *abstraction*, terminating in the medieval view of it as the most general and emptiest concept. Both of these have contributed to the metaphysics of identity that understands being in terms of self-same actuality. One result has been a long, largely unsuccessful history in Western philosophy of struggling to make time or process intelligible.[45]

This alternative approach will further allow us to speak of an ontology of Nature as an "ecology of being" or "eco-ontology." By "eco-ontology," I mean understanding Nature in terms of ways of "inter-being."[46] That is, "to be" is to be related, both actually and possibly. *Natura naturans*, then, is more precisely the object of a concern for the *inter-being of Nature*. The traditional concept of being as "substance" has made us see the world in terms of ultimate "things" which then "possess" attributes. More than a "philosophical theory," this is an entrenched *habit of thought* in western culture. Since Parmenides, the metaphysics of identity has emphasized being over Nature, identity over process, actuality over possibility, substance-attribute over relations. Even when that tradition is overtly critiqued, it reasserts itself. Aristotle, prince of naturalists, critiqued Plato's timeless Forms, but still thought of primary substances as logical individuals, identities, subjects of predicates, and thought of secondary substances, species, as eternal classificatory containers of individuals. His world also ultimately was static with hierarchical groups, an outlook not very conducive for ecological thought. Russell may have rejected a metaphysics of essence, but his logical atoms were still committed to

45. See Bergson's powerful analysis of the problems of conceptualizing or "spatializing" time, the "cinematographic view of existence," in *Creative Evolution*, ch. 4. Ivor Leclerc has offered a detailed historical analysis of the permutations of the problem in the development of modern philosophy of nature in *The Nature of Physical Existence* (London: George Allen and Unwin, 1972). Leclerc sees the modern problem as due ultimately to a loss of the Aristotelian ideas of potentiality and form.

46. This is Thich Nhat Hanh's rendition of the Buddhist term *śūnyatā*, often translated as "emptiness." But what it means is "not absolutely fullness;" i.e., not existing as an absolute separate self-sufficient identity but as arising from relations and capable of coming into relations. *Śunyatā* itself was a Mahayana way of expressing the Buddha's view of existence as "dependent origination," or *pratītyasamutpāda*. See his *The Heart of Understanding* (Berkeley, CA: Parallax Press, 1988), a translation of and commentary on the *Heart Sutra*.

a concept of substantial identities. If we are to develop new, ecologically wise habits of philosophical thought, we must be concerned with developing an eco-ontology, for ontology and metaphysics deal with exposing, exploring and reconstructing the most basic habits of thinking.[47] As this ontology tries to rethink being as inter-being, so it tries to make continuity (especially as temporal process or natural history) more fundamental than identity.[48] The idea of "a world of facts" or universe of "all that is (or is not) the case" is seen as the result of a conceptual and logical abstraction, not as a deep insight into inter-being as process, as "arising and cessation."[49] In trying to articulate the being of Nature, of *natura naturans*, we look for ways to develop relational, polymodal, dynamic habits of thinking—but also to maintain moods of wonder and care.

Though eco-ontology is concerned with thinking out "categories," "generic traits," or "ultimate relations," it does not begin with axioms, principles, or predetermined "isms." It does not begin with "epistemology." It orients itself initially in the key of wonder, "musement," with a concern for discerning continuities. It begins with care as well as with curiosity about Nature. Though "metaphysical," it does not "go beyond" Nature, but *responds* to it and invokes it. We may do so in several distinctive voices, for example, the scientific voice, the humanistic voice, the ontological voice (used here), and the transcendental voice.[50] To invoke Nature with

47. I would not limit describing metaphysics to an attempt to recognize and challenge the deep habits of our thinking. But this is a function of metaphysics that is often ignored. It is the force of inherited habits of thought that renders the so-called empirical (including the phenomenological) approaches limited. Metaphysics engages imagination and tries to see things differently. This is one more reason we cannot dispense with "metaphysics" as a significant part of philosophy, especially in the American tradition, as Charlene Seigfried (to cite one example of many) has urged. See her "Pragmatist Metaphysics? Why Terminology Matters," *Transactions of the Charles S. Peirce Society* 37, no. 1 (Winter 2001): 13–22, and William T. Myers's response, "Pragmatist Metaphysics: A Defense," *Transactions of the Charles S. Peirce Society* 40, no. 1 (Winter 2004): 39–52.

48. See my "Between Being and Emptiness," chapter 3 in this volume, for a comparison of the Western metaphysics of identity with the Buddhist metaphysics of emptiness.

49. In contrast to Greek νοῦς, "insight into true identity," one might think of the Buddhist term *prajñā*, which means "insight" into "emptiness" as "dependent origination," or seeing things in terms of the truth of their becoming and relatedness over against the tendency of the mind to abstract, isolate, and substantialize aspects of process, seeing them (ignorantly) as "substances" or "individuals." Thus one Zen kōan asks, "What was your face before you were born?"

50. The scientific voice is concerned with understanding Nature as "the universe"; i.e., as inquiry into what there is. The humanistic voice beholds Nature as the domain of human existence; i.e., as "world," the home of human history. The ontological voice is concerned with the being of Nature, with *natura naturans* as used here. The transcendental voice is concerned with Nature in terms of self-realization. Examples of thinkers responding to these four voices would be, respectively: Democritus, John Dewey, Spinoza, and Emerson.

one voice does not mean that the others may not also be heard. A voice *may* be exclusive and refuse to hear some or all the others. When the scientific voice becomes exclusive, ignoring or rejecting the others, scientism is often the result. But it need not be exclusory. Many who address Nature in the scientific voice also hear some or all of the others. Ecological thought aims at inclusive invocation. Eco-ontology asks that we integrate these voices as far as possible, that is, that we aspire toward "polyphonic thought." The aim of eco-ontology is wisdom—wise inhabitation of Nature. Thus its inclusiveness seeks to explore dialogue between these voices rather than to be content to leave each and all in solipsistic babble. And to this end an ecological naturalist ontology, one that tries to think the being of Nature, is directed.[51]

Appendix: On the Terms Natura Naturans *and* Natura Naturata

The history of the terms *natura naturans* and *natura naturata* (and the ideas behind them) is quite complicated. They are not even classical Latin. There was no verb *naturare*; the verb "to be born," *nascor* (participle *nascens*), is a deponent verb, passive in form but active in meaning. Thus there could not be two participles, one active, one passive. This complication may have led to the medieval coining of *natura naturans* and *natura naturata* (as if there were a verb *naturare*) as ways of distinguishing "creating" and "created" being. But it would be hard to find a set of terms so drastically, even defiantly changed from one thinker to the next. This has to do, I believe, with the underlying conflict between Neoplatonic and Aristotelian ideas about ultimate causation, the former emphasizing origination as "power" (*dunamis*, δύναμις) the other as actuality (*energeia*, ἐνέργεια).

Anticipations of the distinction can be found in Plato's proposal in the *Sophist* (247 d) to define being as "power" either as "doing" or "undergoing" and in his postulates of the Divine Craftsman and the Receptacle in the *Timaeus*. Likewise, one may point to Aristotle's form-matter distinction and his comparison of nature to a doctor doctoring himself (*Physics* II.8). Plato's "doing-undergoing" or active-passive distinction

51. I would like to acknowledge the helpful input and criticism of Kelly Booth, Jim Garrison, Felicia Kruse, and William T. Myers.

is a pervasive feature of the Stoics' materialistic concept of the principles of nature as active divine reason (Logos) and passive matter. Furthermore, unlike Aristotle, the Stoics consider nature to be a substance, indeed, the only one, so that "doing and undergoing" (τὸ ποιοῦν καὶ τὸ πάσχον) are pervasive "generic traits of nature" in Dewey's terms.

Plotinus (developing insights from Plato's *Sophist*, 247e and *Republic* 509c) places power (δύναμις) above actual being; the One is the generative power whereby actual Being can be (*Ennead* VI.9). Plotinus makes each hypostasis a passive recipient of its higher cause while an active principle for the lower (though the hypostasis of being itself is grounded on the power [δύναμις] of the One, not itself an actuality). Though nature is not ultimate for him, it is whole. The Neoplatonist Eriugena in his *Peryphuseon* (or *Division of Nature*) distinguishes two sets of contraries: uncreated/created and creating/uncreating. From these follow the four divisions of Nature (which include God and creation): uncreated-creating (God), created-creating (Forms), created-uncreating (creatures) and uncreated-uncreating (the Godhead). Weijers sees Eriugena's divisions between nature-creating and nature-created as the source of the *idea* of *natura naturans* and *natura naturata*.

The terms as such first appear in thirteenth-century Latin translations of Averroes' commentaries on *De Caelo*, *natura naturata* referring to all beings composed of potency and act, *natura naturans* referring to God, the ultimate pure act whereby forms are "educed" from Prime Matter. (See Olga Weijers's "Contribution à l'histoire des termes '*natura naturans*' et '*natura naturata*' jusqu'à Spinoza," *Vivarium* XVI, I [1978], 71–80, and Frederick Copleston, *A History of Philosophy*, vol. 2 [Doubleday, 1950], 197–98). They are appropriated by Thomas Aquinas (S. Th. I–II., qu. 85. a. 6) not only to distinguish God as creator (i.e., as pure act) from created being, but God as the act (*actus*) of being whereby other beings can be at all, or the "universal nature" that "intends the good and preservation of the universe" from the "activity" or nature of specific beings that aims at their own proper good.

Spinoza drastically modifies these terms in lines with his ateleological monism that does not separate a divine creator and a created natural order: *Natura naturans* is "that which is in itself and is conceived through itself," that is, infinite substance, "*Deus sive natura*," and *natura naturata* refers to the various modes, primary and secondary, conceived ultimately through *natura naturans* (*Ethics*. I. XXIX. Schol; see also the essay "God,

Man and His Well-being," chs. viii and ix; for the origin of Spinoza's use of the terms, see: Weijers, *op.cit.*, H. Siebeck, "Ueber die Entstehung der Termini *natura naturans* und *natura naturata*," *Archiv für Geschichte der Philosophie* 3 [1890], 370–78, and Paul Oskar Kristeller, "Stoic and Neoplatonic Sources of Spinoza's *Ethics*," *History of European Ideas*, 5, no. 1 [1984]: 1–15.) But for Spinoza and the scholastics, *natura naturans* refers to that which is fully *actual*, the first or ultimate cause.

The recent connotation tends to focus on the *dynamic* meaning of the participles, natur*ing* and natur*ed*. This comes out in the Romantic period (in the works of Schelling, Coleridge, and Emerson). Though borrowed from Spinoza, the term now reflects a Neoplatonic heritage with a Romantic twist. Eriugena, often regarded as a dangerous pantheist (which he was not) for stressing the interrelation of God and creation, had a subversive appeal to thinkers and mystics worried about those who made God utterly transcendent of creation, a concern that grew in the late medieval and early Renaissance period. The idea of God in immanent relation to the world is significantly developed in the fifteenth century by Nicholas Cusanus, who drew upon Greek Neoplatonic sources as well as upon Eriugena. Cusanus does not use the terms, but significantly alters scholastic prioritization of the actual. For Cusanus, God as *coincidentia oppositorum* is ultimate possibility-of-actuality and actuality-of-possibility or the "possible-actual" (for which he coins the term "*possest*," from *posse*, to be able, and *esse*, to be), the simple infinite that contracts into the concrete infinite of the universe (see his *Trialogus de possest*, trans. in Jasper Hopkins' *A Concise Introduction to the Philosophy of Nicholas of Cusa*, University of Minnesota Press, 1978). Cusanus' thought is directly appropriated by Bruno, a real pantheist, in his *De la causa*, where he says God "contracts" into creative primal matter that in turn contracts into the infinite universe. God is the primal power of physical Nature. Bruno is a very likely influence on Spinoza (though Spinoza rejects any idea of power as potential).

Both Bruno and Spinoza are influences on Schelling, who explicitly appropriates the terms, reconfiguring them in line with his absolute idealism. *Natura naturata* means "the totality of objects" regarded as "product"; i.e., "*Nature as object*" (the deterministic universe of science); *natura naturans* is the totality, "Nature," regarded as "productive"; i.e., "*Nature as subject*" (the free ego). (See *First Outline of a System of the Philosophy of Nature, Introduction*, trans. Keith Peterson [Albany: State

University of New York Press, 2004]: 202). Schelling was a major influence on Coleridge, especially in the *Biographia Literaria*, and both Schelling and Coleridge influenced Emerson, who uses the terms in "Nature" (*Essays: Second Series*). Buchler appropriates the terms with echoes of the Romantic usage, but now for the sake of naturalism, not idealism, *natura naturans* meaning Nature as "providingness" or "engendering condition" of orders of natural complexes, *natura naturata* meaning Nature as "the provided, the ordinal manifestation, the World's complexes" (MNC, 100, 276; Buchler's late essay, "Probing the Idea of Nature" is a significant clarification of this idea). As noted, though Dewey does not avail himself of the terms *natura naturans* and *natura naturata*, "doing and undergoing" are generic traits of nature for him. Like Buchler, and unlike the Stoics or Spinoza, nature is not a substance for him, but "an affair of affairs" or *res rerum*.

PART TWO

EROS AND IMAGINATION

FIVE

THE HUMAN EROS

I wish here to explore the relation between our desire to exist meaningfully through action and the question that this poses for philosophy. My thesis is simple: We are erotic beings. Our Eros, however, is neither divine nor animal. It is distinctively human: We are beings who seek meaning imaginatively through each other, and the locus of this transformative encounter is the community. This model of human nature contrasts with the dominant view in analytic philosophy of humans as "minds" consisting of "states," as purely "epistemic subjects" whose primary function is thought to lie in generating propositional claims about the world. It also stands in contrast with more recent postmodern positions that see human existence simply as a function of relations of power.[1]

---

1. The phenomenological ontologies of human nature in the work of Martin Heidegger in *Being and Time* and Maurice Merleau-Ponty in *The Phenomenology of Perception*, however, do have important bearing on these aspects of human nature stressed in pragmatism.

Five Basic Claims

The Delphic injunction, "Know Thyself," asks us to confront some basic, simple realities that challenge such views. I believe five important claims about us can be made: (1) we exist temporally, and the shape of our temporality is dramatically structured through the nature of action; (2) we exist in a human world of culture and not merely in a physical environment; (3) our understanding of ourselves and the world emerges as a dynamic process of learning and growth, and not as a static range of justified true beliefs; (4) our experience is fundamentally aesthetic rather than cognitive; and (5) at the root of our existence is a drive to live with a funded sense of meaning and value, a "Human Eros," as I call it. If these claims are acknowledged, then serious consequences must follow for the practice of philosophy and its self-understanding. Let us begin with the first claim.

TEMPORALITY

We do not exist merely as temporal objects, persisting from one momentary "now" to the next, or even as biological beings continuously proceeding from birth through maturity to death. We exist in the *experience* of time configured by action into a dramatic process whose coherence is expressed through narrative understanding. Our own self-awareness and our consciousness of the world emerge from the infant's prereflective history of desire, experience, and action in which this temporality of our being comes to be presupposed for anything to make sense. Our complex prereflective understanding of time is illustrated, for example, in the modalities reflected in verbs: the "doing and undergoing" of active and passive voices; the tenses (e.g., the perfect of completed actions, the imperfect of actions done but not completed, the future which looms ahead as well as the present immediately at hand); and the moods (subjunctive, conditional, imperative, and indicative). Language exhibits how ontologically intricate our human understanding of time is and how deeply rooted it is in our bodily comportment to the world around us through action. Our lived temporality originates in the prereflective action of the infant struggling to coordinate the body. From the simplest sensorimotor manipulations to highly coordinated projects to ongoing traditions of whole communities, the structure of action builds up a web of interconnected, temporal meaning, a "world." Thus, like a collective historical memory, our temporality pervades the range of experience from infancy to complex cultural webs of interpretive structures that coordinate shared action and constitute the range of ideal objects embraced by the community.

Moreover, action has a *teleological* and *narrative* structure: By aiming at an end to be realized through definite means, action takes on the configuration of having a beginning, middle, and end in which the aim is realized or fails to be. Time begins for us with primitive narratives. The baby reaches for a toy and the toy is either grasped or it is not, whereupon satisfaction or frustration ensues. The action may be minimal but it has dramatic structure. The world is thus *dramatically* encountered as a projected field of possible and actual actions developing in time, and this dramatic embodiment underlies and permeates our tacit understanding as well as conscious, reflective thought.[2] Any theory of human existence, meaning, or knowledge that disregards these features, one that focuses instead on an ideal of formal atemporal correspondence or upon one which epitomizes us in terms of static "states," will only have mystified our most fundamental manner of understanding ourselves and the world.[3]

CULTURE AS ENVIRONMENT

Human beings are also born into *worlds*, not just physical environments. At birth we are as much new members of a community, with its languages, beliefs, traditions, and values, as we are biological beings. Left abandoned or uncared for at birth, we die: That is a *biological fact* about us as a species. Culture is presupposed in our biological existence. The fragile organism of the newborn is vitally bound to its world by the love

2. For discussion of the employment of the bodily "schemata" of action that pervade our cognitive understanding, see Mark Johnson, *The Body in the Mind* (Chicago: University of Chicago Press, 1987) and George Lakoff, *Women, Fire, and Dangerous Things* (Chicago: University of Chicago Press, 1987). The idea of a vital, dramatic embodied understanding as fundamental in human nature was set forth long before, however, by Hartley Burr Alexander. See *The Problem of Metaphysics and Metaphysical Understanding* (1902) and *God and Man's Destiny* (1936).

3. Wittgenstein's *Tractatus* begins with the proposition that "the world is all that is the case." Immediately we are constricted to a factical world of the present tense, a determinate field of "states of affairs" whose significance lies in determination of the truth of propositions. The whole field of human life must be "passed over in silence."

and care it needs to receive. Thus a human birth is more than a biological act; it is a cultural event fraught with all the meaning, mystery, and celebration of a new arrival. A social context of care and cooperation is presupposed along with the physical environment in the very needs of the baby's flesh. And the infant begins to aquire culture through this context of care and love; language first comes to us in the voice of parental love. The infant also transforms a couple into a family and initiates a long process of development on their part. Not only do birth and upbringing result in a new member participating in the world of the culture, but the lives of the caregivers are changed. They are called upon to grow and know themselves in demanding ways. Care is a discipline. As the child develops, new needs develop into an ever-expanding world of affection, attachment, and meaning. A complex emotional world colors the aesthetics of all human relationships; it is directly tied to our actions that sustain or damage the project of care. How we manage to secure and cultivate enriching relationships with others is a primary quest of human life. How we have been raised and treated colors our consciousness as a whole. Again, the standpoint of "epistemology" ignores all this in focusing upon the *individual* as a "knower." This is one of the ghosts of modernity that still haunts us.

LEARNING IS MORE BASIC THAN KNOWING

Third, *learning* and *teaching* are also required for our entrance into the symbols and values of the culture so as to become communicants in its reality. By nature, then, we are not only social beings, lovers, helpers, and protectors, but also teachers and learners. We exist as cultural beings and culture must be passed on. This is also a *biological fact* about us. In addition to the dramatically temporal, care-oriented social structure of our experience, we actually exist by living together in a community bound by meaning-giving traditions, which must be *taught* to be acquired, and without which love, cooperation, communication, and culture would be impossible. From birth we are learners, and the members of our world are teachers. The way whereby we come to inhabit this cultural world is one of constant learning, and in time we become teachers, too. Growth for us is a process of educational transformation. Even if a culture believes that its dogmas possess changeless, absolute authority, each of us spends our first formative years endeavoring to *learn the world*.

Our experience is cast and recast constantly in a developmental process of growth that shapes our adult self-consciousness. This growth process, too, has a narrative structure, and our self-understanding is deeply rooted in this experience. Throughout this process our lives are punctuated by conflicts or problems demanding resolution. These may be temporary, minor shifts in our attitudes or major crises that strike to the core of our innermost being, determining our subsequent attitude toward the world and each other. The "self" is not a "mind," a timeless, ahistorical ground for propositions, a spectator of the world or itself. The process of life belies such a characterization. We understand ourselves as having a history whereby we gradually develop the broad experience and trained habits to function effectively in our physical and cultural worlds. We have struggled to achieve a fluency and continuity in our experience. The "self" is a dramatic process of development.[4]

EXPERIENCE IS MORE AESTHETIC THAN COGNITIVE

Fourth, our encounter with the world is primarily *aesthetic*.[5] Our experience is pervaded with a *sensed* texture of order, possibility, meaning, and anticipation. The world offers itself to us through our capacity to be lured into its aesthetic orders, which in turn become lived meanings. Our immediate experience of even the simplest, most mundane objects resonates with memory and expectation which are directly embodied in the world. If we encounter the day with boredom, arriving at the office and seeing "the same old desk" oppressively heaped with papers, with "Work!," with the cold cup of yesterday's brackish coffee and the dying plant in the windowsill, this suffusion of experience in its complexity and totality must be called aesthetic as much as those moments in which the thrill and beauty of life meets us in a cascade of vibrancy and joy. The pervasive, qualitative horizon of the aesthetic dimension of experience is

---

4. See William James's "The Sentiment of Rationality," in *The Will to Believe, The Works of William James* (Cambridge, MA: Harvard University Press, 1979), 57–89. Also see the extension of this theme in Dewey's "The Reflex Arc Concept in Psychology" (EW, 5:96–110), *Interest and Effort in Education* (MW, 7:151–97); and *Human Nature and Conduct* (MW, 14).

5. I use the word "aesthetic" in a far broader sense than "appealing to a sense of beauty," going back to its rooks in Greek *aisthēsis*, "sense experience." The aesthetic dimension is the qualitative, felt tonality of the world encountered in our living. Heidegger's analysis of "moods" as "attunement" is close to this sense.

always present with us. We seek the possibility of fulfillment; action is a pursuit in response to the lure of the world. The fine arts, Dewey argues, merely raise this dimension of experience to full consciousness. Through the medium of the living human body, we engage in the active and responsive experience of meaning. Human experience engages world and self primarily in the complexity of a pervasive aesthetic awareness: At each moment we are attuned to the world.[6]

THE HUMAN EROS

Finally, I wish to make perhaps the most radical of all my claims: At the root of our lives we manifest a deep-seated drive *to exist with a sense of meaning and value.* Unfortunately, the terms "meaning" and "value" cannot be given precise definition here, the kind cherished by analytic epistemology, for they are understood to denote the richest and profoundest ways in which we exist. Quite simply, we seek fulfillment on a number of levels and flourish when we find it and wither when we do not. A human life that has been denied or stripped of love, friendship, happiness, creative work, curiosity, awareness of mystery and beauty, and, above all, hope, has been destroyed. This drive for meaning and value will allow us to endure suffering and even death for the sake of love for another person or for an ideal. Most literature and many religions take this as their theme, and rightly so. Our lives are projects guided by this most profound human need that truly holds the bonds of community together and constitutes the energy for creative activity of civilization. Our cultural worlds are shared creations whereby human beings seek to fulfill this common drive. Culture is not then simply the web of practices that the anthropologist may categorize. The web itself is a delicate structure opening up a world that enables the human project to continue its quest for meaning. Cultures are "spiritual ecologies." When our meaning-constituting practices and ends are shattered, a crisis ensues, for individuals singly, for groups, or for entire cultures. The loss of all meaning for the individual may generate a hopeless depression ending in suicide or self-destructive behavior; it may direct itself outwardly in acts of

---

6. For a more extensive discussion of the "qualitative horizon" found in Dewey's *Art as Experience* (LW, 10), see my *John Dewey's Theory of Art, Experience, and Nature: The Horizons of Feeling* (Albany: State University of New York Press, 1987).

destructive anger or in the obsessive pursuit of an ideal. A disintegrating culture, as many Native American reservations show, is riddled with anxiety, despair, and confusion. Like individuals, such cultures also may embark upon frantic quests to reassert the values of the past, adopting fanatic ideologies, or may continue to fragment, succumbing to alien values without retaining any coherence of their own. The spread of the Industrial Revolution throughout the world, an event of unprecedented extent and power in its ability to dislocate the values, beliefs, and institutions of cultures, has led to a crisis in meaning and self-understanding for human beings as such.

Culture, then, is the expression of a drive for enountering the world and oneself with a sense of fulfilling meaning and value realized through action. Such a radical impulse I call the "Human Eros." When this drive is frustrated or negated, resulting in the sense of the loss of any meaning or value to our existence, it readily becomes transformed into a highly destructive power which may be directed outwardly or inwardly. One of the primary aims of civilization is to secure conditions whereby this Eros can develop, and it is the function of reflective intelligence in particular to address the crises which threaten it in order to avert its transformation into a drive for annihilation.[7]

Consequences for Philosophy

I begin by noting these five conditions—our dramatic temporality, our social existence, our developmental self, our aesthetic experience, and the Human Eros—because I think that if we hold on to them, serious consequences must follow for philosophy. Much, if not all, of contemporary philosophy is remarkable for the willingness with which it has allowed itself to forget these great, simple facts of who and what we are. Our human temporality is hardly acknowledged in Anglo-American philosophy, while the development of our human consciousness in a process of social care and narrative understanding is ignored in the quest to

7. This alludes to but differs from Sigmund Freud's reductionistic materialism. Though the pragmatic theory of the unconscious is not much developed, it recognizes the capacity of unconscious experience to be "civilized" through intelligent habits. Dewey illustrates this in the operation of such prereflective intelligence pervading and structuring the meaning of experience in works of art (cf. LW, 1:228).

analogize the brain to a computer. Though the theme of temporality once dominated continental philosophy, most postmodern thought has dissolved historical or narrative time into the fictions of social empowerment, which, when deconstructed, expose only the ruptures and reconfigurations of the so-called arbitrary patterns of language and desire. Although Freudian psychoanalysis does concern itself with the complexities of the growth and emergence of the human personality, it adopts a model as reductionistic as that promoted by behaviorism or artificial intelligence theory. Finally, most theories of meaning simply ignore the rich complexity of human life. For example, one must turn, with a few exceptions, not to philosophers but to literary writers, psychologists, and theologians to explore the meaning of love. The versions of materialism in Anglo-American philosophy have nothing to say except to dismiss the cultural world as "folk psychology." Postmodernism also opts for dissolving the self as a construct of sublimated desire, which constantly exceeds and undermines its masks. If we accept these five features of human existence as constitutive, then we must fashion a new path for philosophical inquiry. In reinterpreting ourselves, we must reinterpret philosophy.

Beyond the Community of Contingency and the Community of Power

Before expanding on the emergence of the community through the dialogue of the social imagination, I want to show that the themes discussed have been seriously neglected or misrepresented in the neopragmatist revival. Two instances may be briefly indicated, Richard Rorty and Stanley Fish. Both these thinkers seem to argue, on the one hand, for the importance of imagination and, on the other, for the role of the community in guiding the process of meaning and interpretation. But both have attenuated views of the nature of the imagination, the community, the process of growth, the aesthetic nature of experience, and the human drive for shared fulfillment, so that their "pragmatism" easily turns either into an irrationalist philosophy of contingency and flux, as in the case of Rorty, or into a theory of community and meaning masking the brute force of power, as in the case of Fish.

In *Contingency, Irony and Solidarity*, Richard Rorty sets forth his most forceful vision of the human condition. True to his antifoundationalism, Rorty seeks to expose the vanity of any appeals to some essence of human nature. But here he begins to raise the disturbing political question: What justification can there be, on such conditions, for one social structure, like liberal democracy, over others? His conclusion takes a form of a liberal individualism reminiscent of J. S. Mill. A free society is one that recognizes its nonfoundational character and therefore allows its citizens to be "as privatistic, 'irrationalist,' and aestheticist as they please as long as they do it on their own time—causing no harm to others and using no resources needed by those less advantaged."[8] Whereas Mill justified individual liberty on the basis of its ultimate contribution to progress and general happiness, Rorty sees no "justification" for it at all. Such a view Rorty calls "ironism" because it is committed to certain values, such as the removal of as much pain and humiliation as possible, without having any absolute rational grounds for doing so. What Rorty offers in place of appealing to rational principles is the ideal of developing imaginative sympathy, "the imaginative ability to see people as fellow sufferers."[9]

Rorty sees the development of our imaginative and aesthetic abilities as crucial for the prospects of a free society, but his analysis of imagination and aesthetic awareness is deeply indebted to the Enlightenment position he repudiates. In his discussion of the role of creativity in language, for instance, Rorty wishes to stress the importance of the role of imagination and creativity in shifting the webs of meaning. But because he is so locked into a semantic theory of meaning, he can make no sense of such transformations and so must come to regard any imaginative, creative moment as an irrational intrusion into the rule-governed habits of conventional meaning. This is brought out especially in his treatment of metaphor, which closely follows Davidson's analysis.[10] Metaphoric expression, when it is genuinely novel, is a nonsemantic event; it is like interrupting a conversation to make a face or kiss someone or point to something—anything—which succeeds in "producing effects on your interlocutor."[11] The even flow of linguistic meaning has been suspended by a physical event. Thus, when Dylan Thomas said, "The force that through the green fuse drives the flower / That blasts the roots of trees / Is my destroyer," Rorty believes that at first Thomas had *said* something

8. Richard Rorty, *Contingency, Irony and Solidarity* (Cambridge: Cambridge University Press, 1989), xiv.

9. Ibid., xvi.

10. I am indebted to Mark Johnson for pointing this out to me.

11. Ibid., 18.

quite meaningless, though he had *done* something. Once, however, the poem becomes (somehow) a new set of habits, a familiar sort of expression, memorized and repeated so that it evokes an organized response, it gains meaning but of course has thereby ceased to be an imaginative or creative expression. For Rorty, to say something "without a *fixed place* in the language game is, as the positivists *rightly* have said, to utter something which is neither true nor false."[12]

Note that Rorty cannot explain how such an event *ever* makes sense. Sheer repetition does not establish a convention that makes sense. If one person's hopping on one leg while reciting the Gettysburg Address adds nothing to the content of the speech, neither will it be affected if everyone does it. How then does such an expression become accessible? This is the question Rorty cannot answer because his view of language and meaning is, at the root, one that seeks meaning in the traditional terms of true or false propositions justified by a system of practices, rather than one that takes imagination and process as central. In the compact nature of his style, Dylan Thomas has said, "I am driven by a force of life, the same which drives all living things, and which destroys them." The transformational relations that are set up are between his "green youth" and the life of plants, and so of all living nature. This is a force that also destroys: The word "fuse" connects the implicit image of the stem with a bomb. The movement of the verse goes from flower to root, from youth to destruction, suggesting a temporal process, a development. The powerful totality of the expression is reinforced by the "root-flower" relation. His whole being, then, is in the grip of a force of life which brings blossoming and destruction; while the plant may flower at the top, at the root lies the power of its being destroyed. The expression may not be immediately accessible (and there certainly are instances in Thomas's poetry that may remain recondite), but we can begin to work with the evocation of meaning that the mysterious phrase imparts by exploring the series of transformations and connections, which essentially employ imaginative and metaphoric reasoning. Through this we come into a relation with the poet, who is indicating something about the human condition.

12. Ibid., emphasis added. Note that Rorty ties the question of meaning in general here to some "foundational" truth claim; i.e., meaning is ultimately a matter of *knowledge*.

Rorty cannot make sense of the nature of metaphoric expression, and the entire realm of symbol, mythology, historical interpretation, and the articulation of ideals remain equally opaque to him. Yet this is where most human life is meaningfully lived. Rorty's view of the self is as radically contingent as Hume's (though he strangely lays upon it the Nietzschean injunction of "self-creation"), and his view of the community simply is a contingent web of practices shifting randomly throughout time. Needless to say, this does not give him much to go on for his defense of liberalism, other than an appeal to our contingent, ironic desire not to see others hurt.

This failure to come to grips with the interrelation of imagination and community appears also in the work of a "neopragmatist" literary figure, Stanley Fish.[13] The fundamental problem facing interpretation theory, of course, is whether there ever is something that is "the" true meaning of a text or whether interpretation is a purely relative response. Fish, seeking a moderate position, hit upon the idea that what limits individual interpretations are the accepted practices of the "community of interpreters." In *Is There a Text in This Class?* Fish appeals to this device because though the accepted practices of interpretation shift over time (and thus not only affect what the meaning of accepted literary works may be but also what "literature" itself is and what texts are classified as literary and what are not), there is not an "anything goes" relativism in which anyone's interpretation is as good as anyone else's, at least at a given moment in cultural history. What the text may mean (and may not) and what texts are classified as "literature" is not subjective or arbitrary; it is determined by the standing community of literary authorities. The standards of such a community, however, will shift willy-nilly over time. Though one might be tempted to see such a move as covertly justifying why there must be designated individuals who are empowered by society to read its texts authoritatively (i.e., professors of English), Fish has made the question of community central to the problem of interpretation.

Fish's problem in one sense is the opposite of Rorty's: How to stabilize meaning instead of acknowledging the pervasiveness of contingency. Hence Fish sees the appeal to the community as a crucial step in securing

---

13. Fish subsequently described himself as a "Marxist," though the reasons for this were not terribly clear.

meaning: "Indeed, it is interpretive communities, rather than the text or the reader, that produce meanings and are responsible for the emergence of formal features. Interpretive communities are made up of those who share interpretive strategies not for reading, but for writing texts, for constituting their properties."[14] But what ultimately constitutes a community of meaning for Fish? Nothing but agreeing on a set of interpretive practices, and this itself cannot be further resolved *methodologically*: "[T]here is no single way of reading that is correct or natural, only 'ways of reading' that are extensions of community perspectives. . . . The business of criticism . . . was not to decide between interpretations by subjecting them to the test of distinterested evidence but to establish by political and persuasive means (they are the same thing) the set of the interpretive assumptions from the vantage point of which the evidence will hereafter be specificable."[15] There can only be persuasion and social coercion at the basis of any set of interpretive strategies accepted by a community. Rhetoric, langauge in the service of irrational power, constitutes the community because it is the maker and unmaker of the rules of the game. Thus Fish introduces at the social level the same sort of brute force that Rorty does with his "strong poet" who disrupts the rules of the game, except that Fish's community of interpreters uses force to maintain the rules of the game as its currently stands.

Rorty's and Fish's views indicate how deeply we need to consider both the nature of imagination and community to arrive at an intelligible and humane theory of meaning. But their versions of "pragmatism," instead of drawing upon the insights of the classical pragmatists, like John Dewey, are really more the products of theories of meaning stemming from analytic and ordinary langauge philosophy of the past few decades.[16] The question of the pragmatic result of their position must also be raised. Not only do their views offer a remarkably attenuated view of meaning, imagination, art and the community, but they recommend dubious practices. Rorty's view of the incommensurability of private self-creation with any public concern abandons seeing how public affairs are really implicated

14. Stanley Fish, *Is There a Text in This Class?* (Cambridge, MA: Harvard University Press, 1980), 14.
15. Ibid., 16.
16. See Rorty's confession, in reply to critics, that he is not widely read in pragmatism, "Comments on Sleeper and Edel," *Transactions of the Charles S. Peirce Society* 21, no. 1 (Winter 1985): 39. In *Is There a Text in This Class?* Fish indicates that he has been most influenced by analytic theories of language, especially those of Austin and the later Wittgenstein.

in our private worlds or how our private actions may have broad public consequences. He thus encourages the retreat into a private world of aesthetic description with the hope that it eventuates in a "sentimental education" that somehow bolsters the project of liberal demcoracy. Fish's approach would result in a cynical endorsement of present interpretive methods which must regard any innovation *essentially* as a challenge to an established locus of authority and power. If a community is forged through a rhetoric of power that fixes shared strategies, one rejects the idea of meaningful change or criticism; i.e., *growth*. It also ignores the idea of a community instrinsically founded on the ideas of self-experimentation and a pluralistic imagination. Neither really can make sense of the idea of a community as constituted through an imaginative exploration of the possibilities of meaning resulting in a continuous process of developmental transformation. Nor is there a place for the creation of ideals to be used as critical standards of present practices.

The Community of Social Imagination

I will now explore an alternative approach, developed from Dewey's concept of aesthetic experience and his and Royce's analysis of the community. The idea of the community that emerges is one which through its imaginative, dynamic intelligence actively seeks for conditions that fulfill the deep aesthetic needs of human beings to experience the world with meaning and value in an expressive, reflective, and self-critical way. Our quest for community is also a quest to encounter others; we experience the meaning of the world through each other, and art is a preeminent perfection of this practice. Contrary to postmodern theories, the work of art (alias, "the text"[17]) becomes a medium through which we imaginatively embrace new habits of understanding that give meaning to our old habits by allowing them to develop and grow. Through others we expose the genuine possibilities of the present, which give us intelligent ways of evaluating and developing its tendencies toward fulfilling rather than destructive ends, achieving a continuity of meaningful experience. It is

---

17. What had been usually designated "the work of art" came to be mainly described as "the text" in hermeneutic and postmodern criticism, with the latter even more strangely convinced that a change in critical interpretation of texts would somehow constitute radical political action.

this dramatic, imaginative, embodied, communal engagement of the present in its possibilties as well as histories which allows us to experience meaning, and this is "art."

Culture is a web of highly flexible practices that allow us to enter imaginatively and actively into each other's lives. After acquiring a basic mastery of our infant bodies, we commence the arduous process of social understanding. Gradually we begin to engage the immediate others in our world, those who give us care, and through them we encounter the emerging self we will be. Dewey and Mead have emphasized how we dramatically learn to take the role of the other to develop our sense of self. I wish to stress that this is an imaginative need. We must constantly project ourselves into the stances of many other people to gain an organized perspective of ourselves and become self-reflective. This is more than mere sympathetic substitution of the other for ourselves. The other enters into the creative process of interpretation and understanding that we have of ourselves and the situation. This projection seeks a continuously integrative attitude through the possibility of coordinating common ends of action. We come to experience the meaning of the world only through this process of social interaction. This has the dynamic form of mutual creativity, of ongoing coordination that builds a history of dialogical meaning, which can come to be understood as narrative temporality. The process of meaning involves creative development and ongoing continuity, not mechanical routine interrupted by random change, as with Rorty. In other words, a pragmatic theory of meaning emphasizes imagination because meaning is primarily a process of creative growth and exploration of possibilities that *develop* the situation. The theories of Rorty and Fish make change the result of irrational violence. When human life takes on the pattern epitomized in the theories of Rorty and Fish, it is life on the edge of becoming meaningless, a point at which the destructive force of the frustrated Human Eros will emerge, either outwardly or inwardly.

Let us forget "texts" for a moment. Others enter into the interpretation of my *activities*. Imagine a simple game of catch. I must throw the ball to you. But this is not just aiming and throwing at a target. I must anticipate in my throw the way you will respond, knowing also that you are anticipating my action of throwing. You have dramatically projected yourself into my activity as thrower and I have projected myself into your activity as catcher. This mutual effort to anticipate together creates a dramatic fusion of our fields of action and interpretation through which we can both coordinate our individual activities toward the shared end of playing a game. I do not lose my self-identity through this process; my self-identity becomes more definite because of my ability to take "the social standpoint," as Mead called it. What opens up is a range of possibilities that would not exist if I could not do this, thus creating new projective lines of action that extend from my present circumstances into the future. We both grasp this common end, though we each may perform distinctive but complementary activities (such as the difference between the role of pitcher and catcher in baseball). But without this guiding end functioning as an integrative ideal, we would not be able to coordinate our actions in this manner. If anything, the actions of the other would be regarded as impediments to the realization of our actions.[18]

Most human activity lacks the clearly presented ends of games. (Perhaps this explains why the artifice of games is so popular—games offer clear instances in which such simple ends are set forth and can be rather easily embraced and followed; they are simple models of shared interaction, allowing individuals to experience in an aesthetically vivid manner the dynamic but meaningful projections of participatory interpretation.) Communities are generally bound together by hazier ideals, and we need to find more definite ends to achieve cooperative activity providing a context for the realization of value and a sense of meaning in our lives.[19] The possibility of community, then, lies as much in the ability to search out and discover integrative ends as it does in the conservative practices of its traditions. Indeed, traditions are highly valued largely because they provide such a stable network for guiding and interpreting *future* activity.

The aesthetic immediacy of experience is pervaded by these social features. Our actions aim at ends that fulfill us; we need to be able to make

18. This theory of meaning is discussed by Dewey in chapter 5 of *Experience and Nature* (LW, 1) and by George Herbert Mead in *Mind, Self and Society* (Chicago: University of Chicago Press, 1934); see my *John Dewey's Theory of Art, Experience, and Nature* (Albany: State University of New York Press, 1987), ch. 4.

19. An instance of the tendency of analytic theories of language to seek formalized schemata and then impose them back upon the whole primary phenomenon of experiential meaning is present in the later Wittgenstein's appeal to describing meaning in terms of "language games" governed by conventional rules. Of course, in some senses, language can be seen metaphorically as "game-like," especially where language is used for playing. But language also has many features that are not found in games. And there is more to games anyway than merely following rules.

evaluative, intelligent decisions that can be understood as ways of organizing our present actions toward sustaining and enriching ends. Acting in light of those ends, our activities become imbued with the heightened experience of meaning. Our experience is illumined not only by recognizing it as the outcome of a history but also by seeing the present possibilities of conduct which develop that history: We can act so as to find fulfillment and we find this process an unfolding event of meaning that we inhabit. This theme is forcibly articulated by Dewey in his concept of "an experience." The aesthetic possibilities of experience are not limited to a uniqne class of purely "aesthetic" objects, such as those found in the fine arts. Any activity that succeeds in realizing the possibilities of a present situation so that it becomes pervaded by a sense of completeness, closure, wholeness, and expressive significance exhibits the features of an experience. Dewey stresses the temporal development of any such experience. It is not just that any experience takes time, but an experience constitutes a genuine temporal process having a "narrative structure" of beginning, middle, and end where the parts are organically related to the whole and are the means through which the whole experience is realized. A bar of music, for example, does not merely take time and make noise; when heard as music, it occupies a dramatic moment in a dynamic process, having a relation to the part of the piece which has preceded and to that which is yet to come.

The way an experience fills out time is quite significant. To reiterate: Human time is not a mere succession of moments but rather a process governed by the complex interweaving of developmental, narrative patterns of interpretation built out of the teleological structure of actions. Our activities aim at completion. In some cases, the end lies in a specific goal, such as finding food, reaching for a ball, or removing the hand quickly from a hot dish. In others, we aim at more persistent conditions of equilibrium, such as the maintenance of oxygen in the blood or securing a constant food supply. We organize our world from our earliest days by achieving simple, basic acts of coordination that aim at controlling the body to anticipate the world for the achievement of ends. These acts have a teleological, intentional structure, and as they become connected with each other, new and more complex acts and ends become available as ways of organizing our experience and giving it new meaning. Mastery of simple sensorimotor coordinations links a number of previously discrete acts, such as grasping and arm movement, into new and more complex actions, such as the act of picking up and throwing an object. Gradually these acts form an elaborate and expanding network which constitutes a structural horizon against which consciousness itself emerges. When it does, we characteristically apprehend "the world" not as a static object but as a field within which we must act, as a dramatic context in which we live forward, but also have a past, a history. Through the early years of childhood eventually one comes to understand oneself as living a life in which one's actions greatly determine the meaning and shape of one's existence.[20]

These two points, the imaginative projection into the stance of others and the teleological structure of human experience, may now be combined. Our meaningful experience of the world arises less from purely individual acts than from our social mode of existence. Our social environment acts on us and calls out a social response. We inhabit the world through our imaginative embodiment of others which we learn from their imaginative embodiment in us. The field of intentionality arises from this shared dramatic space in which we struggle to anticipate together. This allows us to communicate and thereby to interpret and understand ourselves so that we can assess, evaluate, and coordinate our particular activities toward a shared world of meaning that is not static or final but in constant developmental play. The teleological structure of these actions gradually engages the complex web of culture, which might be described as the symbolic storehouse of the social imagination. The shape of one's individuality emerges through the appropriation of the culture, which is not merely an environment of coexistent others, but a *world*, a nexus of meanings and values embodied in a range of symbolically interpreted practices through which human beings can be meaningfully present to each other.

A *world* is thus the interpretive horizon within which we encounter and realize our humanity in acts of expressive communication. It extends beyond any group of individuals, embracing traditions, history (sacred or mythic as well as secular and historical), practices, institutions, and the narrative possibilities that are available for individuals to use in the

---

20. See William James's discussion of teleology of intelligence in chapters 1 and 4 of *The Principles of Psychology* (Cambridge, MA: Harvard University Press, 1981). See Dewey's discussions of this topic in "The Reflex Arc Concept in Psychology" (EW, 5:96–110) and *Human Nature and Conduct* (MW, 14).

process of participation in the society. A world allows a culture to have a narrative past and to act in light of a range of ends that define a meaningful, valuable future. It allows for a genuine community to exist through creating the possibility of a process of social interpretation.

Josiah Royce's rich exploration of the interrelation of time and interpretation to the community can illuminate the previous remarks, standing as an important challenge to the idea of interpretive communities offered by Rorty and Fish. Royce acknowledges that a community "is essentially a product of a time process" having a past and a future.[21] Like an individual, a community exists temporally. The interpretive meaning of an individual's present experience is set within a context of memory and anticipation; so too a community is constituted insofar as its members share a *"community of memory"* and a *"community of hope."*[22] The members identify themselves in terms of accepting a certain history as their own, a history that helps explain who they are and articulates a range of values, meanings, and practices. Part of the shared human project of self-understanding requires that we have a shared past as well as an individual past. This is the interpretive act of discerning the "community of memory." But communities, like individuals, live forward: The shared range of hopes and expectations constitutes the "community of hope." These are interpretive horizons without which the community of the present could not exist, and they function as the means whereby a continuous process of action is possible. The nature of the cultural world extends through the social imagination so as to frame a background of a past and the foreground of a future; the community is thus a process with the distinctive temporal structure of *narrativity*.[23] Cooperation alone does not define a community, according to Royce, unless there is an "ideal extension" of the meaning of each member's activity to the community of memory and community of hope which allows for mutual interpretation in the present to be possible and for them all to share a commitment to a common life that generates loyalty and even love. "The time-process and

21. Josiah Royce, *The Problem of Christianity* (Chicago: University of Chicago Press, 1968), 243.

22. Ibid., 248.

23. See ibid., 290. Royce's social hermeneutic emphasizes the constant need for new ideas to interpret the past to the future. By contrast, Alasdair MacIntyre's discussions of community and tradition mostly look backward, except to ensure that future conflicts are resolved so as not to threaten the integrity of the existing tradition.

the ideal extension of the self in this time-process," states Royce, "lie at the basis of the whole theory of the community."[24]

Royce connects this to the nature of interpretation: "A Community . . . depends for its very constitution upon the way in which each of its members interprets himself and his life."[25] Behind the diversity of specific human purposes, there is the need for each individual to make sense of his or her life through the lives of others. Adopting Peirce's triadic semiotic model, Royce argues that interpretation is a constant process with three terms involved, the object interpreted, the sign or interpreter, and the one to whom the interpretation is addressed, the interpretant. This applies as much to my interpretation of my past self to my future self, such as when I recall a promise which thus mediates between my past and future selves and determines the meaning of who I am and will be, as to my interpretation of a text or event.[26] For Royce, the community as such exists as a process of interpretation, mediating past and future through the symbolic configurations of the present. Human temporality as such is *socially* appropriated through the process of interpretation. Time itself is understood as an order of possible interpretation. Temporality is seen to be one of the essential features of human understanding; it is made available through our social imagination.

Furthermore, since each sign calls for a new sign to interpret it, the life of the community calls "in ideal, for an infinite sequence of interpretations."[27] A community exists through a continuous process of generating new meanings which do not rupture with the past so much as render the whole temporal configuration of human existence intelligible. In other words, if meaning originates with our experience of community, we anticipate a future in which new lives and new standpoints are required. Temporal development and novelty are implicated in the idea of process itself. These new meanings cannot be successfully imagined to be mere products of a rhetoric of persuasion masking a will to power; they are anticipated as continuations of our community and as fulfillments of

24. Ibid., 268.
25. Ibid., 274.
26. Royce offers a clear synopsis of Peirce's "semeiotic" in Lectures XI, XII, and XIV in *The Problem of Christianity*, though he does tend to conflate Peirce's idea of the "interpretant" with that of the "interpreter." The promise of Peirce's own, far more nuanced, semiotics for a cultural hermeneutics has yet to be explored.
27. Ibid., 290.

the Human Eros. Of course, communities may be destroyed, their cultural ideals annihilated. But the community as a project anticipates its continuity through an extension into a future that sustains and develops its meaning.

"Man," says Royce, "is the animal that interprets; and therefore man lives in communities and depends upon them for insight and salvation."[28] The "Will to Interpret" is this striving to overcome the radical separation and individuality of each person, thereby constituting a community whereby the meaning of each can be present to the others and to himself as well. The desire to interpret aims at a "community of interpretation," an ideal that gives structure and guidance to the "community of memory" and the "community of hope." Human beings approach each other through the possibility of sharing an integrative world of meaning that allows them to be members of a community, truly present to each other. Interpretation occupies a special function in the community, articulating those symbols whereby there can be shared insight and understanding. As Royce observes, this has tremendous ethical and religious value, for it is "interpretation which is the great humanizing factor in our cognitive processes and makes the purest forms of love for communities possible."[29] By enriching our understanding of our past and articulating possible ideals for the future, we have constituted and extended the community of the present and the meaning it holds for those living within it.

Royce's analysis up to this point poses a serious challenge to the attenuated views of the "community of interpretation" discussed earlier. First, we now can acknowledge the way in which human beings come to inhabit a shared cultural world through the narrative structure of action and traditions which render that world articulate, allowing us to participate as members in the meaning of that world. A cultural world is a narrative web that grasps a horizon of shared meaning. Every culture has a set of stories that serve to organize the "community of memory." These stories are marked out as sacred in archaic and religious cultures. In non-tribal cultures there are also fundamental "myths" that serve the same purpose—essentially any story that functions to define and articulate

28. Ibid., 298.
29. Ibid., 318.

the basic meanings, values, and history of the community.[30] The stories of the discovery of the New World, the flight of the Puritans, the Revolutionary War, and so on, historical facts though they be, serve to define the range of values and meanings out of which a "community of memory" for American citizens is generated, even for those whose American genealogy does not extend that far back. The fight to alter these stories, so as to include the stories of Native Americans, African Americans, Hispanics, and women, is an effort to modify the ideal used to constitute the values and social identities of our culture so that those who have been "faceless" may also be meaningfully present. Many conflicts throughout history are conflicts of stories commanding our ideals because they constitute the meaning of who we are and the world in which we live. Behind these conflicting ideals is the desire for living a shared life of meaning, what I have called "the Human Eros."

Here a more Deweyan conception of community is needed to supplement Royce's idealistic emphasis on integrative transcendence. Communities need a pluralistic orientation to maintain their imaginative creativity and self-interpretation. Instead of the "private project of self-perfection," we need to make the distinctive activities of individuals truly expressive and so shared by others to enhance the intelligence and imaginative horizon of the community. As Dewey stressed, art is a prime example of the way in which highly distinctive visions have not only been shared but have also generated new modes of understanding by showing how seemingly dead-end practices could be radically altered and redirected. The conception of painting as realistic representation was changed by nineteenth-century painters from Monet on by exploring new styles. They did not "rupture vision," though at first they did shock, but ultimately they taught us to see with their styles in new ways. They *educated* vision. The same is true of political reformers who, unlike revolutionaries or hostile enemies who seek to destroy a culture, have managed to reinterpet a culture's meaning through exposing new possibilities in its practices. The progressive inclusion of minorities and women into the full rights enjoyed by all citizens is an enlargement, not a rupture, of the ideal, the meaning, of freedom and equality. Reformers like Martin Luther King, Jr. and Susan B. Anthony have also educated vision: A community

30. I call such stories "Mythoi." See pp. 13–16 above.

is sustained through the continuous process of self-interpretation, that is, self-education.

A community exists, Dewey argues, by developing the art of expression and communication. This is what allows human beings to organize themselves in a variety of ways that expand the horizon of meaning. A rich background of symbolic understanding is needed as well as the trained imagination that explores new modes of response and enters flexibly into the possibilities presented in the encounter with others. A society that trains its citizens to understand and appreciate the diversity of our worlds of meaning is more likely to be able to resolve conflicts in ideals as well as to articulate inclusive ideals that sustain a pluralistic culture. A democratic culture is not a Babel of pure difference held together by the loose, temporary end of the private pursuit of personal happiness; it is a culture that can actively understand a variety of worlds. Mutual indifference as to how each other lives does not prepare one to communicate, much less to understand alternative worldviews. Instead of the narrow ideal of cultural dogmatism, which excludes the meaning of the other, Dewey stresses that democracy flourishes when the aesthetically educated imagination, disciplined through the self-regulation of the experimental method, aims at securing the conditions whereby a community can adapt, develop, and grow.[31]

We can now see the need for theory as imaginative extension of the interpretive ideals that make the community possible, opening up intelligent courses for action and self-understanding. Theory, as Dewey said, liberates practice. It can do this through articulating ideals to be explored rather than by making dogmatic claims for having achieved a fixed, closed system. Insofar as we are constantly caught up in the process of trying to make sense and understand each other, we are rarely faced with pure instances of self-evident intentionality. All who regard intentionality as the perfect lucidity of meaning have simply idealized the product of the fixed, reflex habit. If we focus instead upon the moment of discovery and

---

31. Dewey's idea of the "experimental method" is a continuation of the social hermeneutics of the democratic community. In other words, Dewey conceived of "experiment" far more broadly and loosely than simply as it occurs in science. Unfortunately, the highly constrained meaning it has for the sciences was read back into Dewey's more general use of the term, giving rise to the "scientistic Dewey." For Dewey, science is an extension of the social, imaginative nature of experience as it seeks to educate itself through inquiry into nature. Experimental methodology is a discipline for constant learning and thus provides an important self-limitation in the fallibilistic quest for meaning.

learning, a different view offers itself. Intentionality for Dewey is what points us toward the shared encounter of the future, in its ambiguities as well as in its anticipated stabilities. It is our quest for the community where meaning is aesthetically encountered, where life is lived as narrative development and not as a bare succession of tomorrow after tomorrow: Time can be a tale told by other than an idiot. Our shared strategies of understanding do not have to be masks for the rhetoric of power; they can be instrumentalities toward creative action, lured by the ideal of the aesthetics of meaning, forging a community through hope and memory. Such a community Dewey called "democracy" because it would engage itself in the realization of the distinctive potentialities of each individual toward participatory action and shared benefit. Only through the social can the individual come to be. The result would not be a life entirely subjected to collective ends, as Rorty supposes, but one that can intelligently distinguish between genuinely shared public concerns in need of social direction and those innumerable private transactions that are not.[32]

This indicates a unique function of the humanities in general and philosophy in particular in developing a democratic society. The humanities are the practices that seek to grasp the symbolic life of human existence. They explore the horizons of cultural meaning and so educate the democratic imagination. Through this they enhance the possibility of communication, the understanding of others, and articulate the possibilities for intelligent development and action. Those who are the interpreters of the humanities must be energetically engaged in the task of constituting the community of memory and the community of hope. This also involves the creation of inclusive ideals whereby the present communities may achieve new visions of self-interpretation and greater enhancement of meaningful action. The theory of the humanities posed by Rorty or Fish presents a serious challenge to the role of the humanities in the modern world. It is doubly tragic that they have adopted the name "pragmatism"

---

32. See Dewey's discussion of the community in *The Public and Its Problems* (LW, 2). Dewey's rejection of the individual-social dichotomy undercuts Rorty's efforts to separate the project of "private self-creation" from that of making public policies. For Dewey the distinction of what was private or public was the crucial one to be made, the private being that sphere of actions whose consequences had no far-ranging serious impact and so which could easily be foreseen by the parties involved. Public issues were those that had far-ranging impact and needed oversight. Deciding to modify the rules of chess in playing a private game, such as giving the knight an extra square in its move, needs no public regulation (except perhaps in a tournament). Changing the rules of landing a passenger jet at an airport does have extensive consequences and so needs public regulation.

when it is pragmatism that offers a view of the humanities as central to the cultivation of imagination and the growth of a self-critical community. We need a theory that does not make a neglected riddle of the imagination or community and sees the creation of those worlds of cultural meaning as the expression of a primary human drive to live a life that can embody a value-rich, intelligible existence with others. Our ideals are the sources of our deep commitments and may have the most tragic as well as beneficial consequences. We must foster those which sustain the Human Eros rather than those that evoke its darker nemesis.

The result for philosophy is important. Philosophy, as the preeminent humanistic practice, can serve the Human Eros by articulating those meanings that can secure a community that actively pursues the ideal that human beings can live meaningful lives. But we must appropriate the aesthetic and imaginative aspects of human understanding in order to put philosophy back in constructive dialogue with humanity's quest for meaning, and we must understand the social nature of imagination and the communicative nature of aesthetic expression. The Human Eros possessing philosophy recovers humanism.

SIX

PRAGMATIC IMAGINATION

Pragmatism originated as a movement that sought to clarify meaning in terms of action. We recall the phrasing of Peirce's famous maxim: "Consider what effects, that might conceivably have practical bearings, we conceive the object of our conception to have. Then, our conception of these effects is the whole of our conception of the object."[1] The effort to clarify this maxim might be said to constitute the subsequent history of pragmatism. Whereas there was a tendency in pragmatism to interpret consequentialism in a positivistic sense, it was systematically avoided by its main developers, Peirce, James, Mead, and Dewey, because they were sensitive to the creative, the temporal, and the experimental dimensions of experience. As a result, the meaning of action in pragmatism involved, sooner or later, recognition of the importance of a mode of understanding whereby the actual was reinterpreted and reconstructed in the light of the possible. Human understanding thus conceived is radically different

---

1. *Collected Papers*, 5:402. Future references will be cited in the text as CP.

from the traditional view of either rationality or imagination. First, it is a dynamic, "embodied" view, beginning with the idea of living organic beings acting and learning in a world. Second, it consciously involves a metaphysical standpoint in which the ontological modalities of actuality and potentiality are integrated into the very idea of an "event" or "situation." We cannot imagine either an instantaneous "moment" in abstraction or the universe as a whole purely or even primarily in terms of the Parmenidean third-person present "It is" or "It exists." This can be argued to be pragmatism's most distinctive contribution, especially for a theory of meaning.

The acknowledgment of the importance of what might be called "imaginative understanding" is accompanied in these thinkers by an awareness of the role of the noncognitional or nonpropositional in all our experience; that is, of the aesthetic dimension of meaning and rationality. These themes have always accounted for the richness and humanity in pragmatism's theory of experience, especially when contrasted with empiricisms deriving from more classical models. By integrating the imaginative and aesthetic modes of experience with rationality and action, however, another revolution was achieved. Imagination was often conceived of as a spontaneous, undisciplined faculty at odds with the fixed rules laid down by reason. Because of this assumption, those philosophies which sought to go beyond the traditional view of rationality and truth were inclined to look toward transcendental interpretations of reason and to develop dialectical or unexperimental methodologies. Kant's critical philosophy and its idealist inheritors took this path, which led in the twentieth century to Husserlian phenomenology, Heidegger's phenomenological ontology, and Gadamer's hermeneutics. However much these phenomenologies claimed to be grounded in experience, they either claimed to offer an alternative method of gaining certitude, as with Husserl, or made the question of truth prior to the question of method, as with Heidegger and Gadamer. For the third quarter of the twentieth century, both the "analytic" and the "Continental" trends of thought were destined not only to supplant pragmatism as dominant movements in the United States but also to shape the areas of concern and emphasis of those continuing to develop pragmatism so that where it survived it dwindled to being mainly a theory of cognition and scientific method or was regarded only as a meager approach to the "lived experience" in comparison with those taken up by Continental theories.

Subsequently, it met renewed popularity in the hands of its "postmodern" advocates, many of them former analytic philosophers who had "lost the faith" but still carried with them the presuppositions and interests of their previous incarnations.

Pragmatism, however revived, remains in need of further development of its primary insights. Though Dewey was perhaps the one thinker in this movement who saw these issues and their implications clearly, even he often failed to see how radical they were and how much they clashed with the traditional set of assumptions shared by most philosophers. Dewey's maddening vagueness and sweeping vistas often left a misleading impression that his ideas were insubstantial and confused. The frontiers opened up by the pragmatic movement soon became forgotten and ignored. Now that many within the analytic tradition are turning back to pragmatism, largely out of a sense of the failure of the "Anglo-American" tradition to reduce human experience to a logical or narrowly cognitive procedure, and now that the story of Continental philosophy seems to be a tale of perpetual dissolution as "postmodernism," I think it is important to be reminded that a more adequate theory of understanding is still available, though much in need of development. It will be the primary purpose of my essay first to examine the role of imagination in Peirce, James, and Dewey, and then to suggest the outlines of how such a theory might be developed.

I

First, to return to Peirce's maxim: Despite its beguiling clarity and simplicity, it stood itself in need of much clarification. When James set out to explain this idea, he gave it a characteristic emphasis on the immediate and the personal: "To attain perfect clearness in our thoughts of an object, then, we need only consider what conceivable effects of a practical kind the object may involve—what sensations we are to expect from it, and what reactions we must prepare."[2] By "effects" he meant sense perceptions and by "practical consequences" he meant personal responses, the attitude you or I take toward the object. Pragmatism, in James's hands,

2. William James, *Pragmatism* (Cambridge, MA: Harvard University Press, 1975), 29. Cited in text as P.

was part and parcel of his vitalistic ethics. "There can *be* no difference anywhere," he added, "that doesn't express itself in a difference in concrete fact and in consequent conduct upon that fact, imposed on somebody, somehow, somewhen. The whole function of philosophy ought to be to find out what definite difference it will make to you and me, at definite instants of our life, if this world-formula or that world-formula be the true one" (P, 30).

It was statements like these that irritated Peirce into rechristening his philosophy "pragmaticism," but which also, I suspect, made Peirce recognize the need to clarify his own formulation. Whatever he originally meant, Peirce came to hold that the last thing to be meant by "effects" was sensations; rather it meant general rules whereby the object becomes interpreted by a concept. By "practical consequences" Peirce meant the bearings of the concept on a selfless community of inquirers dutifully laboring through the centuries toward an ultimate description of reality for its own sake, gradually minimizing the idiosyncratic elements each individual investigator inevitably introduced. Even in his early thought we find the expression, "Finally, as what anything really is, is what it may finally come to be known to be in the ideal state of complete information, so that reality depends on the ultimate decision of the community. . . . The individual man, since his separate existence is manifested only by ignorance and error, so far as his is anything apart from his fellows . . . is only a negation" (CP, 5.316–17). By the time of Peirce's papers in the *Monist* (1905–6), we find him interpreting "action" strictly in terms of the "rational purport" or sign properties of any term.[3]

Despite these differences, both Peirce and James acknowledged the importance of understanding the concept of action in light of the possibilities of actual existence, so that an intelligible and dynamic meaning emerged in a temporal process, and both men stressed the significance of the aesthetic, felt, or noncognitive dimension of experience in such a process. Such features were an essential and constitutive element of rationality. A primary instance in Peirce's thought, of course, is his notion of abductive or hypothetical inference. This is the crucial element in scientific thinking for Peirce, being nothing less than the ability of the mind in the face of a body of knowledge and a definite range of problematic data

3. See CP, 5.412 and CP, 5.402nn1–3.

to frame a fruitful explanatory hypothesis out of all the logically possible hypotheses. Whereas induction simply infers a rule—that is, establishes a habit of conditional expectation—"hypothesis substitutes, for a complicated tangle of predicates attached to one subject, a single conception" (CP, 2.643). This involves, says Peirce, a "complicated feeling" because we must see all the predicates inhering in one subject and this is achieved by "a single feeling of great intensity." Like the distinct emotion formed by all musical instruments in an orchestra, "this emotion is essentially the same as an hypothetic inference, and every hypothetic inference involves the formation of such an emotion." In other words, in order to understand the phenomena, the mind must respond to a possible aesthetics of order. "When a man desires ardently to know the truth," says Peirce elsewhere, "his first effort will be to imagine what that truth can be. He cannot prosecute his pursuit long without finding that imagination unbridled is sure to carry him off the track. Yet nevertheless, it remains true that there is after all nothing but imagination that can ever supply him an inkling of the truth. He can stare stupidly at phenomena; but in the absence of imagination they will not connect themselves together in any rational way" (CP, 1.46). Peirce comments that "every single item of scientific theory which stands established today has been due to Abduction" (CP, 5.172).

Abduction, then, is an imaginative effort of understanding, beginning with an "aesthetic-hypothetic" response to the world. It is not completely unconstrained nor is it purely spontaneous, for it must emerge in the course of regular action that suddenly has become so disorganized as to suggest the need for a coherent principle connecting a range of experience that is something more than a mere empirical generalization. The explanation set forth must somehow satisfactorily meet the condition for actually organizing that range of experience intelligibly, allowing us to anticipate the universe with a *more* rational outlook. The "abductive suggestion" does not come ex nihilo but rather emerges from the matrix of experience itself, from "perceptual judgments," as Peirce says (CP, 5.181), aligning this doctrine with the scholastic adage, "*Nihil est in intellectu quod non prius fuerit in sensu.*" True, there is an unpredictable and random nature to the abductive insights we hit upon in trying to understand a phenomenon, but intuition for Peirce must be hedged about with rational, fallibilistic cautions: "The abductive suggestion comes to us like a flash. It is an act of insight, though of extremely fallible insight" (CP, 5.181).

Hence it must be accompanied by a critical and experimental methodology in order for the meaning of the aesthetic-hypothetic insight to become clear. Abduction marks, then, a creative use of the imagination that is consummated in understanding the world rationally, which for Peirce is to say in terms of continuity and "laws of growth" or development. In other words, abduction not only grasps present existence in terms of seeing as part of a range of related phenomena but also interprets the meaning of the present in light of an ongoing history of development, a history that will need constant rechecking and reinterpretation.

The effort to come to grips with the aesthetic of thought explains much of the most recondite as well as outright strange aspects of Peirce's philosophy. As an instance of the former, one might cite his very early, but crucial, article, "On A New List of Categories," and of the latter his distinctive "A Neglected Argument for the Reality of God." Whether we are attempting the most rigorous effort to "precise" or expose the fundamental categories or are allowing the mind the fullest "musement" or play possible, the aesthetic and imaginative dimensions of experience are crucial for abduction. Although Peirce could be said to have neglected the subject of aesthetics, he eventually subsumed logic under ethics and ethics under aesthetics as the highest normative science, the science of the *summum bonum*.[4]

There is one notable aspect of the aesthetic dimension of thought, however, which should be briefly mentioned, Peirce's category of Firstness. This, the primary category, consists of the pure individual suchness unifying any experience considered by itself without reference even to existence. Among the many descriptions Peirce gives of this category, two are "Quality" and "Feeling." From the ontological point of view, the ideal natures included here are pure possibilities. For example, there is an infinite number of shades of blue, not all of which will existentially occur. Peirce considers these natures grasped through the mode of feeling because, being simple, no analysis or comparison, or reasoning of any sort is required to have them. Since these natures constitute the absolute undifferentiated unity of any experience at any moment, they are not to be confused with discriminated objects within experience (as a shade of

---

4. See CP, 5.36 and 5.135–36.

blue might be to a painter choosing which color to use), nor do they strictly speaking exist temporally, that is, as processes; they are absolute states.[5] Whatever further complexity experience acquires through Peirce's other two categories, the existential and dialectical clash of Otherness in Secondness and the lawlike, habit-forming rationality of Thirdness, without Firstness, experience never could have that penumbral unity of feeling that must be present as a substructure for the other categories.[6]

II

Let me briefly indicate a comparable dimension in James's thought. A rather surprising problem must be resolved first. William James was certainly the most mercurial and artistically gifted of the pragmatists. His stress on the creative led him to argue for a cosmos full of untried possibilities, randomness, and freedom so that at times he seems to focus on the irrational and emotional aspect of experience to the exclusion of reason. One would expect to find the themes of imagination and aesthetics dominant there more than in Peirce the logician or Dewey the social psychologist. Yet just as James never wrote on the topic of "aesthetics," so his discussion of imagination is confined to a brief chapter of his *Principles of Psychology*, where it is treated in the classical manner as the faculty of forming images. There is an explanation as well as a solution, I believe. First, just as the artist in James was offended by the uninspired literature on aesthetics (much of it produced in the architectonic systems of German thought, an anathema to James), so the psychologist was wary of transcendentalist or romantic effusions of imagination.[7] The topics that might have appeared under the rubric of aesthetics and imagination in James's work tend to be included with his moralistic voluntarism, his temporal analysis of experience and reason, and his doctrine of pure experience.

5. See CP, 1.306–11.
6. See CP, 1.530.
7. See, for example, *The Will to Believe* (1897 and Dover editions, 69; Harvard University Press, 61). Cited in text as WB. Harvard pagination will follow the corresponding citation in the edition of 1897.

166 EROS AND IMAGINATION

Here I shall focus on the relatively early but absolutely seminal essay, "The Sentiment of Rationality."[8] Indeed, this essay could almost be said to be the breakthrough for James's philosophy that Peirce's "New List of Categories" was for his. Most of the important themes of James's mature philosophy are outlined or anticipated here. The title of this piece alone should be indicative, for James is approaching the question of rationality from the standpoint of determining its psychological marks or characteristics. The question James raises here is: How shall the philosopher-psychologist recognize the ultimate rational conception by which everything else is to be explained? The answer he proposes is "that he will recognize its rationality as he recognizes everything else, by certain subjective marks with which it affects him" (WB, 63/57). These marks include "a strong feeling of ease, peace, rest" full of "lively relief and pleasure." It follows upon the requisite feeling of perplexity or doubt and answers the craving awakened by such a state. It thus has the "feeling of sufficiency of the present movement, of its absoluteness" (WB, 64/58). It is marked negatively by the absence of doubt, of the need for further justification. In other words, it is what allows us to think "with perfect fluency." Like abduction for Peirce, it organizes the mass of phenomena into a cosmos of order. Balancing the drive for simplification, however, James also emphasizes the need for recognizing diversity as such. The life of thought moves from one passion to the other, from diversity to unity and back. Should the self-complete, terminating vision of the Absolute ever be attained, James ironically remarks, since rationality is a *process*, it will only "transcend" this moment and point beyond it toward Nothingness. The question "Why is there something rather than nothing?" will haunt metaphysics with Heideggerian anxiety at this stage; an "ontological wonder-sickness" will be the result (WB, 72/63).[9] Because the "notion of a possible other than the actual may still haunt our

8. An essay with this title was published in 1879–80. Part of it (about one-fifth) was later combined with the companion essay, "Rationality, Activity, and Faith" (1882), and appeared in *The Will to Believe* under the original title of "The Sentiment of Rationality." See the discussion of the publication history by John McDermott in his *The Writings of William James* (Chicago: University of Chicago Press, 1970), 818–19. The essay of 1879–80 appears in the Harvard edition in the volume *Essays in Philosophy*.

9. A fruitful contrast and comparison with Heidegger would be most illuminating just here. In the early Heidegger, at least, the moment in which understanding goes beyond the self-sufficiency of "things" to Nothing reveals the possibility for authentic, "resolute" existence, which is governed by the horizon of the future.

imagination and prey upon our system" (WB, 73/64), it reveals that reality is not ideally grasped as a fixed, timeless actuality, but in terms of a dynamic process. The rationalist or the absolutist simply fails to think beyond the actual in his conception of reality as a fully completed finality; his tranquility, then, is simply a higher manifestation of that of the idiot: satisfaction with the obvious by virtue of obliviousness to the possible. It is an incomplete rationality. Our understanding requires just the themes added by the pragmatic approach for the intelligibility of experience to be manifest.

From the practical standpoint, rationality is not an aimless pointing at the world in blank wonder but the movement of thought itself. Central to a rational claim is that it "awakens the active impulses" and "satisfies other aesthetic demands" (WB, 75–76/66). Our rationality is a process, then, which is driven by an aesthetic eros. For James, this includes a banishment of uncertainty toward the future, a harmonious anticipation of the world acting "congruously with our spontaneous powers" (WB, 82/70). A rational explanation will be one intimately tied to possible courses of fulfilling human action; that is, it will be governed by the prag-matic imperative of the aesthetics of human existence. This is the crucial step for James, for there is no one course set out or preordained that shall constitute which human actions; shall be deemed satisfactory. As James puts it, "although men will insist on being spoken to by the universe in some way, few will insist on being spoken to in just the same way" (WB, 89/75). In particular, James argues that the more rational view is that which says that one's actions actually help realize or constitute a universe which gives meaning and value to our existence. In other words, action is genuinely creative, and so faith is an essential ingredient of any rational, practical view of things. This is more the faith of the artist in the possibilities of his material than of the Puritan in the preestablished will of God or of the mechanist in the iron laws of nature. Faith for the pragmatist amplifies the intelligible structure of the world rather than being in the end submissive to a brute, inexplicable order. In the creative play of reality, the right to believe genuinely exists as a moral experiment. In summary, "No philosophy will permanently be deemed rational by all men which (in addition to meeting logical demands) does not to some degree pretend to determine expectancy, and in a still greater degree make a direct appeal to all those powers of our nature which we hold in the highest esteem" (WB, 110/89).

The rationality of action lies in its acknowledgment of the play of possibility in the present. For action to make sense, not only must this radical temporality be seen as constitutive of human experience, that our experience is a dynamic mediation between the stubborn actuality of the past and the plasticity of the open-ended future, but our temporality is teleologically structured by the life ideals we seek to implement, since it is these that ultimately determine the criteria for the satisfaction of action. "Satisfaction" for James was the counterfoil to any "foundational" theory of truth. This, the most misunderstood idea in the Jamesian philosophy, does *not* connote a *momentary subjective feeling*; rather it is intimately bound up with the *"fluency"* of experience, the capacity for experience to flow not only freely but *meaningfully* from one moment to the next so that the oncoming diversity maintains a *narrative coherency*. Not only must this quality of "satisfaction" endure over a *long period of time* (a lifetime, perhaps, in the case of a "world hypothesis"), but it relies upon establishing an informed and cooperative relationship with nature and one's fellow beings. Satisfaction is nothing less than the manifestation of funded human meaning through action which embodies our own personalized, concrete understanding of appropriated possibilities. It is the meaning of one's life attained through creative struggle. In short, the rationality of "satisfaction" is a dramatic and narrative mode of understanding our own existence. It is this intertwining of possibility and actuality that allows the individual to emerge and persist through action.

It is another major misinterpretation of James to read him as a pure voluntarist, like Nietzsche, in which will acts by itself with no constraints. Though James's emphasis, as noted, is usually upon the impulsive and fluid aspect of reality, an emphasis most needed in the Victorian days of idealism's Absolute and materialism's mechanistic determinism, he does recognize natural and logical constraints. Even in his most widely read and popularly written book, *Pragmatism*, and in the most notorious chapter, "The Notion of Truth," we find James stating, "Between the coercions of the sensible order and those of the ideal order, our mind is wedged tightly. Our ideas must agree with realities, be such realities concrete or abstract, be they facts or be they principles, under penalty of endless inconsistency and frustration" (P, 101/96). When James argued for his "right to believe," he was not introducing a metaphysics of voluntaristic nihilism; what he was doing was exhibiting a definite ontological domain where genuine possibilities existed and were actualized or not because of our belief-affected actions. He was not saying that mere mental wishes, propositions held before the mind's eye, created reality. He was saying that our understanding of our possibilities for meaningful action and our aesthetic evaluation of them mattered. From my most trivial movements to my most momentous life decisions, my deeds actualize one of many possible worlds and genuinely write part of the story of the universe as such.

Thus, action from the Jamesian point of view is a vitalistic poetics; it is the struggle to live in light of a guiding ideal that acts as a projective structure for interpreting difference meaningfully, for shaping human life so that the universe resoundingly answers its genuine needs. The concrete individual stands in a creative relationship with the world, and the world is such that it lends itself to his creative action. While James's attention to the individual in this process is dominant, and surely in contrast with Peirce's emphasis upon the community, James recognizes that the moment of individual action must respond to the hard realities of the world and others. The challenge to the individual is to have wrought meaning successfully from the materials of life, which is to say, to grasp life in terms of its meaningful possibilities and act upon them. The meaningful continuity that results is realized most deeply as that aesthetic fluency of life that is the distinctive mark of rationality. In short, rationality is realized because of the heroic struggle of the creative and imaginative appropriation of the vital possibilities of the world.

III

For Peirce, imagination is crucial insofar as it represents the initial capacity of the mind to respond to an aesthetics of order that leads, ultimately through the community of inquiry, to shared, embodied, explanatory habits of interpretation. For James, the aesthetics of rationality is found in the significance of individual action whereby we can claim certain possibilities as ours and see our lives as genuine actualizations of an ideal.

These themes are expanded and deepened in Dewey's thought. Intelligence for Dewey is nothing less than the effort to see the actual in light of the possible and thereby to be responsive toward liberating ideals of conduct, which, in turn, give a fulfilling continuity, meaning, and coherency to action. In Dewey's thought, imagination is distinctly interpreted as moral imagination. But for Dewey *all* conduct is moral, so that the proper sphere of the moral imagination is life itself. The question for intelligence is to struggle toward an aesthetic ideal of human existence through the dramatic use of imagination. To be sure, imagination must be informed and educated. It cannot successfully operate without either information or structured habits of understanding. But all practical deliberation, according to Dewey, also operates by relying on a tacitly sensed horizon of experience that determines the sense-giving awareness of context essential for any particular action to have meaning. Thus the themes of dramatic imagination and aesthetic awareness are complimentary aspects of the same event.

Dewey's treatment of imagination is difficult to summarize. The topic appears ubiquitously in his writings, but nowhere does he offer a focused, sustained treatment. To elucidate his views thoroughly would involve a lengthy scholarly task. It must suffice here simply to sketch some dominant characteristics.

First, imagination emerges as an extension of activity; when an engaged habit governing overt action is impeded, the goal of the activity is transformed into a conscious ideal, not simply because action is frustrated but because consciousness is a reconstructive organ of action itself. The awareness of the intentional structure of the activity, in other words, functions to reorganize the blocked action so that it may complete itself successfully. As Dewey says, "This thought is not what is sometimes called thought, a pale, bloodless abstraction, but is charged with the urgent force of habit."[10] Intelligence blossoms forth in the passionate desire for objective, embodied completion. Imagination is thus a condition for any intelligent action.

It is to be noted also that imagination emerges as a thoroughly temporal or modally complex event: It arises *in* an ongoing activity already structured by the fundamental narrativity of any act (that of having a beginning, middle, and end); it also arises in consciousness as a *crisis* of that activity, carrying within itself the contradiction between what is and what ought to be; i.e., between actuality and possibility, necessity and contingency. The imaginative moment, which marks the birth of consciousness itself for Dewey, is pregnant with the range of all temporal

---

10. *Human Nature and Conduct* (*Middle Works*, 14 [Carbondale: Southern Illinois University Press, 1983]), 39.

moods springing from the structures of our active embodiment: perfect, imperfect, present, future, conditional, subjective, and imperative. Usually this problematic or tensive aspect of experience does not emerge fully articulated—when it does (as in ordinary, everyday "problem solving," such as: "Where did I leave my glasses?") we have a secondary instance. Originally the conflict is undergone in its full aesthetic force. We are stunned and confused; we "don't know what hit us." Intelligence begins to operate as a search to determine "what's going on" before it can secure the proper key to determine reconstructive activity.[11]

As projected completion of action, imagination seeks to understand the actual in light of the possible in a dramatic or experimental way. Possibilities are engaged as possibilities *of* a continued meaningful activity. This is also to say that they are alternative interpretations of activity. For pragmatists, the meaning of action is determined by futural teleology rather than a priori intent. Thus, the *meaning* of an activity which has been projected into the reconstructive movement of imagination is also at issue. Imagination must contend with the alternative possible meanings of the situation: Possibilities will present themselves not in a neutral light but as candidates for being the meaning of our actions. They stand as perspectives from which the possible values of the situation emerge—hence the distinctly "moral" significance of imagination for Dewey. Our capacity to view the present from a number of possible points of view offers the basis from which more fulfilling values may emerge and be implemented in reconstructive activity. By dramatically engaging these options in imagination, we can anticipate the meaning of the situation.

This is why Dewey argues that in moral deliberation ends as well as means come under consideration. It is not that we "choose" which end to pursue on the basis of some subjective "desire" that arbitrarily gives it "value" (the emotivist view that still haunts most contemporary moral theory, not to mention moral practice). Rather, it is that imagination allows the aesthetic nature of the ends it reveals to operate upon us as part of the environment—of the imaginatively extended environment. Dewey says, "The 'object' which then presents itself in thought as the goal of desire is that object *which, if it were present,* would secure a re-unification

---

11. This is the point of Dewey's pivotal article "The Reflex Arc Concept in Psychology."

of activity and the restoration of its on-going unity" (MW, 14:172). The end of action ceases merely to be the outcome and becomes instead a "pivot of action" integrated into the event and determining of its own outcome, the "end-in-view," which becomes the anticipated meaning of the action itself. Thus meaning becomes consciously embodied when action undergoes reconstruction through the art of imagination. The selected course does not simply stand on its own; it exists surrounded by a penumbra of other options, other possibilities, which have been rejected, "roads not taken."

This is why art is such a significant form of activity for Dewey. The artist strives to make each moment of the creation of his work a meaningful, selected option that contributes toward the meaning of the whole. A great work of art exhibits its "choices" in terms of being especially meaningful; other choices simply would not have done so well. A poet, for example, cannot place down just *any* word; it must be the *right* word. If that "rightness" does not show itself in the structure of the whole poem, the work of art does not have that inner coherence to generate in the reader a responsive sense of meaningful selection and continuity that is the basis for "an experience," the aesthetic value of the whole.

For imagination to operate, then, it must reveal the "extended environment" of a situation. That is to say, in order to understand a situation, we must not only grasp its actualities, but its possibilities. Those possibilities are ontologically part of the situation. In reflecting upon a situation, we are still *within* that situation; we cannot step outside of it except through the course of action. Our understanding of the situation as such, then, cannot be achieved by simply objectifying it and analyzing its structure, the way philosophers have traditionally undertaken the task of "proving" the existence and nature of the world, for example. To be in a situation—to be in the world—is a condition of understanding. The way understanding appropriates the situational nature of the world and itself must be through some kind of awareness that illuminates the horizonal context of our objective, focal concerns. Though this horizonal understanding is always present as a condition of any conscious thought or practical activity, it is usually tacit, according to Dewey. Nevertheless, when our imaginative and aesthetic experience becomes heightened, such as in encounters with works of art or any experience conducive to "an experience," this otherwise tacit but pervasive meaning-giving horizon becomes sensed *through* the engagement with the medium of the work or the world. Dewey points especially to aesthetic and religious experience as prime instances where this awareness becomes conscious. Dewey describes this pervasive horizon as the "pervasive quality" permeating our experience, either unconsciously or explicitly felt in varying degrees; in either case, it operates to be the underlying sense of continuity and meaning.[12] This aesthetic and imaginative mode of understanding is a precondition for any cognitive or analytic one. In one of his most significant essays, "Qualitative Thought," Dewey writes:

> There are paintings, buildings, novels, arguments in which an observer notes an inability of the author to sustain a unified attention throughout. The details fall to pieces; they are not distinctions of one subject-matter, because there is qualitative unity underlying them. Confusion and incoherence are always marks of lack of control by a single pervasive quality. The latter alone enables a person to keep track of what he is doing, saying, hearing, reading, in whatever explicitly appears. The underlying unity of qualitativeness regulates pertinence or relevancy and force of every distinction and relation; it guides selection and rejection and the manner of utilization of all explicit terms. This quality enables us to keep thinking about one problem without our having constantly to stop and ask ourselves what it is after all that we are thinking about. We are aware of it not by itself but as the background, the thread, and the directive clue in what we do expressly think of.[13]

As noted, Dewey is very sensitive to the moral implications of this idea: Only to the extent that deliberation functions within an imaginatively rich environment will its operations be responsive to the possibilities—the possible *meanings*—of the present. Not only is imaginatively impoverished intelligence only capable of apprehending a smaller number of possible courses for action, but the tacit dimension determining the context of conscious meaning is a narrower and more limiting horizon. It should be born in mind as well that this is not merely a private matter for Dewey. We only deliberate with ourselves because we have *deliberated with others*. The tacit horizon shared by a *community* limits the nature of any discussion and provides for the very possibility of communicating

---

12. See *Art as Experience* (*Later Works*, 10 [Carbondale: Southern Illinois University Press, 1987]), 197; 194 in the original and LW, 5 Capricorn editions.
13. LW, 5:247–48.

at all. Thus the problem of imagination is first and foremost a question of *social* intelligence, of cooperative creativity, so to speak. For Dewey, it was the essence of the liberal, democratic community that it incorporated this dynamic view of intelligence in its public institutions, especially in its schools. The democratic community for Dewey is the community that understands itself as creatively pursuing life as art. The problem of human liberation and freedom is a collective problem, having as much to do with our capacity to generate shared, social ideals that organize action toward the ends of human fulfillment as with our technical control over the physical medium of our natural environment.

IV

Such, then, is a brief sketch of the significance of imagination in the three major pragmatists. What does this indicate for a pragmatic theory of imagination? First, it obviously rejects the two dominant views of imagination in the philosophical literature: the Aristotelian and the Romantic. Whereas "imagination" usually functions in epistemologies as simply the psychological property of having images of absent or nonexistent objects, a view going back to Aristotle's account of *phantasia*, the Romantics, like Schelling and Coleridge, tend to treat imagination as a power of primary and unlimited creativity, acting above and beyond any discursively rational understanding. The pragmatic view offers a radically different outlook. Imagination is neither merely an extension of the passive capacity of sensation, subsumable under preestablished rational categorial structures, nor is it a purely intuitive source of novelty. It is a mode of action and as such seeks to organize experience so that it anticipates the world in a manner that is meaningful and satisfying. In more human terms, it is an essential and necessary element in our perpetual project of making sense of life.

The concept of action in pragmatism has been misinterpreted because its critics (as well as some of its less able defenders) fell prey to a limited version of behaviorism. As we have seen, action for Peirce, James, and Dewey always involved more than the mere reaction to stimulus; none could be said to hold a mechanistic theory of action or thought— indeed, everything these thinkers said would throw such a view into doubt. Second, although pragmatism was concerned with questions of truth and knowledge, these issues were always seen from a much broader standpoint than that of an epistemology of cognition. Even Peirce, by far the one who concentrated most on the problem of knowledge, translated "epistemology" into a social theory of inquiry primarily governed by abductive reasoning. Third, by its emphasis on the practical, pragmatism did not conversely imply a neglect or rejection of theory, for this would be to maintain just the dualism between theory and practice that was to be overcome. In other words, imaginative as well as rigorous conceptual interpretations were intrinsic requirements of action. Peirce, James, and Dewey all developed metaphysical philosophies in recognition of this need. Finally, in its analysis of action, pragmatism stands at once as an ontology of human experience in which the historical and cultural matrix of actuality as well as the future as an immanent constitutive presence of possibility are significant in understanding. This involves the twofold need of a hermeneutic of historical experience as well as a creatively critical appropriation of the present in light of the future.

As far as the first requirement goes, the problem of reductionistic behaviorism, now promoted under the name of "neurophilosophy," can be met with an emergentistic and transactional view of human nature. While biological and organic conditions provide the material for human meaning, the content of meaning in the human world can never be translated into stimulus-response associations or, as the latest trend would have it, to neurological synapses. Neurons are not persons although persons have neurons. Here the emphasis must be on viewing nature itself as a creative process in which novel types of order emerge from more basic and elementary conditions but which display features not exhibited by the more basic, constitutive elements. As Dewey himself observed, this is only good empiricism: Nature does seem to produce elements from energy, life from elements, and consciousness from life. There is no more intelligibility in reducing human consciousness to an isolated biological event than there is in explaining the significance of the Great Pyramid of Khufu solely in terms of how many tons of limestone were moved to build it.

To meet the second requirement, an emphasis must be put on the role of the noncognitive aspect of human meaning. Experience, as Dewey repeatedly insisted, is not even *primarily* an affair of knowing. While this cuts against the grain of most contemporary Anglo-American philosophy, two important developments stand as possible exceptions. First, the later work of John Searle has acknowledged the significance of a large noncognitive "Background" of practical experience that extends beyond the contextual "Network" of intentional states implied in any overt intentional state. While Searle denies that the "Background" is part of meaning, he recognizes its indispensability:

> The Network shades off into a Background of capacities (including various skills, abilities, preintentional assumptions and presuppositions, stances, and non-representational attitudes). The Background is not on the *periphery* of Intentionality but *permeates* the entire Network of Intentional states; since without the Background the states could not function, they could not determine the conditions of satisfaction.[14]

Aside from Searle's denial that this Background has meaning, this bears a remarkable similarity to Dewey's notion of the articulated web of habits that constitute the "pervasive quality" that is immanent in any conscious experience.

More important, however, and far more pragmatic in tone and outlook, is Mark Johnson's *The Body in the Mind*. Whereas Searle simply acknowledges the Background, Johnson insightfully explores some of the primary structures that constitute it and which arise from the precognitive structures of our embodiment. Johnson tackles head-on most of the analytic assumptions about the primacy of cognition and argues that intelligence is more an affair of the adaptive, imaginative organization of experience by virtue of which it gets intelligibility as well as fluency. Thinking is fundamentally metaphorical, argues Johnson, and this places the issue of imaginative structures (or "image schemata") as central for any view of rationality. "Without imagination," says Johnson, "nothing in the world could be meaningful. Without imagination, we could never reason toward knowledge of reality."[15]

Imagination for Johnson is embodied. By this he means that there are dynamic patterns rooted in the activity of the living body by means of which we preconceptually understand the world. These bodily structures, in turn, are metaphorically elaborated to provide the basis for conscious and conceptual meaning. It is because of these schemata that

---

14. *Intentionality* (Cambridge: Cambridge University Press, 1983), 151. Quoted in Johnson, *The Body in the Mind*, 188.
15. *The Body in the Mind* (Chicago: University of Chicago Press, 1987), ix. Cited in text as BM.

we "understand" or "have a world" at all, argues Johnson (BM, 102). In a very Deweyan manner, Johnson presents a view that opposes any dualism between imagination and conception; imagination, the human effort to organize experience and mediate the transition from past to future, from old to new, is an integral part of our ordinary life, though it is capable of great refinement and conscious development, as we see both in the sciences and the arts.

To take up the final two points very briefly: I think it is obvious now why the pragmatic theory of "practice" or "action" must stand for a synoptic theory of experience in which imagination and speculation are regarded as essential moments of action; otherwise we will be condemned to divorce theory from practice and to accept a narrow, truncated, and unfruitful view of action at that. Nor can pragmatism afford to be ahistorical; experience is temporal and social, which is to say historical and cultural. Whereas initial efforts in developing this dimension of pragmatism were undertaken by John Herman Randall, Jr., this is still largely an unfulfilled agenda. A philosophy of history and of historical consciousness, a philosophy of culture in all its diversity, is the most pressing demand for pragmatic theory. Such a theory alone will save us from perennial attacks by neoconservatives who oppose any historicist as well as any functionalistic view of intelligence and education. Human beings seek to live lives of meaning and value by virtue of sharing cultural, symbolic universes that determine the significance of action. "Action," whatever else it may mean, must include the historical experience of cultures as well as those metaphorical and symbolic schemata that constitute those contexts of interpretation by means of which we apprehend aesthetic and imaginative patterns of fulfillment for human life. These patterns allow us to define and encounter problems as well as to evade, reinterpret, or resolve them as best we can. If we are to explore the possibilities of the present for the ends of human liberation, we must come to grips with the powerful and inertial force of the interpretive habits that constitute the human world of culture and give life and breath to every conscious, cognitive symbol we use.

Perhaps more important than "cognition" is the idea of "understanding." Once again, Johnson provides a valuable discussion:

> [U]nderstanding is not only a matter of reflection, using finitary propositions, on some preexistent, already determinate experience.

Rather, *understanding is the way we "have a world," the way we experience our world as a comprehensible reality.* Such understanding, therefore, involves *our whole being*—our bodily capacities and skills, our values, our moods and attitudes, our entire cultural tradition, the way we are bound up with a linguistic community, our aesthetic sensibilities, and so forth. In short, our understanding *is* our mode of "being in the world.". . . Our most abstract reflective acts of understanding (which may involve grasping of finitary propositions) are simply an extension of our understanding in this more basic sense of "having a world." (BM, 102)

The similarity between this view and Dewey's is quite striking, I believe. Johnson's only problem lies in establishing some connection between the prereflective intelligence of the lived body and the blossoming of meaning in the inter-subjective social realm. Here, I think, the pragmatists' emphasis on the emergence of meaning in shared activity would be useful.

Not only is an enriched conception of "action" vital for any robust development of the pragmatic tradition, but it looks toward two other important philosophical developments. Alasdair MacIntyre's appeal to the concept of "narrative" as a broader and more fundamental category than the old cognitivist idea of "explanation" and to the legitimizing function of cultural traditions has far-ranging implications for any historicist contextualism. Martha Nussbaum's defense of an Aristotelian idea of "practical wisdom" as the outgrowth of an emotionally rich experience combined with a morally educated imagination, vitally nurtured by reason in action, has a great deal of affinity with Dewey's idea of intelligence. What both these thinkers lack, however, is the emphasis on the future as the reconstructive field of action. MacIntyre looks back wistfully to a polis that never was; Nussbaum seems stymied by the inherent value of emotional sympathy with opposing moral claims. Here, I believe, Dewey has something to teach them. But these are themes to be explored some other time.

In conclusion, I have simply tried to explore three main points. First, in the major pragmatists, action involves modes that are aesthetic, imaginative, creative, and noncognitive. We cannot look to psychological reductionisms, such as behaviorism, or utilitarian theories of practicality to clarify the meaning of action, for those will only obscure it through narrowness. Rather, we can look to recent work exploring the image-schematic structures at work in our preconscious bodily organization of experience, such as Johnson's *The Body in the Mind*. This still leaves as unfulfilled what is perhaps the most significant theme for a complete pragmatic theory of action, a treatment of historical and cultural experience.

SEVEN

JOHN DEWEY AND THE MORAL IMAGINATION

Beyond Putnam and Rorty toward an Ethics of Meaning

The last decades have witnessed an important series of changes in Anglo-American philosophy, not least of which has been the revival of an interest in the classical phase of American pragmatism. The work of the pragmatists seems once again to speak to the current philosophical dilemmas. Former "analytic philosophers" like the late Richard Rorty, Joseph Margolis, and Hilary Putnam came to embrace some form of neopragmatism. By and large, however, this revival has come in the domain of epistemology and the debate on realism. I would like to show here how a reappraisal of an aspect of pragmatic moral theory may have importance in a relatively promising but still undeveloped topic in contemporary ethics, the topic of "moral imagination" as a key feature of ethical reasoning and behavior.

The impact of Alasdair MacIntyre's *After Virtue* and Martha Nussbaum's *The Fragility of Goodness* in the 1980s indicated that the dominant assumptions of modern ethical theory were undergoing critique. Both MacIntyre and Nussbaum sought to reintroduce the classical

Aristotelian concepts of "character," "happiness," and "virtue," though in very different ways. MacIntyre (in *After Virtue*, at least) argued for the need of a general "narrative" view of action to reestablish the idea of character (since he then found Aristotelian teleology impossible to accept). The proper issue for moral philosophy should not be judging the moral value of some kind of *act* per se, but seeing any act, as Aristotle did, as an expression of the more fundamental dispositions of the agent's *character*, which MacIntyre there construed as an ongoing narrative that determines the meaning of specific actions.[1] Nussbaum's *The Fragility of Goodness* stressed the tragic contingency of conduct, the artistic nature of ethical judgment, and the importance of feeling as crucial in our very ability to understand moral situations, not to mention their importance as essential features of our moral character and actions.[2] Both of these thinkers advocated a reconstructed version of Aristotelianism without really coming to grips with the issues any such position must face in a Darwinian view of nature. MacIntyre, having converted to Catholicism, went on to advocate Thomism and took a view of the historical development of philosophical traditions as mutually unintelligible; Nussbaum turned more to application of her theory to literature and to social issues rather than explore what a theory of human teleology might mean today.[3] One of the advantages of the Deweyan view of ethical theory lies, I believe, in successfully accommodating the very features which they wish to salvage while also directly appropriating an evolutionary view of nature, compatible with Darwinism broadly conceived.

Thus, after summarizing the aporias in the modernist theory of ethics, I will examine the idea of a moral imagination in two "postmodern"

1. Alasdair MacIntyre, *After Virtue*, 3rd ed. (Notre Dame, IN: University of Notre Dame Press, 2007). See especially chapter 15, "The Virtues, the Unity of a Human Life and Tradition." The crisis of contemporary moral theory is the theme of Bernard Williams's *Ethics and the Limits of Philosophy* (Cambridge, MA: Harvard University Press, 1985).

2. Martha Nussbaum, *The Fragility of Goodness* (Cambridge: Cambridge University Press, 1986). See especially chapter 1, "Luck and Ethics."

3. See their subsequent studies: Alasdair MacIntyre, *Whose Justice, Which Rationality?* (Notre Dame, IN: University of Notre Dame Press, 1989), and Martha Nussbaum, *Love's Knowledge* (New York: Oxford University Press, 1990). Nussbaum has explored the possibility of a moderate theory of human essence in "Non-Relative Virtues: An Aristotelian Approach," *Midwest Studies in Philosophy*, vol. 13 (1988). She lists eight common features of the human condition: mortality, the body, pleasure and pain, cognitive capability, practical reason, early infant development, affiliation (or a sense of fellowship) and humor. But even so, she has not addressed the metaphysical arguments a theory of essence must face with respect to Darwinism and evolutionism.

discussions by Hilary Putnam and Richard Rorty. Both of their accounts are inadequate as they stand and would benefit from a more robust form of Deweyan pragmatism. After describing how Dewey's own theory incorporates the theme of a moral imagination in a way that surpasses theirs, I will briefly indicate how it goes on to address the two issues which MacIntyre and Nussbaum have stressed, namely, the idea of a narrative view of character and the importance of the affective-aesthetic dimension of moral perception and action. In this way I wish to indicate Dewey's contribution to the ongoing debate in what has come to be known as "virtue ethics."

The Origin of the Problem in the Modern Era

I argued in the previous chapter that the pragmatic tradition represents an important development of the theory of imagination in Western philosophy.[4] The two dominant views of imagination were either that of classical philosophy, which saw it as the faculty of producing copies of sensible objects (really a power of "imaging"), or the romantic view of it as an irrational, arbitrary, creative power capable of generating entirely new objects, concepts, or symbols. The transitional figure, of course, is Kant, who began by regarding imagination as a somewhat mysterious but necessary synthetic power in linking concepts to percepts and ended by making it a power to modify, perhaps create, concepts.[5] While thinkers in the both the classical and modern traditions, like Plato and Descartes, saw imagination as a source of error or, like Aristotle, at best as a lower, necessary condition of thought, the romantics and their inheritors made it the source of creativity, transcending discursive reason as well as convention for insight into a "transcendental" reality.

Pragmatism, by contrast, treated imagination as the capacity to understand the actual in light of the possible. It was thus intrinsically linked to the view of experience and action as temporally ongoing, transformative events. Imagination was a *creative* exploration of *structures* inherited from past experience which thereby allowed the future as a horizon of

4. See "Pragmatic Imagination," chapter 6 in this volume. See also the thematically related essay "The Human Eros," chapter 5 in this volume.

5. See Mark Johnson's fine discussion of this in his *The Body in the Mind* (Chicago: University of Chicago Press, 1987), ch. 6, "Toward a Theory of Imagination."

possible actions, and so of possible meanings, to guide and interpret the present. Imagination was manifest as the *growth* and *continuity* of meaning. It was neither mere copying nor radical creation *ex nihilo*; it was the transformation or reconstruction of experience in a changing world that nevertheless admitted of general stable features. As a phase of action, imagination was an essential feature of environmentally engaged rationality or "intelligence," as Dewey termed it. Needless to say, this had immense consequences for any theory of "knowledge." In effect, it changed the "theory of knowing" into a "theory of learning." It also had fundamental influence on what would constitute moral reasoning and the aims of ethical theory.[6]

The classical views of imagination and reason naturally affected these last topics. Moral action was a *mimēsis*, a successful enactment, of a general *type* of good—this much Plato and Aristotle had in common. For Plato (as Diotima says in the *Symposium*), virtue lies in the ability of mortals to "give birth" to copies of Beauty-Itself; the moral life is the *mimēsis* of this Form of Forms, governed by the degree of our recollection of it. (Hence, the propriety of Alcibiades' eulogy of Socrates' virtuous *life* after Socrates' speech on the *theory* of virtue.) Aristotle saw virtue as the successful realization of the natural type endorsed by the species; wherever happiness was to be found, it was always *human* happiness, individually exhibiting the universal features found everywhere. At times Plato tended toward seeing moral reasoning as aiming toward a quasi-mathematical exactitude, at least as a purely theoretical science then to be applied to specific circumstances, while Aristotle saw it more as a deliberative skill relying on well-trained habits developed from healthy natural dispositions. But both men saw moral reason as the means of organizing the whole *psychē* so that it performed its appointed task, its *ergon*, well. Virtue (*aretē*) was the human being "doing well" (*euprattein*), an activity which *completed* or *perfected* the individual as much as possible.

---

6. In *Art as Experience*, Dewey says, "Only imagination elicits the possibilities that are interwoven within the texture of the actual" (LW, 10:348; hereafter cited in text as LW, 10). Elsewhere, he describes it as the "spontaneous carrying power" ideas possess (LW, 6:115–16). It is "testing in thought" (LW, 8:193). His most important discussion is in *Human Nature and Conduct*, where it is described as "dramatic rehearsal" for possible environments (MW, 14:132–40). In *The Quest for Certainty* and *A Common Faith* he stresses imagination as the origin of unifying ideals of conduct (see LW, 4:239–45 and LW, 9:29–36).

Any given action was ethically significant in terms of the perfection of character it revealed as its origin and cause.

The modern era, having dispensed with Aristotelian teleology, had to rethink ethics almost from the ground up. A mechanistic view of nature looked toward universal, abstract "laws" governing each event at every moment; the question was to find which law any given phenomenon exemplified. With Bacon, the idea of moral action itself became that of applied physics, a technology of human happiness. His own *New Atlantis* hints at this futuristic ideal, a utopia of materialistic acquisition, but the applications of the mechanistic model to ethics and politics was carried out most dramatically in Thomas Hobbes's *Leviathan*. The scientific revolution led eventually to a position radically different from that of classical ethical theory, a position which constitutes the underlying paradigm for subsequent theories. That paradigm is of discrete, individual events obeying absolute, universal laws. Whatever the differences, deontological and utilitarian theories have in common the emphasis upon establishing universal moral *principles* and their application to specific *instances*. Like his scientific counterpart, the moral theorist sought the "universal law," natural or nonnatural, which ought to be exemplified in any moral act to be counted as good. Likewise there was now an emphasis upon the moral value of the isolated *act as such*, considered by itself without any reference to the agent's character or "*psychē*." A moral life would be simply the succession of events obeying a universal law; the whole question of the importance of "moral feeling" would be dismissed as an irrelevant "psychological question." (The school of "moral sense" was, in its own way, an acceptance of the model while rejecting the existence of universal laws.)

Aristotle, for example, would have seen an all-important distinction between one individual who felt genuine empathy for a child he had rescued from drowning and one who may have done the same deed for the sake of duty alone in spite of a loathing for children; Kant would have admired the latter as illustrating the pure force of the categorical imperative without the possibly confusing motives of sympathy or personal happiness being implicated; Bentham would find the pleasure experienced by rescuer and child as mere factors in the hedonistic equation. For Aristotle, the act would be important because it revealed the true good-hearted courage and social feeling of the agent's character; this is one reason why, he says, one cannot really determine happiness, much less the moral meaning of any given act, without seeing it in terms of the *life* of a human being. For Kant or for Bentham, the value of the act lies solely in terms of its exemplification of the rule, its conformity either to the categorical imperative or the greatest happiness principle.

For the utilitarian and the deontologist, practical reason must simply correctly determine the proper rule for action and apply it whenever the opportunity presents itself. There is no particular continuity to the life of a human being, considered from the moral point of view; it is a series of independent actions that reveal the same rule consistently applied or misapplied or not applied at all. There is nothing for the imagination as such to do. Indeed the modernist suspicion of imagination as confusing the senses and reason seems at work here as strongly as anywhere. If it is introduced, it is merely to assist the ends of utilitarian calculation or rational intuitionism. Aristotle, it must be noted, doesn't have much to say about it either, but he does stress the need for practical experience and education of desire in the development of a virtuous character and finds in works of literature a significant mode of moral education precisely because in them we grasp the meanings of human life through the types of characters portrayed.

What is the problem with the rule-oriented approach? It doesn't really allow us to grasp the *character* of the moral agent, at least in any sense more profound than his or her "reasoning" and motivations at any given time. MacIntyre has even argued that it is impossible to assess the intent of any act by considering it in isolation from its context, which is to say, the agent's life narrative. But there is a deeper problem lying with the very attempt to ground judgments upon rules. How do we really decide whether an act falls under a rule or not? Either this procedure is itself guided by a rule, in which case an infinite regress opens before us, or it is not, in which case we are face-to-face with some primary intuition that we have applied the rule correctly. It becomes especially problematic when one is confronted with a *new* situation that is radically different from one's previous experience. This, of course, is one of the most common features in ethical dilemmas. But a deontologist like Alan Donagan can only speak of "unformalized analytical reasoning" supported by a set of core cultural beliefs understood in themselves, at least those core cultural beliefs of the Judeo-Christian tradition, which, he thinks, comes close to getting the concept of morality right.

Legal theorist Steven Winter uses as an example the debate over whether judges, in deciding court cases, merely apply or actually interpret the law. The more the "original intent" literalists in this debate argue, the clearer it becomes, I think, that deciding *any* case must count as an act of interpretation and therefore of modifying the meaning of the law, even if only by rendering a general law more determinate. "Vehicles" are forbidden in certain parks. But should skateboards, items not in existence when the park laws were written, count as "vehicles"? Is using a skateboard in a mall like driving your car on a sidewalk? Here I think most of us agree that the judge tries to use his or her understanding of the various laws about vehicles and the needs of personal freedom to determine a situation that had not been anticipated prior to the invention of the skateboard. In our courts, it should be noted, judges working in a common-law tradition are interested not merely in applying rules but also in establishing a working continuity with previous decisions and the life of the culture itself and know that when they decide the case they have established the basis for precedent. They are, I would say, trying to think in those temporal, historical terms that are so necessary for the concept of character in moral thinking. They are imaginatively extending the meaning of the law in light of resolving a problem in which a number of old values and new have come into conflict.[7]

Moral Imagination in Putnam and Rorty

The problem with the conception of morality as merely getting the rules and instances right indicates, then, that perhaps the role of imagination is worth investigation. With the exception of Dewey there is little or no mention of imagination in the role of moral thinking until quite recently. We have a brief but interesting acknowledgment of the importance of imagination in R. M. Hare's *Freedom and Reason*, which takes an important step beyond Hume's ethics of sentiment. Unfortunately, as soon as Hare acknowledges imagination he qualifies it so much as to make it negligible. He notes that imagination assists us in correctly applying the

---

7. See Alan Donagan, *The Theory of Morality* (Chicago: University of Chicago Press, 1977) and Steven Winter, "Transcendental Nonsense, Metaphoric Reasoning and the Cognitive Stakes for Law," *University of Pennsylvania Law Review* 137, no. 4 (1989): 1105–1237.

universalizability principle, because to do so we have to imagine ourselves in the situation under dispute from a number of different perspectives; this helps us reveal any latent contradictions in our assent to the
principle.[8] With the utilitarian principle in mind, to act so as to realize
happiness in others, I must try to imagine what makes them happy; in
other words, I must imagine myself *to be* them, and not merely imagine
myself, with my own likes and dislikes, in their places (FR, 126–27).
Finally, Hare argues that imagination serves the cause of liberalism
against that of fanaticism insofar as literature educates the socially important sympathies of the public. Of course, the fanatic can use works of
imagination, too. Thus, says Hare, fiction is ultimately bound by truth
conditions that only experience can reveal. In a poignant passage, Hare
(who had been a prisoner of the Japanese in World War II) says the
following:

> For story-books, though they help to stimulate our imagination, do
> not by themselves help us very much, to separate what is really likely
> to happen from what is not, nor to assess the probable frequency of its
> occurrence. For this, some experience of actual moral perplexities,
> and of actual consequences of certain moral choices, is a necessity.
> A few months spent as a coolie building the Burma railway is worth
> more to one's moral thinking than the reading of a great many novels
> or even factual reports about underdeveloped countries. (FR, 183)

If we merely limit imagination to works of fiction, Hare's appeal to real
experience is quite sound. But he has already indicated that part of
the value of experience lies in its imaginative use in our reflection upon
present problems. Even so, Hare sees imagination as little more than a
subjective faculty providing a supplementary "sentimental education,"
which merely helps us apply rules with greater finesse. Hare does not say
how this is possible.

In *The Many Faces of Realism*, Hilary Putnam devotes his third Carus
lecture to "Equality and Our Moral Image of the World." Here he rejects
the formal, a priori mode of Kantian ethics, yet wants to preserve what it
secured, the fundamental values of liberty, autonomy and respect for persons. Lacking any foundational principles like the categorical imperative

---

8. R. M. Hare, *Freedom and Reason* (New York: Oxford University Press, 1963). Hereafter cited in
text as FR.

or the idea of rational persons, he appeals to the power of "moral images." Putnam finds, for example, Kant's arguments against fanaticism interesting and successful in a way Kant did not intend:

> My claim, then, is that Kant is doing what he would have called "philosophical anthropology," or providing what might be called a moral image of the world. He is not simply providing arguments for the third formulation of the Categorical Imperative . . . he is also, and most importantly, providing a moral image of the world which inspires these, and without which they don't make sense. A moral image, in the sense in which I am using the term, is not a declaration that this or that is a virtue, or that this or that is what one ought to do; it is rather a picture of how our virtues and ideals hang together with one another and of what they have to do with the position we are in. It may be as vague as the notions of "sisterhood and brotherhood"; indeed, millions of human beings have found in those metaphors moral images that could organize their moral lives—and this notwithstanding the enormous problem of interpreting them and of deciding what it could possibly mean to make them *effective*. Now moral philosophers generally prefer to talk about virtues or about (specific) duties, rights, and so on, rather than about moral images of the world. There are obvious reasons for doing this; nevertheless I think it is a mistake. . . . What we require in moral philosophy is, first and foremost, a moral image of the world, or rather . . . a number of complementary moral images of the world.[9]

I quote this remarkable paragraph at length because it not only marks an extraordinary advance from Hare's view, but because Putnam has had virtually nothing else to say about what a "moral image" is or how it works.[10] Let us analyze what at least he does say. First, a moral image is *an image of a world*, not a sentimental identification with some other individual in a particular situation. Second, he claims that without such images our rational arguments *don't make sense*. Imagination is clearly

---

9. Hilary Putnam, *The Many Faces of Realism* (Chicago: Open Court, 1987), 51–52.

10. Since this essay was written, Putnam has more openly embraced pragmatism, especially Dewey's version of it, and has written more about issues in moral philosophy from that point of view, without, to my knowledge, returning to the question of the imagination and the role of the moral image in ethical thinking. See *Ethics without Ontology* (Cambridge, MA: Harvard University Press, 2004) and *The Collapse of the Fact/Value Dichotomy* (Cambridge, MA: Harvard University Press, 2002).

something more than fine-tuning for rationality here. Third, Putnam states that such *images organize our moral lives*, however vague they may be by rational standards. They have immense pragmatic value for guiding and illuminating human conduct. Finally, he claims that in moral theory we need *several complementary images*. Moral thinking operates within a pluralistic context rather than through a unifocal theoretical stare.

We have to think for ourselves, says Putnam, about what-it-is-to-be-human without having a preordained end, a fixed human essence limiting that freedom, and the way we do this is by imaginatively exploring desirable and undesirable possibilities. For example, Putnam uses Huxley's *Brave New World* to illustrate by description of a moral image of the world what is intrinsically wrong with the utilitarian project. This shows us, he says, what is wrong with such an outlook far more effectively than any rational argument. Once it has been described concretely enough, we just wouldn't desire that kind of world. This is not simply the old emotivist view that somehow irrational desires have been manipulated by irrational images. Putnam's point is that the moral image is the way we organize our *rational* responses to the claim of some principle. The novel gives us a *world* whose meaning of what-it-is-to-be-human is clear; on seeing that world imaginatively, utilitarian arguments *don't make sense*; this image cannot effectively *organize* our lives. It is a one-dimensional, not a *pluralistic*, image.

I wish Putnam had said more here, especially about *how* moral images organize our world and guide rationality in spite of their vagueness, but he has not. If I understand the thrust of his point, the problem of human values is essentially aesthetic and imaginative, especially insofar as we are morally pluralistic creatures. Unlike Hare, Putnam sees the moral imagination playing a vital role in our thinking as well as acting, though he leaves us simply with this tantalizing fragment.

The late Richard Rorty, however, has said a good deal more in *Contingency, Irony and Solidarity*. Rorty's main concern in this work is to persuade us that there is not and cannot be a reconciliation in the conflict between our private desire for self-creation and our public sense of moral duty, though this has been the aim of all "moral metaphysicians" from Plato on. Some writers, like Habermas and Dewey (to use Rorty's examples), try to show us the values of solidarity; others, like Kierkegaard and Nietzsche, show us what the value of "private perfection" or "a self-created, autonomous human life" can be.[11] Since these two aims cannot be conjoined by theory discovering a rock-bottom human essence, "The closest we will come to joining these two quests is to see the aim of a just and free society as letting its citizens be as privatistic, 'irrationalist,' and aestheticist as they please and as long as they do it on their own time—causing no harm to others and using no resources needed by those less advantaged" (CIS, xiv). John Stuart Mill couldn't have put it better: Reconcile conflicting desires by reconciling them so they do not conflict!

Rorty wishes to present us with his moral image of liberal society, an ironist utopia that realizes the incommensurability of values, admits its own historical contingency, and yet sticks to the guns of its ideals. Ever since Hegel (and in spite of what Hegel himself said), historicism has cast doubt upon the claim that there is a deep core to the self that is not through and through a product of the weavings and contingencies of history. Thus Hegel (who saw history as the necessary unfolding of the Absolute), for Rorty, is *malgré lui* the first great ironist: "I use 'ironist' to name the sort of person who faces up to the contingency of his or her most central beliefs and desires. . . . Liberal ironists are people who include among their ungroundable desires their own hope that suffering will be diminished, that the humiliation of human beings by other human beings may cease" (CIS, xv).

Since appeals to principles and arguments have no function in this brave new world, the role of imagination acquires a dimension previously unknown in Anglo-American moral theory:

> In my utopia, human solidarity would be seen not as a fact to be recognized by clearing away "prejudice" or burrowing down to previously hidden depths but, rather, as a goal to be achieved. It is to be achieved not by inquiry but by imagination, the imaginative ability to see strange people as fellow sufferers. Solidarity is not discovered by reflection, but created. It is created by increasing our sensitivity to the particular details of the pain and humiliation of other, unfamiliar sorts of people. Such increased sensitivity makes it more difficult to marginalize people different from ourselves by thinking, "They do not feel it as *we* would," or "There must always be suffering, so why

---

11. Richard Rorty, *Contingency, Irony, and Solidarity* (Cambridge: Cambridge University Press, 1989). Hereafter cited in text as CIS.

not let *them* suffer?" This process of coming to see other human beings as "one of us" rather than as "them" is a matter of detailed description of what unfamiliar people are like and of redescription of what we ourselves are like. (CIS, xvi)

This is why public works of imagination are so important—Rorty includes here TV, movies, the comic book and docudrama, and especially literature. In his liberal utopia, Rorty urges that we move toward narrative and away from "Truth," seeing our culture as simply shifting webs of vocabularies in transition, forever open to alternative descriptions and redescriptions.

It is impossible, says Rorty, to produce a reason that will actually make us *care about,* much less understand or respect, another person. The important thing for the liberal ironist is to *notice* suffering when it occurs. To be capable of doing this, one needs a trained, sensitive imagination: "For the liberal ironist, skill at imaginative identification does the work that the liberal metaphysician would like to have done by a specifically moral motivation"; the liberal ironist wants "to increase our skill at recognizing and describing the different sorts of little things around which individuals or communities center their fantasies and their lives" (CIS, 93). I think Rorty is right here, for many—most—societies provide themselves with moral images which *prevent* ordinary, well-intentioned *good* people from noticing suffering in others. The movie *Driving Miss Daisy* was filled with poignant examples of the petty humiliations endured by a good man from a good woman, deriving simply from the unnoticed "moral givens" of their society, which encumbered any possibility for genuine friendship between blacks and whites. The Bhagavad Gita offers an elaborate justification for why the caste system is to be respected and endured—to change it would be to go against the laws of karma. The dominant moral images of women in most societies are another instance; by a tacit acceptance of a "natural order" a dominant sex is prevented thereby from even *noticing* injustice in social empowerment and inequality of opportunity. A liberal society, then, would stress training in our ability to notice such things, the petty as well as the great.

Imagination here is absolutely central to the Rortian project. Yet in a way it is a retreat from Putnam's position back toward Hare's idea of a "sentimental education," except since there are no principles, a sentimental education is all one has. For Putnam, the moral image organizes our world and gives us a basis for reasoning. The major function of the imagination, for Rorty, is to avoid hurting others, especially by humiliating them. Rorty has projected in his utopia a world in which the major moral problem is how my private aesthetic project may somehow interfere with yours. I do think that Rorty has hit upon an important insight in his insistence that to understand the world of other people, especially people who are very different from us, the imagination has tools available that reason alone lacks. The key for his society to work is an imaginative education that allows one to grasp different contexts and enter into the standpoint of the other. But there is really nothing more; dialogue aiming at solving problems with the other is not part of Rorty's utopia, simply continuing conversation and the avoidance of humiliation. Nor does Rorty have anything to say about Hare's quiet observation that the enemy of peaceful liberalism can use imagination, too. The Nazis, the Ku Klux Klan, and others have vividly trained people, especially children, to hate individuals they previously would not have noticed or known.

Obviously a great deal hangs upon Rorty's concept of language, redescription, and imagination. The first part of *Contingency, Irony, and Solidarity* is devoted to these topics, and I cannot do more than briefly state that his conception of change in language is that of a radical, irrational shift. The language in place is constituted by a fixed vocabulary; against this the "radical poet" or "utopian revolutionary" introduces strong poetic, metaphoric shifts. Initially these are pure ruptures in the field of meaning. Rorty here sides with Davidson's view of the meaninglessness of metaphoric shift. To give Rorty's discussion:

> Davidson puts this point by saying that one should not think of metaphorical expressions as having meanings distinct from their literal ones. To have a meaning is to have a place in the language game. Metaphors, by definition, do not. Davidson denies, in his words, "the thesis that associated with a metaphor is a cognitive content that its author wishes to convey and that the interpreter must grasp if he is to get the message." In his view, tossing a metaphor into a conversation is like suddenly breaking off the conversation long enough to make a face, or pulling a photograph out of your pocket and displaying it, or pointing at a feature of the surroundings, or slapping your interlocutor's face, or kissing him. Tossing a metaphor into a text is like using italics, or illustrations or odd punctuation or formats. (CIS, 18)

Everything Rorty says here about the irrationality of metaphors applies to what he says about imagination. If, by definition, meaning and rationality are identified with *fixed* habits in place, anything new is meaningless, until, of course, it becomes a fixed habit and ceases, by definition, to be new, and so either imaginative or metaphorical. Rorty's view, like Hare's, reflects the heritage of positivism's radical dualism between cognitive meaning and emotive meaninglessness, only Rorty has given up the cognitive side of the doctrine, leaving him with little but emotivism. He recognizes the need for some kind of viable, humane social order, but he has no way of explaining how a moral imagination is educated or how it works. Creativity is as mysterious for him as for the romantics; the creative shifts in language can only be absurd entrances into the fixed mechanism of routine speech habits. When did an absurdism redirect thinking or enlarge vision or help direct action or reevaluate a previously cherished value? Ironically, Rorty's postmodernism plays upon the very conceptual notions introduced by modernism.[12]

But what if thinking were a transitional activity rather than an operation of merely applying rule to case? What if imagination establishes continuity with existing habits, revealing their capacities to grow meaningfully and give fulfillment and direction to them? This sort of irrationalism would collapse. Intelligence would be an art of seeing the actual in light of the possible and of discerning possibilities by developing dynamic structures in experience. It would be imaginative, and imagination would be primarily exhibited in the dynamics of social communication and cultural expression rather than in a private, internal subjectivity. This of course is exactly what Dewey's theory of experience offers.

Dewey's Theory of Moral Imagination

In this section I wish to indicate some of the ways in which Dewey thought that imagination was absolutely central to the problem of moral intelligence. I might as well say "the problem of intelligence" because Dewey thought that all conduct was "moral" and that drawing a sharp distinction

---

12. See my criticisms in "The Creative Community and the Aesthetics of Human Existence," in *Frontiers in American Philosophy II*, ed. Robert Burch (College Station: Texas A & M, 1993). A more extensive critique can be found in Mark Johnson, "Good Rorty, Bad Rorty," unpublished manuscript.

between moral and prudential reasoning was one of the underlying problems in contemporary theory. For Dewey, human beings are cultural creatures caught up in a dynamic interplay with their organic surroundings and their communicative systems. These latter are the cultural symbols and habits that are passed on and developed from generation to generation and so radically transform human existence. It is the human capacity to learn rather than know which so impressed Dewey. Furthermore, the quest for knowledge and for cognitive certainty is not, in his view, the ultimate agenda for human living. We act in order to realize on a deeper, aesthetic level a sense of meaning and value in our very existence. Knowledge may play a crucial role in this, but in the last analysis, for Dewey, we are creatures seeking a kind of dynamic, embodied fulfillment that goes far beyond generating mere propositional attitudes and other abstractive cognitive needs. As active beings, we are in constant touch with the *possibilities* of our situations. Indeed, this is Dewey's definition of intelligence: to see the actual in light of the possible. This is also his definition of imagination. Imagination is rooted in the organic embodiment of our existence and flowers in our highest consciously articulate moments.

This was why action was such a fundamental issue for the pragmatists. It was not that they wished to glorify utilitarian "practical" activity over against theory; rather, it was that through understanding action as a temporally complex event—an event with actualized past and possible future interweaving in the transitional point of the present, that one managed to show the *integration* of theory and practice in the process of existence itself. In this analysis, the role of imagination becomes pivotal, for it is a phase of activity—that phase in which possible activities are envisaged in relation to our own situations, thereby amplifying the meaning of the present and creating the context from which present values may be criticized, thus liberating the course of action in itself. This theme is most emphasized by Dewey's work.

In his analysis of moral conduct, Dewey places an Aristotelian importance upon the role of habit. Habits are dispositions to *kinds* of activity by marking out general avenues of conduct. They organize our responsiveness to the world, interpreting it in a dynamic, temporal way, so that the world takes on a structure as a field of dramatic meaning for us. We walk into a room, for example; we do not just see "space," but space-through-which-we-can-move. Chairs are *seen-as* "sitable," and so on. Psychologist

James J. Gibson has built a complex "ecological theory of perception" around the phenomenon that, in order to act in the world, organisms must grasp objects in terms of their "affordances," or avenues of interaction.[13] Habits have an intrinsic developmental structure to them, a *narrative structure*, I would say, for they are not merely serial operations but are inherently organized toward resolution, giving them beginnings, middles, and ends; this constitutes a narrative or dramatic teleology.[14] Habits are not passive tools lying ready-to-hand for our use; they are organized, energetic, primed responses pressing to come into play as the shifting contexts of the world may allow, and they are disposed to growth. The consequence is important. "All habits are demands for certain kinds of activity," says Dewey, adding, "and they constitute the self" (MW, 14:21).

What Dewey means by this cryptic remark is that the self is no mere contingency of history, as Rorty thinks, but neither is it some complete Cartesian substance. Rather it is a continuous process of organization that develops within a historical context. It does not merely shift from one vocabulary to the next, but *grows* through the appropriation of possibilities to achieve an integrative way of acting. This is what constitutes character for Dewey. It is a process of continuous growth.

> Were it not for the continued operation of all habits in every act, no such thing as character could exist. There would be simply a bundle, an untied bundle at that, of isolated acts. Character is the interpenetration of habits. If each habit existed in an isulated compartment . . . character would not exist. That is, conduct would lack unity, being only a juxtaposition of disconnected reactions to separate situations. But since environments overlap, since situations are continuous and those remote from one another contain like elements, a continuous modification of habits by one another is constantly going on. A man may give himself away in a look or a gesture. Character can be read through the medium of individual acts. (MW, 14:29–30)

This is close to Aristotle: The act as such, because it is caught up in a connected process or activity, has significance—moral significance—because of the character it reveals. But instead of a preordained end

---

13. See James J. Gibson, *The Ecological Approach to Visual Perception* (Hillsdale, NJ: Lawrence Erlbaum Associates, 1986).

14. John Dewey, *Human Nature and Conduct* (MW, 14:15). Hereafter cited in text as MW, 14.

determining the continuity, there is more of a narrative development, such as MacIntyre deems important. Character for Dewey is not just the sedimented habits of the past, the expressive actions of the immediate present, or the tendencies toward future action. To be sure, it is all of these: but it is above all the flexible ability to *integrate* the possibilities of the present by using the organized experience of the past in reconstructing present action. Character realizes its continuity *through* the moral imagination. In this process it becomes essential to discover new values, especially as older values come into conflict. Thus, character is our moral imagination in action.

Habits are not static or mechanical tendencies to repeat the same action either, according to Dewey. They are expansive and developmental. Having been put into operation in one situation, a habit will be all the more likely to come into play in a wide variety of situations and become progressively linked up with *other* habits. Imagination emerges as the need for habit to expand and integrate itself with the whole body of behavior. It is our ever-insistent need to anticipate the world by reading it as a dispositional set for our actions. In this sense, imagination is temporally complex, an operation in the present, establishing continuity with the past, anticipating the future, so that a continuous process of activity may unfold in the most meaningful and value-rich way possible. Imagination uses educated habits developed in the domain of social interaction.

It is important to note here that imagination is intimately connected to perception, action, and intelligence. Imagination is not the negation of the perceptual present for a fictitious image. It symbolizes for us the *meaning* of possible activity. The capacity to interpret a situation in terms of possibilities in turn requires an organized body of experience upon which to draw. The richer the background of habits is, the more nuanced and complex our perception of the world is. The eyes of a child and a naturalist may receive similar light waves, but their worlds have different depth of meaning.[15] Habits also help us focus on the highly relevant features of a situation, thus simplifying it. Where a novice chess player

---

15. In *Human Nature and Conduct*, Dewey says, "The more numerous our habits the wider the field of possible observation and foretelling. The more flexible they are, the more refined is perception in its discrimination and the more delicate the presentation evoked by imagination" (MW, 14:123).

debates dozens of moves at each turn, the grandmaster sees two or three. Imaginative extensions develop out of our understanding of past meanings; they cannot be radical Rortian (or Davidsonian) ruptures. The redirection of a course of action can be meaningful as the *growth of conduct*. It is illustrative of Dewey's theory that, contra Davidson and Rorty, the kinds of actions mentioned—kissing, pointing, slapping—are meaningful parts of any communicative activity, unless, of course, they are performed by a madman.

Deliberation, an important phase of moral conduct, uses imagination in exploring the possibilities of a situation. These possibilities help determine the meaning of that situation. Thus deliberation helps us assess and evaluate as well as understand the dilemma at hand.

> Deliberation is an experiment in finding out what the various lines of possible action are really like. It is an experiment in making various combinations of selected elements of habits and impulses, to see what the resultant action would be like if it were entered upon. But the trial is in imagination, not in overt fact. The experiment is carried on by tentative rehearsals in thought which do not affect physical facts outside the body. Thought runs ahead and foresees outcomes, and thereby avoids having to wait the instruction of actual failure and disaster. An act overtly tried out is irrevocable, its consequences cannot be blotted out. An act tried out in imagination is not final or fatal. It is retrievable. (MW, 14:132–33)

In effect, imagination constitutes an extension of the environment to which we respond. By reading the possibilities of the present, the present situation is itself transformed and enlarged.[16] By looking into the possibilities and responding to them, we come to assess the present ongoing situation. It is thereby possible to act so as to effect continuity and development, growth, of the present, rather than simply mark another abrupt shift in the play of redescription of vocabularies.

---

16. Again, *Human Nature and Conduct*, "We do not act *from* reasoning; but reasoning puts before us objects which are not directly or sensibly present, so that we then may react directly to these objects, with aversion, attraction, indifference or attachment, precisely as we would to the same objects if they were physically present. In the end it results in a case of direct stimulus and response. In one case the stimulus is presented at once through sense; in the other case, it is indirectly reached through memory and constructive imagination" (MW, 14:139).

Imagination thus has the central ability to generate new values, according to Dewey. It is important to insist again that imagination is a social activity. Just as we learn to talk to ourselves because others have talked to us, so we learn to reflect and deliberate before we act because we have been taught to. This is what education aims for, the internalization of social activities. We have to learn how to take others into our considerations and we do so through a variety of means, not the least of which are stories. The self is born from such a process of "taking the role of the other," as George Herbert Mead put it.[17] One of the primary ways in which imagination is used is in understanding oneself in light of the other. By anticipating the responses of the other, we can control our own actions to communicate; gestures can thus become symbols. The personal imagination is a further refinement of the social imagination.

In confronting a situation in which we are faced with competing values, we undertake an exploration of the possibilities of preserving both of them before we apply any abstract principle. To hit upon a mode of activity that successfully keeps both values offers the meaningful extension of the situation we are looking for. In this process various rules may certainly be applied. But for Dewey rules legitimately function as tools or devices for projecting further lines of action or reminding ourselves of the continuity with past action which is important to keep. Rules and principles are ways of keeping experience organized and of picking out certain values which we wish to realize.[18]

To take a simple, perhaps all-too-simple, example: Think of two children fighting over a ball, each insisting that he or she wants to play with it. One way of resolving the situation is the might-makes-right way and letting the stronger child have the ball. Another would be to apply some abstract principle (such as property rights: Give the ball to the child who owns it). A third would be to try to find an *integrative value* that preserves the previous values that come into conflict (desire for

---

17. This is most completely worked out in Mead's *Mind, Self and Society*, though a synopsis of the theory is outlined in the fifth chapter of Dewey's *Experience and Nature*.

18. As Dewey says, again in *Human Nature and Conduct*, "Principles are methods of inquiry and forecast which require verification by the event; and the time honored effort to assimilate morals to mathematics is only a way of bolstering up an old dogmatic authority, or putting a new one upon the throne of the old. But the experimental character of moral judgment does not mean complete uncertainty and fluidity. Principles exist as hypotheses with which to experiment. . . . The problem is one of continuous, vital readaptation" (MW, 14:164–65).

possession of the ball, in this case). Here one might try to persuade the children to learn to play the game of catch. In this way, the ball is not only used by each child, thus sustaining the original value, but *additional* values are also discovered through the activity: sharing, the joy of the new game, and, above all, friendship. I do not wish to suggest that all moral dilemmas offer such an easy resolution. What I am trying to indicate is that the *discovery* of new, integrative values is a primary aim of the moral imagination, an aspect not even acknowledged by the modernist rule-oriented theories of morality.

This leads to Dewey's point that morality is not a fixed code based on some one ultimate value to which all others must be reduced but is rather the possibility for meaningful growth and development in our conduct:

> Morals means growth of conduct in meaning; at least it means that kind of expansion in meaning which is consequent upon observations of the conditions and outcome of conduct. It is all one with growing. . . . In the largest sense of the word, morals is education. It is learning the meaning of what we are about and employing that meaning in action. The good, satisfaction, "end" of growth of present action in shades and scope of meaning is the only good within our control, and the only one, accordingly, for which responsibility exists. The rest is luck, fortune. . . . "Present" activity is not a sharp narrow knife-blade in time. The present is complex, containing within itself a multitude of habits and impulses. It is enduring, a course of action, a process including memory, observation and foresight, a pressure forward, a glace backward, and a look outward. It is of *moral* moment because it marks a transition in the direction of breadth and clarity of action or in that of triviality and confusion. Progress is present reconstruction adding fullness and distinctness of meaning. (MW, 14:194–95)

This is the core of Dewey's theory of ethics. It offers a model radically different from those of the dominant traditions: *Morality is concerned with the growth of meaning through action.* It aims for a continuous process of integration in which new values can be discovered. This process cannot be guided merely by duty, pleasure, freedom, the universalizability criterion, self-interest, or any other single end. A plurality of values, however incommensurate, must be integrated. That dynamic integration is character. To acquire sensitivity to the developmental meanings of events, which define the significance of the situations in which we find ourselves and the values they possess, is what I have called here "the moral imagination." A moral imagination requires experience, a body of developing habits, education, an ability to understand the way other people think and live, and the ideal of discovering through cooperative action solutions to conflicts. It is the ability to see the meanings at issue in a given situation. It is the moral imagination which thus continually strives to create those ideals that offer the possibility of directing situations toward ends that are most fulfilling. This is what it is to have a moral character.

The Moral Self

The moral self, for Dewey, cannot be conceived as some absolutely isolated, unchanging entity, a source of propositional attitudes, free actions, emotive ejaculations, or rational commands. It is a process of growth ecologically connected with its biological and cultural world. Thus its moral life cannot be summarized by merely looking at some given "act," which is then assessed in terms of some absolute "law." Neither can it be judged in terms of a changeless human essence. Still, Dewey can agree with Aristotle that acts establish the habitual basis for character, and established habits become the conditions whereby future acts tend to be generated. From this process, the self arises. "The self is not a *mere* means to producing consequences because the consequences, when of a moral kind, enter into the formation of the self and the self enters into them." Consequences and conduct, Dewey adds, "form, reveal, and test the self."[19]

The nature of moral conduct is analogous to a process of artistic creation. One begins with a set of material conditions out of which the result must be produced, and each step in that process has an integral effect on the final product. If there are meager conditions or a thoughtless or ignorant process of creation, the chances of a satisfying work are not large. Likewise, for a meaningful self to emerge, it is better for the cultural conditions to be rich, and for the creative process itself—the moral life of the individual—to be cultivated with care. A moral life, in other words, reflects the complex interplay of the cultural world into which one is

---

19. John Dewey and James Tufts, *Ethics*, 2nd ed., 1932 (LW, 7:286). Hereafter cited in text as LW, 7.

born, constituting the matrix of meanings from which one's life is generated, the natural dispositions and talents one has for understanding and creatively developing those meanings, and the training (or blunting) of that talent by whatever education one receives in the art of moral living. A self may develop that is a careless, arbitrary self for many reasons. The culture may be fundamentally ignorant of factual matters in its world, deciding, for example, to go to war because of the markings of a goat's liver. The individual may have received no training in the formation of a sense of responsibility born of habits of reflection. Or the person may by temperament have a flighty, erratic disposition, acting irresponsibly no matter. These may all produce arbitrary actions, and the result will be a self (or perhaps a whole culture) in which the integration of meaning becomes difficult or impossible. Alasdair MacIntyre, and the sociological studies inspired by his work undertaken by Robert Bellah and his colleagues, criticizes our culture's vocabulary as morally impoverished, *turning* people into emotivists, making them live emotivist lives.[20]

Thus for Dewey, moral conduct must seriously explore the "self at issue" in any decision or general mode of conduct. "In committing oneself to a particular course, a person gives a lasting set to his own being. Consequently, it is proper to say that in choosing this object rather than that, one is in reality choosing what kind of person or self one is going to be. . . . Below the surface, it is a process of discovering what sort of being a person most wants to become" (LW, 7:287). In this sense, then, "the self reveals its nature in what it chooses." The most important theme for moral theory to recognize, asserts Dewey, is "the *essential unity of the self and its acts*" (LW, 7:288). This unity is not preestablished, but, to repeat, an ongoing process constantly at risk. This is why, on Dewey's view, children are held morally responsible in varying degrees at different times. The young child does not intend to be "selfish," for it is not intending perhaps anything more than to respond to immediate desire. He or she is *taught*, however, the *meaning* of types of behavior so that, at a later date, one is held accountable for being selfish or not.

A certain range of virtues opens up as a result of these considerations. If the self is a dynamic process in which culture, education, and

20. See Robert Bellah et al., *Habits of the Heart* (Berkeley, CA: University of California Press, 1985), and *The Good Society* (New York: Knopf, 1991).

readjustment to a changing world are conditional features, then those habits, and the ethical theories endorsing those habits—which treat the self either as an independent, nonnatural fixed entity or a passive, reactive, arbitrary collection of impulses—are hindrances. Those habits, by contrast, which keep the self open to change, enable it to see itself as a process, and allow it to communicate with others and to attend to the art of experience with care will be highly important.

> Except as the outcome of arrested development, there is no such thing as a fixed, ready-made, finished self. . . . Our personal identity is found in the thread of continuous development which binds together these changes. In the strictest sense, it is impossible for the self to stand still; it is becoming, and becoming for the better or the worse. It is in the *quality* of becoming that virtue resides. We set up this and that end to be reached, but *the* end is growth itself. (LW, 7:306)

There is a constant interplay, Dewey says, between "the old, habitual self," upon which we can fall back and "rest our oars," and the "growing, enlarging, liberated self," which "goes forth to meet new demands and occasions, and readapts and remakes itself in the process" (LW, 7:307). This tension exists in the society as a whole as well. This is why a proper continuation of this discussion would turn toward the ideal of the "democratic self" and the "democratic virtues," which Dewey thought important. It would also include the significance for democratic education in training the imaginations of the young to be morally rich. It must be enough for now, however, to note that the core of the democratic virtues lies in the ability to learn the art of living meaningfully, cultivating experience so that society can intelligently act for those consummatory experiences which realize the deepest sense of embodied value and meaning in our existence. These themes are treated in Dewey's educational and political work and, above all, in his discussions of aesthetic and religious experience: *Art as Experience* and *A Common Faith*.

It is important to remark here that Dewey summed up his discussion of the virtues and moral conduct under the term "love."

> The mere idea of a catalogue of different virtues commits us to the notion that virtues may be kept apart, pigeon-holed in water-tight compartments. In fact virtuous traits interpenetrate one another; this unity is involved in the very idea of integrity of character. . . . Another bad consequence of treating virtues as if they were separate from one

another and capable of being listed one by one is the attempt to cultivate each one by itself, instead of developing a rounded and positive
character. There are, however, in traditional teachings many remind-
ers of the wholeness of virtue. One such saying is that "love is the
fulfilling of the law." For in its ethical sense, love signifies completeness of devotion to the objects esteemed good. (LW, 7:257–59)[21]

Dewey then applies this idea of love as the ultimate integration of the
growth of character to the classical virtues of temperance, courage,
wisdom, and justice. Love realizes temperance by paying attention to the
whole range of interests rather than just some immediate, pressing desire.
It promotes courage by evaluating obstacles in light of the ultimate ends
we seek. It embraces wisdom as the consideration generated by sympathy
for those affected by our conduct. And such a complete interest is the
only means to bring about justice insofar as justice is impartially concerned with the common welfare. Love is the ability to guide the self in
light of the ideal of those complete, integrated interests that it not so
much has as is. Love is the virtue of character itself.

That love is the ultimate function of the moral imagination is brought
out in the startling passage concluding *Art as Experience*:

> Shelley said, "The great secret of morals is love, or *a going out of our
> nature* and the identification of ourselves with the beautiful which
> exists in thought, action, or person, not our own. A man to be greatly
> good must imagine intensely and comprehensively." What is true of
> the individual is true of the whole system of morals in thought and
> action. While perception of the union of the possible with the actual
> in a work of art is itself a great good, the good does not terminate with
> the immediate and particular occasion in which it is had. The union
> that is presented in perception persists in the remaking of impulsion
> and thought. The first intimations of wide and large redirections
> of desire and purpose are of necessity imaginative. Art is a mode
> of prediction not found in charts and statistics, and it insinuates
> possibilities of human relations not to be found in rule and precept,
> admonition and administration. (LW, 10:351–52)

---

21. For a more extended discussion of this theme in Dewey, see Steven Rockefeller, *John Dewey:
Religious Faith and Democratic Humanism* (New York: Columbia University Press, 1991), 483ff.

The key to moral conduct for Dewey is the capacity to discover the aesthetic dimension of human existence. This does not mean simply creating those ideals which by their lure allow people to act cooperatively for mutually fulfilling ends, though that is certainly included. It also means the ability to understand others and oneself in terms of the aesthetics of character, a palpable, concrete insight into the meaningful continuity of our lives. This embraces seeing the possibilities of others and oneself as well as the realized actualities. To love another includes awareness of that individual's ability to *grow*. This is particularly true in parental love of children, and it extends into healthy adult relationships as well.

Dewey's theory of character clearly provides those central features of moral understanding that both MacIntyre and Nussbaum have empha-sized, without the limitations their own positions seem to entail. The idea of character as the continuity of a developing process certainly can incorporate the "narrative" context for understanding intent which MacIntyre looks for. But Dewey does not have to retire to the dogmatic view that only self-enclosed "traditions" working out the preordained coherence of their positions provide the context of "rationality." He does not end either with MacIntyre's belief that we must be fanatically commit-ted to some grand tradition to escape confusion or with his false dilemma of "Nietzsche or Aristotle." Dewey, like Nussbaum, stresses the impor-tance of the contingent and tragic in moral life and that this life must be mutually realized rather than treated as an isolated project of the solitary self. Like her, he sees imagination and aesthetic understanding as primary modes of moral perception and reasoning. But while Nussbaum seems caught in something closely resembling an ethics of sympathy, vaguely urging us to act so long as we feel for the other, Dewey has a robust theory of experimental moral conduct, conflict resolution, and the pluralistic, integrative ideals of the democratic life. While Dewey would entirely agree with Nussbaum's incorporation of works of literature as prime instances where our moral understanding can be educated, he is not limited to literature. Indeed, at times Nussbaum seems almost to equate the moral life with reading. Dewey would find in this a tendency to isolate art from life. The thrust of Nussbaum's position, though, points toward a Deweyan integration of art and life.

Much more work, obviously, needs to be done. While Dewey has offered, in my view, the most comprehensive theory of the moral life of any of the "postmodern" thinkers, his account remains vague especially in the notion of habits as developmental structures which organize experience. A major contribution toward giving this concept a concrete, rigorous articulation has been carried out in Mark Johnson's work, *The Body in the Mind* and, more significantly, *Moral Imagination: Implications of Cognitive Science for Ethics.*[22] Johnson, building on the cognitive semantics of George Lakoff, sees the nature of meaning as inherently imaginative, an extension of the creative dynamism of our organic embodiment. There is good empirical evidence that our verbal, cognitive processes are structured by extending and developing many implicit structures of the living body. He has extended this work into exploring how image structures, especially metaphoric schemata, organize and guide our moral reasoning.

> We human beings are imaginative creatures, from our most mundane, automatic acts of perception, all the way up to our most abstract conceptualization and reasoning. Consequently, our moral understanding depends in large measure on various structures of imagination, such as images, image schemas, metaphors, narratives, and so forth. Moral reasoning is thus basically an imaginative activity, because it uses imaginatively structured concepts and requires imagination to discern what is morally relevant in situations, to understand empathetically how others experience things, and to envision the full range of possibilities open to us in a particular case.[23]

Johnson explicitly recognizes that this is a "Deweyan conception of morality."[24] By looking at how specific metaphoric structures organize our moral thinking and shape our moral vision of the world, Johnson has opened up a vast project which has direct implications for pragmatic ethical theory.

To conclude, the failure of the modernist approach to ethical theory has led to some important, new developments, mainly focused around the reintroduction of themes found in the classical theories, such as character, without much successful confrontation of the dilemma posed to those theories by Darwinism. So far, most of these have operated

22. See Mark Johnson, *Moral Imagination: Implications of Cognitive Science for Ethics* (Chicago: University of Chicago Press, 1993).

23. Johnson, *Moral Imagination*, preface.

24. Johnson, *Moral Imagination*, acknowledgments.

without any awareness of the contribution of Dewey's own ethical theory, which was developed in a consciously Darwinian manner. The centrality of imagination in recent theory, too, points toward Dewey as providing an adequate theoretical framework within which most of the topics in ethical theory must be reconsidered.

The implications of taking such an approach are extensive. Not only might ethics as a philosophic discipline escape the arid discussions of the deontological-utilitarian debate, but the issue of how moral reasoning is developed through cultural symbols, stories, myths, and religious systems remains to be explored. Connections with cognitive semantics on the one hand and sociological and anthropological studies on the other would make the field of ethics a study of the imaginative and practical ways human beings actually construct and live meaningful lives. Nor would this remain a descriptive approach. The focus on imagination reveals that we are constantly creating our worlds, for better or worse, and this is an art that must be attended to with care. Dewey once described democracy as the art of being able to listen to others. At least, listening to other people's stories is the beginning of our ability to understand and communicate with them, and so is the first step of social intelligence.[25]

25. See for example the series of studies by sociologist Robert Coles, *Children of Crisis*, 5 vols. (Boston: Atlantic, Little, Brown, 1964–80), and especially his book, *The Call of Stories: Teaching and the Moral Imagination* (Boston: Houghton Mifflin, 1989). I have explored the implications of this theory for education in my essay, "The Moral Imagination and the Aesthetics of Human Existence," cited in note 4. However far an art of the moral imagination may go toward overcoming misunderstanding and conflict, I wish to stress that the fundamental possibility for conflict and tragic failure of intelligence is ineradicable for the Deweyan view of morality.

This essay owes much to discussions with my former colleague Mark Johnson. His *Moral Imagination: Implications of Cognitive Science for Ethics*, referred to above, contains his own important exploration of this subject. See also Steven Fesmire's *John Dewey and Moral Imagination: Pragmatism in Ethics* (Indianapolis: Indiana University Press, 2003) and Gregory Fernando Pappas, *John Dewey's Ethics: Democracy as Experience* (Indianapolis: Indiana University Press, 2008).

EIGHT

EDUCATING THE DEMOCRATIC HEART

Pluralism, Traditions, and the Humanities

Though Dewey is frequently recalled primarily as an educational theorist, it would be better to remember him as a philosopher who located every aspect of his thought within the general problematic of the nature and purpose of the democratic life. Dewey's theory of education is guided by his conception of what a democratic culture must be. Every political and educational theory reflects fundamental commitments about human nature and what constitutes a well-lived or meaningful life. In this essay, I intend to sketch a portrait of Dewey's ideal of democratic culture and to discuss its bearings upon the role of the humanities and the value of cultural traditions, the place of "pluralistic" education within this debate, and ultimately the character of the cultural imagination that is at the heart of democratic civilization. Contrary to the scientistic interpretations of Dewey, I will argue that the humanistic and aesthetic values are central. We cannot dismiss the importance of traditions in the name of pluralism. That is, we cannot have genuine pluralism merely by recognizing diversity or by offering a smattering of superficial details about various cultures. Pluralism involves a rigorous, deep, and wide exposure to the dimension of human symbolization. This dimension is mainly imparted through the imaginative and narrative structures that traditions provide. The humanities thus are central to the Deweyan ideal of democratic education. The aim, in short, of democratic education must be to provide a rich, imaginative, and above all aesthetic vision of the worlds of meaning that human beings have created, thereby allowing the ultimate project of civilization to be more fully discerned—the creative quest to experience the world with a funded sense of meaning and value.

This claim may appear to conflict with two themes that often appear in characterizations of Dewey's theory of education: the importance of allowing learning to develop from a connection of information with the daily experience of the child and the significance of the scientific method of shared inquiry and experimentation as the guiding habit for intelligence. Two unwarranted consequences are often seen as following from these assumptions. The first is that the idea of a historical tradition with its remote figures and events and its expression in a canon of literature, art, and philosophy must be dismissed in the name of what is "relevant" to the student's contemporary experience. The second is that the arts and humanities must take a secondary place to the sciences, especially the applied sciences. To the extent the humanities are admitted, they too must submit to a version of the scientific method. The final, overall conclusion seems to be that Dewey envisioned an educational curriculum that would be most appropriate for democracy as one that is radically antihistoricist, unsympathetic to the humanities, utilitarian, relativistic in its moral values, and devoid of content for the sake of the experimental method.

While most Deweyans would realize this to be at best a caricature of Dewey's true position, it is often used by those who take a sharply critical approach to his ideas, from political and religious conservatives to intellectuals like Mortimer Adler, E. D. Hirsch, Allan Bloom, and Alasdair MacIntyre. Such people defend the need for moral absolutes for any society to function, the importance of a tradition to form a sense of cultural identity and purpose, and the unique ability of the humanities to impart such values and ideals. It is true that Dewey attacked the idea that education should be irrelevant to those living today or that moral values should be imparted or justified simply by appeals to the past or the *ipse dixits* of the great and dead. It is also true that in his effort to point to an alternative conception of intelligence Dewey all too frequently appealed to what he called the scientific or "experimental method." Dewey's battles were with aspects of late Victorian civilization, especially its facile appeal to absolutes, inevitable progress, and the self-evident nature of "higher" ideals. Against this, Dewey's emphasis on experience, method, and practice was meant as a corrective. But when his arguments are taken out of that context and placed within our own world of late positivist civilization, they seem to be uncritical endorsements of what came to be thought of as "the" scientific method and the technological civilization spawned by it. Viewed from our "post-modern condition," Dewey may seem no longer radical, but filled with the optimistic naiveté and faith in technological progress that the moral and political experiences of the twentieth and early twenty-first centuries seem to have called into question. This is a major reason why it is crucial to understand the Deweyan view of the arts and humanities. Another is that the only alternative theories that seek to do justice to them are indifferent or hostile to science (like hermeneutics) or promote the fallacies of Victorianism under a new banner (like MacIntyre). One of the great advantages of Dewey's ideas today is that they offer the possibility of a humanistic theory of technology.[1]

The contrast between Dewey's understanding of what the "experimental method" is (or, rather, *methods* are) and how it relates to the sciences in particular and the positivistic approach cannot be discussed here. If closely examined, it would become evident that instead of incorporating the humanities into the sciences, Dewey had really placed the sciences more within the broader issues of the humanities. Indeed, several studies have revealed the close affinity between the Deweyan conception of science and views put forward by contemporary feminists.[2] The most salient feature of the contrast between the Deweyan concept of inquiry and positivism is found in the very idea of method itself. Whereas positivism aspired toward a universal methodology based on mathematical logic and "value free" data, Dewey, like Aristotle, held for a variety of

1. See Larry Hickman's *John Dewey's Pragmatic Technology* (Bloomington: Indiana University Press, 1989) and my own essay, "The Technology of Desire," in *Studies in Technology*, vol. 8, ed. Paul Durbin, 1991.
2. See studies by Lisa Heldke, "John Dewey and Evelyn Fox Keller," in *Hypatia* (1987), vol.2, no.3 and Eugenie Gatens-Robinson, "Dewey and the Feminist Successor Science Project," *Transactions of the Charles S. Peirce Society* (1992) vol. 27, no.4.

methods, each tailored for its appropriate subject matter, and denied the possibility or even desirability of removing values from the nature of inquiry; without values, no data would be discovered.[3] Dewey rejected both the absolutist defense of the humanities as a repository of eternal values by which contemporary life must be measured and to which it must conform and the positivist dismissal of everything as meaningless that could not fit into its attenuated, formalistic methodology. Given this, what is the Deweyan understanding of the nature and purpose of the humanities, the value of appropriating cultural traditions from the past, and the study of diverse cultures? In what way do the responses to these questions fit in with the ideal of the democratic life?

It is best to begin with an analysis of Dewey's conception of democracy, a theme to which he returned many times in a variety of contexts. First, Dewey says that "a democracy is more than a form of government; it is primarily a mode of associated living, of conjoint communicated experience."[4] Initially, this must mean a commitment on the part of the state to equality of opportunity, especially with regard for opportunity for education. But the education must be such that it fosters a democratic form of life. Dewey points to two prominent aspects of democratic culture: There must be recognition of common ideals and there must be a wide, flexible range of points of contact with other groups, enabling cooperation and communication. The former liberates conduct because it allows activity to become participation. The second allows social action to be ready for change and to meet conflict in a constructive rather than violent manner. Thus blind obedience and rigid narrowness of interests are both anti-democratic cultural tendencies. As Dewey summarizes:

A society which makes provisions for participation in its good of all its members on equal terms and which secures flexible readjustments of its institutions through interaction of the different forms of associated life is in so far democratic. Such a society must have a type of education which gives individuals a personal interest in social relationships

3. It is helpful to remember that the two memorable works that appeared in the positivistic series on "The Unity of Science" were highly critical of that idea: one was Dewey's *Theory of Valuation* (an attack on emotivism and the fact-value distinction), the other Thomas Kuhn's *The Structure of Scientific Revolutions*.

4. *Democracy and Education* (MW, 9:93). This point is also extensively made in *The Public and Its Problems*.

and control, and the habits of mind which secure social changes without introducing disorder. (MW, 9:105)

Dewey believed that at the root of human existence there was a desire to experience life in a way that was value-rich, meaningful, and in which our sense of the world and ourselves was vividly realized on the deepest levels. This experience was not necessarily cognitive so much as a total integration of feeling and meaning embodied and expressed through activity in some medium that was socially expressive. Experience became charged with a sense of fulfillment and meaning when it was growing and expressive. The skills to develop such experiences Dewey alternatively called "education" or "art." Quite simply, the aim of life is to experience the world on a deep level; i.e., aesthetically. While Dewey devoted many works, such as *The Public and Its Problems* or *Freedom and Culture*, to the question of democracy, perhaps the most important discussion of what lies at the heart of his social and political theory is in *Art as Experience*. The aesthetic experience as analyzed in that work describes the fullest realization of the human quest for embodied meaning. If any other work expands Dewey's main ideas of the aesthetic in the direction of their social implications, it would be *A Common Faith*, where life itself becomes the medium for the embodiment and experience of ideals.[5] This is why Dewey said that there is no end outside of education than life itself. The democratic concept of education is thus radically opposed to all narrower views, from isolated ivory tower views, where education is isolated from life in general, to utilitarian assumptions that education aims at some specific, "socially useful" skill or vocation.[6]

Democratic culture would be one that consciously aimed at providing as many people as possible the materials and arts whereby they could construct meaningful lives. For Dewey, this means that the individual would be able to understand and communicate with other members of society, and be able to engage in shared activities that fulfilled all of the participants. This cannot be misconstrued as the skill for joining groups or accepting their beliefs; it is not a call for conformity. Though Dewey stressed the importance of community, he also stressed the importance

5. See "The Spirituality of the Possible in John Dewey's *A Common Faith*," chapter 11 in this volume.
6. See *Democracy and Education*, Chapters 8, 20, and 23.

of creative individuality. For a person to develop and give life to the community, that individual must be able to take a dynamic approach to
the group, and the group must foster the individual potentialities of its
members.[7] Thus, a critical attitude to the past would be combined with
a creative approach to the future. One of the most significant aspects of a
democratic society for Dewey is its ability to question practices and beliefs
as well as formulate new ideals whereby action may be directed to consummatory ends. The two are related, for one cannot criticize experience without using an ideal of some sort. A broad, realistic basis is needed as well as
a commitment to pursue an ideal of human life. Ideals cannot be unques-
tioningly inherited. They must be created, tested, and reformulated.

Dewey finds a crucial role for history in such an educational program.
Dewey was highly critical of the presentation of history as divorced from
contemporary life. As far as the *mere* past is concerned, Dewey is blunt:
"Let the dead bury the dead" (MW, 9:221). He goes on: "But knowledge
of the past is the key to understanding the present. History deals with
the past, but this past is the history of the present." This should not be
misconstrued as studying history only for what is *a priori* determined
to be "relevant" to today's current interests, a common error made in
reading Dewey at this point. Rather it is the breadth and depth of the
historical perspective that opens up what the *contemporary* situation
really is. "Geography and history," Dewey writes, "are the two great
schools for bringing about an enlargement of the significance of a direct
personal experience" (MW, 9:226). The idea is to show how present-day
things (like technology, government, science, and so on) have *evolved*
from radically different forms. Dewey would shift history away from
"dynastic" and military accounts to a more complex view of cultural
process. While introducing the topics of technological and economic
history, it is important to note that Dewey especially stresses "the most
neglected branch of history," that is, "intellectual history" (MW, 9:224).
History is the history of *ideas* that have shaped the worldviews within
which human beings have had to forge the meanings of their lives. This
would reveal, as perhaps no other subject, the great task for civilization
itself, the creation of meaning in the world.

---

7. Once again, this is why *Art as Experience*, which tends to stress the idea of individual creativity
and expression, is a valuable counterbalance to much of Dewey's social writing.

It is important to note here that this provides Dewey with the unique concept of a *democratic* or pluralistic tradition. Alasdair MacIntyre has argued that rationality does not operate in a historical or cultural vacuum, that it needs, specifically, a "tradition" within which to operate. That is, reason needs to be working out fundamental assumptions and overcoming conflicts over a historical span so that it aims toward an integrated worldview. Not all cultures have traditions, according to MacIntyre. They may have customs, but they do not necessarily have the implicit capacity to articulate internally coherent, integrated worldviews. MacIntyre believes, in other words, that each tradition has the capacity to have an unfolding dialectic, an internal development working out of its central conceptions. While I shall return to discuss MacIntyre's position later, one comment must be faced here. MacIntyre rejects the idea that modern liberalism can provide such a tradition or, if it could, that its philosophical outlook could make that tradition function effectively in the employment of reason. MacIntyre believes that the individualistic view of self-interest and the formal conception of reason have permanently disabled democratic societies from constructing coherent worldviews.[8] While Dewey would agree with much in MacIntyre's critique of Enlightenment liberalism, he offers an alternative view of democracy and what a democratic, pluralistic tradition must be.

Dewey's critical and creative approach also contrasts with the widespread conception of "tradition" found in most cultures, a concept that still persists in most discussions in educational theory. Most cultures throughout history only focus on their own traditions and regard the values and ideas embodied in current institutions and symbols as the only acceptable forms of living. The result has often been that, in building up the sense of the worth and meaning of one's own culture, all others have been denigrated. Alien peoples are devalued because of cultural as well as racial differences. The names by which most Native American tribes call themselves usually can be translated as "the people" or "the human beings"; all other human beings (including all other Native American tribes) are thereby ranked one step lower. I recall my father explaining the migration of peoples across the Bering Strait, the ancestors

---

8. See *Whose Justice? Which Rationality?* (Notre Dame: University of Notre Dame Press, 1989), Ch. 17.

of Native Americans, to a Jemez Pueblo Indian he knew. The fellow listened attentively and then said, "That's very interesting. I've always wondered where all those *other* Indians came from. Of course my people came up through the sacred opening in the earth at Jemez." The Chinese refer to their country as *Chung Guo*, "the Central Kingdom." This was not merely a case of geographical centrism: those peoples inhabiting the periphery were "barbarians." "Barbarian," of course, is a Greek word used to refer to all those who did not speak Greek. Hebrew culture distinguished itself from all others on the basis of the deity it worshipped; all other cultures were degraded as "heathen" or "gentile." In the Renaissance nationalism gradually evolved as the basis of a collective identity, English, French, German, and so on. People who found value in cultural systems outside those of the group or who took a critical attitude toward the group's own beliefs and values that lay at the core of the shared identity are often seen as constituting a real threat. Beliefs about religious or racial purity justifying the superiority of one group over all others are world-wide, from the recently concocted notions of white supremacists to the immensely ancient beliefs the Japanese hold about themselves. The martyrs to religious, scientific, and political freedom were regarded as dangerous individuals because they seemed to challenge a system of symbols and meanings whereby the lives of a people derived everything that made them valuable and significant. Tradition, in short, has provided mainly a basis for constructing the fundamental "we-they" mentality of most cultures. MacIntyre's concept, however refined, is fundamentally the same. This, obviously, cannot be a democratic view of tradition.

Though the idea of democracy arose in the seventeenth century primarily as a national concept, the rights of a specific "people" from which sovereignty derived, it quickly evolved into a universal conception of the "rights of man." In its attempt to become universal, Enlightenment theorists looked toward science and mathematics as examples of formalistic systems. The concept of political rights became distinguished from the specific cultural beliefs, customs, or symbols that constituted the meaningful world for the members of that society. The result, exemplified above all in Kant, was that the concept of "rational agents" as "rule followers" who exercised "choice" over their actions became the dominant model of what "persons" were. To the extent pluralism was admitted on such models, it was on the basis of Madisonian arguments about the desirability of a diversity of conflicting interests to prevent powerful majority blocs from forming. Freedom, for Madison, was the result of nobody easily gaining or maintaining a position of power; the fundamental political problem was to distribute power and make it oppose itself, the famous theory of "checks and balances."[9]

Under this model, a plurality of cultural beliefs and practices could be allowed because they were *irrelevant* to the capacity of individuals to function as citizens. The Jeffersonian ideal of "the pursuit of happiness" was conceived as the search for private, individual pleasure—a far cry from Aristotle's view of happiness or *eudaimonia* ("doing well" rather than "feeling good") as the basis of the political order.[10] In separating religion from the state, for example, there was no ideal that it was desirable to have a diversity of religions in the culture. The use of religion as a basis for political oppression was vivid in the minds of the *philosophes*. Enlightenment universalism was behind a great part of the American experiment in political liberty. Immigrants were expected to "become American" when they arrived, an ideal many embraced enthusiastically, while others struggled with the double consciousness of their national, ethnic or religious identities and their newfound American selves.

This Enlightenment ideal has come under severe criticisms, beginning with those offered by Marxism and fascism and ending with those made by postmodernism and neoconservatism.[11] Dewey himself could be cited as one of the major critics of this ideal, though in his case it was as a defender of democracy and liberalism rather than as a would-be gravedigger. Dewey was especially critical of the formalistic concept of reason and personhood that had emerged with the Enlightenment. The challenge he faced was to accommodate democracy to (1) a concept of individuality as social, (2) a concept of reason as pervaded by feeling, and (3) a concept of diversity as integral rather than tangential to the life of democracy itself. But Dewey, unlike many other critics of the Enlightenment, retained the *philosophes'* sensitivity to the nature of oppression and tyranny, emphasizing that the ideals must always be tested by experience and not ideological purity. Nor would Dewey have much

9. See *The Federalist Papers*, 10 and 48–52.

10. See the discussion of the phrase "pursuit of happiness" by Garry Wills in his study of the Declaration, *Inventing America* (New York: Doubleday, 1978).

11. Two prominent examples of "postmodern" critics are Theodor Adorno and Michel Foucault. Both provide negative critiques of modern society without believing that any constructive model can be offered in its place.

use for the popular postmodern stance of simply seeing the role of philosophy as a negative critic of power, cynically unmasking its constructs without providing some alternative direction for organized action.

At the core of Dewey's concept of democracy are the interrelated ideas of community and creative individuality. Human beings need to have established social contexts to have a sense of their own selfhood. We develop our self-awareness through the dialogue of parent and child and gradually acquire the means of communication as part of this ongoing interplay. Communities, then, are primarily groups of people who can *communicate* with each other. Communication, however, is not even primarily the transference of information; nor is the ultimate objective necessarily mutual agreement. These are aspects of some types of communicative action, but communication itself is more inclusive and rich. It is the open space, the event, created by languages (verbal and nonverbal) whereby humans can share experiences and be with each other in a meaningful way.[12] Very often it means a *shifting* of perspectives and recognition of the *diversity* of roles within any communicative process. While the aim may be to integrate and coordinate perspectives that at first may seem conflicting or exclusive, this is not the same as the formalistic ideal of reducing all perspectives to a mono-focal identity. If there is agreement achieved as a result of the process, the process itself is part of the *meaning* of that understanding and cannot be jettisoned as a "mere means" for getting there.

A comparison can be made to human vision. We perceive a world that has formed objects in three-dimensional space. Psychologists like Jean Piaget and J. J. Gibson, as well as psychologically informed philosophers like Maurice Merleau-Ponty and John Dewey, have noted that we perceive objects because the eye is in constant motion. Experiments in which one eye was closed and the other prevented from moving resulted in the subjects having difficulty in recognizing or focusing on objects in the visual field. An object has edges as a result of the eye adjusting its readings back and forth.[13] Likewise we perceive depth because we have a view of

12. Again, Dewey's analysis of artistic and aesthetic expressiveness in *Art as Experience* provides an important insight into what he means by "communication." Art is the highest example for Dewey of this activity. An experienced artwork is not merely physically proximate but meaningfully present.
13. See Jean Piaget's *Psychology and Understanding*, Maurice Merleau-Ponty's *The Structure of Behavior* and J. J. Gibson's *An Ecological Approach to Visual Perception*.

the world from two slightly divergent perspectives. Loss of one perspective flattens out the field as a whole. Dewey himself was fond of stressing that in vision we have the whole living, moving body implicated in each act— the world perceived through the eyes is a world of projected motion, action, response, and possible adjustment.[14]

Communication takes this one step further. There is no common neurosystem linking one communicant to another. The medium here is symbolization and expression. Both Dewey and his colleague George Herbert Mead worked out a sophisticated analysis of how communication requires that all members of the process imaginatively project themselves into the situation from the *other's* standpoint so that they can interpret the response or meaning of *their own* possible actions.[15] If I am throwing the ball to you, I must try to see myself as you to help gauge my pitch; you as the catcher must project yourself into my role as pitcher. I understand myself as "pitcher" only by incorporating imaginatively how you respond to my possible actions as catcher. This is how I try to grasp the *meaning* of my possible gestures or actions, and vice versa. Most communication, of course, is far more subtle and complex than this example indicates. But, as in the case of the eyes mentioned above, there is mutual adjustment and coordination whereby a vague or indeterminate situation becomes clearer, especially as a field of action. The process of communication is possible because of the use of imagination in reconstructing experience. It involves the capacity to see one's own perspective from other points of view, to "take the standpoint of the other," in Mead's phrase, and, above all, to integrate these diverse perspectives into one organized, mutually responsive activity through the use of symbols. Diverse viewpoints are not reduced to the same; they are reinterpreted in light of a common ideal that is large enough to make use of the diversity as well as the commonality.

The importance of diversity to this process is immediately evident. The aim of intelligence is to comprehend the meaning of situations in terms of their actualities and more so in terms of their possibilities. The possibilities of situations constitute the meanings the situation may have, depending upon the course of conduct chosen, especially upon those

14. See, for example, "The Reflex Arc Concept in Psychology" (EW, 5:96–110).
15. See Dewey, *Experience and Nature*, chapter 5, and George Herbert Mead's *Mind, Self, and Society*.

who may be affected by it. An argument may lead to a conflict lasting throughout a lifetime, leaving its residue of malice and resentment. Handled differently, it may become the basis of a friendship or at least of greater compassion and self-knowledge. Dewey's position is not that we construct the meaning of situations out of the whole cloth of our subjective insights and hopes. The situation is a feature of the world with which we are involved. There may be aspects of it that transcend our individual understanding or to which we are blinded by our own personal habits and dispositions. The complex topography of situations is better discerned through a variety of participants who do not share exactly the same outlook. But diversity is not enough: These diverse points of view must be in communication with each other, otherwise they become reduced once again to isolated individual perspectives, like two eyes without a common brain.

While most political and social theorists have regarded cultural diversity as a problem to be overcome (or, in Madison's case, as a vice that can be turned, in spite of itself, into a virtue), Dewey regards it as the reservoir of a greater social intelligence. (Aristotle likewise objected to Plato's ideal of an intellectual elite ruling because there was a greater wisdom, he thought, in the moderation and breadth of common intelligence in a collective polity.)[16] For this reservoir to be available, there must be a capacity of the members of the society to recognize the nature of diversity as a resource, to enter imaginatively into the alternative perspectives as much as possible that communication may occur, and for all members to be guided in light of a common ideal, which for Dewey would be the democratic life itself.

It should be clear by now that this democratic ideal cannot be the bland hope that all ethnic, religious, or individual differences be cast aside for the empty formalism of "becoming American" or whatever abstraction that is used instead. On the contrary, for this ideal to work, there must be a concrete, vivid, factually rich, and aesthetically sensitive awareness of the symbols, histories, and traditions at play. Communication is impossible otherwise. The democratic ideal cannot be the Madisonian faith that the arithmetic sum of everyone's self-interest will mechanically result in freedom, conceived only as the negative freedom from tyranny.

16. *Politics*, 1281a, 40ff.

Democratic education must aim at training the cultural imagination. By learning about how other peoples have constructed meaningful worlds, how they have expressed those meanings in art, literature, religion, and philosophy, we develop essential tools for democratic communication.

Not only do we learn to see ourselves from the standpoint of the other, we learn to understand the meanings of things in contexts. Those who urge the teaching of religion in the schools, for example, assume that this will recognize a universal belief in God, the transcendent Being of Judaism, Christianity, or Islam; if they realized that exposing students to a well-developed course in world religions would impart the awareness that in such religions as Buddhism, Confucianism, or Taoism there are no corresponding concepts of "God" or "soul," they might vociferously oppose the teaching of religion in the schools. The only way to develop an understanding of concepts is to see how they have been expressed and used in a variety of historical and cultural contexts. "Democracy" is not a univocal term covering a Native American tribe, the Athens of Solon or Pericles, the England of Locke or Mill, or the United States of Dewey. Even if some element can be found in common, it is probably not the most important aspect of each case.

One vital part of democratic education, then, is the exposure over a long period to the histories and cultures of diverse peoples in the world, especially as embodied in the arts and humanities. The languages of Paleolithic cave painting, Greek drama, Chinese poetry and ink-brush painting, Gothic architecture, Hindu sculpture, and so on open up the world at its most expressive level. Cultures comprehend themselves through aesthetic expression, and it is through such expressions that we begin to approach them. Simply seeing a Greek Zeus next to a Gupta Buddha and a French twelfth-century crucifix can teach more about the conceptions of the divine than many sermons or lectures. Verbally we can say that the Zeus is the essence of balanced, energetic power, the Buddha of inward tranquility, the Christ of human suffering, and transcendent spirit; such shorthand descriptions are inadequate to beholding the works themselves.

The rich awareness of cultural pluralism must be counterbalanced by an equally rich understanding of the nature of democracy as a cultural as well as a political movement. Naturally, this involves an understanding of the development of democracy in its historical contexts, the alternative political systems that have contested it, and a realistic emphasis upon the tragic failures of democracy. Jefferson could write that "all men are created equal" while recognizing that slavery would persist in the new political order. The brutality experienced by suffragettes at the hands of democratic governments is another example. Merely focusing upon a recital of the lapses between an articulated ideal and its limited implementation can result in cynicism. A realistic idealism will appreciate the power of ideals to shape history while maintaining a tragic sensibility to the blindness we may exhibit at any time; it needs an energetic, compassionate heroism. Thus, one of the central themes of democratic education must be not only a capacity to impart appreciation of diverse cultures and traditions, but an understanding of political history.

Together, with the exposure to the arts and humanities of other cultures as well as one's own and with an astute appreciation of the political nature of history, we approach perhaps the most important theme in Dewey's conception of intelligence: to grasp situations as processes. A process is not merely a string of events deployed in time, a mere succession without development. Process involves what Dewey calls "continuity." Most frequently Dewey used the term "growth" as a synonym; this is fine if one remembers that death and fate are elements as well. A life can end as well as begin, and in its course can encounter things that impede or defeat it. Abstractions are immensely useful; Dewey fully acknowledged that. But it is all too easy to substitute them for the complex experience that they were taken from. This is because it is easier to symbolize them and talk about them, and they do in fact help us guide and control the world. When this happens, we end up with a concept of the world composed of ultimate unities (substances, sense data, bare particulars, or whatever) and formal laws (ontological, epistemological, or logical categories) governing them. Both the concepts of "self-identical unit" and of "formal law" are essentially *atemporal*, pure logical identities. Process and change become "problems" at this point and extreme theorists will simply dismiss "genetic explanations" or try to assimilate disciplines like history to mathematics. The result, as William James pointed out, is like trying to capture the nature of a stream by lining up a series of pails filled with water: The process itself is gone. The Deweyan approach, by contrast, insists upon the pervasive nature of temporality (even in mathematics). Dewey struggled to articulate how this view of intelligence differs from the other (by far the dominant model in Western civilization), though with limited success.

There has been a recent recognition of the importance of "narrative understanding" by thinkers as diverse as hermeneuticists like Hans-Georg Gadamer and Paul Ricoeur, ethicists like Alisdair MacIntyre and Martha Nussbaum, and cognitive theorists like Jerome Brunner and Mark Johnson. I believe it is helpful to look here for something close to what Dewey was seeking. Being able to place something in a narrative gives us a different understanding than simply seeing it as an instance of a formal law, and a great deal of our moral, not to mention conceptual, understanding is transformed when we can do so. Thomas Kuhn, working with the formalistic model, saw the transformation from one dominant paradigm to another as an irrational shift because there were no governing laws to translate the members of one conceptual system into another. The sun, for Ptolemy, was a planet; for Kepler, it was one of many stars. The two paradigms determined that different people saw different entities. Kuhn's own paradigm dictates that the shift from one system to the other is irrational because there are no formal laws of translatability. Yet, as MacIntyre has argued, on looking back to the crisis of astronomy in the fifteenth century and to its subsequent development, we can tell a coherent *story* of how the "problematic situation" (to use Dewey's phrase) occurred, how intelligence (not "reason" in the formal sense) sought alternative explanatory models in a sensible fashion and not in a randomly "irrational" way, and how the result was a new, productive way of organizing and understanding the phenomena.[17] What connects the transition from one paradigm to the other in retrospect is the narrative coherence of the process. MacIntyre, of course, is utterly oblivious to the fact that his own astute analysis of this issue neatly fits Dewey's classic description of the "phases of inquiry" and it is unlikely that he would be pleased with the similarity.

In *Whose Justice? Which Rationality?*, MacIntyre argues that "reason" must be seen as grounded upon a developing historical tradition. Fundamental paradigms of rationality are only gradually worked out as inner tensions and conflicts present themselves and are resolved. But whereas Dewey, in making a similar point, would stress the contextual nature of intelligence, its reliance upon a vast world of preconceptual,

17. See Alasdair MacIntyre, "Epistemological Crises and Narrative Explanation," *The Monist* 60, no. 4 (1977): 453–72.

interactive experience, and its constant reconstructive movement, MacIntyre falls prey to the formalistic problems that he had tried to solve in Kuhn. Traditions for MacIntyre are historically unfolding Kuhninan paradigms; there cannot be any meaningful translation from one to the other. No "dialogue" between competing traditions is possible. For an individual to be genuinely open to another tradition is for that individual to be in existential crisis, without any means for intelligently deciding which tradition is correct or even for comparing them. Traditions may "overhear" other traditions, but only insofar as they can reinterpret alien ideas into their own internal dialectic. In the end, for MacIntyre, we stand within one tradition or another as an act of fatality or a leap of faith. Thus, MacIntyre's attempt to introduce "narrative" understanding essentially ends up with the problem to which it was introduced as a solution, except that now we have a more complex theory of paradigms as historically unfolding through their own internal dialectic.

Such an approach, while providing an interesting historical view of reason in the face of the purely formalistic theories spawned by positivism, is hardly a fruitful model for those interested in developing a democratic understanding of cultural pluralism. MacIntyre is openly contemptuous of modern "liberalism" and its pluralism. He believes that pluralism on such a view must be essentially the same as the Enlightenment's acceptance of diverse "pursuits of happiness" without any common or uniting theme other than satisfaction of self-interest. It is in short a pluralism of indifference or, at best, a kind of cultural smorgasbord offering the members of a society a variety of competing cultural beliefs to be chosen only by mere personal preference or satisfaction. MacIntyre is convinced this model cannot work because he holds—correctly, I believe—that neither human beings nor human reason can function in atomic isolation.

Here is where Dewey's understanding of social inquiry and intelligence offers an important alternative to MacIntyre's own view of rationality, which has ended, as I said, back where it began: In the end, rationality for MacIntyre is a finished paradigm, internally consistent and indifferent to any other ideas. However much MacIntyre stresses the idea of "history," it is as a process toward a fixed, ideal end. Deweyan intelligence, by contrast, does not see the essence of reason in a finished product, but in the ability to connect experiences meaningfully; i.e., *to grow*. It sees process as continuity achieved through the interplay of order and contingency, in which ambiguity and real potentiality for alternative developments are present. This allows for a broader conception of tradition, in which a variety of symbolic connections are possible. "Coherence" is not merely the province of dialectical rationality. The "coherence" of a work of art is a texture of feeling and meanings that are not primarily cognitive at all. Most cultures seek to provide this *aesthetic* sense of the texture of meaning in human lives. The coherence achieved through rational debate is only one kind of coherence, from Dewey's standpoint.

Likewise, pluralism is integral to the idea of an ongoing process. Dewey is willing to sacrifice the ideal of aiming toward a final, ultimate, rationally tight textbook of "answers" to problems. This was a false ideal of rationality to begin with. If our problems are genuinely contextually generated, they must be understood historically, it is true, but so must any "answers" proposed to meet them. As Gadamer has said, answers are meaningful only as responses to questions; it is the dialogical process that constitutes understanding, not the intermediary tool of devising formalistic systems to help us organize knowledge. Thus "openness" (which Dewey sometimes calls a "willingness to listen") is an essential part of his conception of rationality or intelligence. Deweyan "reason"— intelligence—must be emotional and imaginative. The old use of "heart" is perhaps closer to his meaning than the modern idea of "mind." We must try to enter into the full meaning of situations, not merely a "cognitive" understanding of them. Our imaginative ability to shift from one perspective to another facilitates the process of communication and brings diverse perspectives into a *working* relationship, even though there may be a degree of *conceptual* vagueness as a result. "Open-mindedness is not the same as empty-mindedness," says Dewey. "To hang out a sign saying 'Come right in; there is no one at home' is not the equivalent of hospitality." Instead, he argues there is a receptivity that is willing to let "experiences accumulate and sink in and ripen, which is an essential of development" (MW, 9:183). Instead of teaching people to develop merely their own powers of self-justification, we need to develop our capacities to hear others, genuinely to listen to them. Listening does not mean uncritical acceptance, just as it does not mean being automatically judgmental. It is, as Dewey said, a capacity to take the other's point of view into our own and through it to enlarge our understanding of the situation. Only insofar as we have developed our ability to enter imaginatively into the worlds of meaning that human beings have constructed to make sense out of life, can we begin to listen to the richness of experience itself. Only then can we even begin to hear ourselves.

It is at this point that the ultimate goal of the democratic ideal presents itself, the ideal that all humans desire to live lives fraught with meaning and value and that this is the aim of civilization itself. We are responsible for creating, implementing, and criticizing the meaning of life. "Democracy" is the name of the culture that takes this responsibility self-consciously. Democratic civilization is the "culture of experience," as John McDermott has said. It explores the world of possible meanings through which we may achieve a political wisdom about the best lives possible. The method of democracy is art applied to life. The first step must be in enlarging our capacity to imagine and feel as well as understand conceptually. The arts and humanities are crucial in this endeavor: "they supply organs of vision" (MW, 9:238). But they also supply what Dewey might have better called "organs of hearing." If democracy has any hope, I believe it must lie in encouraging this capacity of people to hear, to have a creative silence that opens them to the fullness of the world, as well as encouraging the active search to find cooperative ways to develop this richness and share it with others.

PART THREE

AESTHETICS OF EXISTENCE

"LOVE CALLS US TO THINGS OF THIS WORLD"

Santayana's Unbearable Lightness of Being

One of the most fascinating and totally unproductive exchanges between two major American philosophers commenced with Santayana's review of Dewey's *Experience and Nature* and Dewey's rather testy rejoinder, "Half-Hearted Naturalism." Santayana's review was perversely insightful, highlighting in Dewey's metaphysics just about everything Santayana detested about America: pragmatism, metaphysics, idealism, romanticism, optimism, the busy foolishness of industrial democracy, naiveté. Dewey's outlook was irredeemably "boyish" and "near-sighted," focusing on the human foreground rather than upon nature, which herself had no foreground or background. Dewey's "naturalism" was tainted with the loathsome bacillus of idealism; it lacked a discipline of spirit in which nature's power was acknowledged but not worshiped. Ideals, said Santayana, are not magical causes in the bosom of matter. Only the materialist, like himself, seeing nature for what *it* was, could love the ideal for what *it* was: lovely, alien, and indifferent. Santayana, Dewey shot back, was a dogmatic materialist, "kneeling before the unknowable," with a "broken-backed" rather than robust naturalism due to an intellectual "hang-over" from Platonism and its resulting dualism.[1]

It is not my purpose to rehash this debate and fault each philosopher for misunderstanding the other. I wish instead to explore a theme that is shared by Dewey and Santayana in their attempts at a "naturalistic metaphysics," or, to use Santayana's preferred term, "ontology." The role of the aesthetic I find particularly crucial. I hope to show how Santayana approached the question of "Nature" or "Being" through this avenue. I will also indicate briefly at the end that Dewey's and Santayana's very different conceptions of the aesthetic may account, ultimately, for their very different philosophies. The moral I draw from this is that the aesthetic may well prove to be a more important domain of philosophical inquiry, especially for metaphysics, than hitherto suspected. I will state for now, broadly and indefensibly, that I take imagination to be central to the philosophical enterprise and, granting this, the traditional idea of ontology must be rethought.

In this sense, Dewey and Santayana might be regarded as "postmodern philosophers," a term I am sure makes Santayana's shade in Limbo wince in disgust. "Postmodern" is used in the sense in which one questions the modernist assumption that science or a scientific epistemology is the driving force of philosophy or that "being" is to be identified with the object of scientific knowledge. But I do not mean that Dewey and Santayana deny the possibility of knowledge, the value of science, or the possibility of progress, though here Santayana is far more conservative and skeptical than Dewey. The purely negative, "deconstructive" aspect of postmodernism is alien to their thought. Perhaps, rather than perpetuate the simplistic rhetorical division of philosophy into "modern" and "postmodern" phases, it would be better to contrast those philosophies that are "epistemic" in orientation—including those that are primarily concerned with "deconstructing" epistemic claims—with those that are "aesthetic" in orientation. In this sense, both Santayana and Dewey, I would contend, are aesthetic philosophers, putting philosophy to

1. See George Santayana, "Dewey's Naturalistic Metaphysics," *The Journal of Philosophy* 22 (1925): 673–88, reprinted in *The Philosophy of John Dewey*, ed. Paul A. Schilpp, and in *Obiter Scripta*, and John Dewey, "Half-Hearted Naturalism," *The Journal of Philosophy* 24 (1927): 57–64, included in *Later Works* 3 (1984): 367–84.

service toward the end of a life incarnate with wisdom and beauty, a "spiritual life," if you will.

Before treating Santayana directly, I will make some broad claims about the classical conceptions of ontology found in the Greeks.[2] I find myself in company with Martin Heidegger in designating Parmenides as the "fateful" figure for Western thinking. It was Parmenides who enumerated the various signs (*semata*) of Being (*to eon, esti*): uncreated and deathless, without past or future, "since it *is* now" (*epei nun estin*), one, indivisible, continuous, everywhere alike, at rest, limited, whole, nameable, necessary, immanent to the mind (*nous*) rather than the senses: in short, it is "full" (*empleon*), complete, and so *perfect*. It is alone what is thinkable and knowable, "For *Being* must be the same for thought and speech" (DK, 6, 8). The location of the primary (or for Parmenides, only) sense of "Being" is the present third person singular, "it-is," the impersonal "now." But this carries with it the sense of a process brought to final actualization. The guiding metaphor in this description is that Being is "full" and "complete," hence it has no "emptiness" or "need." It is "perfect" in the sense of perfec*ted*: brought to fulfillment, "finished" in the way a work of art is when to add or detract would ruin it. The "is" is that of determinate finitude, not open possibility. Whatever modifications would be introduced by subsequent classical ontology, they would be undertaken in light of accepting Parmenides' ontology of perfection. Being came to be most fully exemplified in what is perfect, and perfection means that it is "self-sufficient" (needing nothing beyond itself and so self-caused and self-sustaining). It also means that it is without change, movement, or growth; that is, it is "timeless," an ever-present *now*, which does not have a history or a future. Plato and Plotinus apply this canon to the Forms; Aristotle to his divine principle, the Unchanging Changer; Democritus to his material atoms; Origen and Augustine to God.

Because Being is conceived here as that which is *essentially finished*, it can be thought of as *finite*, that is, as something whose nature is *fixed*— something which has no potentiality in it because it is realized. From a temporal perspective, in terms of tense, its sense is not the present so much as the perfect, denoting some action that is over and done, completed,

---

2. For a more in-depth discussion of this see "Between Being and Emptiness: Toward an Eco-ontology of Inhabitation," included in this book.

brought to an end. The "necessary" character lies, I am suggesting, in that what is "timeless" is really presented in terms of something that is *past*; what is done is done and cannot be changed. The "necessity" of Being is really the necessity of the past. Parmenides shattered the implicit connection of *phusis*, of growth and development, with "reality" or Being, that about which a *logos* was possible. The *logos* of Being now became "logic," not *historia*, "natural history." But in fact the idea of "perfection" relies upon the assumption of time, process, and development toward some end. Parmenides, in making Being "perfect," was in fact thinking of a process that *had been perfected*, and so it was in principle knowable with certainty. As Hegel's system attests, nothing is so certain as the past. He tried to see the future as if it were already accomplished history, and so it took on a "necessary" modality in his eyes. But the problem, as Kierkegaard (and James, following him) says, is that while we may *understand* backward, we *live* forward. If you want an absolute science of Being—that is, to regard Being as fundamentally something that is *known*—it helps to think of Being as that which has no future to it; i.e., as something which is "perfected." If, on the other hand, you have the pragmatist's sense of the future, your ontology had better have multimodal dimensions in which chance, individuality, and growth have a share.

The implications of collapsing the finished, perfected past into the idea of an "eternal present," which was necessary, finite, and "sayable" (capable of being brought into the domain of *logos*, "rationality"), resulted in the identification of Being with the Knowable. Put another way, the primary way in which Being manifested its true essence was through instantaneous grasp of intellectual insight (*nous*). Conversely, given the understanding of Being as the completed and fully articulated, knowledge itself came to be understood as that which "came to rest" in this luminous vision. Ideally, "metaphysics" would be a demonstrative science based upon first principles realized through such a direct insight into the nature of Being *qua* Being. That is, knowledge itself was epitomized in the notion of a *completed science* rather than a *process of inquiry*.

It was one of the projects of modernity to reformulate the categories and concepts of classical metaphysics so as to fit the needs of the emerging new science. However much Aristotle's concepts of form and matter, actuality and potentiality, hierarchical causes and internal principles of self-development or change came to be jettisoned, the fundamental commitments stated above remained. Physics aspired to a science of nature whose substance, in itself, was changeless, and whose laws of motion were ideally expressible in the transformational equations of mathematics, and an equation is inherently timeless. For matter to be *known*, it had to be conceived in the classical manner as something essentially fixed and determined. Motion in the world machine, for Descartes, Leibniz, and Newton, had to be introduced from without: if not *Deus ex machina*, then *Deus extra machinam*: God outside the machine! For example, Newton's atoms are essentially inertial, capable of receiving but not of initiating motion.[3] The irony of the modernist project was that from Galileo on, it had tried to impose Plato's timeless realm of mathematically precise forms onto the physical world, where Plato had kept the precise realm of Being distinct from the inherently imprecise realm of Becoming.

I will not tell the long tale of the unraveling of the project of modernism, from Kant and Mill to Heidegger and the later Wittgenstein, to Foucault and Kuhn, to Derrida and Rorty. Their apparent consensus seems to be that metaphysics is a mistake, and at least for the postmodernists, "Philosophy" is at an end. Instead I would like us to consider an alternative: that from the beginning metaphysics had been ravished by an aesthetic ideal, that of perfection, and that the prospect of future metaphysics may lie more with our susceptibility to other forms of ravishment, to falling in love again, perhaps more wisely this time. If our condition as human beings is, as I maintain, suffused by an aesthetic horizon, not itself finite, focused, or at rest and yet a condition of all we can delimit and cognize, then we may find that imagination is at the root of all meaning and that the quest of metaphysics may not be to seek completion in a perfected science but to open up the possibility of an art of existence, of a wisdom which is polymodal in its understanding of Being and governed by an eros of aesthetic existence rather than by the ideal of the "mastery of nature."

Though Plato, obviously, had connected the themes of desire and beauty to the question of Being, and there are echoes of this throughout the medieval tradition (as when Augustine calls God, "Beauty, so ancient and so new"), the "aesthetic" has not on the whole been taken seriously as an approach to ontology, at least in Anglo-American philosophy,

---

3. See Ivor Leclerc's fine discussion of the problems of modern philosophy of nature giving an account of motion on non-Aristotelian principles in his *The Nature of Physical Existence* (Atlantic Highlands, NJ: Humanities Press, 1972).

although I believe it could be shown that it has always been *used*.[4] *Aisthēsis* for the Greeks meant perception of the changing world of nature; there was no topic designated as "aesthetics." The term "aesthetics" was the coinage of Alexander Baumgarten in the Enlightenment and it intended to address those judgments leading to "inferior *knowledge*, clear without being distinct," *cognitio inferior, clara sed non distincta*. That is, "aesthetics" was born as a poor sister to epistemology. It is here, I believe, that the comparison of Santayana's and Dewey's approaches can be of value to us. If our ways of understanding ourselves and our world are fundamentally constituted through an aesthetic awareness, our prereflective understanding of the "aesthetic" may well determine the ontology we articulate. Santayana and Dewey begin with radically different understandings of the aesthetic and end up with the conflict that they have over "naturalistic metaphysics" as a result of this.

When Dewey published "The Postulate of Immediate Empiricism" in 1905, he was, I believe, entirely aware of his radical break with the Western tradition, which identified the nature of reality with the object of knowledge.[5] The "postulate" that "things are as they are experienced *as*" led Dewey to the claim that things may be experienced in a variety of ways *other* than as the outcome of a process of inquiry. To claim that Reality was only what it was for a *knower*, Dewey stated, is "the root paralogism of all idealisms" and "if not the root of all philosophical evil, at least one of its main roots" (MW, 3:160). 1905 was also the year in which the five volumes of *The Life of Reason* began to appear. In his introduction to *The Life of Reason* (appearing in the first volume, *Reason in Common Sense*), Santayana wrote, "the Life of Reason is another name for what, in the widest sense of the word, might be called Art" because impulse and ideation are fused so that action is expressive and aims at happiness. Moreover, "Every genuine ideal has a natural basis. . . ."[6] But, even so, Santayana was careful to point out that

> This ideal, far as it is from actual realisation, has so dazzled men, that
> in their religion and mythical philosophy they have often spoken as if

---

4. See Augustine, *Confessions*, 10:27. This statement may seem unfair to the whole Platonic tradition as well as to such German idealists as Schelling and Hegel. Nevertheless, the aesthetic is there treated at best as a facet or moment of complete Being.

5. "The Postulate of Immediate Empiricism" (1905: MW, 3), reprinted in *The Influence of Darwin on Philosophy* (1910). See my essay "The Aesthetics of Reality" chapter 1 in this book for further discussion of this important article and its place in Dewey's development.

6. *Reason in Common Sense* (New York: Scribner, 1905), 6–7. Hereafter cited in text as RCS.

it were already actual and efficient. This anticipation amounts, when taken seriously, to a confusion of purposes with facts and of functions with causes. (RCS, 7)

Both Santayana and Dewey rejected the claim of idealism, that the ideal is the real. But for Dewey, this opened up the possibility for reconceiving what is meant by "Reality as something *not* equated with the object of knowledge and reconceiving knowledge as something other than a "science of causes" in the modernist sense. For Santayana, who accepted "nature" as the object of scientific knowledge, as a domain of causes or power, the moral was to avoid making "ideals" into causal powers; a careful distinction between the two must be observed. Because ideals are not causes they are "unnatural." For Dewey, ideals are part of nature. The implications of these divergent views would be worked out in the mature works of both thinkers: with Dewey's *Experience and Nature* (1925/1929) and *Art as Experience* (1934) and Santayana's *Scepticism and Animal Faith* (1923) and *Realms of Being* (1927–1940).

I begin by focusing on the role of imagination in Santayana's earlier period. At the beginning of *The Life of Reason* we get a natural history of the genesis of reason itself, since it is a living thing that has a life. Reason emerges gradually from the flux of preconscious nature. Consciousness itself, however, is by no means inherently "rational." It begins "lost in its objects" and even when it thinks it cares for itself, "it really cares only for its ideals." Practical concerns are peripheral: "[T]he core is an irresponsible, ungoverned, irrevocable dream" (RCS, 49). Dreaming is prior to thinking; perception is merely the first school of our birthright lyric madness on its way to normalcy. As Santayana astutely comments, the failure of British empiricism was in trying to get ideas from experience, but "the great difficulty in education is to get experience out of ideas" (RCS, 51). Indeed, our only hope lies in the possibility for the dream to become orderly and productive of a happy life.

Thought itself for Santayana does not arise from innate logical principles but from a prerational "witches' brew" (RCS, 65). It develops with the spontaneous ability for experience to become infused with memory and, by action, anticipatory of immanent ends. "Thought is a form of life," says Santayana, "and should be conceived on the analogy of nutrition, generation, and art" (RCS, 67). It comes to sense the order of the world in a rhythmic, progressive way, rather than by inherent empty intuitions of Euclidean space and Newtonian time. Repetition of the same sound is not mere succession of identity; it is the growing *insistence* of the experience, as in the tolling of a bell. The important point here is that the patterns in experience emerge as *growing forms*, which *imaginatively* and *creatively* shape the experience as it develops:

> It is not identity in the substance impressed, but growing complication in the phenomenon presented, that makes possible a sense of diversity and relation between things. The identity of substance or spirit, if it were absolute, would indeed prevent comparison, because it would exclude modifications, and it is the survival of past modifications within the present that makes comparisons possible. We may impress any number of forms successively on the same water, and the identity of the substance will not help those forms to survive and accumulate their effects. But if we have a surface that retains our successive stampings we may change the substance from wax to plaster and from plaster to bronze, and the effects of our labour will survive and be superimposed upon one another. It is the actual plastic form in both mind and body, not any unchanging substance or agent, that is efficacious in perpetuating thought and gathering experience. (RCS, 70–71)

I quote this passage at length because it contains an important clue, one that I think Santayana himself eventually ignored. Our imagination need not be thought of as a faculty *opposed* to reason; rather, reason itself can be seen as our imagination at work in making sense out of the process of the experience of an organism in constant interplay with its world. There may be any number of possible patterns that can be developed from our active, embodied existence, which quite effectively "organize" our lives. Our ability to exist not merely from moment to moment but to have a past and a future that are actively fused in the creative transfiguration of the present means that we cannot evade our pervasive temporality. In a more Heideggerian way, we might say that human temporality is our "Dasein," our "Here/There-Being." This temporality gets narrowed to the vanishing point and so misunderstood and devalued in the claims of Parmenidean ontology, in which "Being" is the perfected present of a completed deed, the ultimate "fact" (or *factum*: something which has been accomplished and is no longer underway). Santayana, however, read the moral differently, in a way that, with the wisdom of hindsight, prefigures the direction of his later ontology. The discipline of nature upon the imagination leads ultimately to a distinction between two realms:

> When reflection, turning to the comprehension of a chaotic experience, busies itself about recurrences, when it seeks to normalise in some way things coming and going, and to straighten out the causes of events, that reflection is inevitably turned toward something dynamic and independent, and can have no successful issue except in mechanical science. When on the other hand reflection stops to challenge and question the fleeting object, not so much to prepare for its possible return as to conceive its present nature, this reflection is turned no less unmistakably in the direction of ideas, and will terminate in logic or the morphology of being. We attribute independence to things in order to normalise their recurrence. We attribute essences to them in order to normalise their manifestations or constitution. Independence will ultimately turn out to be an assumed constancy in material processes, essence an assumed constancy in ideal meanings or points of reference in discourse. (RCS, 73–74)

This passage clearly prefigures Santayana's later distinction between the realms of matter and essence, with the former eventuating in scientific knowledge and technology, the latter contributing to the free disport of the life of spirit. But a deeper issue is involved here: The discovery of essence is possible only with the systematic, categorial *separation* of the aesthetic from the temporal existence of the animal body and its situation. Essence is intuited only when time and knowledge are given over to their proper domain:

> To catch the passing phenomenon in all its novelty and idiosyncrasy is a work of artifice and curiosity. Such and exercise does violence to intellectual instinct and involves an aesthetic power of diving bodily into the stream of sensation, having thrown overboard all rational ballast and escaped at once the inertia and the momentum of practical life. (RCS, 75)

Aesthetic apprehension is due to an ability to *exclude* or *suppress* the world, the body, and time. It requires an ability to concentrate on the passing phenomenon as a pure object, disregarding its order of genesis or its semiotic import. Santayana's later conception of Being arises from this interpretation of the aesthetic, and many of the differences we can find between his philosophy and Dewey's can be traced to their different ways of interpreting aesthetic experience and its relation to the world. Before contrasting Dewey's own approach, I would like, briefly, to examine Santayana's ontology and his theory of intuition, which is the basis for his conception of the "spiritual life."

Scepticism and Animal Faith marks an introduction to the later system; it is a strange and unusual book for Santayana—a laborious, technical "philosopher's book." It serves to introduce the later system by asking the reader to undergo a self-imposed discipline of skeptical reduction, the result of which will reveal the nature of matter as "that-which-is-not-essence," an unintelligible urgency of power, a dynamism of external relations, and the nature of essence as "that-which-is-not-matter," a limpid, luminous domain of possible objects of intuition, each self-enclosed by necessary internal relations and sublimely indifferent to nature. By this progressive disillusionment, Santayana wishes to reveal the possibility for the liberation of spirit.

Santayana's ontology, then, is not written from some sort of "value-neutral" standpoint or methodology. As he himself says, "My philosophy is like that of the ancients, a discipline of the mind and heart, a lay religion."[7] By clarification of the "basic categories of common sense," he undertakes to discern the various meanings of the word "is" not to show the structure of Being as it stands in itself or to some all-knowing subject, but to show the basic, useful distinctions for the possibility of living a spiritual life. The aim is not a supreme science of sciences or even an extension of cosmology; the aim is wisdom. His system, then, can be described as a "grammatology of Being." The result should be for us, readers of *Realms of Being*, a new kind of life, a *vita nuova*, in which aesthetic apprehension is actively cultivated, for it is the only salvation that we will know. The good news is that it lies close at hand; it merely needs disentangling from all that would distract or disperse it, all that would make us submerge the radiance it offers in the worries and concerns of a struggling animal in the mechanical flux of nature. The key to the kingdom is intuition.[8]

But what is this "intuition"? Santayana says, "By intuition I mean direct and obvious possession of the apparent, without commitments

---

7. *Realms of Being* (New York: Scribner, 1942), 827. Hereafter cited in the text as RB.
8. I have developed this claim in "Santayana's Sage: The Disciplines of Aesthetic Enlightenment," in this volume.

of any sort" (RB, 646). It is "always with us, but dispersed" (RB, 647); hence the aim should be to gather it together. But all activity is a function of the realm of matter. The act of intuition is based on the nutritive and gestational conditions of the mothering psyche; in itself it is, like any organic action, "a process and not an image, an event and not an idea, an existence and not an essence" (RB, 648). Yet somehow it transcends the lowly origins of its birth and, though itself a temporal, existential, embodied event, concentrates the object of its attention into a timeless unity, recognized and enjoyed simply for being only what it is.

Spirit is thus "the fruition of an organ" and requires a vast, slumbering preconscious "vital background" (RB, 650). Yet it does not realize itself if it does not ignore all the biological hullabaloo that makes it possible. It lives only in the appropriation of essences. But how is this possible? By "synthesis," says Santayana.

> Intuition is in some sense always a synthesis, even when the datum is an inarticulate feeling, like a scent or a pain. . . . Yet the word synthesis is highly ambiguous and misleading, like other Kantian terms that have become convenient or indispensable. The danger is that what occurs in the realm of matter should be interpreted by literary psychology as occurring in the realm of spirit. In the realm of spirit there is no machinery, nothing compounded, dynamic, mysterious, or latent; therefore there is no synthesis at that level. . . . A synthesis may therefore be said to have occurred, but not in consciousness. (RB, 651)

The grand error of idealism lies in just this transference of the act of synthesis from the body to its blossoming effect: take Husserl as an example.

The peculiar consequence of all this for Santayana's position, however, is that in no sense can consciousness or spirit be said to be "autonomous"—self-governed, self-determining, a master of its own destiny. It lives and dies by the grace of its animal host. So in what sense, then, can even "literary psychology" be of any use in helping others to awaken to the possibility of the spiritual life and sharpen their aesthetic powers of concentration? At best, Santayana says, intuitions may return to the same vicinities of the Realm of Essence, each mortal intuition discerning a new face or aspect of a field of related essences, such as we would find in mathematics or in an author's exploration of a certain literary world, like

Lear's kingdom or Tolkien's Middle Earth. There may be ways in which intuitions can be organically cultivated, suggests Santayana. But

> successive intuitions can never be synthesized. They are events, they are unsubstantial, they blaze for a moment and vanish into nothing. But the deliverances of those moments may supplement one another as descriptions of the object, or as mere experiences; and a subsequent intuition, springing from the organic soil so tilled and fertilized, may repeat those intuitions or variations of them in a fresh description of the object, or poetic suggestion of it in its wholeness and in its destiny. Imagination may thus evolve, and knowledge may increase, not by an impossible synthesis or breeding together of dead intuitions, but by the training of organisms and the complication of instruments, orchestrating a richer but no less fugitive life in the spirit. (RB, 652–53)

Consciousness for Santayana is a type of sublimation. But it can unmask its pretenses, and at its best, it rejoices in what light it finds at its disposal. The spiritual life is one in which we learn to concentrate upon the pure aesthetic character of the infinite experiences close at hand, which so silently offer themselves to the busy, bypassing dwellers of the world. "Art" is not to be identified with the high culture of the museum elite for Santayana any more than for Dewey. As for the Zen master, the Buddha-nature or its transitory suchness of each thing needs only to be noticed with purity of insight; the only thing that can see it is the "no-mind," the purely present attention, of the enlightened being. In a late letter, Santayana recalls the great art historian Bernard Berenson running into him in Venice and blathering on about a Veronese exhibition "as if we were still in the 1890s," while ignoring a beautiful sunset such as Veronese would have loved to paint.[9]

I think now we can see that Santayana's aesthetics falls in line with the tradition of post-Kantian formalism, including the "art for art" movement, Clive Bell's doctrine of significant form, and Susanne Langer's impressive extension of it. The aesthetic stands revealed when the practical world is somehow pushed into the background and something that is "pure" and "only itself" stands forth. Santayana's Realm of Matter is very

---

9. Santayana to Mrs. C. H. Toy, Oct. 10, 1929, in *The Letters of George Santayana*, ed. Daniel Cory (New York: Scribner, 1955).

much the Hobbesian world of mechanical cause and effect promising the possibility of some technological control; his Realm of Essence is very much the Platonic world of contemplative selfsame objects, but unlike Plato's Forms in that they are not objects of cognition and inhabit a free, unstructured realm, an ontological Hollywood rather than a systematic "great chain of Being." Essences for Santayana form no ultimate domain for a theoretical science to explore by painful dialectic and then axiomatically expound. They stand in paradoxical, contrasting, surprising, humorous, or hostile relationships submitting only to the rule of the law of identity—the anarchist's law of only being yourself that was the motto of Rabelais' Abbey of Thélème.

Thus, I find, in the end Santayana accepted the Parmenidean thesis, changing it only in that for him "perfection" meant "emptiness" or "freedom" of existence and its sordid moral and epistemological imperatives. Essences were static, self-identical, timeless objects, only irrelevantly connected with the world. The moment in which they were manifested, though itself in time, mysteriously conjured the sense of time suspended. Because he conceived of the aesthetic as the "lightness of Being," the illusion of floating the magician performs, it liberates us from the weighty concerns of our existential lives and personal selves. As in a performance, intuition is an event in which time somehow seems to stand still, and the disconnected plurality of a madly whirling world consolidates, briefly, into a luminous mask of unity and order, evoking a cry of astonishment and selfless love.

Santayana's ontology and conception of the aesthetic is predicated on a different kind of *life* than Dewey's naturalistic metaphysics and doctrine of consummatory experience. I cannot draw out the comparison extensively here, but some brief remarks are possible. Dewey agrees with Santayana about the naturalistic basis of the aesthetic: "Every living experience owes its richness to what Santayana well calls 'hushed reverberations.'"[10] But Dewey insists that these reverberations cannot be dismissed from the apparition of the aesthetic itself. This includes two aspects that I think Santayana ignores: the temporal nature of the aesthetic as process and the penumbral, circumambient nature of the unifying quality, the "felt horizon," which gives the experience meaning.

10. *Art as Experience* in *Later Works*, 10:23 (Carbondale: Southern Illinois University Press, 1987). The passage from Santayana is found in *Reason in Common Sense*, 65.

As to the first, Dewey says, "Art celebrates with peculiar intensity the moments in which the past reenforces the present and in which the future is a quickening of what now is" (LW, 10:24). The past and future are constitutive features of the present, so that we experience the aesthetic as the *consummation* of a process: Time is not merely a condition, but part of the *felt meaning* of the experience. The experience has finitude because it has this sense of drawing together and fruition. Its closure is one of development: ". . . its close is a consummation and not a cessation. Such an experience is a whole and carries with it its own individualizing quality and self-sufficiency. It is *an* experience" (LW, 10:42). Hence Dewey's well-known description of *an* experience as a *process*: "In such experiences, every successive part flows freely, without seam and without unfilled blanks, into what ensues. . . . There are pauses, places of rest, but they punctuate and define the *quality of movement*. They sum up what has been undergone and prevent its dissipation and idle evaporation" (LW, 10:43, emphasis added).

There is a pervasive sense of the whole, which contextualizes each of the phases *as* phases of *its* development. This is the unifying quality for Dewey, but it does not have the character of a bare identity: "The existence of this unity is constituted by a single *quality* that pervades the entire experience in spite of the variation of its constituent parts" (LW, 10:44). Aesthetic quality is a pervasive qualitative sense of unity in the *temporal* sense of having a transformative growth within it. Its unity is that of *continuity* rather than bare *identity*. Continuity involves the idea of a process in which changes take place, but nevertheless contribute to a whole narrative order. The notes with which a symphony ends are not necessarily those with which it begins. But the beginning has developed and carried us through so that the ending is a closure of a meaningful event and not just another rupture in nature. The aesthetic, for Dewey, not only can but must embrace the world and acknowledge its history and its worldly connections.

Thus Dewey's sense of form, as "*the operation of forces that carry the experience . . . to its own integral fulfillment*" is different from Santayana's concept of form as static (LW, 10:142). Form is the function of interest, says Dewey. In his criticisms of formalists like Roger Fry, he says that without the focusing interest of our embodied perception, there would be no form to see (LW, 10:93). Nor is the aesthetic quality a mere datum, without any further depth than its own simple facade. We do not perceive mere "data," but *meanings*, and these point to the web of contextualizing relations immanent in the focus of any aesthetic experience. It is in ordinary experience that this horizon is forgotten or ignored, but in the aesthetic it is brought to the fore.

Finally, in contrast to Santayana's solitary moment of pure intuition, Dewey must see the aesthetic as an engagement in which a dialogue of expression and response goes on, even if it is only within ourselves. The rhythms of the social self continue in our solitary moments, shaping the objects of experience into expressive forms, as at the very least *potential* objects of communication and sharing.

Though I cannot expand upon this theme now, I think this is why Dewey's metaphysics, like Santayana's, is connected to an art of imagination. If imagination is not a mechanical process, thematically irrelevant to the intuition of spirit, but itself a dynamic way in which possible developments of order are projected from our current experience, then intelligence does "make a difference" in the existential world without invoking transcendental egos. Just such a view of imagination has been jointly proposed by Mark Johnson and linguist George Lakoff. By their account, making sense of the world involves a network of dynamic paths of making significant connections. These originate in our preverbal experience, deriving from the active structures of our animal embodiment, such as the patterns we get from being vertical, symmetrical, bipedal beings. They call these patterns "image schemata." As Johnson explains, "An image schema is a recurring, dynamic pattern of our perceptual interactions and motor programs that gives coherence and structure to our experience."[11] One of the major implications of this view is that "rationality" is inherently and irrevocably built upon using these patterns across a variety of experiences; in other words, our rationality is essentially metaphorical. Metaphor is

> conceived as a pervasive mode of understanding by which we project patterns from one domain of experience in or to structure another domain of a different kind. So conceived, metaphor is not merely a linguistic mode of expression; rather, it is one of the chief cognitive structures by which we are able to have coherent, ordered experiences that we can reason about and make sense of. (BM, xiv–xv)

11. Mark Johnson, *The Body in the Mind* (Chicago: University of Chicago Press, 1987), xiv; hereafter cited in the text as BM.

One example here might help. We have the structure of "Source-Path-Goal," which shapes our understanding of "Action." This becomes elaborated in understanding something like a process of growth or development: for example, the seed "aims" at becoming the plant. We thereby get the idea of the end of a process as the *consummation* of a beginning. We also have the idea of full-empty from our biological existence as creatures that can *be* full or hungry. What may have happened with Parmenides, from this standpoint, is that the "meaning of Being" was read through the schema of "full" and "consummation" (as *perfect*, recall), but it was then detached from the idea of process. If we went back to Parmenides' "signs of Being," we would see not so much a "rational argument" as a series of metaphors guided by an image schema which implicitly relies on the ideas of organic processes.

What if we took the whole living body and its image schemata as the field for discerning "Being"? From such a basis, the meaning of Being would look very much, I think, like Dewey's plan for a transactional, ecological metaphysics. We are constantly connecting various fields of meaning, actively structuring and reconstructing them. We are always imaginatively constituting our world, and so we are guided by a plurality of possible meanings that are not so much intellectually discerned and cognized as aesthetically felt, immanent senses of the situations we are in. The question of metaphysics is intrinsically bound up with the aesthetics of human existence. The aesthetics of our existence is also that of the world that draws us to it through our projects. We experience the world through an eros for meaning that cannot be divorced from life. The "generic traits" of nature are discerned so as to guide us toward a life of wisdom in which dualisms are avoided and intelligent distinctions are made so that the material conditions of our social lives are secured for the end of sharing the world in that embodied beauty called love. And "love calls us to things of this world," as poet Richard Wilbur says. However much we may find ideals of purity and disembodiment alluring, it is "better to accept the waking body."

In his poem "Love Calls Us to Things of This World," Richard Wilbur gives us a symbol of the Santayanan ideal of the purity of disembodied beauty in the vision of fresh laundry drying in the morning sunlight:

> The eyes open to a cry of pulleys,
> And spirited from sleep, the astounded soul

> Hangs for a moment bodiless and simple
> As false dawn.
> Outside the open window
> The morning air is all awash with angels. . . .

Their billowing in the breeze gives an almost intoxicating sense of pure freedom:

> Now they are flying in place, conveying
> The terrible speed of their omnipresence, moving
> And staying like white water; and now of a sudden
> They swoon down into so rapt a quiet
> That nobody seems to be there.

But this is also a world without love—and so Wilbur turns toward the Deweyan world of embodied beauty, which bears with it fallibility and the sense of the precarious reality of the world.

> Yet, as the sun acknowledges
> With a warm look the world's hunks and colors,
> The soul descends once more in bitter love
> To accept the waking body, saying now
> In a changed voice as the man yawns and rises,
>
> "Bring them down from their ruddy gallows;
> Let there be clean linen for the backs of thieves;
> Let lovers go fresh and sweet to be undone,
> And the heaviest nuns walk in a pure floating
> Of dark habits,
>   keeping their difficult balance.[12]

---

12. Richard Wilbur, *The Poems of Richard Wilbur* (New York: Harcourt Brace Jovanovich, 1963), 65–66.

TEN

MOUNTAINS AND RIVERS WITHOUT END

The Intertwining of Nature and Spirit in Emerson's Aesthetics

East and West

In many ways Chinese and Western philosophy offer a series of vivid contrasts going all the way back to their respective origins, so that the very idea of philosophy itself stands in contrast. The West begins with the Greeks and their speculative wonder at nature. The original question for them is: What is the originating principle of nature? This prefigures the central concern of Western philosophy with knowledge and science. The origin of Chinese philosophy focuses upon fundamental questions of political and ethical philosophy. The original question for them is, How can we discovery the Way? These two different origins gave rise not only to different conceptions of the central issues of philosophy, but also to how philosophy should be conducted and what sort of person the philosopher should be.

This paper was prepared originally for an APA panel session devoted to the topic of "Integration and Transcendence in Chinese and American Philosophy"; Tu Weiming addressed the topic from the Chinese side, I from the American, with comments by Robert Neville.

This contrast is perhaps sharpest in the role of aesthetics. In the West, aesthetics (for which there was not term until the eighteenth century) is not regarded as a very important, much less central, part of philosophy. Metaphysics, ethics, and logic have constituted the core of Western philosophy.[1] Platonism's ontology of the beautiful is the noble exception, but it made the ideal of beauty the mark of transcendent true being, a theme extensively carried out by Plotinus, for whom the Beautiful ceased merely to be a criterion and became the lure whereby the soul was "oned" with the One.[2] In Christianity this becomes the yearning of the soul for God. *"Sero te amavi, pulchritudo tam antiqua et tam nova, sero te amavi!"* says Augustine.[3] Contrast the transcendent yearning in Augustine's utterance with the matter-of-fact statement of the Daoist, Guo Xiang (or Kuo Hsiang in the old Wade-Giles transliteration): "The music of nature is not an entity existing outside of things."[4] In a similar vein, Greg Whincup observes, "The essence of Chinese poetry is emotion linked to landscape. Chinese poets make the natural world an expression of human emotion. This is more than just a convention. The unity of man and nature is part of the traditional Chinese perception of the world."[5] Classical Chinese thought focused on living in harmony with the Dao. Confucianism in particular turned to art as essential to cultivating the *junzi* (*chün-tze*), the "gentleman" or noble scholar. For Confucius, *The Book of Odes*, having come from a distant age when humans were in harmony with the *Dao*, was therefore a canon for wholesome values; similarly music and social forms of propriety (or "ritual") manifested and maintained our open-hearted humanity. The arts attuned the scholar to humanity. With the other four of the "Five Classics," it was regarded by Confucius as the foundation of philosophy. If the Daoist rejected the art and ritual so central to Confucianism, it was to experience more purely and intimately the

---

1. This goes back to the divisions of the Stoa, but even Kant repeats it, though he himself included aesthetics as part of one "leg" of the critical tripod in *The Critique of Judgment*.

2. See *Enneads* I.6 and V.8.

3. "Late, late, have I loved thee, Beauty, so ancient and so new." *Confessions* X.27.

4. *Sources of the Chinese Tradition*, vol. 1, ed. Wm Theodore de Bary, Wing-Tst Chan, and Burton Watson (New York: Columbia University Press, 1960), 240. Even the one point where Western philosophy says something like this, namely Pythagoreanism and its "harmony of the spheres," shows the fundamental contrast, for number "orders" and "governs" nature and philosophy turns to mathematics as a catharsis to purify the soul. Guo Xiang (d. 312 CE) edited and wrote a commentary on the *Zhuangzi / Chuang-tze*.

5. Greg Whincup, *The Heart of Chinese Poetry* (New York: Anchor Books, 1987), 7.

great spontaneous harmony of nature itself. But perhaps culture and nature are not so opposed, especially if it is natural for humans to be artistic. As Guo Xiang says, genuine music is in nature.

It is no surprise that the Western and Chinese images of "the philosopher" should contrast as well. The Western philosopher since the beginning of the modern period seeks analytical methodologies; that is, *regulae*, as a means to "the mastery of nature." We know nature to master it. The result for Anglophone philosophy is the obsession with epistemology and symbolic logic. Philosophy becomes a manipulation of concepts by symbols. Contrast this with the philosopher as *junzi* (*chün-tze*) who tries to cultivate his spirit, who plays music seriously with his whole heart, and whose brush may as easily paint a landscape and write a poem as write philosophy. The Confucian philosopher seeks above all to cultivate his heart-mind (*xin* or *hsin*), for this is what realizes the central virtue of benevolence or human-heartedness (*ren* or *jen*). One's person becomes music to be in harmony with the Way. Or contrast the Western "master of nature" armed with science with the Daoist rogue, for whom philosophy is one with intuition, laughter, and spontaneity.

In the understanding of "art," too, there is sharp contrast between East Asian and Western art traditions. Art in the West, at least since the Renaissance, has been the assertion or expression of creative individual ego, summed up in the idea of the genius. Western art is not demure, but commands attention. It is form dominating matter as the intellect and will dictate. East Asian art is the result of attained harmony of spirit; it is quietly receptive and, like the "empty" space in ink landscape painting, invites the viewer to enter the work with plenty of room for one's own imaginative interplay. Individual style, be it the misty, dark forms of Mi Fu (Mi Fei) or the linear traceries of Ni-Zan (Ni Tsan), is not assertion of self but an achievement of harmony between self and world.[6] The participatory nature of art finds a marvelous example in those paintings called "Mountains and Rivers without End." These are long scrolls meant to be gradually unrolled, depicting an ongoing journey, which the viewer can take in imagination, walking along mountain paths, crossing streams on rustic bridges, and resting at inns or temples along the way. The viewer

---

6. Mi Fei or Mi Fu (1051–1107) and Ni Tsan or Ni Zan (1301–74) were painters of the Song and Yuan Dynasties respectively. Mi Fei is known for misty, dark landscapes, Ni Tsan for clear, finely drawn ones.

is invited into the world of the painting. More often than not, a Western painting or sculpture is an assertion and frequently a wall challenging the viewer. (The epitome of this is perhaps found in the work of sculptor Richard Serra, whose pieces are made out of slabs of raw sheet metal. His massive wall-like *Tilted Arc*, which was installed in Federal Plaza in 1981, was eventually removed because of complaints made by those who worked nearby and used, or tried to use, the plaza.) This is not to ignore the vein of nature-oriented art in Western history, especially since the romantic era. Indeed, the opening toward experience of nature is one of the great contributions of Romanticism. Nevertheless, in philosophy and art, there are sharp contrasts between the West and China.

Chinese and American Philosophy: The Aesthetics of Living

In spite of these profound differences, I do think there can be a significant connection between classical Chinese thought and Western philosophy, especially that of some classical American thinkers. There is an important part of the American philosophical tradition that places emphasis upon the aesthetic aspect of experience as crucial for self-realization and sees philosophy as ultimately concerned with this life of vitalized experience. In other words, "aesthetics" should be understood first and foremost as the "aesthetics of human existence," as I have termed it.[7] Three major examples of thinkers in this tradition are Emerson, Dewey, and Santayana. But we can detect an aesthetic strain in Jonathan Edwards' insistence on the primacy of seeing the "excellency" of things, the "consent of being to being," as the essence of grace.[8] In other words, if one is in the state of grace, one sees the world as beautiful, as God sees it. Aesthetic phenomenology pervades Peirce's idea of Firstness as well as James's radical empiricism. Stanley Cavell's "moral perfectionism" and Richard Rorty's

---

7. See Thomas Alexander, "The Human Eros," chapter 5 in this volume, and "John Dewey and the Aesthetics of Human Existence," *Classical American Pragmatism*, ed. Sandra Rosenthal (Urbana: University of Illinois Press, 1999).

8. "There has been nothing more without a definition than excellency, although it be what we are more concerned with than anything else whatsoever." And: "This is a universal definition of excellency: The consent of being to being, or being's consent to entity." *The Mind*, no. 1 (1723), in *A Jonathan Edwards Reader*, ed. John Smith (New Haven, CT: Yale University Press, 1995), 22, 26.

ironism may be counted as diluted contemporary examples. Dewey summed up this approach when he said,

> To esthetic experience, then, the philosopher must go to understand what experience is. For this reason . . . the theory of esthetics put forth by a philosopher . . . is a test of the capacity of the system he puts forth to grasp the nature of experience itself."[9]

Moreover, the themes of integration and transcendence form part of the central dynamism in this tradition. Dewey's aesthetics is decidedly one of integration; the consummatory experience is a cumulative realiza- tion of the possibilities for deep, qualitatively expressive meaning achieved through the interaction of human beings with each other and with nature. The aesthetics of the later Santayana is one of liberation, seeking escape from the "realm of matter" as well as the needs of the petty ego for liberation into the fictive "realms" of essence and spirit. Though Santayana perversely insisted on calling himself a "Platonist" of sorts, art for him bears some comparison with the Buddhist view that stresses the impermanence and insubstantiality of the world. Both of these moments, integration and liberation, are present in Emerson's thought, and are equally significant for him. They constitute a dynamic polarity between spirit and nature, fusing in his concept of "character," the realized self, as the transformative medium where both God and world become living symbol. The human spirit is the perpetual act of creation.

Dewey's naturalism is a nonreductive one in which creativity, emer- gence, and the ontological possibility of ideals are at its heart.[10] In *A Common Faith*, Dewey stressed the religious implications of this view, arguing for the importance of the religious orientation to existence or Nature, including a meaningful way of invoking the idea of "God," much to the concern of his followers.[11] Thus Dewey picked up the theme of "integration," one of the aims of Confucian views of art. Santayana, even though he embraced materialism and fervently rejected idealism of any sort, was, in one sense, far more of a "transcendentalist" than Emerson,

---

9. *Art as Experience*, (LW, 10:278).
10. I have discussed Dewey's metaphysics of aesthetic experience in my *John Dewey's Theory of Art, Experience, and Nature: The Horizons of Feeling* (Albany: State University of New York Press, 1987). Dewey's naturalistic humanism or emergentism is the central theme of his major book, *Experience and Nature* (LW, 1).
11. *A Common Faith* (LW, 9).

with his detached, timeless "realm of essence" and "realm of spirit."[12] While articulating a concept of a life of spirit, of perpetual possibility of aesthetic awareness, Santayana removed it from all earthly connection so that it might be free, a discipline of liberation. But while the theme of integration can be found in Dewey and liberation in Santayana, it is Emerson who regards both as important.

In all three thinkers we find, then, the idea of "lived aesthetics" as a central concern for realizing human existence, with the topics of integration and liberation reflected in the tensive relation between nature and spirit.[13] Only in a very secondary sense is "aesthetics" related to issues normally included in philosophical discussions of the topic, which focus on the nature of fine art and our experience of it. In a way, then, this approach may be compared with the Chinese view of the aesthetic as an "attainment" of spirit, primarily a discipline of existence and experience. Because Emerson holds these two aspects of integration and liberation together, unlike Dewey and Santayana, who emphasize one over the other, my focus here will be on Emerson. What I propose is that Emerson desires for philosophy to eventuate in transformative vision of ourselves-in-nature.

Furthermore, Emerson offers the possibility of what might be called a "spiritual aesthetics of nature." Of course, this is more fully developed by Henry David Thoreau. But Thoreau's work grows directly out of Emerson's. Not only do these thinkers establish a point of contact with the East Asian tradition, but the implications of aesthetic philosophy have a more imminent bearing. We are at the point in history when we must collectively care for the ecology of the planet. I do not think we come to care for things unless we can behold them and love them in their wonder and beauty. If we are to live with an ecological wisdom, I think it will be because we have encountered nature with a deep aesthetic engagement that not only makes us care for it, but makes us realize it as the

12. One might argue for the influence of the enigmatic figure of Schopenhauer, upon whom Santayana wished to write for his dissertation until Royce objected. There is something of that high pessimism that is present in Santayana's later thought, especially in terms of "the realm of matter." Both Santayana and Schopenhauer turned toward Platonism and Hindu philosophy for solace and insight.

13. By "spirit" I mean the fulfillment of human existence in the creative and receptive engagement with the world. It is meant to be inclusive of Emerson's concept of character, Dewey's description of "God" as the transformative interrelation of the ideal and the real, and Santayana's idea of spirit as a witness to essence.

home of spirit.[14] Thus I believe this topic has serious bearing on the way
Western philosophy has been practiced.

The Importance of Romanticism

Before directly turning to Emerson, we should pause and reflect how
deeply Western culture carries with it a spiritual alienation from nature
and how anomalous this is when compared with other cultures' worldviews. Most cultures around the world and throughout history have
experienced the world as holy. By this I mean that people experience
aspects of the world as aesthetically profound relationships that connect
them with vital meanings.[15] The world is "home," *oikos*. Not far from
where I grew up in Albuquerque, New Mexico, you could see the
beautiful form of *Tsoodzil*, "Mt. Taylor," one of the sacred directional
mountains defining *Dinetah*, the Navajo homeland, and in the Navajo
worldview, a living being, Blue Turquoise Boy. A traditional Navajo
home has the doorway facing east so that the first act of the day is wel-
coming Dawn Boy in a sacred manner, with an offering of pollen or corn-
meal. The Navajo pray: May I go with Beauty before me / May I go with
Beauty behind me / May I go with Beauty above and below me. The idea
of beauty for the Navajo, *hozho*, is not an "aesthetic" concept; it refers
primarily to living in harmony, the "health" of moving along the path of
a human life, which involves feelings of connection and relationship to
family, nature, gods, and the past: *sa'a nakai, bikhei hozho*—as it has long
been, so may it be always done in *hozho*. Part of the beauty-way involves
giving and sharing, remembering and passing along the traditional
stories and songs, being a dynamic passageway for *nilchi'i*, the Holy
Wind, the spirit of life, which is process. The very act of breathing is being
connected—being a vessel for this spirit.[16]

---

14. I realize Romanticism is not a popular approach in contemporary philosophy, but I think the
Romantic movement contains the one thing in the Western tradition that we need—and the one
with which we might connect with the traditions of integration and liberation in Asian thought. For
this reason, too, Emerson is a key figure.

15. Even in Hinduism, where the ideal of transcendence as liberation (*moksha*) is ultimate, the
Hindu experience of the world is in terms of embodied holiness; God is *here*, not "away," and we
need to see and feel that.

16. Richard Farella, *The Main Stalk: A Synthesis of Navajo Philosophy* (Tucson: University of
Arizona Press, 1990), and James Kale McNeely, *Holy Wind* (Tucson: University of Arizona Press,
1991).

Platonism, Neoplatonism, and those "isms" influenced by them made the beauty of the world a shadow of the Beautiful-itself. At least Plotinus was willing to defend the beauty and goodness of the world against the pessimism of Gnostic dualism.[17] For Plotinus, nature was the final outpouring of the cascade of forms from the One. With the rise of modernity, the holiness of the world as an aesthetic home has been fading away. In 1611, John Donne wrote,

> And new Philosophy calls all in doubt,
> The Element of Fire is quite put out;
> The Sun is lost, and th'earth, and no man's wit
> Can well direct him where to looke for it.
> And freely men confess that this world's spent,
> When in the Planets and the Firmament
> They seeke so many new; then see that this
> Is crumbled out againe to his Atomies
> 'Tis all in pieces, all cohaerance gone;
> All just supply, and all Relation . . .[18]

The death of the medieval cosmos was not just an intellectual change, the shift of one "paradigm" for another, but a cultural trauma involving a dislocation in feeling and embodied relationship to the universe. Shortly after Donne wrote his poem, Descartes composed Le Monde, setting forth the modernist vision of nature as a vast, soundless, colorless machine performing mathematical equations, an ocean of power that could be mastered by science guided by the spectral, disjoined "thinking thing": us. The project of the "mastery of nature," as Descartes calls it in the Discourse, now presents us with the literal, not just metaphorical, possibility of the "death of nature" as a result of the success of the project of modernity. Philosophy, in general, has understood itself in terms of this project.

The analytic movement has enshrined the idea of the philosopher as scientist, as the mathematical logician, the clarifier of scientific theory, the empirical investigator of ordinary language and the exponent of "the-mind-is-the-brain-is-a-computer." For a century now, the various "analytic trends" have adopted without question the modernist assumption

---

17. See Plotinus, Enneads, II.9, "Against the Gnostics."
18. John Donne, An Anatomie of the World, "The First Anniversary," a poem nominally commemorating the death of Elizabeth Drury.

that the aim of philosophy is knowledge and the aim of knowledge is to give us mastery of nature. However much "postmodernism," whether of the European or home-grown Rortian variety, may protest the presuppositions of modernism, it has done *nothing* to reconnect humans to the aesthetics of the world. If anything, it has intensified the sense of meaninglessness and cynical alienation. From a pragmatic point of view, postmodernism is as ecologically irresponsible as modernism, except that technology actually does cut down trees and cynicism doesn't care. A responsible ecological philosophy cannot spring from postmodernism. This is one reason why I think that the Romantic movement is such a valuable, if mixed, part of our heritage, with implications for philosophy insofar as it gave us a radically new way of experiencing nature and ourselves and found thereby a renewed experience of the divine that was existentially transformative.[19]

It has been one of the features of recent philosophy to be dismissive of Romanticism or thinkers associated with it, such as Schelling—or Emerson. Postmodernism focuses on such figures as Nietzsche mainly out of a concern for developing its "hermeneutics of suspicion." It would be more than odd to claim that postmodernism has sought to reconnect us to nature as a sustaining source of spiritual realization. The impact of Romanticism has largely been elsewhere than philosophy. The extreme to which positivism was willing to go to dismiss the whole emotional and spiritual life should be a symptom of something deeply wrong. Even if the movement itself has passed away, we still see most of analytic philosophy devoted nearly exclusively to problems in epistemology. In American thought, it was the Transcendentalists—above all, Emerson—who embraced Romanticism and celebrated the creative, intuitive power of "the Reason" over against the analytic faculty of "the Understanding."

Emerson: Liberation and Integration as Self-Realization

Whether or not one classifies Emerson as "philosopher" as well as "thinker," his influence on the subsequent major figures of classical

---

19. Wordsworth's and Coleridge's *Lyrical Ballads* (1798) can be read as consciously offering itself as the antidote to Donne's alienation and as beginning to articulate a vision that evolved into Wordsworth's great poem *The Prelude* (1805/1850). See Isaiah Berlin's *The Roots of Romanticism* (Princeton, NJ: Princeton University Press, 2001).

American philosophy is unquestionable.[20] Though Dewey was not a "Transcendentalist," he accorded Emerson the highest respect.[21] The intimate relation of nature and spirit—indeed, the ascension of spirit through nature—is the subject of Emerson's first book, *Nature* (1836). This theme is explored in a variety of directions throughout the two series of *Essays* as well as in various addresses (including the notorious "Divinity School Address" given at Harvard in 1838, which kept him from being reinvited as a speaker there for nearly thirty years). Emerson's break with Christianity as an institution was for the sake of a revived spirituality of experience.[22] Like the existentialists a century later, Emerson was concerned with the problem of human alienation—alienation from nature, from self, and from God. He saw two reasons for this: the dead weight of tradition that obscures our own creative power and the reigning materialism in science. These are both results from a lack of the use of imagination on our part. The "Transcendentalist turn" was to affirm our own capacity to "enjoy an original relation to the universe" and so rediscover ourselves and God. In *Nature*, Emerson says,

> The axis of vision is not coincident with the axis of things, and so they appear not transparent but opake. The reason why the world lacks unity, and lies broken and in heaps, is because man is disunited with himself. He cannot be a naturalist, until he satisfies all the demands of the spirit. Love is as much its demand, as perception. Indeed, neither can be perfect without the other. In the uttermost meaning of the words, thought is devout, and devotion is thought.[23] Deep calls unto deep. But in actual life, the marriage is not celebrated. There are innocent men who worship God after the tradition of their fathers, but their sense of duty has not yet extended to the use of all their faculties. And there are patient naturalists, but they freeze the subject under the wintry light of the understanding. Is not prayer also a study of truth,—a sally of the soul into the unfound infinite? No man ever

20. See Russell Goodman, *American Philosophy and the Romantic Tradition* (Cambridge: Cambridge University Press, 1991).

21. John Dewey, "Emerson—The Philosopher of Democracy" (MW, 3:185–92). Dewey's own work takes a significant turn just after this essay as a result of, I believe, his reexposure to Emerson at a crucial period in his own development.

22. In this respect much like Dewey's aversion to "religions" in favor of the "religious" quality of experience they often inhibit rather than generate.

23. Heidegger likewise draws attention to the etymological relation of "thought" and "thank" (*Denken, Danken*); see *What Is Called Thinking?* Part II, Lecture iii.

prayed heartily, without learning something. But when a faithful thinker, resolute to detach every object from personal relations, and see it in the light of thought, shall, at the same time, kindle science with the fire of the holiest affections, then will God go forth anew into the creation.[24]

The key here is the phrase "axis of vision": the solution lies in *how* we experience ourselves and the world. The method Emerson proposed was to turn away from dead custom and belief toward nature, and thereby we could discover for ourselves the inherent metamorphosis of symbols that constitutes the presence of spirit in experience. *Nature* was written as a sort of "discipline" of ascension to regenerate our own capacity for original vision, and it begins with a paradoxical dualism of "Soul" and "Nature" as the "me" and "not me."[25] As the lower ego is transcended, the "not me" changes from opacity to transparency. The eye itself has a synthetic power to grasp vistas as wholes within a defining horizon and permeated by a constitutive mood so that "all mean egotism" vanishes.[26]

Emerson proceeds to overcome our experiential alienation through stages of "correspondence," or what might be called "analogous understanding"; that is, degrees of seeing ourselves in nature and vice versa. He does this through the ascending topics of "Commodity, Beauty, Language, and Discipline." Our technologies are extensions of natural forces; beyond this the world appears as beautiful in its own right, and the interplay of eye, light and object is the basis for the beauty of art, virtue and intellect.[27] "A work of art is an abstract or epitome of the world. It is the result or expression of nature, in miniature."[28] Nature is the basis of language, but nature itself is "symbol of the spirit."[29] Our experience is fraught with presence and suggestive meaning from the beginning, and

---

24. Emerson, *Nature*, in *Essays and Lectures* (New York: Library of America, 1983), 47.
25. Ibid., 8.
26. Ibid., 10. Hence the fortunate or unfortunate image of the "transparent eyeball."
27. Emerson clearly follows the ascension of Eros in Plato's *Symposium*.
28. Emerson, *Nature*, in *Essays and Lectures*, 18.
29. Ibid., 20.

these symbols grow throughout our lives.[30] In symbols we experience meaning as *metamorphically* alive.

This explains Emerson's own chosen style for writing, so often dismissed or treated condescendingly by "professional philosophers." Regenerative language must be poetic, and images, symbols, not only speak, but *think*.[31] The world is a growth and metamorphosis of meaning, and this *life* of meaning is the presence of spirit in nature. This is the ultimate discipline of nature: "The visible creation is the terminus . . . of the invisible world."[32] From the embodied context of our existence come the ideals of civilization, the arts, sciences, and philosophies. Beyond this is the interconnection and unity of all things, a "central Unity," which for Emerson was the pervasive, creative immanence of God, intuited holistically by "the Reason," not analyzed by "the Understanding." Thus, "Nature is made to conspire with spirit to emancipate us."[33]

Emerson's *Nature* was not only full of his enthusiasm for idealism, but had it ended with chapter 7, "Idealism," it would have seemed to soar off into the heavens. If so, it would only have been another avatar of Neoplatonism (which Emerson studied and admired) and so a philosophy of pure transcendence.[34] What is distinctive in the concluding chapters, "Spirit" and "Prospects," however, is Emerson's insistence that it is the act of "creative individuation" in the world that constitutes the life of God, and this leads him to break with Neoplatonism for an emphasis on immanence. Emerson's goal was the regeneration of human experience

30. In an essay, J. R. R. Tolkien says that one power "fairy stories" have—that is, stories that truly come from *Faërie*, "the Perilous Kingdom"— is "recovery" of our own nature:
"We should look at green again, and be startled anew (but not blinded) by blue and yellow and red . . . Recovery . . . is a re-gaining—regaining of a clear view. . . .We need, in any case, to clean our windows; so that the things seen may be freed from the drab blur of triteness or familiarity—from possessiveness. . . . And actually fairy-stories deal largely, or (the better ones) mainly, with simple or fundamental things, untouched by Fantasy, but these simplicities are made all the more luminous by their setting. . . . It was in fairy stories that I first divined the potency of the words, and the wonder of the things, such as stone, and wood, and iron; tree and grass; house and fire; bread and wine." "On Fairy-Stories," in J. R. R. Tolkien, *The Tolkien Reader* (New York: Ballantine Books, 1966), 57–59.
31. The imaginative and metaphoric root of reason has been extensively explored by philosopher Mark L. Johnson and linguist George Lakoff. See Johnson and Lakoff, *Metaphors We Live By* (Chicago: University of Chicago Press, 1983).
32. Emerson, 25. See: "Idealism is a hypothesis to account for nature by other principles than those of carpentry and chemistry," 41.
33. Ibid., 33.
34. Thomas Taylor's translated selections from *The Enneads* was among Emerson's favorite books.

in the world, not the "flight of the alone to the Alone." The true "axis of vision" to be attained was a perpetual, creative act of vision with "new eyes" linking human being and nature; this was "God go[ing] forth anew into the creation."[35] This meant the continuous reestablishment of new, unique "angles of vision." In other words, the epiphany of the Divine requires a *plurality* of individually realized relations—it is a dynamism of ever-adjusting *perspectives*, just like our own vision, which depends on two eyes with different angles constantly adjusting back and forth across the visual field; this is how objects come to have visual form.[36]

Emerson's emphasis upon the need for spirit to actualize itself in concrete relationship with nature comes out in his understanding of the purpose of art and the role of "exemplary" individuals, like "The Poet." It is the creative individual who is more important as an inspiration to us than the "art" (or art objects) he or she produces. As Dewey would say later, Emerson insists on the latent creativity in the act of experience itself. In "Art," he comments, "Because the soul is progressive, it never quite repeats itself, but in every act attempts the production of a new and fairer whole. . . . What is that abridgment and selection we observe in all spiritual activity, but itself the creative impulse?"[37] Human experience is the "self-explication" of nature and the artist uses his own creative vision to generate similar creative powers in others. Historically, art has been an "education" in the perception of beauty. "We are immersed in beauty, but our eyes have no clear vision."[38] Works of art train our powers of perception to behold the beauty of the world itself: the "excellence of all things is one."[39] Painting and sculpture are "gymnastics of the eye" that transform how we see ordinary objects, people, and scenes, and, ultimately, how we see ourselves. Great works of art "restore to us the simplest states of mind; and are religious. Since what skill is therein shown is the reappearance of the original soul, a jet of pure light, it should produce a similar impression to that made by natural objects."[40] To find beauty in

35. Emerson, 47.
36. Experiments that take the Cartesian one-eye perspective and fix the eyeball from moving make the subject increasingly uncertain of the location and eventually the nature of the object they are seeing. See Maurice Merleau-Ponty, *The Structure of Behavior*.
37. "Art," *Essays: First Series* in *Essays and Lectures*, 431. Dewey makes much the same point in *Art as Experience*.
38. Ibid., 432.
39. Ibid., 433.
40. Ibid., 434–35.

the world we "must carry it with us, or we find it not." The end of art is not to add to the number of objects in the world but make our perception of the world artistically and aesthetically alive: "Nothing less than the creation of man and nature is its end. . . . A true announcement of the law of creation . . . would carry art up into the kingdom of nature, and destroy its separate and contrasted existence."[41] Again, anticipating Dewey, Emerson criticizes the idea of art as separated from the ordinary and useful, segregated as moments of "pleasure," "solaces and compensations," or "voluptuous reveries" apart from living. We create beauty from "religion and love" rather than by the pursuit of pleasure.[42] We better "serve the ideal" from the start in daily existence, in "eating and drinking"; then beauty will be found in "the railroad, the insurance office . . . the galvanic battery, the electric jar, the prism."[43]

Emerson's well-known but not well understood individualism of "self-reliance" is a discipline of self-transcendence toward a receptive and creative relationship toward the world. The "self" that is to be "relied" upon is the "deep Self," the creative influx of the divine that reconstitutes the nature of perception and rejuvenates the "angle of vision" whereby things are seen in their transparencies; it is fundamentally a call to a new way of experiencing the world. "Our faith comes in moments; our vice is habitual. Yet there is a depth in those brief moments which constrains us to ascribe more reality to them than to all other experiences. . . . Man is a stream whose source is hidden."[44] For Emerson, this connection with the hidden source was the root of his experience of divinity, which did not vanish in an ineffable cloud of unknowing but in a renewed capacity to see the world as whole and alive:

> We live in succession, in division, in parts, in particles. Meantime within man is the soul of the whole; the wise silence; the universal beauty, to which every part and particle is equally related; the eternal ONE. And this deep power in which we exist, and whose beatitude is all accessible to us, is not only self-sufficing and perfect in every hour, but the act of seeing and the thing seen, the seer and the spectacle, the

41. Ibid., 435, 437–38.
42. Ibid., 439.
43. Ibid., 440.
44. "The Over-Soul," in *Essays and Addresses*, 385. See, for example, the story Wordsworth tells in Book I of *The Prelude*, in which he takes a rowboat at night and, in rowing up to a cliff beneath the stars, has a dim stirring of the divinity within and above nature.

subject and the object, are one. We see the world piece by piece, as the
sun, the moon, the animal, the tree; but the whole, of which these
are the shining parts, is the soul.[45]

In other words, the theophany of God lies in the fulfillment of an experience that achieves a spiritual aesthetics of nature: "From within or from
behind, a light shines through us upon things, and makes us aware that
we are nothing, but the light is all."[46] And: "The soul looketh steadily
forwards, creating a world before her, leaving words behind her."[47]

Emerson often explicitly used the term "metamorphosis" to express
this idea, but it is implied in his use of "form" as well. He uses "form," for
example, in speaking against materialism; he complains that we no longer
have a "doctrine of forms," but have a dualistic philosophy that sees us as
"put into our bodies, as fire is put into a pan, to be carried about."[48]
Furthermore, the world is regarded as a field of objects, of literal meanings, rather than as a multisymbolic realm of meaning in which spirit can
realize itself and the world. "For," says Emerson, "we are not pans and
barrows, nor even porters of the fire and torch-bearers, but children of
the fire, made of it, and only the same divinity transmuted, and at two or
three removes, when we know least about it."[49] The true nature of form
lies in *trans*formation; this is why form is to be understood as "symbol"
rather than as "essence." Symbols are dynamic, not fixed identities, and
their dynamism lies in their power to grow and to liberate, to allow spirit
to escape the shell of the past for a new incarnation.[50]

Thus Emerson finds the figure of "the Poet" as a representative person
to be herself a symbol because she reveals to us the true relationship we
have to nature. Most people, says Emerson, "cannot report the conversation they have had with nature," but the poet "traverses the whole scale of
experience."[51] It is the duty of "the Poet" as the "Sayer" of the Universe to
know that "Beauty is the creator." Before there is expression in language,

45. Ibid., 386.
46. Ibid., 387.
47. Ibid., 388.
48. "The Poet," 447.
49. Ibid.
50. See the account of the sculptor of Phosphorus in "The Poet," 458–59. See also "The Over-
Soul," 389.
51. "The Poet," 448.

the poet has a "whole new experience."[52] This is the establishing of that "original relation to the universe" that had been called for at the beginning of *Nature*. Thus the poet becomes more important for revealing the possibility of human experience in general to have that relationship than for any particular artistic product. In other words, the poet stands, for Emerson, as a way of existing and experiencing. Our meaningful experiences are not drawn from thin air but are found in the primary interactions we have with the qualities of the world. The poet experiences the symbolic depth of things as inherent in their being. It is in this sense that Emerson says "the soul makes the body": "Here we find ourselves . . . in a holy place. . . . We stand before the secret of the world, there where Being passes into Appearance, and Unity into Variety."[53]

As Dewey would say, Emerson finds the roots of meaning and value constituting experiences in the *aesthetic* contact with the objects of our lives. For example, the oldest known forms of art, the great Magdalenian cave paintings, show a spiritual connection between the hunter and the creature that gives its life in the hunt. Modern hunting, as expression of power over nature, is the result of the general "detachment and dislocation" from nature. For Emerson, it is the poet "who re-attaches things to nature and the Whole."[54] This is a perpetually needed activity, for the forms that were expressive symbolic connections in the past are the dead literalisms of today. The symbol is the way in which the "angle of vision" is achieved, for "all symbols are fluxional; all language is vehicular and transitive, and is good, as ferries and horses are, for conveyance, not as farms and houses are, for homestead."[55] The symbol, then, is a process of growth, of transformation, of metamorphosis.

Emerson's "angle" or "axis of vision" is not an epistemological standpoint arrived at by a careful analytical methodology but an act of self-realization in which the "I" that stands off from nature becomes the medium of the spirit giving life to nature and of nature giving embodiment to the spirit. Of course we can find here the exaggerations and extremes of Romanticism—the idea of will as the root of personality or the suggestion that the value of nature lies only in its potential for spiritual meaning.

52. Ibid., 450.
53. Ibid., 453.
54. Ibid., 455.
55. Ibid., 463.

Chinese philosophy, I think, would see this as an unfortunate and unnecessary reflection of the West's emphasis on individualism and see nature as material for use. It would insist, against the Romantic emphasis on "creativity," on the value of receptivity, which is not to be confused with passivity. Yin is not *hulē*; it listens and its yielding is a response, like a lover's touch. We must admit that Romanticism is shot through with the needs and anxieties that gave birth to the modern. Yet—and perhaps because of these tendencies—it has acted as a counterpoint to modernism. It has been the West's way of hearing "the music of nature." Emerson's (misunderstood) statements on "self-reliance" must be put in the context of what "self" one is relying upon and how. It is the higher self, or the deeper, creative self, if you prefer, and it demands the eradication of all "mean egotism." Furthermore, we access it through receptivity and silence, not by Promethean act of will. Emerson calls this "intellect receptive."[56] If the artist inspires us by her ability to express and bring meaning to life, more importantly, the artist shows us how to listen, be open, and through silence renew that "axis of vision."[57]

Aisthēsis

As I indicated, Dewey and Santayana, both naturalists though in very different senses, followed different sides of Emerson's "aesthetics" as a way of experiencing and existing, Dewey pursuing the theme of integration, Santayana that of liberation. I can only briefly indicate how they both retained the centrality of the aesthetics of existence in their philosophies. Dewey quite severely limited the concern for knowing and contextualized it within the more important concern for experiencing.[58] The theory of inquiry was a modest aspect of the theory of experience, the wholeness

56. This is worked out in some detail in "Intellect," an essay Dewey especially admired for its insights into the "unsaid" or "silent logic" in thought ("Emerson—The Philosopher of Democracy," in MW, 3); see Dewey's own emphasis on this at the end of Chapter 2 in *Art as Experience* (LW, 10).

57. "Happy is the hearing man; unhappy the speaking man. . . . The waters of the great deep have ingress and egress to the soul. But if I speak, I define, I confine, and am less. . . . The ancient sentence said, Let us be silent, for so are the gods. Silence is a solvent that destroys personality, and gives us leave to be great and universal" (*Intellect*, p. 426).

58. This is why it is incorrect to label Dewey by the term "instrumentalism." Instrumentalism is the part of Dewey's philosophy that pertains to inquiry; his philosophy of experience is far broader than concerns with "knowledge," as "The Postulate of Immediate Empiricism" (LW, 3) and *Experience and Nature* (LW, 1) explicitly say. See chapters 1 and 2 above.

and depth of which was treated in Dewey's understanding of "the con-summatory" and aesthetic—hence his claim that the test of any philosophy of experience is its understanding of the aesthetic. The aim of knowledge and education and politics and ethics should be the realization of meaning and value as experiential, consummatory events in human experience. What we needed was to see how what happens in the arts is capable of happening in the range of human experience, and often does, though without the recognition of it as "art." The most significant way to do this is by developing habits of aesthetic perception, both in the sense of realizing the consummatory as well as in seeing its possibilities. Through our care of the expressive potential of the world, we can come to realize it as experienced meaning and value. On a social and cultural level this becomes the ability of communities to integrate themselves with the possibilities of their environments. In Deweyan terms, we see nature's actualities in terms of possibilities, and realize that we are involved to the core of our being with the potentiality of process.

Santayana is enough of a modernist to hand over the "truth" of nature to the physical sciences, which, however, are themselves to be poetically and pragmatically understood. We never "know" the realm of matter—the realm of causality—but our scientific symbols come to terms with it. So be it. The ends of life are elsewhere. The realm of spirit is unconcerned with the ebb and flow of events, with the needs, desires, anxieties, and fears of the psyche struggling in the world. Taking a step back and simply acknowledging the stupendous, poetic beauty always before us achieves a liberation from all that. The second we abandon concerns for "integration" we see the simple, luminous purity of the nonexistential realm of essence. This is to achieve "spirit," and spirit offers itself as a way, a life, and a "realm of spirit." The life of spirit was a discipline of transcendence of the psyche for this joyful impersonality, this gratitude of beauty everywhere. Still, like Dewey, Santayana saw the "aesthetic" primarily as a way of experience, an art of existence.

To be sure, in looking at these three figures of Emerson, Dewey, and Santayana, we can observe how very "Western" they can appear when contrasted with their East Asian counterparts. I think the East Asian tradition has a great deal to teach us, especially in terms of getting us beyond our endemic voluntarism as well as our obsession with "knowing." Perhaps the classical American tradition has something to say as well in terms of the potential significance of the individual, the presence of possibility in existence, and the vitality of passion.

I conclude by saying that one of the responsibilities of contemporary philosophy is to address the "inhabitation" of the planet—the responsible, caring "walking in beauty" of our species with the earth. To this end, I have proposed that developing what might be called a "spiritual aesthetics of nature" is paramount. Our being is primarily one of the experience of the world as lived and suffered, not as known. We exist as relational beings, not as autonomous substances, and our primary relationship to the world is "aesthetic"; that is, it is noncognitive, tonal, affective and expressive, and conditional for any "conscious," much less cognitive, functions. Given the limitations of the word "aesthetic," I call this mode of experiencing the world *aisthēsis*. Cultural traditions tacitly and explicitly educate their members from infancy on to develop special forms of *aisthēsis*; that is to say, they teach fundamental ways of engaging with, of experiencing the meaning of the world.[59] The symbols, language, customs, habits of a culture shape the *aisthēsis* of the world for its members. More specifically, how we experience something, the *aisthēsis* with which we engage it and how it manifests itself in the world, largely determines how we treat it and think about it. Humanity is now entering into the phase of its history where we simply must take care of the earth—and with this phase comes the need to develop global habits of understanding and communication. Philosophy, of all disciplines, should be primarily concerned with this, whatever else it does. Can we articulate an *aisthēsis* of nature that can be a home to "spirit"? And is this an opportunity for genuine dialogue between American and East Asian philosophy?

---

59. This is necessary in fulfilling what I have described elsewhere as "the Human Eros," the primary drive we have as human beings to experience the world with meaning and value.

ELEVEN

CREATING WITH COYOTE

Toward a Native American Aesthetics

In this essay, I want to address the problem of creativity largely through the eyes and voices of Native North American traditions. The theme of creativity, however, is so deeply tied up with fundamental commitments of the West that I will have to postpone the examination of the Native American traditions for a brief synopsis of what I take to be the key schematic structures or "tropes" that dominate Western discussions of "creation." (Indeed, the term "creation" predisposes us already toward a certain way of understanding coming-to-be; "origination" might be a better general term in which "creation" represents one way of thinking about coming-to-be.) These will be the Hebrew, Hellenic, and romantic ideas of creation as act of will, as achievement of form, and as the expression of individual imagination or genius. Native American traditions offer radically different models, ones that do not stress the "lone creator" manifesting his or her individuality through an act of will that results in perfect form. Initially I look at four points of contrast Native American "creation" models offer to the Western: (1) as a collective enterprise, (2) as a process that stresses cooperation and evocation over command, (3) as an experimental and progressive process, and (4) as resulting in an open-ended product that does not look to the achievement of perfect form as the goal but to a sacred living presence fraught with power, ambiguity, and a degree of indetermination. Perhaps even more important than these various themes is the overall idea of "ceremonial renewal." Art as ceremony aims to reintegrate human beings with the aesthetics of a "way of life" that embodies a wisdom tradition. Finally, we should consider the figure of "the Trickster"—of Coyote, Raven, Rabbit, Glooscap—as a significant approach to the idea of creativity.[1] The Trickster is a morally ambiguous crosser of boundaries who for that very reason illumines those boundaries; his transgressions often result in fundamental acts of "creation." Trickster also opens up the role of chance, fallibility, and blindness that attend all existence.

I present these themes because I believe that Native American traditions have a great deal to teach us, if we can listen to them, about the living presence of the sacred and its relation to art, community, and dwelling in nature, themes that have been lost in modernity and whose loss is celebrated in postmodernism. Walter Benjamin rejoiced in the loss of the "aura" of the sacred in the work of art (for as a Marxist he thought that mass-produced, decentered arts like movies helped undermine bourgeois concepts of "critical authority"). But mass art has not uplifted or liberated us. Likewise, Jean-François Lyotard hailed the antirealism of postmodernism as the point where the individual frees herself from the domination of a social construct, which is all there is to "reality" anyway. He is not clear why it is good to be "liberated" from reality or why this is a greatly comforting achievement of our civilization.

Before moving on to discuss the classic creative tropes of Western civilization, I would like to discuss in more general terms why I think philosophy could and should address what I call "wisdom traditions," especially Native American wisdom traditions.

---

1. Sam Gill offers cautionary suggestions about the tendency of scholars to talk about this personage, so-called, of "*the* Trickster"; it is better, he says to talk about specific Tricksters in specific narrative contexts. See "Trickster" in his *Native American Mythology* (Oxford, 1994).

The Importance of Wisdom Traditions

In recent years, a small group of philosophers has been exploring themes in Native American philosophy. There are several reasons for this. First, though most professional philosophy has dispensed with any conception of the pursuit of wisdom, those of us who have not see great value in the interaction between philosophy and what can be called "wisdom traditions." Among these traditions can be counted those of the Original Nations of the Americas. Wisdom traditions are concerned with teaching human beings how to live wisely and well *as* human beings. That is to say, they are concerned with what is perhaps the most creative task there is, transforming a creature who is biologically human into one who is a fully realized human being living a *life*, that is, having an awareness of the relationships of meanings and values that sustain a human existence in the world. Wisdom itself can be understood to be a living of life in recognition of the larger forces that affect our condition along with an insight into the individual, unique, and transitory situations that demand our attention and, perhaps, embody all that is precious or meaningful in our existence. It involves living with such an awareness of these things that these truths, great and small, are vitally present to us in our experience. Symbol, myth, and ritual are far more effective means to achieving this living awareness than rational arguments or propositions. In fact, there may be many sophisticated, rational philosophies that miss wisdom completely. The various methods wisdom traditions employ are woven together in the daily practices of conduct, language, and culture so naturally as to be hardly the object of reflective concern. Philosophy itself grows from such traditions when they do become objects of critical reflection. From this come the methods of philosophy proper: questioning, criticism, conceptual exploration, linguistic articulation, new insights, and systematic speculation. When philosophy loses connection with its roots in the question of wisdom, it becomes something else to which the name "philosophy" is misleadingly attached.

When wisdom traditions face conditions in which they are challenged, such as rapid change or suddenly being confronted by alternative practices and values, they have three choices. They may seek to escape their problems by denial, focusing on a rigid traditionalism. They may develop a bifurcated or "double consciousness" (to use W. E. B. Du Bois's expression), an unresolved set of inner identities internalizing the clash of cultures. Or they may enter the domain of philosophy and gain a critical and reflective stance toward *both* traditions. Neither of the first two approaches, I believe, can succeed where the challenging set of values is that of contemporary Western culture, now overwhelming the world. There simply is no place left to hide for a culture that hopes to seal itself off.

Rigid traditionalism, the *conscious* struggle to return to the ways of one's ancestors without deviation, is itself a reaction to and so a product of modernism and change. Fundamentalist Christianity is a similar case in point; it is a contemporary reaction to contemporary culture. As a movement it is less than a hundred years old and adopts a one-dimensional approach to reading the Bible that has more to do with the fact-oriented, literal way of reading and writing that characterizes modernism in everything from scientific reports to newspapers. Symbolic depth is lost along with the idea of a multidimensional approach to reading. Similar fundamentalist reactions can be found in Judaism and Islam. Thus fundamentalism, social conservatism, and rigid traditionalism are forms of denial due to the failure to come to terms with a world that has changed and which seems to put the values and meanings of one's culture at risk.

I do not take these reactions lightly. Human beings have traditions because we desire to experience the world with meaning and value; this is our "Human Eros," as I have called it. Cultures are "spiritual environments," worlds of meaning that allow this Eros to be fulfilled. When the core ideas and values of a culture are challenged, a fiercely negative and potentially destructive force (call it "Eris") arises. Thus, I believe, it is highly important for those peoples whose wisdom traditions are now, and which have been, affected by the crisis of modernity to engage philosophy, at least that part of philosophy still concerned with wisdom. It is to be hoped that philosophy may mediate this important tension and discover ways in which the wisdom of those wisdom traditions may enter into philosophical consciousness and show that there are better ways to handle modernity than capitulation, escapism, double consciousness or fundamentalism. In turn, philosophy may discover resources to help it work its way out of the tradition of modernism; it may rediscover itself as being "a friend of wisdom" instead of an epistemology industry.

Hebrew, Hellenic, and Romantic Origination Tropes

The question of "creativity" or "creation" may be a case in point. These terms evoke two different though related Western traditions, the one being the Judeo-Christian concept of God as creator, the other being the "creative individual," the Romantic idea of the artist inspired by a creative imagination that transcends the old forms. Along with these two, there is a third tradition involved in thinking about art that derives from the Greek concern with the role of form in constituting beauty. Unlike the first two, here the focus is not on the *process* that brings form about but on the *product* understood as form organizing and prevailing over matter. When Hellenism is combined with the Judeo-Christian concept of God, as we see in Augustine, form becomes the eternal ideas in God. When Romanticism transposes the idea of God as creator into that of the human creative genius, the genius is one who creates *new forms* that overthrow the old. Let us look at these three influential models more closely.

With the triumph of Christianity the story of the creation in Genesis came to occupy a central way in Western culture of conceiving of "how things came to be," so much so that we tend to approach other origin stories as "*creation* myths" that are then measured by our expectations.[2] The account in 1 Genesis is remarkable in its insistence that the universe is the result of a lone deity's fiat and is then pronounced good. There are three oddities in the Genesis story here. (1) While many non-Western societies place value on a divine origin of the cosmos, it is unusual to find one that places supreme value on an *individual* divine creation, as the Hebrew tradition does. Most origin stories speak of creation as a collective project. Next (2), the universe comes about by the lone deity speaking: Let there be light, and there was light. This "Let there be" phrase (simply the verb *yehi* in Hebrew) is clearly a command, not a wish or request or call. This is an important point, given the narrative structure of the stories in the Bible, for they are filled with commands.

---

2. *Origin* stories around the world use a variety of core metaphors: sexual intercourse, birth, growth, speech, searching, tool making, and so on. We always ask of these other accounts "*Who* made X? *What* was it made out of?" The origin story from the Finnish *Kalevala* has Blue Teal flying wearily over the waters searching for a place to nest and lay her golden eggs, from which the world will hatch. "*Who* made Blue Teal? *What* were the eggs made out of?" we ask and miss the point of the metaphor.

("Commandment" is a key trope in Hebrew culture, just as "Logos" is in Greek culture and "Freedom" in ours.) Third (3), there is judgment. At the beginning the earth is "unformed and void," a worthless waste, and darkness is over the face of "the deep."³ God, or "Elohim," begins to "create" (*bara'*) by blowing as a wind over the waters, followed by creative command: "God said, 'Let there be light'; and there was light. God saw that the light was good." Here, then, is a certain model for origination: A single being takes a formless "waste" and by commanding a thing to be causes it to exist; then it is judged and found to be good.

The pattern of Command-Act-Judgment is repeated as a narrative structure in stories throughout both testaments, especially in the more complex form: Command-Act (usually disobedience)-Judgment-Atonement-Covenant. The Garden of Eden story, which follows the account of creation, has it. God commands Adam and Eve not to eat of the fruit of the Tree of Knowledge. They disobey. God's judgment follows: They are expelled and forced to work and die. The fact of judgment is also of importance, for the question concerning something's existence is one of moral worth: Is it good or bad? The eschatology of the New Testament envisages a "final judgment" as a coda to the original act of creation. So here is *one* way of understanding origination: as "creation." Lone authority and unchallenged power, a command to exist, and a judgment cast in moral terms of "good" or "bad" fuse together in this influential model. It is *one* way "origination" can be thought of. But for the Western tradition, it represents a primary model and so pervades our thinking about "creativity" as such.

Our understanding of creation is also influenced by Hellenic and Romantic ideas. In contrast to the Hebrew emphasis on power, command, and will, the Hellenic stresses form, order, and reason. As Hesiod tells it in his *Theogony*, there is no lone deity imposing "good" order on a worthless waste; there is a gradual emergence of order *in* the cosmos. It begins with χάος: It is the first thing that *comes to be*. This is not "chaos" in our sense—for what is there to be "disorderly"? It means "the Opening." (The Indo-European root of χάος, *gheu-*, is echoed in our words "gap" and "yawn.") As such it is *not opposed* to order, to κόσμος, but is rather

---

3. Hebrew: *tohu va vohu*, a "formless waste"; see Jeremiah's use of it to describe Israel after the Babylonians were done with it: Jer. 4:23–27. See *The JPS Torah Commentary: Genesis*, commentary by Nahum M. Sarna (Philadelphia: Jewish Publication Society, 1989), 6.

that vital, dynamic matrix *out of which order comes*. It is the place or space *in which* cosmic order can be achieved. An appropriate image might be a blank canvass waiting for paint or an empty stage waiting for the drama to begin. The narrative structure of the *Theogony* tells of the achievement of greater and better order; the cosmos becomes more civilized and reasonable. Zeus surpasses the previous deities Ouranos and Kronos in his ability to establish κόσμος, an order that is beautiful, fair and intelligible. In battling against Typhon ("chaos" in our sense), Zeus exhibits the triumph of excellence, ἀρετή. Hesiod concludes the poem listing Zeus's many offspring, embodiments of order like the Hours and Graces, and has Zeus "swallow" or internalize Metis, Wisdom. The story of the universe is one of movement toward form: *Chaos-to-cosmos*.

Plato and Aristotle merely take this temporalized narrative and make it ontological, form organizing matter so it can achieve being, limit, and excellence. When the idea of an ultimate divine being as "cause" (αἰτία) is introduced, whether Plato's demiurge, Aristotle's unmoved mover, or the Stoics' cosmic Logos, its rational nature is what is stressed. Its divinity lies in bringing about rational order, cosmos. There is no command or act of will. Instead there is the progressive realization of limit and proportion. This is the triumph of λόγος; it does not *impose* order by force; order is what allows something to achieve its proper goodness, its excellence. Language as λόγος plays a role, but this is not the language of command. Because something has limit and order, it can be understood by λόγος, hence it can be put into speech. Speech is "rational" (*ratio* in fact being the Latin cognate for λόγος). This is developed in Greek philosophy. For Parmenides, even though time and the cosmos as such disappear, intellect (νοῦς) has insight into Being because is it limited. Its necessity is utterly logical. Plato gives a mythic account of creation in his *Timaeus*, but here, too, the Demiurge does not create by act of will but by *knowing* Forms, which he then attempts to emulate in pliable, restless matter. The Demiurge does not *force* form onto matter but *shares* it because it is good.

From this comes the concern with the constitutive nature of form as beauty in Western art. Art, τέχνη, is the craft or skill to make formed things and the form expresses the being of what something is. Hence we have the classical concept of "creation" as the attainment of form. Classicism always tends to emphasize the object of art rather than the persona of the creator.

This is the key to the tension in Western art between the "classical" and "romantic" traditions: The former turns toward the Greek ideal and makes the artist one who achieves form through mastery of skill; the latter has the Hebraic element of creation by act of will so that the artistic genius is one who creates a new form that shatters previous forms.

Romanticism transfers the act of genuine creation to human nature, which had formerly been reserved for the divine.[4] Sometimes this is regarded as the divine element in human existence, as for William Blake or Samuel Taylor Coleridge. Creation comes through an artist's act of will. In his effort to translate the beginning of the Gospel of John ("In the beginning was the λόγος"), Goethe's Faust significantly changes it to "In the beginning was the *deed*!" Like the Hebraic version, the Romantic creator is alone. He is the genius who, like God, creates something that is new that then establishes *new* criteria of what is good. The true artist does not create by conforming to preestablished forms; his creation over-throws them. Thus imagination—creative imagination—trumps reason. It is the artist's work—the embodiment of his genius—that creates value. But in an inversion of the Garden of Eden story, it is the Romantic creator who is outcast. The ordinary masses of people do not realize the significance of the artist's creation and fail to understand his genius so that he is an exile from the world of power, money, and recognition. The Romantic concept of creation is also connected with the ideas of individuality and freedom derived from the democratic revolutions of the seventeenth and eighteenth centuries. So we now have the ideal of the creator as the lone individual who is enacting free individuality in unconventional expression. Outside of a theological context, this is what "creativity" has come to mean in most Western societies. The ideal of the individual as a rebel against conformity, a center of creativity, is not only a standard theme of modernism but also postmodernism. Lyotard's "The Postmodern Condition" is about as pure a statement of Romantic anarchism as one could want.

Here, then, we have the major tropes of three traditions that character-ize our understanding of creativity and creation: as command of will, as achievement of form, as imaginative expression of transcendent genius.

---

4. In the Tanakh, the word "create," *bara'*, is used exclusively of God's action. See the JHP commentary, 5.

We may turn now to the question of origination in Native American cultures to find that these are not the only possible tropes. And the consequences for the question of "creativity" can be quite important.

Native American Origination Tropes

What would our "aesthetics" and our "philosophy of creativity" be like if Native American concepts of origination had worked as deeply within our tradition as the Hebrew, Hellenic, or Romantic ones? Linguists have noted that originally there does not seem to be a word in Native American languages corresponding to our term "art." This does not mean that the various Native American cultures lacked any concept of "art." They were and are highly artistic. But there was not a special activity called "making art" distinguished from other activities. Similarly, Native American languages did not originally have words corresponding to our word "religion"—which is not to say they had no religion but that it pervaded daily life. If one turns to the various Native American origin myths, the predominant tropes that emerge are quite different from those found in the West.

I will discuss only four here. First, I want to contrast the West's idea of the lone creator, either as all-powerful (the Hebrew notion) or as rational knower (the Hellenic), with the Native American view that power and wisdom are to be symbolized by a group, community, or, especially, a council. Second, I contrast the Hebrew model of creation by command with what might be called a model of "cooperative evocation," whereby things are invoked or evoked into being. Third, the idea of coming-to-be in Native American origin stories is more a process of experimentation and gradual improvement over a process of time in which a variety of contributors may participate. This may be contrasted with the Hebraic model in which what God makes and pronounces as "good" becomes broken through disobedience or with the Platonic view that existence depends on and proceeds from "the Good." Finally, the outcome, "the world," is not regarded as something that must obey the laws of the creator (the Hebrew concept), achieve finalized perfect form (the Hellenic concept), or be a pure original expression of individual imagination (the romantic concept). Rather, "creation" is a living process that must have a degree of open-endedness and indetermination to have vitality.

With these four themes, then, we might easily find a source of very different ways of looking at what we call "creation" than through the traditional tropes inherited from the sources of European civilization. The overall approach might be called "ceremonial evocation," which becomes the basis of a wisdom tradition. Finally we must note the idea of creation by "Trickster." Tricksters are morally ambivalent but very powerful; their ability to generate wisdom lies in revealing the nature of boundaries often through their misguided schemes and misfortunes. Yet from these misadventures often very important, even holy, results may follow.

CREATIVE WISDOM AS COUNCIL

First, let us look at figure of the cosmic creator. One of the striking contrasts with Western models that Native American approaches exhibit is that one finds at the outset the strong importance placed upon collective deliberation as a symbol of power and wisdom. In Native American origin stories, the cosmos is often the result of a council working together. Even in those accounts where there is a single original being (itself often of a dual male-female nature, as with the Zuni creator Awonawilona), frequently the first act of that solitary being is to create helpers. There is no more eloquent example than the Mayan Popul Vuh, or Book of Council. The scene starts out not with the watery "waste" of Genesis but with an oceanic stillness, a murmuring hush, as translator and interpreter Dennis Tedlock suggests.[5] In this primal setting there is only sea and sky and those beings in them. In the water are three male and female pairs of gods, the Maker and the Shaper, the Lord and Plumed Serpent (Quetzal or Gucumatz), and the Mother of Life and the Father of Life.[6] They "are known as great knowers, great thinkers in their very being" (Tedlock, 64). In the beginning they are floating luminously in the watery abyss. There is also a celestial god, Heart of Sky (himself a three-in-one deity consisting

5. Dennis Tedlock, *Popul Vuh: The Mayan Book of the Dawn of Life* (New York: Simon and Schuster, 1985, rev. ed., 1996), 221; this is his gloss on the beginning phrase, "Now it still ripples, now it still murmurs, ripples, it still sighs, hums, and it is empty under the sky." See also Adrian Recinos, *Popul Vuh: The Sacred Book of the Quiché Maya* (Norman: Oklahoma University Press, 1950), and Allen J. Christenson, *Popul Vuh: The Sacred Book of the Maya* (Norman: University of Oklahoma Press, 2003). All three editions have extensive notes.

6. The exact number of gods is difficult to determine; Christensen argues for three primary pairs (60n11).

of Hurricane, Newborn Thunderbolt, and Sudden Thunderbolt). The book insists on how at first all is "at rest," "still," and "calm." For the "creation" to begin, there must be a council. Heart of Sky comes to Sovereign and Plumed Serpent "and they talked and they thought and they worried. They agreed with each other, they joined their words, their thoughts" and they "conceived the growth of life," that is, of all that is to be (65). "How should the sowing be, and the dawning?" they ask. "Let it be this way, think about it: this water should be removed, emptied out for the forming of the earth's own plate and platform, then should come the sowing, the dawning of sky-earth" (65). After a council is formed, then it *deliberates*; it asks *questions*: How may a *process of vital growth* begin?

The Pawnee origin story as recounted by Alice Marriott and Carol Rachlin has a single original being (of dual male-female nature) whose first act is to create helpers. "First in the world was the Power. He was everywhere and nowhere. He was thought and planning; he was man and woman. He had everything that was and would be. 'I need helpers,' said the Power to himself, 'There can never be a world unless I have others to help me.' He stretched out the four fingers of his right hand and they became four stars. He put the Morning Star in the East, with the Sun to help and advise him. He set the Evening Star in the west, with the Moon to guide her. And the South Star and the North Star he put in their places in the heavens with the smaller stars as their helpers, because they are not as powerful as the Morning and Evening Stars."[7] Though there is a lone primal being (of dual nature), this being's power is a power to know how to get help. The first helpers, the sacred stars of the four directions, are thus also themselves in need of helpers, the Sun, Moon, and lesser stars. The wisdom needed to set up a good "committee," in which deliberative thoughtfulness and cooperation are vital, is different from commanding.

The brief but elegant origination story of the Pit River Nation (as told by Jaime de Angulo, who reports it as a dialogue with his informant "Bill") goes as follows. Bill says, " 'It was like there was nothing everywhere but a kind of fog. Fog and water mixed, they say, no land anywhere and this here Silver Fox. . . .' 'You mean Coyote?' 'No, no, I mean Silver Fox. Coyote comes later. You'll see, but right now Silver Fox was wandering

7. Alice Marriott and Carol K. Rachlin, *Plains Indian Mythology* (New York: Penguin-Meridian, 1985), 16.

and feeling lonely. . . . "I wish I would meet someone," he said to himself, the Silver Fox did. He was walking along in the fog. He met Coyote. "I thought I was going to meet someone," he said.'" Well, Silver Fox and Coyote decide to walk together, because it's better for people to travel together, "they always say." And eventually they decide to make the world, which they proceed to do by *dancing* it into existence.[8] Dancing not only functions as a communal action but, as will be seen, also as a form of evocation.

A number of origination accounts begin with Coyote in similar circumstances, usually either walking around or floating on a log in a watery expanse. The version of the Crow Nation has Coyote wanting someone to talk to, whereupon he sees two ducks. Is this all there is, he asks, or do you people think there is something more? The ducks respond, "We think there might be something deep down below the water. In our hearts we believe this." Then there is an "earth-diving contest," perhaps one of the oldest types of origin stories in Native North America. One animal after another tries to dive down deep enough to get some of the mud at the bottom. This is successful with the fourth try, and once obtained can be used to generate the whole earth.[9] This story has plural creators and conceives of origin as the *discovery* of something hidden and difficult to get. Creation here is search and discovery.

CREATION AS EVOCATION

The second major facet of these origin accounts I wish to emphasize is that, in addition to the creative act being a communal endeavor, it is an act of evocation, of calling something forth, not command. "Evocation" must be understood not only to be the use of a creative word to call something, but also other cooperative metaphors, like dancing or building. The fundamental attitude involved is not that of a "will-to-dominate" but of a "summoning-by-showing-respect" or providing a *receptivity* within which something can appear, become manifest. The resulting relationship is not a top-down relation of dominance to subservience

<hr/>

8. John Bierhorst, *The Red Swan* (Albuquerque: University of New Mexico Press, 1992), 42–43.
9. *American Indian Myths and Legends*, Alfonso Ortiz and Richard Erdoes, eds. (New York: Pantheon, 1984), 88. Compare Barry Lopez, *Giving Birth to Thunder, Sleeping with His Daughter: Coyote Builds North America* (New York: Avon, 1977), 4ff.

(with the possibility of "disobedience") but one of mutuality, each part demonstrating its proper respect to the other in spite of differences in power or importance. Let us look at the stories I have mentioned already.

In the Popul Vuh, we saw that the gods of the watery abyss and Heart of Sky were "thinkers" and elders in a council. As with the Hebrew Genesis, the creation is through the word, a "phatic act." But the nature of the spoken word is different, being more an *evocation* than a "command." "And then the earth arose because of them, it was simply their word that had brought it forth. For the forming of the earth, they said 'Earth.' It arose suddenly, just like a cloud, a mist, now forming, unfolding (*upupujeik*). Then the mountains were separated (*xtape*) from the water, all at once the great mountains came forth" (Tedlock, 65–66). This sounds similar to the "creation by command" in the Bible to our ears, but the use of speech here is evocative—calling something forth. The word *upupujeik* carries the sense of clouds forming around a mountain, and *xtape* refers to the way they can part to reveal it. Tedlock adds, "It is as if the mountains were there in the primordial world all along and were revealed, little by little, as the clouds parted" (226). The "word" here is not a command but a disclosure. By saying something's name it responds; it comes forth. The word as primal name is sacred because it connects directly with the being of the thing. This is what makes the act of prayer a sacred act and governs the strict rules most societies have regarding the use of names, especially names that are expressive of one's inmost identity. It is an entirely different matter whether your truest name is said respectfully or with a tone of command. Native American cultures are highly sensitive to this issue, and one can trace the importance of these themes, naming, evocation, manifestation and respect, as the core of origination. In short, the primordial gods do not dominate, but discover the magic of sacred utterance.

In the Pawnee story, after Power makes the four stars and their helpers and has placed them in their proper quadrants, he-she says, "Now show yourselves," and they become bright. "You shall be known as the lodge poles of the heavens. It is your job to hold up the sky and you shall stand as long as the sky lasts. And when men are made, you shall teach them how to make sacred bundles for worshiping me. You shall teach them to build their houses in the domed shape of the sky, and to set the four lodge poles at the points where the roof beams are placed. Everyone will know what you can do, because although our feet touch the earth, your heads touch the sky."[10] Again, with our own cultural tradition operating as an "interpretive horizon," this may sound like God giving commands. But the process is that of *establishing a home*. The star helpers frame the basic structure of the cosmos as a *dwelling*, a divine house, within which life can be born and grow. The human home will be a symbolic representation of the cosmic home. The message of this story is that a community of powers creates the world as a home within which life itself is generated, nurtured and continued. A home is also an evocation, a preparation and invitation to dwell. The rest of the story recounts how the winds, lightning-beings and thunders-beings become helpers of the stars as priests who make the land and plants appear by rattles and songs; finally human beings are made from the first woman born to Morning Star and Evening Star and the first man born to the Sun and the Moon. The Pawnee annually have a ceremonial retelling of this story as an act of communal renewal.

As already noted, the Pit River story with Silver Fox and Coyote expresses evocation in terms of dancing together. As the informant says to Jaime de Angulo, "Well, this Coyote he says, 'What are we going to do now?' 'What do you think'?' says Fox. 'I don't know,' says Coyote. 'Well, then,' says Fox, 'I'll tell you: Let's make the world!' 'And how are we going to do that?' 'We will sing," says Fox. So there they were singing up there in the sky. They were singing and stomping and dancing around each other in a circle. Then Fox he thought in his mind, clump of sod, come!' That's the way he made it come: *by thinking*."[11] Fox throws the clump into the clouds while they dance with their eyes closed. Eventually they open their eyes and see something. Then Fox thinks about stretching. The next time they look they see the earth, whereupon they both jump down into their creation to finish it. Fox and Coyote are complementary opposites, rather like the Yin and Yang of Daoism: Fox being the aspect of "the right way things should be done so that the power is able to work" and Coyote being the "Trickster" force that dwells beyond the "right" way. Together they make up the world.

10. Marriott and Rachlin, 16.
11. Bierhorst, 43.

CREATION AS EXPERIMENTAL PROCESS

The third point is that the process of creation is not one in which the thing created is immediately perfected or complete. Rather most Native American origination accounts tell of a process of experimentation whereby the original thing becomes gradually the way it should be. Again the Mayan Popul Vuh gives us a primary example, too long to recount in detail here. After the world is evoked by the primordial powers, they embark upon the main object, the creation of beings that can know and keep the sacred calendar and know the names of the deities. But there are a series of failures before this happens. The first beings they make can only hoot and cry, and so they are dismissed to become the animals. The second effort is made from mud and cannot keep its form.[12] The third group is made of wood; these beings can talk and make things, "but there was nothing in their hearts, in their minds, no memory of their mason and builder . . . they did not remember Heart of Sky. And so they fell, just an experiment and just a cutout for humankind."[13] Their tools rise up against them, grinding them, and they become the monkeys. Finally human beings are produced—at first too perfectly, for they can see to the ends of the earth like the gods. So their vision must be limited before the creation is perfected.[14]

This process of collaborative experimentation may remind us somewhat of the Greek notion of κόσμος slowly emerging from χάος, but we should be careful. First, Native American origin stories usually emphasize the presence of fallibility and imperfection as part of the heart of things. This is different from a struggle or ἀγών that ultimately achieves a controlled balance of powers, which is what we find in the Greeks. One humorous example of this is a story of human genesis told by the Miwok nation. Note that though it begins with the trope of a "wisdom council," in this case the council is dysfunctional. The collective wisdom is due to Coyote being able to *listen* to what each animal says.

> After Coyote had completed making the world, he began to think about creating man. He called a council of all the animals. The animals sat in

12. Tedlock wonders whether the tellers of the story at this point were consciously criticizing the Genesis account (since they were recounting it to a priest after the conquest). Obviously, a mud creature in the Yucatan would fare less well than in the Mesopotamian desert.

13. Tedlock, 70.

14. As in Genesis, once having eaten of the fruit of the Tree of Knowledge, the fear is that Adam and Eve will eat of the fruit of the Tree of Life and be like God.

a circle, just as the Indians do, with Lion at the head, in an open space in the forest. On Lion's right was Grizzly Bear; next Cinnamon Bear; and so on to Mouse, who sat at Lion's left. Lion spoke first. Lion said he wished man to have a terrible voice, like himself, so that he could frighten all animals. He wanted man also to be well covered with hair, with fangs in his claws and also very sharp teeth. Grizzly Bear laughed. He said it was ridiculous for anyone to have such a voice as Lion, because when he roared he frightened away the very prey for which he was searching. But he said man should have very great strength; that he should move silently, but very swiftly; and he should be able to seize his prey without noise. Buck said man would look foolish without ant-lers. And a terrible voice was absurd, but man should have ears like a spider's web, and eyes like fire. Mountain Sheep said the branching antlers would bother man if he got caught in a thicket. If man had horns rolled up it would give his head weight enough to butt very hard. Then Beaver talked. Beaver said man would have to have a tail, but it should be broad and flat, so he could haul sand and mud on it. Not a furry tail, because they were troublesome on account of fleas. Owl said man would be useless without wings. But Mole said wings would be folly. Man would be sure to bump against the sky. Besides, if he had wings and eyes both, he would get his eyes burned out by flying too near the sun. But without eyes he could burrow in the soft, cool earth, where he could be happy. Mouse said man needed eyes so he could see what he was eating. And nobody wanted to burrow in the damp earth.

So the council broke up in a quarrel. When it came Coyote's turn, he said the other animals were foolish because they wanted man to be just like themselves. Coyote was sure he could make a man who would look better than Coyote himself, or any other animal. Of course he would have to have four legs, with five fingers. Man should have to have a strong voice, but he need not roar all the time with it. And he should have feet nearly like Grizzly Bear's, because he could then stand erect when he needed to. Grizzly Bear had no tail, and man should not have any. The eyes and ears of Buck were good, and per-haps man should have those. Then there was Fish, which had no hair, and hair was a burden much of the year. So Coyote thought man should not wear fur. And his claws should be as long as the Eagle's so that he could hold things in them. But no animal was as cunning and crafty as Coyote, so man should have the wit of Coyote.

Then every animal set to work to make a man according to his own ideas. Each one took a lump of earth and modeled it just like himself. All but Coyote, for Coyote began to make the man he had talked of in the council. It was late when the animals stopped work and fell asleep. All but Coyote, for Coyote was the cunningest of all the animals, and he stayed awake until he had finished his model. He worked hard all night. When the other animals were fast asleep, he threw water on the lumps of earth, and so spoiled the models of the other animals. But in the morning he finished his own, and gave it life before the others could finish theirs. Thus man was made by Coyote.[15]

Thus, unawares, all the animals have contributed to the final result, though at the price of their individual egotism. This story carries with it two important implications—that we humans are related to all the animals and that one of those animals that had a large hand in making us was Coyote, who is prone to misadventure and foolish mistakes, although as in this case he also has his own wisdom.

The idea of creation as a gradual process is also central in the origin stories of the Southwest Pueblo cultures and those influenced by them, such as the Navajo, Apache, and Kiowa. These focus around the idea of emergence, the original, largely unshaped first "people" being in a dark "first world" that is left behind for a second, third, and fourth world. The previous worlds are left behind because of some form of social conflict that must be resolved, so that by the time the fourth world, this world, is reached, a proper way of life is realized.

THE WORLD AS LIVING PROCESS

The final key theme I wish to present is that the resulting product, the *ens creatum*, is not a finished or perfected being in the Greek sense of something that has achieved a completed form, something perfectly limited whereby it can be isolated as a "self-identical thing" with a fixed nature that can be expressed in λόγος, a definition that sums up its essence. The tendency of Greek thought was toward making the ultimate reality an individual being, an οὐσία, whose nature was to be complete.[16]

---

15. From Raymond van Over, *Sun Songs: Creation Myths from around the World* (Denver: Mentor Books, 1980), 40–41; this story is very similar to the Crow creation of man also included in this anthology (see pp. 56–60) in which Raven as well as Coyote participate.

16. Plato's Forms are "individuals" qua beings, because each is ultimately "itself" (αὐτός), though "universal" in relation to the things that come to be. The problem of relating something so self-enclosed and yet also a member of a group may have led to the class-based logic of Aristotle. One wonders what might constitute a Native American logical form that involves open-endedness and growth—perhaps Peirce's or Dewey's views may come close to this possibility.

But Native American traditions tend to see everything ultimately in terms of life, and this implies a degree of indeterminacy, unpredictability, and room for others to take constructive part.[17] A Native American myth from the Snohomish people of the Northwest, an account for the plurality of languages (especially diverse around the Puget Sound area), shows the need for a deliberative council and cooperative action in order to improve the world as left by the "creator." The emphasis here is the need for the creatures to participate in the act of creation itself.

> In the beginning, the Creator and Changer made the world. He created first in the east. Then he slowly came westward, creating as he came. With him he brought many languages. He gave a different language to each group of people he created. When he reached Puget Sound, he liked it so well that he decided that he would go no farther. But he had many languages left. These he scattered all around Puget Sound and to the north, along the waters there. That is why there are so many different languages spoken by the Indians in the Puget Sound Country.
>
> These people could not talk together, but they soon found that they were not pleased with the way the Creator had made the world. The sky was so low that the tall people bumped their heads against it. Also, sometimes people climbed high up in the trees and went into the Sky World.
>
> One time the wise men of the different tribes had a meeting to see what they could do about lifting the sky. They agreed that the people should try to push it up higher. "We can do it," a very wise man of the council said, "if we all push at the same time. We will need all the people, and all the animals and all the birds when we push." "How will we know when to push?" asked another of the wise men. "Some of us live in this part of the world, some in another. We don't all talk the same language. How can we get everyone to push at the same time?"
>
> That puzzled the men of the council, but the last one of them said, "Why don't we have a signal? When the time comes to for us to push, when we have everything ready, let someone shout 'Ya-hoh.' That means 'Lift together' in all our languages."

---

17. The οὐσία of Greek ontology is also to be conceived of as alive. Plato ultimately put life into the forms (see Plato's *Sophist*, 248e–49), Aristotle conceived his primary example of being as an organism (hence his insistence that the Unmoved Mover is a "life"), and Plotinus (following the passage from the *Sophist*) made his Second Hypostasis a world of living intelligence. But this idea of life is very different, I contend, from the open-ended view in Native American traditions.

So the wise men of the council sent the message to all the people and animals and birds and told them on what day they were to lift the sky. Everyone made poles to push against the sky, poles from the giant fir trees. The day for the sky lifting came. All the people raised their poles and touched the sky with them. Then the wise men shouted, "Ya-hoh!" Everybody pushed, and the sky moved up a little. "Ya-hoh," the wise men shouted a second time, and everybody pushed with all his strength. The sky was lifted a little higher. "Ya-hoh," all shouted, and pushed as hard as they could push. They kept on shouting, "Ya-hoh!" and pushing until the sky was up to the place where it is now. Since then, no one has bumped his head against the sky, and no one has been able to climb into the Sky World. . . .

We still shout "Ya-hoh" when doing hard work together or lifting something heavy like a canoe. When we say "Hoh," all of us use all the strength we have. Our voices have a higher pitch on that part of the word, and we make the *o* very long—"Ya-hoh!"[18]

The world itself does not attain a finished aspect. The inhabitants are all part of an ongoing "creation"; that is, a life. Space does not allow for a wealth of illustrations here—indeed all the stories of human beings, heroes, and spirits would illustrate the unfolding, dynamic narrative of existence in this worldview. In the Mayan Popul Vuh, for example, it would be represented by the story of the Hero Twins. Perhaps one simple nonmythic illustration will suffice: the Navajo rug. In Navajo weaving it is important to leave the pattern irregular or broken at one point (English is driven to speak of this as an "intentional flaw"). This is the essence of the work of art, however, being the "spirit line." In the world view of the Diné (i.e., "Navajo"), the world is pervaded by *niłchi'i*, "the Holy Wind," the ubiquitous power of life itself. All beings, from the great Holy People themselves to the most mundane "below earth person" (like the ants), share in this sacred breath. It is because it is moving that it can connect and heal. Hence the ritual healing designs we call "sand paintings" must be open, not just so the sacred powers may enter, but so they can also *leave*. This is crucial, for it is the characteristic of witches and skin walkers to try to entrap the power and keep it for themselves alone. It is because this power moves and is dynamic that the world has the characteristic of

18. "Pushing Up the Sky," in Ella Clark, *Tales from the Pacific Northwest* (Berkeley: University of California Press, 1953), 148–49.

hozho, of "going in beauty" or "environmentally attuned process." Evil, *hoxho*, is what tries to stop this process (hence one aim of witchcraft is to prevent aging or acquire individual power or wealth).[19]

Art as Ceremonial Renewal

THE TRICKSTER

The theme that the world is inherently open for further creative action introduces the importance of risk and chance as key elements in understanding existence—hence the importance of the Trickster throughout the various North American traditions, be it Inktome the Spider (Lakota; Wihio in Cheyenne), Raven (Northwest), Glooscap (Northeast), Nanabush or Manabozho (South Central), or Coyote.[20] This figure is disobedient and holy, powerful and foolish, wiser than he knows and perhaps than is good for him, but limited by his personal desires and willingness to rely on chance rather than thought.[21] He is the power of creation, revival, learning, and, above all, laughter, which is so central to Native American spirituality. The Trickster is the one who can explore the boundaries of the world and embrace contradictions and opposites. He may suffer, but he never dies—or if he does, he always comes back. Embodying transformation, he can occasionally open up the creative magic of the world and, in spite of himself, cause something good. Trickster is perhaps another way to think of the creative process, for not only is that process one of exploration of boundaries, surprise, and transformation, but it allows us to experience in imagination consequences that would be undesirable in reality.

Trickster is also a way of thinking about the appreciator of the artwork. We are not just changed by art, but the experience itself is one of transformation and metamorphosis. The work calls us into its world; it is a portal, not a surface. And if we have the power to enter into it, like the

19. See John R. Farella, *The Main Stalk: A Synthesis of Navajo Philosophy* (Tucson: University of Arizona Press, 1984), and James McNeeley, *Holy Wind in Navajo Philosophy* (Tucson: University of Arizona Press, 1973).

20. Always remembering Sam Gill's warning that this "person" may be the creation of Eurocentric science–or better, the product of chance encounters between Euro-American scientists and Coyote himself, as Barre Tolkien recounts in Barry Lopez's *Giving Birth to Thunder, Sleeping with His Daughter*, xi–xii.

21. Indeed, many stories have Trickster create death by betting that a stone will float.

shaman, we will be transformed and, perhaps, bring back to our shared existence something of the power of that spirit world that can heal and enliven.

Conclusion

My main point is that by exploring the Native American wisdom traditions—which those of us who are philosophers who still care about wisdom should do—we can arrive at a wealth of challenging and illuminating key tropes that often differ considerably from those we have inherited from Judeo-Christian, Hellenic, or Romantic and modernist sources. Instead of the usual ideas one assumes that go with the idea of "creativity," which I have been exploring here, such as creativity being an expression of individuality, brought forth by "will" and achieving perfect, finished form, we find the ideas of creativity embodied in a council of wise people, evoking, not commanding or willing the "*ens creatum*" (or *ens evocatum*), experimentally proceeding, often with mistakes that must be corrected, and resulting in a being that is alive and full of its own inde-terminate potentiality. Instead of the hierarchical power relationship of Creator-to-Created, we find instead a web of relations of respect. Given that the world is one where we need to think more about community and less about individualism, more about ecological harmony than domination (even as "stewardship of the earth"—an idea I find rather patronizing), one where growth and learning should be more prized than enclosed, rigorous systems that can then be pitted against each other, and, above all where the value of laughter as well as respect should be part of our spiritual attunement with the world, I think the traditions of the original nations of this place—Fourth World, Turtle Island—should gain our attention, our ears. After all, they have been speaking to us for quite a while now.

TWELVE

TRICKSTERS AND SHAMANS
Eros, Mythos, and the Eco-ontological Imagination

This essay is at once an effort to present something of a synopsis of views I have been developing over the past decade as well as to articulate that aspect of them that falls under the area of *aisthēsis*, by which I mean the "aesthetic" reconceived as ecstatic, transformative existence. *Aisthēsis* is a mode of participatory existence in which the immediacy or texture and symbolic depth of the world stand forth with illuminated intensity, defining in its transitory and metamorphic way both world and spirit.[1] It is at once a concrete actualization, a full engagement, an awakening of the world that funds the human drive to experience meaning and value. In this way, it also becomes a crucial part of a humanistic ecology, or "eco-ontology" in my terminology, that takes our qualitative and affective orientation to existence as crucial. As such, *aisthēsis* imaginatively discloses a "spiritual environment"—our disposition to those

---

1. Used here rather close to Santayana's sense, "Spirit is the *witness* of the cosmic dance" (*Realms of Being* [New York: Scribner, 1942], 562). But, unlike Santayana, I think it also "dances," else how could it be a "witness"? *Spirit* in this wider sense is the aesthetic experience of meaning and value.

aspects of the world that carry symbolic depth for our lives. *Aisthēsis* is the access intelligence has into the meaning of the world. For this reason, a deep aesthetics holds out the promise of an ecological reconstruction of philosophy.

In focusing on *aisthēsis* so conceived here, I intend to contrast it with those concepts more familiar to readers of Western "aesthetics," using in particular the figures of the Trickster and Shaman instead of the traditional topics encountered in aesthetics: "imagination," "art," "artist," "work of art," and "creativity." Ecstasy and laughter are participatory and transformative experiences that overcome the dualities of the world. The aims here are to establish an aesthetic primacy to philosophy and to indicate the importance of archaic modes of experience for aesthetics. In doing so, we open up a significant alternative to the range of "postmodern" modes. In this way, philosophy may serve the needs of an emerging global civilization that must undertake as its primary responsibility care for the world. And the roots of care lie in the deep and intense experience of the world on the aesthetic level.

Before going any further, I have to acknowledge my indebtedness to Mark Johnson's work and mentorship. Although my approach and concerns are more speculative and less tied to the issues of cognitive philosophy, I believe that we both are trying to orient our philosophical thinking in terms of the living vitality of embodied human existence. And both of us take the aesthetic as the fundamental "philosophical category," the stone that was thrown away that shall be the cornerstone, as Mark said to me one day. The ideal of finding in the aesthetic a testimony to the richness of our embodied existence guides what follows, though I have turned more to myth and civilization than cognitive studies.

Aesthetics and Shamanism

Let me begin by stating a fairly common textbook description of "aesthetics." This is the area of philosophy that concerns itself with problems of art and beauty and the judgments made about them. As one of the most recent branches of philosophy, it is one of the least significant (attested by its frequent omission in introductory textbooks). Indeed, it often is regarded as an area of applied epistemology, applied philosophy of language, applied cognitive theory, or applied ontology. To the extent possible, philosophy tries to shed its beams into this area of ideas that may be clear if not distinct. The results stress such themes as "aesthetic distance" or "disinterested pleasure," "purposiveness without purpose," "necessary satisfaction without a determining judgment," and so on. Imagination is a faculty of conceptual creativity. The work of art is a representation with some kind of semantic structure, an expression, or maybe, in a postmodern vein, an attack on "reality." The artist is valued for the individuality or subjectivity of her point of view. The contemporary artist must be, above all, unique; each work must be unique.

Now I will recount an experience. I was sitting in the dentist's office waiting for my son and happened to see an article in *National Geographic* (Feb. 2001) on "Bushman paintings"; that is, rock art pictures of animals and hunters, not unlike the great Magdalenian cave paintings from northern Europe some thirty to twenty thousand years earlier. Europeans had "read" these "crude" Bushman paintings as "representations" of "hunter-gatherer life." New scholars began to realize how seriously such imported Western ideas had missed the reality of this art. "For the San [i.e., Bushmen] rock paintings weren't just representations of life; they were repositories of it. . . . They put paint to rock and opened portals to the spirit world. . . . For the rock was not merely a canvas but also a veil between the material and spirit worlds, and paintings helped pierce that veil."[2] Though the San quit making such works more than a century ago, some groups still practice "trance rituals" that help us understand how these works were used. By dancing and singing (and hyperventilating), shamans would induce trances, interpreted as the "boiling" of their spiritual power that would enable them to journey into the "spirit world." There they might transform into animals or half-human/half-animal beings (such as are represented in the rock paintings). The shaman would undertake this "journey" in order to return to his people with some beneficial power, which would need to be preserved in discussion and, at one time, pictorial embodiment. "'This is what I looked like in the spirit world,' they might say as they painted a portal to that place of being."[3]

---

2. "Paintings of the Spirit," David Lewis-Williams, *National Geographic* 199, no. 2 (Feb. 2001): 118–22. Lewis-Williams subsequently expanded his study in *The Mind in the Cave* (London: Thames and Hudson, 2002) and (with Jean Clottes) *The Shamans of Prehistory: Trance and Magic in the Painted Caves* (New York: Harry N Abrams, Inc, 1998). See also Joseph Campbell's description in *The Power of Myth*, "The First Story-tellers," 87.

3. Ibid., 124.

As Mircea Eliade says in his definitive study *Shamanism: Archaic Techniques of Ecstasy*, "The shaman, and he alone, is the great master of ecstasy," so that he defines shamanism itself as identical to "technique of ecstasy."[4] "Ecstasy" here carries something of its root meaning: a "standing outside or beyond oneself."[5] During this trance, the shaman experiences a journey into another realm, "a region of the sacred inaccessible to other members of the community," where certain important spiritual powers are encountered in a beneficial way for the sake of the community. A shaman, through a deeply personal experience brought on by his unique ability, is nonetheless an intermediary who undertakes these journeys to restore or maintain the "health" of the "soul" of the community and to keep it in proper relationship to the life-giving, symbolic powers that sustain it.[6] The shaman, moreover, experiences the world as having a *depth* to it, which is vital for the functioning of life in its daily aspects. The world is not to be understood merely as its calm surface appearance, its bland literal meaning, but as a dynamic, mythic depth of great power. This may be entered through a "portal" in which one undergoes radical, but not disjunctive, transformation. And the phenomenon of transformation itself is revealed to be more the truth of the world than any fixed identity.

I was planning an aesthetics course when I read this article, and I was struck by the remarkable change in perspective that occurred when what seemed to Western eyes to be a flat, decorated surface covered with animal and human figures, such as we might "aesthetically appreciate" in a museum or gallery, that is, *a decorative flat surface with objects that could be recognized*, was experienced as a *portal* into an ecstatic realm, a realm that changed *us* and, later, allowed us to *help others*. Indeed, this description struck me as far truer to the nature of art and the artistic consciousness than the facile array of concepts encountered in aesthetics textbooks. What would happen if we took the shamanic experience as in some way fundamentally akin to the aesthetic, where the aesthetic transcends the decorative impulse to become an ecstatic, revelatory

4. Mircea Eliade, *Shamanism: Archaic Techniques of Ecstasy* (Princeton: Princeton University Press, 2004), 4.
5. Latin *ecstasis* is borrowed from Greek ἔκστασις, which ranges in meaning from "displacement" to "astonishment" to "trance."
6. "The shaman is the great specialist in the human soul; he alone 'sees' it, for he knows its 'form' and its destiny," Eliade, 8.

communion of self and world? Are not the intense experiences under-gone by shamans, perhaps to a far lesser degree, a component of the way human beings encounter the world in its profoundest sense? Have not the deepest experiences of our lives been both revelatory and transfor-mative? I was also led to reflect on the ways in which human beings experience the sacred and to reflect, in particular, on the tremendously rich body of myth, especially myths of origination (or "creation myths"). Is it not puzzling that perhaps the most ancient and greatest human art form, mythology, is never discussed in the philosophical discipline of "aesthetics"? Perhaps the earliest human thinking actually does concern itself with "creativity" and it has expressed these ideas mythically. Thus it seems to me that anyone concerned with the issues surrounding the theme of creativity might want to undertake a reflective inquiry into the archaic imagination and its forms of experience and expression. And this is what I intend to do in the context of my own philosophical theory, focusing here on the figures of the shaman and Trickster and leaving the question of creation myths for another time.

The Ecstatic Body and the Vita Humana

In order to proceed, I must give some summary of my position, beginning with an amplification of Mark Johnson's idea of embodied imagination.[7] Johnson has ably shown that the tropes of bodily life pervade our cognitive and linguistic understanding and that our thinking is necessar-ily metaphorical and imaginative. The upright, balanced, breathing, and seeing body gives us a rhythmic logic without which our high abstrac-tions would have no substance or sense. As such, the thesis advanced by Johnson (and George Lakoff) has been effectively applied against "disem-bodied" objectivist and purely linguistic concepts of meaning. But the "body" is much more than the "organism." It is the medium of symbolic understanding and existential mystery. What I would like to explore is the sense in which the body may be the vehicle of an ecstatic (and comic) aesthetics of mytho-poetic existence.

---

7. See Mark Johnson, *The Body in the Mind* (Chicago: University of Chicago Press, 1987), and, with George Lakoff, *Philosophy in the Flesh* (New York: Basic Books, 1999).

First let us reflect that the "body" is in fact the whole of human life conceived of as a structured process, the Vita Humana, borrowing a term from my grandfather.[8] The body, in short, is a "Life" of transformation in which the world's capacity for taking on new and deeper meaning is fundamental for our sense of ourselves. At the most obvious level, our embodiment means being born, having the experiences of the neonate, the infant, toddler, child, adolescent, young adult, and so on. This arc of embodiment is one of transformation and reconfiguration of selfhood. In our endeavor to view the living body as the dynamic origin of meaning, we may go beyond the various ways in which simple acts of standing or falling, being well or ill, seeing or being "in the dark" constitute a source for image schemata or other tropes that articulate experience for us. The human body in the arc of its existence gives us a dramatic understanding of the world as the enactment of life itself. A humanistic philosophy must take seriously the ways in which human beings have symbolized the meaning of life and expressed the idea of the world as "cosmic drama."[9] The Vita Humana points toward a philosophical anthropology that engages world cultures and the symbols they have used to render in conscious experience our vital embodiment. The phenomenon of our own existence is itself an ecstasy of the world, a mystery, a transformation, and this has a great deal to do with our perception of "meaning."

The Human Eros

The Vita Humana points toward a key theme, which I have designated "the Human Eros."[10] As a thesis of philosophical anthropology, I make the following claim. The dynamics of embodied living point toward a drive for the qualitative experience of meaning and value throughout human existence. We must encounter this sense of meaning aesthetically, that is, as the qualitative sense of the world and of our lives in it.

8. See Hartley Burr Alexander, "The Great Art Which Is Philosophy," in *Contemporary American Philosophy*, vol. 1, ed. George D. Adams and Wm. Pepperell Montague (New York: Macmillan, 1930), esp. 96ff.: "For the finality of aesthetic rationality is...no less than the life-form of the body itself."

9. This term (as well as the substance of the thought) here comes from Hartley Burr Alexander's *God and Man's Destiny* (Oxford: Oxford University Press, 1936). See chapter 2, "Drama as the Cosmic Truth."

10. See "The Human Eros," chapter 5 in this book.

A simple way to understand this claim is to reflect on what it takes to destroy a person's ability or desire to live, ranging from loss of a sense of self-worth to experience that is empty of value, beauty, love, or acknowledgment. When the Human Eros is not fulfilled, we die or avenge it. (One of the most humiliating forms of degradation is that those whom society makes "unpersons" are not even *seen*; a great deal of social conditioning lies in developing techniques for avoiding awareness of the suffering of others.) When this Eros does not succumb to negation, it transforms into Eris, the drive toward destruction and death.[11]

The various phases of the Vita Humana engage this Eros in different ways, and the whole array of civilization, in its diverse forms, is primarily an effort to meet this need. Eros was the generative/creative force in Hesiod's *Theogony*, the golden "limb-loosening" principle that evoked Cosmos out of Chaos.[12] And so I use it here as the creative power in our experience that seeks to fill the pregnant "space" or void of "Chaos" with the limited and articulate order of a fulfilled life.[13] But Eros aspires beyond itself as well. Plato called "Eros" a daimon, or spirit, which was the great intermediary between the mortal and divine realms, keeping the two from falling asunder (*Symposium* 202 e). It suffused all human endeavors so that all deeds and actions were "poietic," that is, conceived in some intimation of what was beautiful, and giving birth to "offspring" of the spirit as well as the body that sought to be *mimēseis* or "enactments" of this ideal in some faithful way. In this sense, I take Eros to be a power of seeking meanings and values that, when taken as patterns for living enactment, raise human life toward creation and self-transcendence. Eros is the drive that appropriates the symbol-giving structures of embodied

---

11. See Viktor Frankl's account of his effort to preserve a sense of the meaning of life in the Nazi concentration camp, *Man's Search for Meaning* (New York: Simon & Schuster, Inc., 1984). Unlike Freud, I do not take a reductive approach to Eros, nor do I find an "aggressive instinct" as its counterpart, since aggression is a reaction. See Erich Fromm's discussion in *Greatness and Limitations of Freud's Thought* (New York: Mentor, 1980), ch. 4. Aside from Fromm's reductive approach, Eros is not some principle of aggregation. It seeks to encounter meaning and value, not in generic abstraction but concretely as moments of life, in "consummations," as Dewey called them.

12. Hesiod, *Theogony*, l:120ff.

13. In Greek, "Chaos" did not mean disorder (for there was nothing before it) so much as "pre-order;" i.e., the "opening" or "space" that *allows* the drama of the cosmos to unfold; in this sense the "stage" is the "Chaos" of the play. But the primordial powers of the emergent world are just that: *powers* in need of form and limit in order to become productive and so good and beautiful to behold.

existence and frames them into various "tropes." These are pivotal themes in a culture's core pattern or "constellation" of dominant ideas that sustain and develop its sense of the structure of the world as a meaningful and value-imbued domain, or "cosmos."

Thus, Eros is the architectonic drive of civilization. Human beings experience meaning and value only within a symbolically constituted world or "cosmos." Just as we require a physical environment that sustains organic existence, so we require a cultural environment to experience meaning and value concretely. The Human Eros, then, seeks to enframe a cultural ecology for the sake of an aesthetics of existence. One aspect of the project of philosophical anthropology, so conceived, is the study of those cultural worlds that have sustained and served the Human Eros throughout time. One of the great contributions philosophy can accomplish is to turn toward a global inquiry into the heritage of civilization. This would mean the abandonment, however, of conceptions of philosophy as governed by some sort of pure methodology that legitimizes narrow and parochial notions of "experience." The world is now passing through one of its most crucial periods, and the need to create the outlines of a meaningful, value-rich civilization of global dimensions is upon us. Philosophy can play a key role in this, when undertaken as a humanistic ecology, a discipline that would require literacy in history, religion, literature, and art around the world and would teach in order to enlarge our students' imaginations and not just their analytical powers. In this way, aesthetics may be one of the most neglected aspects of contemporary philosophy.

Eco-ontology

While the Human Eros and the Vita Humana determine a philosophical anthropology, there is an ontological side to this position as well. The live body exists *in* an environment. Western ontology, since Parmenides, has been dominated by the idea of identity as a fundamental sign of Being or substance, with the result that being is thought of as changeless and disconnected. As Aristotle says, unity and essence are universal for substance, for to be and to be one are equally predicated of substance. This idea derives, I believe, from the commitment to making being fundamentally logical. I have explored this commitment and the problems it continues to have for a genuinely ecological conception of being elsewhere.[14] From a pragmatic standpoint, logical identities are ideals, that is, tools for dealing with certain kinds of problems, like those of identifying. When hypostatized into underlying substances, however, they distort the interrelated and transformative character of nature. That is, they mask the ecological dimension of "inter-being." Buddhist metaphysics acts as a wonderful resource in counterbalancing this tendency with its emphasis on the inherent "emptiness" (śūnyatā) of all things, their "dependent co-arising" (pratītya-samutpāda), that becomes evident when one focuses upon the elements (dharmas) of events with insight (prajña). In this mode, events are reveals as events, arising from conditions, being conditions themselves, and passing into further conditions. But they also stand forth with an utterly distinctive, if transitory character (tathatā). Whereas the Greek concern for eidos was due to an interest in truth, as "that which is honest, sincere, dependable" (alētheia), the Buddhist emphasis on emptiness was for the sake of cessation of grasping and compassion (karuṇā).[15] If Western ontologies err in commitments to identity as the truth of substance (whether logical or material), the aims of Buddhist metaphysics can err in the emphasis on impermanence.

An ecological ontology is concerned with understanding beings in terms of environmental relations and natural histories. "Doing and undergoing," as generic traits of existence, give an ontology that is both qualitatively immediate and relationally mediated. "Situations" are ranges of interactions of varying degrees and modalities, inherently transformative, but capable of realizing continuous histories, which, in human existence, can achieve consummatory—that is, aesthetic—experience. Eco-ontology endeavors to see process and metamorphosis at the heart of things, and undertakes the task of responsible intelligence in sustaining the diversity as well as the stability of environmental being. That is to say, the aim of eco-ontology is care of the world. It is humanistic in designating human being as a locus of meaning, but sees human existence and so meaning as interwoven with the world.

---

14. See "Between Being and Emptiness: Toward an Eco-ontology of Inhabitation," in this book.

15. Greek ὰληθεια is "truth" in the sense of "one who speaks the truth"; i.e., someone who is trustworthy and dependable. The root meaning is "not to escape notice," which in the human context means not to forget one's promises or obligations. This is evident in Homer's *Odyssey*, in which Odysseus must determine cautiously those servants who have remained loyal, that is, "true," and those who have not.

The implications of this position for an ecstatic aesthetics are that we are inherently in the world as a transformative process and its qualitative dimension is capable of radical connection to the ecology of our existence and can be experienced in a consummatory manner. We are capable of making experience symbolic of the way we are in the world, and this symbolism can be "undergone" or "had" as "*an* experience." Imagination, then, is a way in which we dramatically connect ourselves with the world in its deep as well as immanent aspects. Art breaks through dualities, being a "portal" into the aesthetic environment; boundaries are transgressed and creative change becomes possible. Imagination is also the power we have of constructing symbolic meaning in our existence and so serving the Human Eros. A primary way this is done is through Mythos.

Mythos

Another key theme I emphasize is the importance of "Mythos" in our understanding of self and world. Unlike the common usage of "myth" to denote a "false" or untrustworthy story, Mythos designates those stories that are taken as constituting our identities. These narratives can range from highly symbolic to empirical and historicist, but it is their use that I designate as mythic. A Mythos tells the constitutive events whereby something significant came to be. We all have core stories that we use to define ourselves individually, as families and as whole peoples. Mythoi are "true" in this sense primarily, aside from their literal referentiality. They are modes of self-understanding and meaning. Thus, while the event that a Mythos relates may be in the historical past, it "exists" in terms of its power in making us what we are or the world as it is.[16] Mythoi are condensed and symbolic and help us determine a fundamentally affective relationship to the world. The different Mythoi different cultures have are at heart habits of aesthetic existence, teaching ways of seeing (or not seeing), feeling, even dreaming. In looking, then, at the central Mythoi of a culture, we are investigating the major ways in which

16. In one sense, here I am following Mircea Eliade's understanding of myth (as in his *Studies in Comparative Religion* and its numerous derivative studies, such as *Myth and Reality*). But I reject his rather dualistic and structural way of schematizing "myth" as in a separate domain of "sacred time." The sacred, on my more Deweyan account, is a potential qualitative depth of the world rather than a "breakthrough" or "hierophany" of another realm.

that culture has designated and described those constellations of tropes that constitute its cosmos. That is, we are seeing how it frames the ecology of the world as an environment of meaning and value for the Human Eros. We are now ready to consider the importance of those tropes of shaman and Trickster as modes of eco-ontological wisdom for an aesthetics of existence.

Shamans and Tricksters

Let us recall the dilemma of our concept of the "aesthetic" and the experience of the shaman. The shaman does not have the "aesthetic attitude," we would say; he does not distinguish the "representation" from the reality; he does not experience the nonpurposive intellectual pleasure of aesthetic emotion. With this approach, the best one might hope for is that of Cassirer who saw in mythic experience a "confusion" of art and science that became clarified with the progress of civilization.[17] But consider another possibility: the shaman has merely intensified a form of experience that is incarnate in our flesh and used to help create and sustain a domain of meaning that helps a group of people exist with a heightened sense of the significance and value of their world. He has inhabited the world through the mode of imagination in a way that has given him an ecstatic wisdom that reconnects his people aesthetically to the world as they inhabit it. Moreover he has experienced in himself the profound mystery of transformation, how he and the world of daily experience can be reconfigured as powerful and sacred to the core. The shaman understands the world and himself as metaphoric power, as the possibility of significant relation. It may be that here we have more insight into the true origins of art—and philosophy—than we think. Our experience of the world may have everything to do with its transformative magic and its revealing a domain of possible significant relations. Ecstasy, then, is an aesthetic negation of dualism and so becomes a mode of profound reconnection with genuinely positive relationships that sustain our connections with the world on an affective level.

Ecstasy is one way of achieving this; laughter is another. Let us take a look at the well-known figure of the Trickster. Being most familiar with

---

17. Ernst Cassirer, *Myth and Language*, trans. Susanne K. Langer (Harper and Brothers, 1946).

the Native North American versions, I will focus my remarks on them. Tricksters are sacred beings who are the subject of laughter. Laughter involves the coexistence of contraries, and Trickster figures are powerful because they are able to transgress boundaries (including those of life and death) and persist. The Trickster often acts out of socially unacceptable motives, lust, greed, ignorance, or pride, and may be humiliated, injured, dismembered, or "killed" (until he comes back). But, by playing across the limits of the forbidden, Trickster allows himself to become not only an object lesson for those who stay within the norms but also a very powerful creator and healer. The world is often a paradox, combining order and disorder, and the role of the Trickster becomes significant in looking at the world as this sort of interplay rather than as a fixed and ultimate harmony. A Pit River Nation story has the world grow from the dual dancing of Silver Fox and Coyote, who both leap into their creation at the end. In many stories, Trickster is responsible (intentionally or not) for making the world or some significant part of it, like human beings or tobacco.[18]

One story from the Crow Nation tells how, when human beings were to be made, a council of all the animals was called.[19] Each animal spoke, from Bear and Mountain Lion down to Ant, each stating that the human being must be made to look just like himself. Coyote alone was silent. The council broke up with each animal making a mud version of what Human was to look like, but Coyote took a little from each animal and combined them in his model, then destroyed the others as the animals slept. In the morning the Sun gave life to Coyote's model and it became—us! Note how Coyote's ability to transgress boundaries here comes across as the ability to be open to the possibility of otherness and of creative integration. Each animal is caught up in his own self-enclosed vision, not only exclusive of the others, but of genuinely new creations. The result, our own being, becomes more significant in light of this story, for we humans have a little of every other creature in us (including Coyote and Sun)—something that connects us to them as relatives. The upshot of this myth not only gives us an account of Trickster wisdom—the ability to refuse to admit boundaries for creative possibilities—but also shows how, through myth, we develop

18. See Paul Radin, *The Trickster* (New York: Schocken Books, 1956), Åke Hultkrantz, *The Religions of the American Indians* (Berkeley: The University of California Press, 1980), 34–35.
19. See the previous chapter, "Creating with Coyote."

a primary aesthetic relationship to the animal kingdom as a "*kin*-dom." It also warns us of the Coyote part in us, our talent for getting into trouble, and reminds us of the life-giving part of the holy Sun, which is also in us.

In another story, Coyote is responsible for the tobacco plant, the means by which human beings send messages to the sacred powers. The origin of this Eucharist is Coyote's anus. It seems Coyote was cold one day and squirmed inside a hollow log. When he woke up, he was stuck. He could see out of a hole and called on a bird to help make it larger so he could get out. But the bird made too much noise and Coyote told it to go away. After a few more similar tries in which the hole does get larger, Coyote decides he must take himself apart to get out and begins tossing body parts out of the hole. After he has tossed his innards out, Crow comes along and says, "Hey, Coyote! You shouldn't throw good stuff like this away. I'll eat it." Coyote frantically tries to stop Crow from eating his innards, but by the time he gets out, most of his stomach and intestines are gone. Reconnected, Coyote discovers he is very hungry and begins to eat everything in sight—except it all falls out (and tobacco grows up where this happened). He tries stopping up his anus with some pine gum, but a spark from a smoldering pieces of grass from a forest fire sets it alight and he runs off—even today you can see that black spot under Coyote's tail. Like the Christian Eucharist, the medium of communion comes from a dismembered and reconstituted holy being, except where there are tears in the former, here there is laughter.

One of the truly impressive things about Native American religious consciousness is the central way in which it integrates humor into the experience of the sacred. This is especially evident in the social institutions of the sacred clowns in the Pueblo societies of the Southwest, the *koshare*, *koyemshi*, or *newekwe*. They often appear in costume during the most important ceremonies and are viewed as having a healing, cathartic function in their society. The koshare paint their bodies with broad black-and-white stripes, embodying the contrariety of life, which they themselves transcend.[20] Their ability to "transgress" is often depicted as

---

20. The members of the *koshare* society are often people who have survived terrible trauma, physical or psychological. See Barbara Tedlock, "The Clown's Way," in *Teachings from the American Earth: Indian Religion and Philosophy,* ed. Dennis Tedlock and Barbara Tedlock (New York: Liveright, 1975), 112, and "Boundaries of Belief," in *I Become Part of It,* ed. D. M. Dooling and Paul Jordan-Smith (New York: Parabola Books, 1989), 126.

the ability to "take in" or eat gluttonously as well as ingest quite unacceptable things. Likewise they are able to say and do things that violate the rules of respectable Pueblo society, even mocking priests and gods. The purpose, though, is to restore a sense of health, which involves a harmony born of balance between opposites. Barbara Tedlock recounts one episode from a ceremonial at the Pueblo of Zuñi just after the first moon landing, an event that had caused great distress because of its sacrilege. The newekwe threw one clown up to the moon (a nearby roof), and then the clown jumped off into the arms of doctors armed with huge needles while he gave a ludicrous report of what he had seen up there.[21]

According to the Zuñi, says Tedlock, worry lodges in the stomach and causes most illness, so that laughter is indeed a restoration of health. The sacred clowns of the Pueblos, says Tedlock, undertake "private shamanic journeys on the Milky Way," and they are known as "the wisest and most fearless people in the entire Pueblo." They paint their bodies with broad black-and-white stripes, representing the Milky Way, which was the sacred path traveled by Payatamu, the son of the Sun. His job was to awaken his father every day, but one day he had his head cut off playing a game with a mysterious woman. His relatives—the animals— looked for his head until the lowly Mole found it and they put it back on—backward. The Sun rose, but now because Payatamu did everything backward, he was now called Ne-payatamu and became the founder of the clown society.[22] The clown refuses to exist within established polarities—and indeed loves to reverse them. His "'medicine' is nothing but common filth."[23] This reversal acts as a form of release, and so it restores balance, harmony, and happiness, which are sacred feelings in Pueblo society.

The shaman and the Trickster are holy beings in a worldview that recognizes distinctions but realizes the truth of transformation underlying them. And both have something to say about the nature of art, the artist, the aesthetic, imagination, and the world. Through these figures we see that the ordinary world is something to be transcended in a moment of ecstasy (which includes the experience of humor), so that its transformative power becomes manifest when it is in danger of becoming contained in

---

21. Barbara Tedlock, "Boundaries of Belief," in *I Become Part of It*, 127.
22. Ibid., 127–28.
23. Barbara Tedlock, "The Clown's Way," in *Teachings from the American Earth*, 113.

rigidly defined boundaries between objects. These moments, whether experiences in some other "spirit world" or in the enactments of social transgressions by clowns, are sought out not just for their revelatory power into the dynamism of a mythic worldview, but because they are capable of restoring and intensifying meaningful relationships within the ordinary world. Our world is reconstituted, like Coyote, with its sacred power understood. (This is operative in our modes of tragedy and comedy, by the way, which play with the ideas of the destruction of sustaining boundaries, tragedy proceeding to destroy them and in so doing destroying the participants, comedy suddenly averting their destruction and consummating the reconstituted world in the marriage of laughter.)

Aisthēsis

The Shaman and the Trickster tell us that human life is a ceremonial enactment of cosmic meaning. The structure or form of our lives, the Vita Humana, is at heart a mystery of transformation, for we not only pass through the transformations of neonate to infant to child and so on to old age and death. We ourselves are transformations of the universe into life and of life into death. The very carbon of our bodies holds within it a history of the life and death of ancestral suns. And, as far as we can tell, the cosmos itself is but such a transformation. Symbols, rituals, myths, and religions are means whereby we endeavor to remind ourselves of the mystery of being, though this mystery itself comes to us in the naked immediacy of each moment. To live with the awareness of the immanent possibility of the sacred is the aim of the spiritual life; that is, as Thoreau said, to be awake.[24] In this mode of philosophical reflection, the primacy of the aesthetic is at once apparent. For here we must admit the role of our affective attunement to the world and its qualitative horizon as conditions of thought, and imagination and symbol as the centers of our transformative, meaningful response. This part of philosophy places its hand directly on the beating heart of the world and reminds us, as philosophers, to remain true to the calling of our discipline, which has

---

24. "The light which puts out our eyes is darkness to us. Only that day dawns to which we are awake. There is more day to dawn. The sun is but a morning star." The conclusion of Henry David Thoreau's *Walden*.

managed to become ever more remote from the impulses that give rise to it in the first place.

Let us remember the great Magdalenian cave paintings from the end of the last Ice Age some twenty thousand years ago. Here, if not in the crude burials or cave bear altars of the Neanderthals, are the first stunning testaments of the emergence of the human mind. It is a world fully engaged with the mystery of life, its sacred meaning, and its almost overwhelming immanence. The caves were no more dwellings than the paintings were "pictures." As André Leroi-Gourhan has effectively argued, they were temples where initiations occurred, rituals that transformed the identities of young boys forever. Entering the cave is a return into the primal womb of the earth, the mother of all living things; the paintings are encountered suddenly looming up out of utter blackness, huge and alive. There, tribal shamans, like the one pictured in the cave of the Trois-Frères, themselves dressed up as composite animal and human beings, induced experiences that would change the boys into men, so that when they emerged again, were reborn, they would be prepared to enact the role of hunters who revered and blessed the animals they killed. Indeed, aside from the series of female fertility figurines, the image of the "sorcerer" of the Trois-Frères is the first image we have of ourselves.

Perhaps one of the key steps in developing an ecological world civilization is to develop once again those primary powers of aesthetic ecstasy that project us beyond the surface of the world into its imaginative heart and, like the shaman, to return to our human comrades with those transformative visions that keep us emotionally as well as symbolically connected with the immanent mystery of existence. Trickster offers us laughter as a wisdom for overcoming duality and for understanding the world as a creative mixture of the precarious and the stable. Transformations are paradoxes and human life is a series of transformations, at once serious and comic. Philosophy is itself guided by a reckless and creative Trickster spirit, easily crossing boundaries to discover the unforeseen consequences. If ecstasy connects us to a deep world so powerfully that it changes us, laughter releases us from imprisonment in a given form. Thus I think that an ecological philosophy that cares passionately about this life and this world is also in need of the clown's wisdom to eat anything and survive in its journey across the Milky Way, that is, the arc of existence.

PART FOUR

SPIRIT AND PHILOSOPHY

THIRTEEN

SANTAYANA'S SAGE

The Disciplines of Aesthetic Enlightenment

Entréme donde no supe
y quedéme no sabiendo
toda ciencia trascendiendo
I came into the unknown
and stayed there unknowingly
rising beyond all science.

—San Juan de la Cruz / St. John of the Cross,
trans. Willis Barnstone

Reading Santayana

In his "General Review" at the end of *Realms of Being*, Santayana observes that "my philosophy is like that of the ancients a discipline of the mind and heart, a lay religion."[1] I intend to take this remark seriously and to explore what "a discipline of the mind and heart" means. Santayana was a careful writer, so already we should remark on those three key words: "discipline," "mind," and "heart." This theme provides a guiding focus for understanding Santayana's later work and illuminates what might appear to be the excessively eclectic nature of his ontology. In his intellectual autobiography, "General Confession," Santayana states that his family was "remarkably staunch in our complex allegiances, combining

---

1. George Santayana, *The Realm of Spirit* (New York: Scribner, 1940), 272 (= *Realms of Being*, 827), hereafter cited in the text as RS/RB. *The Realm of Essence* will be cited as RE.

them as well as logic allowed, without at heart ever disowning anything."[2] This is true of his philosophy as well. But the question remains *how* Santayana never "disowned" the contending elements of his philosophy.

The principle of his philosophical allegiances, I believe, was nothing less than the realization of a "lay religion" that provided for spiritual liberation through a systematic discipline, and his work deserves to be read and understood from *this* point of view. The discipline of spirit was, moreover, an aesthetic one closely connected with the artistry as well as philosophy of Santayana's texts. Our assumptions of how to read a text often determine what we understand it to mean. Too often Santayana's texts are read (by philosophers, at least) as if they were just like those texts produced for the professional academician. By this I mean texts written for those involved in the ideal of impersonal, institutional search for objective truth by means of careful argument, systematic integrity, and pervasive criticism. Such texts are neither written for "spiritual liberation" nor does their form have to be beautiful. In this light, Santayana is often erroneously judged as a "bad philosopher" or, at best, a "literary philosopher," someone who *could* have been a "good" philosopher if he had only been more "serious" and more rigorous in his arguments, more responsive to his critics, less seduced by his natural flair for expression. Those who believe Santayana could have been a philosopher, if only he had wanted, point to his sophisticated, critical understanding of the work of Moore, Russell, Husserl, and Heidegger long before any of his colleagues teaching in American universities.

Aside from the fact that Santayana *was* a good philosopher in the ultimate sense (i.e., one who offers a "disciplinary vision" that enlarges the human sense of wisdom), perhaps we should not read his texts as if they belonged to the life of the academic philosopher. If there is one clear fact about Santayana's life, it is that at the first moment he was able, in 1912, he firmly rejected the career of the professional philosopher. He chose instead not to pursue another "career" but a *life*, a "spiritual life," as he came to call it. His writings thereafter, such as the meditations collected in *Soliloquies in England*, are products of a *vita nuova*.

---

2. "General Confession," in *George Santayana*, 2nd ed., Library of Living Philosophers, ed. Paul A. Schilpp (Greensboro, NC: Tudor Publishing, 1951), 3. Hereafter cited in the text as GC.

From this context, Santayana's commitment to *writing* must be understood as part of living a certain kind of life that, as far as he was concerned, achieved his own individual "salvation." After 1912, at least, he did not write to advance his career, to win verbal victories over other philosophers, to add to knowledge in any scientific sense, to gain popularity with avant-gardists, to be canonized or anthologized, or to leave his grand system for a wiser posterity that would revere his name. He wrote— and wrote well—because he loved to and because it was vital to the life of spirit; giving expression to thought through the medium of his style was a means of achieving liberation. He wrote for himself and for anyone who wished to live in this realm. In this sense, then, his texts must be read as tools, like Buddhist sutras, helpful toward living a certain kind of life somewhat at odds with the typical professional academic life. The "doctrines" he teaches are those that are *useful* to hold *if* one is aiming at a special result, a "spiritual liberation" of a very specific type. In light of this end, Santayana offers "dogma," as any religious discipline might (and he characterized himself as a dogmatist), but from the standpoint of other ends, Santayana rejects dogma, and indeed he was one of the most tolerant and uncontentious of philosophers, allowing others their own poetic symbols and styles of normal or lyric madness. He was a pluralistic dogmatist. What do his texts look like read from this perspective?

Santayana as a Hellenistic Sophos

An immediate and obvious analogy can be drawn to the ancient Hellenistic schools and their competing ideals of the "*sophos*," the sage or individual who has achieved a state of spiritual emancipation and clarity by unswerving embodiment of philosophical principles as living tools. Against the contingency of existence, the Hellenistic sage sought to cultivate a character marked by unperturbed equanimity (*ataraxia*) and independent self-sufficiency (*autonomia*) realized though a discipline of living (*askēsis*). The various Hellenistic schools debated the means to achieve this end, leading to their disagreements in the related topics of metaphysics and epistemology. This is an important theme that forever separates the disputes among the ancients and those of the moderns, whatever "arguments" they may share. The ancient schools pursued philosophy as a means of realizing virtue—any epistemological argument was ultimately understood in terms of an ideal of personal completion or happiness. Moderns, such as Bacon, Descartes, and Hobbes, saw the pursuit of knowledge as a means of gaining power over nature through a technology of judgment. Though one can discern through their writings an ideal of the "wise man" (as one who can acquire and use the power of nature, the *magus*), this ideal is usually left implicit. Thus the ensuing debates in epistemology from the seventeenth century to today result from the project of natural science unrelated to the question of virtue or personal salvation. This is what forever separates contemporary from classical skepticism, for example, though similar arguments may be used.

The Hellenistic schools, on the contrary, placed virtue as central. The Stoics required absolute conviction for the elimination of our passive, emotional reactions (*pathē*) to fortune: Thus they *had* to advocate those doctrines that would help one attain a rational certitude toward unpredictable events and help destroy unquiet emotions. The Skeptics, on the contrary, found the idea of absolutely certain knowledge a source of disquiet and anxiety, and so they achieved peace through a complete suspension of the power of belief, "holding off" the claims of the world (the literal meaning of the famous "*epochē*"). Skepticism *had* to reject Stoic epistemology because if the Stoics were right, then tranquility could not be realized. But to live happily, tranquility *had* to be realized. Therefore, the Stoics *must* be wrong. And so skepticism attacked the possibility of knowledge for the sake of a tranquil life.[3] The Epicurean community, in a sense, constituted the first "monastery" (from *monas*, "solitary"); i.e., a place to shut out the unmanageable troubles of political life—an amazing change, given the political orientation of classic Attic philosophy—and to secure in their garden, amid friendships, the simple

3. See John Michelsen's comparison of Santayana with the *sophos* of the ancient skeptical school of Pyrrhonism in "George Santayana: A Pyrrhonian Sceptic of Our Time," *Overheard in Seville*, no. 11 (1993): 30–40. Michelsen says that the "most important point to be made in an attempt to situate Santayana correctly . . . is as an antique sage, or ancient philosopher in modern guise" (32). Michelsen's reading seems rather at odds with that given in the same issue of *Overheard in Seville* by John Anton, whose article "Santayana and Greek Philosophy" looks primarily at the early Santayana of *The Life of Reason* and its more Hellenic, rather than Hellenistic, ideal. My own approach, taken here and in the companion essay, "Santayana's Unbearable Lightness of Being: Aesthetics as a Prelude to Ontology" (in this volume), is to see Santayana's development from 1912 to 1923—the period of his departure from America and the impact of World War I and its aftermath—as one from the Hellenic ideal Anton describes to the Hellenistic ideal Michelsen depicts in his comparison of Santayana with Pyrrhonian skepticism.

physical conditions for quiet happiness and gentle pleasures.[4] In order to find release from pain, superstition *had* to be eliminated. Therefore, the system of Democritus *must* be true, for it offered the best means to disregard various Orphic or Platonic myths of the afterlife. Acceptance of Democritean materialism was a conditional necessity for living an Epicurean life.

The dogmas espoused in all these schools were, quite literally, *tools* for realizing the life of the sage. There are numerous other examples: The writings of most Asian and medieval philosophers fall into this category, as do"nonphilosophical" texts like *The Cloud of Unknowing*, the *Spiritual Exercises* of Loyola, or the sermons of Meister Eckhart. In their concern for the life of the reader, these texts differ profoundly in their approaches from philosophical works stemming from the modern period down to today's various movements. Even so, one might discern behind the modernist texts a constructed ideal individual, such as Descartes' dispassionate, methodical knower aiming at truth. If there are major exceptions to this modernist shift, one would have to look at authors like Spinoza, the existentialists, or, perhaps, individualists like Søren Kierkegaard, John Stuart Mill, and William James.

Santayana's texts, especially in his later phase, exhibit features more akin to the premodern traditions. Prior to World War I, Santayana had entertained the more sanguine Hellenic ideal of a "life of reason" mutually realized by members of society in order to create an "island" of cosmos amid the engulfing "chaos" of nature.[5] More and more, perhaps due to his close-hand experience of the effects of the First World War in England, witnessing the slaughter of a generation, he came to disavow this possibility, turning instead toward the question of the spiritual life. This transition can be found in his "farewell essays" in *Character and*

---

4. It might be argued that Plato's Academy, established outside the walls of Athens, might be the "first monastery," but its mission was absolutely political. Its physical removal (in contrast to Isocrates' school in the heart of Athens) can be seen as the required isolation needed by a new political organization to organize its ideology, its membership, and remain unmolested by the established powers it aims to challenge. The Epicureans, by contrast, looked back to a prepolitical state of nature, ruled by a rustic anarchy, that gave rise to society and civilization from a combination of animal needs and ignorant fears and desires. See Lucretius, *De rerum natura*, 5:925ff. (the basis of Rousseau's *Discourse on the Origin of Inequality*).

5. "The universe, apart from us, is a chaos, but it may be made a cosmos by our efforts and in our own minds.... Civilization is precarious, but it need not be short-lived," "A Religion of Disillusion," in *Poetry and Religion* (New York: Charles Scribner's Sons, 1900), 245–46.

Opinion in the United States and *The Genteel Tradition at Bay*, as well as in the haunted meditations *Soliloquies in England*, especially in "Tipperary," in which the jaunty optimism of the World War I song is set against his own disillusionment and foreboding sense of things to come. Santayana did not abandon the idea of creating an island of spiritual cosmos amid universal chaos, but he restricted its limits to the personal life of spirit attainable in each of us. Santayana achieved this cosmos in *writing*, thereby inhabiting a realm which, though immaterial, impotent and non-existential, set spirit free.

In *Platonism and the Spiritual Life*, he produced a lucid enchiridion of his new, starker ideal, claiming that "one of the great things always possible is the spiritual life."[6] Indeed, the spiritual life was so inconsistent with the moral or political life that one of the dangers of a social utopia, he said, would be that this ideal would become lost and totally obscured—at worst, confused with the real. The greatest threat to the spiritual life was for it to be bound up with "moralism" (as happens in Platonism or Christianity): the identification of impotent values with "causes." This replaces naturalistic physics with illusory metaphysics and binds the spirit at the moment of its liberation with distracting demands.[7] The ideal stands forth perhaps best when it can be utterly contrasted with the real. But if reality is so antithetical to vital aims, the spiritual life is existentially unattainable. Thus, as a *possibility*, the spiritual life "is always with us, but dispersed over occasions that continually confuse and interrupt it" (RS, 93/RB, 647). The question is how to realize the possibility.

In trying to identify the nature of the spiritual life, Santayana is also forced to develop a concept of "the sage." This is more than the literary ideal of the complete life that any text on ethics might advance. To one interested in happiness, the "sage" is the author of any given text in philosophy. That is, different texts are products of different ideals of wisdom, and any philosophical author *uses* this ideal to formulate the perspective (and so the *arguments*) that constitute the text itself. Examples would

6. George Santayana, *Platonism and the Spiritual Life* (New York: Scribner, 1927), 1. Hereafter cited in the text as PSL.

7. See *The Realm of Spirit*, 191 (= RB, p. 745): "Suppose the prophecy came true and we began to live in the Millennium or in the New Jerusalem. As we walked those golden streets and gazed at those crowned and white-robed phantoms that discoursed music in eternal peace, the still solitary spirit within us might well ask whether all this was not a dream, whether the heart was not deceived and disappointed by it, and whether reality possessed no other dimensions."

be the "erotic dialectician" of Plato's *Dialogues*, the "systematic inquirer" of the Aristotelian corpus, the "believer who seeks understanding" of Augustine's works, Nietzsche's Zarathustran ironist, or the later Wittgenstein's philosophical therapist.[8] Kierkegaard consciously created different authorial personae for different texts. One of the clues in interpreting various philosophical systems, then, is not so much to compile the web of arguments used for any position, but to discern the shape of the *sophos* who stands dark and shadowlike behind the luminosity of the words themselves. To find "the sage" rather than the existential author of a text is to have the hermeneutic key to its universe. It is perhaps one of Santayana's strongest claims to greatness that he recognized this in his work. The sage behind the Santayanan texts, I believe, is one who has risen above the pursuit of knowledge for the sake of pure aesthetic vision; his arguments and doctrines must be put in that context.

The Aesthetic Discipline of the Sage

What, then, *is* the discipline of the sage for Santayana? Traditionally, the philosopher has undertaken the Socratic quest for knowledge as the absolute good, seeking through some rigorous intellectual method (e.g., dialectic) a means for the gradual possession of a system of timeless truth. The philosopher thus had to subordinate all personal interests and passions to the universal claims that came to define what was meant by "rationality" in the West. Eros had to be redirected for Plato and completely removed for Descartes. Objective reason, as Foucault would say, was the result of a discipline of the body. The Platonic inheritance identified the quest for wisdom with the quest for "science," for systematic, demonstrable knowledge of Being based on absolutely correct insight. Santayana, it is true, rejects the thought that philosophy should be idiosyncratic, arbitrary, or "personal" (it shouldn't even aspire to be the expression of an historical epoch, as with Hegel). He states that his philosophy is founded upon "a certain shrewd orthodoxy with the

---

8. For an attempt to read Nietzsche's writings as authored by a self-consciously created persona, see Alexander Nehamas' *Nietzsche: Life as Literature* (Cambridge, MA: Harvard University Press, 1985).

sentiment and practice of laymen maintain everywhere" (SAF, v).[9] "In the past or the future," he says, "my language and my borrowed knowledge would have been different, but under whatever sky I had been born, since it is the same sky, I should have had the same philosophy" (SAF, x). This must be squared with his rejection of the possibility of a system of universal knowledge built upon absolutely certain foundations, for knowledge was nothing but "faith mediated by symbols" (see SAF, ch. 18).

The discipline of the sage is not a discipline of the rational intellect arriving at objective first principles. Rather, it is a discipline in which our moral concerns are transcended through the power of concentrated *aesthetic apprehension* or, as Santayana would later refer to it, "intuition." Though Santayana, like William James, abjured any admiration of the philosophical subject known as "aesthetics," his philosophy (again somewhat like James's here) was radically oriented toward an aesthetic ontology of the human existence.[10] The questions of philosophy will focus upon their relation to this ambition, and the distinctions which Santayana's philosophy draws will be tools that serve this end. In short, the philosophical life must be directed toward developing a "philosophical imagination." "Does not modern philosophy teach that our idea of the so-called real world is also a work of imagination?" asks Santayana; "the question is which imaginative system you will trust. . . . [A]ll systems may be used and, up to a certain point, trusted as symbols" (GC, 8).

Let us begin to treat this issue by discussing the origin of Santayana's ideal of the sage in terms of those thinkers who deeply influenced him. I obviously cannot attempt to cover all the philosophical doctrines that influenced Santayana's own system, Indian as well as European. Rather I will be concerned with the various figurative modes that contributed to Santayana's *ideal* of the philosopher as a textual persona or construct of the *sophos*. This will disclose the steps or "moments" of the "discipline of the mind and heart" in Santayana's method leading to liberation through intuition or aesthetic concentration.

9. See *The Realm of Spirit*, 273; (=RB, 287) and the famous preface to *Scepticism and Animal Faith* (New York: Charles Scribner's Sons, 1923) hereafter cited in the text as SAF.
10. See "General Confession," 20: "But in philosophy I recognize no separable thing called aesthetics; and what has gone by the name of philosophy of art, like so-called philosophy of history, seems to me sheer verbiage."

I think we can distinguish four major archetypes that contribute to Santayana's ideal of the sage, though at first the members included, even under one archetype, may seem to be strange fellow travelers, indeed. Santayana designate the term "trope" to refer to the pattern of an event, "the form of its flow," "the essence of that sequence seen under the form of eternity" (RM, 102/RB, 294). Perhaps we can understand the various archetypes of the *sophos* in the same sense: the essence of a dynamic movement, a form of a kind of life. These archetypal tropes had to be passed through in a certain order, like the Stations of the Cross. Each presents its own "discipline" needed on the way to Santayana's "ultimate religion," the "religion of disillusion," the liberation of spirit into its own, "the realm of spirit."

THE DISCIPLINE OF MATTER

Three figures were formative influences on the young Santayana and spoke deeply to those receptive tendencies in his psyche: St. Augustine, Schopenhauer, and Lucretius. Santayana rarely mentions Augustine, though we know that at one time or another he relished *The City of God* and *The Confessions*.[11] But the presence of Augustine pervades the Spanish Catholicism in which Santayana was immersed in his early years in Spain (but not raised—his father was a free thinker) and with which he felt a great deal of sympathy. Santayana admired the nobility of the repudiation of "the world, the flesh, and the devil," the high Castilian scorn for the world, as he calls it in his autobiography. Augustine saw the world and the "lust" for it (*libido*) as the effort of man to set himself up without God, to secure temporal goods and the necessary means for them by a faith in his own powers. This was *superbia*, the sin of Lucifer. Atheist though he was, Santayana seems to have adopted a very Augustinian view of the futility of worldly loves. Like Augustine, there was a very "Manichean" or "Gnostic" side to Santayana, which Anthony Woodward has sensitively described.[12] The world is what lures the soul

11. See Letters: to Henry Ward Abbott, Jan. 16, 1887 (in Daniel Cory, *The Letters of George Santayana*, 17) and to Daniel Cory, Mar. 13, 1938 (in McCormick, *George Santayana*, 378).

12. See Anthony Woodward, *Living in the Eternal* (Nashville: Vanderbilt University Press, 1988), esp. 116ff.

away from what truly unifies it, giving it false objects of love which only slip away, thereby dispersing or disintegrating the soul in time. For Augustine, when the Soul "recollects" itself through *memoria* it gathers itself toward a transcendence of time in an act of absolute, timeless insight. This theme is paralleled in Santayana's description of the Realm of Matter as one of constant, turbid "distraction." The psyche can only arrest this through arriving at the "solipsism of the present moment," where the timelessness of essence reveals itself. This is what gives birth to the very possibility of the liberation of spirit.

Augustine was a theistic Platonist; his atheistic counterpart in the history of philosophy is Arthur Schopenhauer. Santayana wished to write on Schopenhauer for his dissertation and allowed Royce to dissuade him, alas, to write on Hermann Lötze instead. For Augustine, the will had a natural end in God; for Schopenhauer, the will had no teleological direction but was its own self-predator. It is interesting that for Schopenhauer, as for Santayana, Platonism and art became an epiphenomenal means of escape in which at last will dissolves into a will-less state of nonidentity. It was thus essential, in order to achieve transcendence, that the violent, purposeless, and cruel aspects of nature be emphasized. To a certain extent, Santayana shared this view of nature. He was baffled by his Columbia enthusiasts who held (and who thought he held) a more romantic view of nature. Herbert Schneider recalled Santayana once saying, "Well, you fellows from Columbia will never understand me. You still talk of me as a naturalist, and I am not a naturalist." John Herman Randall, Jr. remembered him saying, "I *hate* nature!"[13] Instead of reading "will" as something rational (as for Kant or Fichte) or as the dictator of its own values (as for Sartre), Schopenhauer thought it a completely impersonal and incomprehensible force. Schopenhauer was not a materialist, but it is easy to see how this view of the "will" as an inhuman power easily translated itself into Santayana's view of the "the realm of matter."

Though Augustine and Schopenhauer had very similar views of the material world (and both considered matter in itself irrational), each offered a different therapy—faith in a transcendent God or high aesthetic pessimism. Santayana chose another course. Moderating these two rather imbalanced influences on him was the naturalism of Epicurus, told in ringing Latin poetry by Lucretius, whose *De rerum natura* Santayana

13. *Dialogue on George Santayana*, ed. Corliss Lamont, (New York: Horizon Press, 1959), 73.

carried about with him as a student at Harvard so that he "learned the great passages by heart." Later, Santayana would write one of his most brilliant and self-revelatory essays about Lucretius.[14] Lucretius represented for Santayana the possibility of a "spiritual materialism," regarding nature as a materialistic maze without a plan, while living without resentment, fear, or rancor. If it was a mighty, meaningless spectacle, it was also cathartic for human vanity, and at least a temporary ally and friend. The Epicurean sage, safely secure in "the high-walled temples of the wise," said Lucretius, could look upon the struggles of men as one watching a battle from a high mountainside:

> O wretched minds of men, O poor blind hearts!
> How great the perils, how dark the night of life
> where our brief hour is spent! Oh not to see
> that nature demand no favor but that pain
> be sundered from the flesh, that in the mind
> be a sense of joy, unmixed with care and fear![15]

The key for Epicurus was the use of Democritean atomism to remove the worst fear from human life: the fear of supernatural religion. As our century would venerate Freud, so Lucretius saw Epicurus as a healer of the most elusive and painful affliction in human existence, self-torment. Santayana, too, found dogmatic materialism the key to removing the anxieties introduced by any moralistic metaphysics which confounded "essence" with "power." Perhaps he also appreciated Lucretius as discovering the fundamentally poetic nature of what passed for scientific truth.

Thus, in this first archetype we find the sage as one who takes a pessimistic, irrationalist view of nature but quells the subsequent anxiety through Epicurean detachment and naturalistic explanation. Though matter may be scorned, it is also to be acknowledged and respected. Though the discipline may begin with disillusionment, the aim is to escape pain and find a pure, tranquil, lucid joy. To do this, the nature of the material must be described in such a way that the purity of essence can exhibit itself.

---

14. George Santayana, *Persons and Places* (New York: Charles Scribner's Sons, 1944), 239. See also letter to Abbott cited in n.11 above. The essay on Lucretius is in *Three Philosophical Poets*.

15. *De rerum natura*, II, 1, 14ff., trans. Frank Copley, *On the Nature of Things* (New York: W. W. Norton & Co., 1977).

THE DISCIPLINE OF THE INFINITE

The second archetype is closely related, and Santayana found it embodied in the figure of Spinoza. Santayana's esteem for Spinoza is reflected in his public "swan song," the lecture "Ultimate Religion," which was given in the Spinoza house in 1932 and marked the tricentennial of Spinoza's birth.[16] From one approach, Spinoza was a thoroughgoing determinist, but he also saw philosophy as a means of liberation from the human bondage of the "affects," not so much by a Stoic suppression of emotion, but through a rational identification with infinite substance, transforming the negative affects into the positive feelings of joy and intellectual love. The philosopher, for Spinoza, is one who understands the inevitable and comprehends the finitude of any relative context through the infinite itself. The infinite, through which all things are to be conceived, is the key for human liberation. In the last analysis, the infinite is unlimited *power*.

Such a concept forces us to go beyond any absolute sense of good and evil. "Good and evil" are relative, human terms and not aspects of Substance. A sense of "abashment"—Santayana's word—before the infinite helps liberate us from personal care. Spinoza thought that human reason could identify with his infinite substance, *Deus sive natura*. Today, since we no longer have Spinoza's confidence in the inherent rationality of Nature (as is evident from the first trope), Santayana asks us to "imagine the truth to be as unfavorable as possible to your natural presuppositions; so that the spirit in each of us may be drawn away from its accidental home and subjected to an utter denudation of supreme trial." Confronted with its absolute impotence, spirit can come to be "attracted to all facts by the mere assault of their irrational presence and variety. It watches all that happens with a certain happy excitement, even at the most fearful calamities," so that here, in a sense, will and intellect can, as Spinoza wished, coincide.[17] The sage transcends the relativity of the world through the encounter with the infinite. But the infinite deploys itself in two ways for Santayana: as the infinite, mysterious power of nature (which

16. To see the esteem in which Santayana held Spinoza, compare Santayana's tercentenary essay on him with that given for Locke the same year and published in *Some Turns of Thought in Modern Philosophy* (New York: Scribner, 1933).

17. "Ultimate Religion," in *Obiter Scripta*, ed. Justus Buchler and Benjamin Schwartz (New York: Scribner, 1936), 282, 286. Hereafter cited in text as UR.

abashes human endeavor) and as the infinite realm of essences (which abashes the human intellect). Through these moments, while moral or intellectual ego may be limited, the possibility for freedom and joy are revealed.

THE DISCIPLINE OF ESSENCE

Though Spinoza did not believe there was an ultimate "good" as cause of nature, at least in any human sense of "good," he did believe that nature was a rational structure, conceived through itself and manifested in the attributes and the modes. Human reason could grasp this completely. Santayana's skepticism rejected this possibility. And yet he turned toward classical Platonism or, more precisely, Neoplatonism. The "realm of essence" and the "realm of matter" must be firmly and conclusively distinguished (not "separated," as Santayana observes, for essences do not exist).[18] In *Platonism and the Spiritual Life* we clearly see the emergence of the third and fourth archetypes of the sage: the third being found in Plotinus' turn toward form (rather than the political orientation of Plato himself) and the fourth in the startling conjunction of the Hindu notion of *Nirguna-Brahman* (Absolute-Preconscious-Spirit-without-Quality) and Aristotle's concept of *nous*, or actualized insight.

Plato (and Aristotle and Plotinus after him) clearly erred, Santayana said, in believing that form could function as a magical, "magnetic" cause[19] (PSL, 9). Forms or "essences" have no causal power; they do not exist; matter exists. But they are indeed the "most real" things, if by "real" we mean "most valuable." Moralists like Plato wish to make values causal, existential powers. In spite of his "Platonism," Plato is first and last a political thinker, and his metaphysical ideas are proposed for the sake of that end: "To this descendent of Solon the universe could never be anything but a crystal case to hold the jewel of the Greek city" (PSL, 27).

---

18. See "Apologia Pro Mente Sua," in Schilpp, 525: "I do not separate the two [essence and existence], I merely distinguish them." Only matter is self-subsistent; essences are entirely existentially dependent upon the realm of matter, though they constitute an independent logical universe. But their ontological dimension is merely "grammatical," a function of the discernment of Spirit. Hereafter cited in text as Ap.

19. See Santayana's humorous critique of Aristotle's four causes in "The Secret of Aristotle," in *Dialogues in Limbo* (New York: Charles Scribner's Sons, 1948).

Plotinus advanced over Plato, according to Santayana, in overcoming that ultimate political purpose and transforming Platonism into a genuinely spiritual life. "In the unclouded, synthetic, believing mind of Plotinus this chastened mythology crystallized into the most beautiful of systems" (PSL, 23). I don't think Santayana offers a higher compliment to any philosopher than this; the only implied term of criticism used is "believing." Removing this feature from Neoplatonism was Santayana's self-understood advance over Plotinus. The realm of essence, once discovered, need not be put to use as a blueprint for moral endeavors in nature. Instead it offers an alternative home for spirit in which it can find rest and delight.

It was impossible for Santayana to love nature: What he loved was the Good and the Beautiful—here he sided with Socrates against Democritus.[20] But there was a peculiar result to the single-mindedness of Socrates' quest. As we can see in his cynic followers, Socrates' "fervid utilitarianism has a strangely revolutionary force: in squeezing the world to get every drop of pure good out of it, it leaves the world worthless and has to throw it away; nothing remains but the immediate good of the spirit" (PSL, 22). Here, then, comes the moment of the Neoplatonic sage. Unlike Plato's erotic philosopher who seeks to "give birth to Beauty" (as Diotima explains), Plotinus was, we hear, "ashamed to be in a body."[21] Rather than attempt to create a derivative icon of the Beautiful-itself, the Plontinian lover seeks to become *unified* with it. Through dialectic, the philosopher rises to the hypostatic realm of *nous*, gaining immediate insight into the infinity of Forms and, beyond that, seeks their cause in the "flight of the alone to the Alone," achieving union with the "unspeakable" (for that is the original meaning of "mystic") principle of the One "beyond Being," an absolute power or *dynamis*.[22] Not knowledge, but union, is the virtue of the Neoplatonic *sophos*. For Santayana, the "Good" loses its moral force and simply becomes the Beautiful.

20. See letter to Robert Bridges, Aug. 8, 1925, in Cory, 222–23, and letter to Sterling Lamprecht, Nov. 15, 1933, in Cory, 284–85. In the latter, Santayana says, "Moreover, my position [in *Dialogues in Limbo*] is that of the *Stranger*, which Democritus disowns. . . . Democritus, having thought he had discovered 'Reality', thought he must worship it. I am in that respect a disciple of his enemy Socrates and worship only the beautiful and the good."

21. See Plato, *Symposium*, and Porphyry, "Life of Plotinus," in Plotinus, *Enneads* (printed in volume 1 of the Loeb edition).

22. These themes—the infinity of Forms, the nature of the One, and the mystical union—can be found in R. T. Wallis, *Neoplatonism* (Indianapolis: Hackett Publishing Co., 1995).

In addition to changing Plato's love of the good into the love of the beautiful, making love a flight from nature with no return, I must mention a strange interpretation Santayana gained from his study of Plato's *Parmenides* with Henry Jackson of Trinity College, which gave the cast, I hazard, to his whole later ontology. Perhaps Santayana, like young Socrates in the first part of the dialogue, was shocked to realize that, insofar as any self-identity qualifies as an essence, there will be all sorts of essences, including those of "ignoble things," such as mud, hair, and wax. But it was Jackson's interpretation of the second, dialectical part of the dialogue, says Santayana, that "had an important influence on my philosophy, because it helped me to see that Being, the One, the Many, etc. were names of categories, not of existent things, so that all cosmological theories relying on dialectic (such as that of Leibniz) were sophistical."[23] Ontology is a product of grammatology, so to speak. This may be characterized, then, as developing the idea that the "sage" is the lover of forms or essences taken as moments of grammatical insight; that is, as pure appearances without substantial existence other than as they arise in intuition. We have seen that Santayana dismissed the notion of the realm of Forms as an object of moral attention. Now, this new point completely removes the Platonic notion of approaching the realm of Forms as a search for knowledge. There is no knowledge in essences. The sage, as we might say, "deconstructs" metaphysics. But this is done in order to preserve the purity of essences. The realm of essence blossoms forth simply as itself without moral imperatives or cognitive claims attached, a field of amazement and delight. The sage likewise appears as the pure lover and not as the moral reformer or the practitioner of a false science. The life of spirit opens up.

23. *My Host the World* (New York: Charles Scribner's Sons, 1953), 25. For the influence of the first part of the *Parmenides*, see letter to Thomas N. Munson, S. J., Mar. 12, 1948, in Cory, 373: "Capital of course were Platonic Ideas: especially the undeveloped suggestion at the end of the first part of Plato's *Parmenides* about 'ideas' of filth, rubbish, etc., which the moralistic young Socrates recoils from as not beautiful, making old Parmenides smile. That smile of Parmenides made me think." Oddly, Santayana adds, "But the most exact anticipation of my 'realm of essence' I found in a quotation from an Arabic philosopher, whose name I have forgotten in the Life of Avicenna by the Baron Carra des Veaux." The philosopher may well have been Avicenna himself, who made a radical break with Al-Farabi's emanationist Neoplatonism, distinguishing existence from essence and speaking of an "indefinite" number of essences. See Bernard des Veaux, *Avicenne* (Paris: F. Alcan, 1900). Santayana goes on to note the influence here of the Platonism of G. E. Moore and Bertrand Russell.

THE DISCIPLINE OF SPIRIT

Santayana's interest in Hindu philosophy is well known, especially in the school of *Sānkhya* (often connected with that of *Yoga*), which argued for a strict dichotomy between a primal creative force or natural power, *prakriti*, and a reality composed of passive, observing monadic consciousnesses, *purusha*.[24] More might be developed from a comparison here to Santayana's own realm of matter and realm of spirit. But I wish to draw attention to Santayana's appropriation of another aspect of classical Indian thought more associated with the *Upanishads* and the system of *Vedānta*: the ultimate principle of Brahman (or "Brahma," as Santayana refers to it). This he regards as the permanent possibility of spirit or potential spirit. With this he appropriates something of Aristotle's view of *nous*, which becomes one with its object in the act of knowing. Spirit does not "know" for Santayana, but when it is awake or actual it is one with its vision.[25]

While matter remained for Santayana as the only possible meaning for "existence," he was willing to ascribe "Being" to the other realms of essence, truth, and spirit. The realm of essence consists of infinite pure possibilities of intuition. The realm of spirit is the realization of some of those possibilities into self-contained intuitive moments. Thus, in a way, the realm of essence considered in itself is the sleeping possibility of the awakened spiritual life. "Brahma is sometimes likened to deep sleep and Nirvana to nothingness," he says at one point (PSL, 81). This was the analogy that Santayana saw to the Hindu principle of Brahman, the ubiquitous, indescribable, unconscious source of Being. "Brahma is all things yet none of them," he says, for to *be* one of them, it would have to be realized (RS, 114/RB, 668). As the Upanishads say, it is "not this, not that." More precisely:

> The vital background is far more stable, far wider, than the flash of feeling. . . . Thus when the Indians tell us that in deep sleep we return to Brahma, we may say that from the point of view of spirit they

24. Again, Anthony Woodward has briefly discussed this influence on Santayana. See *Living in the Eternal*, 98–100.

25. Technically, "Brahma" is one of the three ultimate gods in the Hindu pantheon, the creator, counterpart with Vishnu, the preserver, and Shiva, the destroyer. These three are manifestations of the primal source, *Nirguna Brahman*; i.e., undifferentiated Brahman.

are describing the birth of spirit itself, representing the absence of consciousness as consciousness in a perfectly placid, equable, infinitely potential equilibrium. Logical vacancy would thus cover vital repletion. So we too, looking . . . from the outside, may well feel that spirit actually slumbers in all things, in a deep sleep inclined to waking, a sleep, as it were, under tremulous eyelids. (RS, 96/RB, 650)

This feature of Santayana's system bears some similarity to the idea of the "potential intellect" (*nous pathētikos*) in Aristotle's philosophy, the way in which, in a sense, "the mind is all things" in its potential state.[26] The potential intellect is the individual's capacity to actualize the essential forms and their principles that constitute objects of scientific knowledge. Likewise, Santayana conceives of the individual organic psyche as providing the material conditions whereby some particular essence may be actively intuited, though without its being constituted as an object of knowledge. Santayana also objects to Brahman as the ultimate object of the quest for the sage's inmost self, "Atman," for this would be to leave the realm of essence in a mere state of potentiality. Santayana's Hellenism breaks through here. He agrees with Aristotle in valuing the actual, determinate intuition of form over the Hindu view of the ultimate bliss of *Nirguna Brahman.* "Nothing could be more worthless to spirit," he writes, "than spirit dozing" (RS, 101/RB, 655). "As for me," writes Santayana, "I frankly cleave to the Greeks and not to the Indians, and I aspire to be a rational animal rather than a pure spirit" (RE, 65/RB, 65).

For Aristotle, when *nous,* or direct insight, is actualized, completed and fully "energized" as *energeia,* it becomes one with its object, the form. The actual intellect is in no way a personal "self," for it is nothing but this direct apprehension. (Hence the doctrine made infamous by Averroes that there can be no personal immorality, even though the agent intellect eternally thinks eternal things.) This activity is also "timeless" in the sense that it is no process of becoming (*kinēsis*) but rather a fully complete accomplishment of the being as such. This matches Santayana's description of intuition, as the "perfect function of spirit" which by its generative impulse "tends to become pure" (RS, 92/RB, 646). It is "the perfect

26. See *De Anima,* III, 5–7, esp. 431b20. Aristotle does not actually use the term *nous pathētikos,* though he describes its functions. It was conjecturally used by the Greek commentators as a term corresponding to his *nous poietikos.*

SPIRIT AND PHILOSOPHY

actuality" of organic life, having no end outside itself other than the very appearance or essence which constitutes its awareness (RS, 95/RB, 649).

Now Aristotle, as I have noted, shared with Plato the belief that essences were "causes" in the highest sense, a point that Santayana completely rejects. The final moment, then, for Santayana, is for spirit to transcend its psychic origin, to suppress the tendency *to believe* arising from the needs of a personal, organic, existent being, and to achieve a purely non-committal, *aesthetic* apprehension of essence. The world is not "rejected" so much as suspended from concern, "bracketed" or "held-off" in an *epochē*, as the ancient skeptics taught. The only way for the utter simplicity and purity of the essence to be apprehended is for any external concern, judgment, or need to be absolutely excluded from consciousness. It is for the sake of this end, indeed, that the whole of Santayana's ontology, including the elaborate reduction of belief in *Scepticism and Animal Faith*, is organized.

In intuition, spirit attains the fullness and definiteness of the Greek view of wisdom while also losing the ego, or at least egoism, in the purity of nonexistence as in *Vedanta*. (Though even the Vedanta contrasts *Saguna-Brahman*, "Brahman-with-qualities," which gives itself to the "play" of illusion, *līlā*, from *Nirguna-Brahman*, "Brahman-without-qualities;" i.e., beyond distinctions). The divine life, which Aristotle ascribes to the Unmoved Mover, belongs to spirit, with the qualification that, since spirit doesn't "value" one essence over another, it can play over the infinite field of form rather than single-mindedly concentrate on its own, singular perfection. But as pure intuitions Greek and Hindu systems are on a par:

> We might arrange them in a circular or a spiral order, from intuition empty to intuition filled with all truth; for according to the Indians, who know more about this than we do, deep sleep, being perfect bliss, must be a kind of intuition, yet empty; and I think an intuition filled with the truth (about which we know more than they did) would be perfect bliss too, if our whole psyche were absorbed in conceiving that truth, with no other wish subsisting. And in that case it would be indifferent that this truth happened to be true rather than mere poetry, since it would be only as poetry that the spirit would entertain it. Pure intuition, even when filled in with infinite detail, would thus revert to the perfect peace of pure Being. (RS, 113/RB, 667)

These, then, are the figurative modes, or tropes, of the sage: the disillusioned materialist, the one humbled before the infinite, the pure lover of essences and the selfless moment or act of spirit accomplishing itself through aesthetic intuition. One might add to this the discipline that occupies the third volume of *Realms of Being*, namely, the discipline of truth. Though truth refers to that realm of essences that have been existentially instantiated in the realm of matter, absolute in itself (contrary to any pragmatist theory, as Santayana argued), I believe it is somewhat tangential to the discipline of the spirit which aims at liberation. In Santayana's system, it functions more as a corrective to idealist as well as pragmatist doctrines, either one of which could mark a danger for spirit, distracting it either toward a "duty" to think the Absolute and reproduce it dialectically or to confuse the mere need-governed perspectives of the animal psyche with the impersonal independence of nature.[27] Now that the four tropes of the Santayanan sage have been described, let us examine how they establish a "discipline of mind and heart."

Disillusionment, Insight, and Aesthetic Liberation

I posed the question at the beginning of this essay as to what was the method to be followed in order to arrive at the standpoint of the sage, of liberated spirit. By examining the tropes of the sage, we can sketch out the "moments" whereby the possibility for genuinely aesthetic insight can be recognized. The discipline will be one of imagination in which both the "heart" (that is, one's passions and moral aspirations) and the "mind" (our cognitive powers in the service of animal faith) undergo a certain humiliation in order that both may be purified of the "world" and set free to enjoy existence in playful charity. Absolutely central will be the use of the features of Santayana's ontology to achieve utter purity in aesthetic apprehension of essence. The various themes are really techniques of purgation or purification designed to leave a clarified aesthetic residue.

First, in terms of the trope of materialistic pessimism, we discover three important moments: (1) *the skeptical reduction of belief to animal faith,*

---

27. John Lachs argues that rather than constituting its own irreducible realm, truth "is, in fact, reducible to matter and essence and represents the area of their intersection. Santayana may well have been more accurate, therefore, if he spoke only of three realms and used truth as a neat example to demonstrate the explanatory power of his categories." In *George Santayana* (Boston: Twayne Publishers, 1988), 140. In fact, Santayana originally drafted his work as *Three Realms of Being*; see letter to Mrs. Frederick Winslow, Dec. 6, 1912, in Cory, 120–22.

which thereby allows faith to be revealed as faith, as "trust" (Ap, 517), (2) *the disclosure of the bifurcation between existence and essence*, and, finally, (3) *the humiliation of spirit before matter*, whereby it recognizes its utter impotency and loses all hope of completing itself through moral projects. Santayana wrote *Scepticism and Animal Faith* as the introduction to his later system. In addition to sketching out the themes elaborated in *Realms of Being*, the book is a "spiritual exercise," using the skeptical reduction as a discipline that allows the reader to *make use* of the ontology. One should not "follow Santayana's argument" in the book so much as *perform* it. By forcing the reader's consciousness to focus only on the pure datum of the passing moment, one achieves the insight that the *idea* of change itself is a static essence and that, consequently, there can be no essence or self-identity ascribed to that which by nature must be absolutely "other," that is, constituted by nothing but external relations. This is why matter is incomprehensible, "unseizeable," a "whirligig," "contingent," "groundless," and "irrational."[28] Santayana's "Gnostic" descriptions of the realm of matter are well known, but this is a *necessary* description for the sake of creating a spiritual reaction. "Nothing is able to banish the world except contempt for the world," he says (PSL, 85). Spirit thus "withdraws from that vain and horrible struggle and makes for peace, or even for non-existence" (RS, 104/RB, 658). Spirit claims for itself a sense of "intellectual honor," and if it cannot truly *know* matter, then it will not degrade itself by pretending it does (SAF, 10). Its honor will have to be found in what it can apprehend, and this allows it to recognize the fundamental ontological distinction between essence and existence. But with this distinction comes also the acknowledgement that essence is completely powerless to be a cause and that power, force, compulsion, and blind necessity are integral aspects of matter. The only possible response, then, is submission to nature. That is to say that the very moment spirit awakens to know itself as that which can intuit essence, it also admits its utter impotency.[29]

The second moment of Santayana's discipline of heart and mind comes with the discovery of the realm of essence and the subsequent project that it sets for spirit proper, including spirit's own self-knowledge. The stages

28. These descriptions come, respectively, from Ap, 500, "Religion of Disillusion," 241, PSL, 35.
29. See "Ultimate Religion," in *Obiter Scripta*, 286.

here are (1) *the discovery of essence as mere appearance,* (2) *the discovery of the infinity of the realm of essence,* and (3) *the discovery of spirit.* With the recognition of matter as unknowable brute power or substance also comes the recognition of essence as that which is capable of apprehension, for each essence reveals an inner necessity, that of absolute self-identity. The realm of essence itself, unlike the realm of matter, avoids contingency only by logical necessity. Santayana sees this as similar to the traditional insight of Platonism. But Platonism succumbed to a superstitious physics in believing these essences to be causes in light of their importance. By his materialism, Santayana can now let the essences stand forth simply as pure appearances. They are not entities requiring belief from us—they are *not objects of belief* at all, but objects of aesthetic concentration, only to be enjoyed for what they are (Ap, 526). Moreover, as pure possibilities for intuition, they inhabit a *continuum of infinite possibility.* The realm of essence does not exist, though it has "reality" (that is, "importance for us"). It is constituted by entities which are characterized by being absolutely distinguishable; indeed that is their *being*: they are "distinguishabilities." It is the act of spirit that (to use Whitehead's apt phrase here) "atomizes the continuum." Intuition brings the essence into existence, marking it off from anything else. Thus the realm of essence is truly infinite in both senses of the term: as that which is *apeiron* or indefinitely potential and as that which is without limit and incapable of being "passed through" in any finite, temporal process.

These features of the realm of essence set a further discipline for the spirit's mind and heart. Spirit finds itself with a realm for its home, whose condition for entrance is rejection of the world. Spirit begins to know itself in its intellectual contempt of matter and admiration of essence. "Spirit, since its essence is to aspire, comes to life at the foot of the ladder" (PSL, 73). But spirit also discovers the realm of essence as a domain of "infinite tasks" (as Husserl would say). If the realm of essence laid an imperative upon spirit to be *known,* this would indeed be a source of despair. "But quantity is not a category important to spirit . . . it is indifferent to the endless multiplicity of things, existing or not existing, which may lie beyond its ken. It is not anxious, like an animal soul hounded by curiosity and fear, to dominate and possess everything. . . . As Dante says, there is no envy in these spheres" (PSL, 75; see *Paradiso,* III.76). What *is* important is that spirit should merely see each essence against the whole field of infinite possibility: "The eye of spirit, in its virtual omni-science, sees the visible in its true setting of the invisible." Essences are to be enjoyed, not owned, so that passionate desire is transmuted into care-free attention: "Spirit chills the flesh and is itself on fire" (PSL, 86). In this way, both the tropes of the Platonic lover of essence and the Spinozistic dweller in the infinite combine to awaken spirit to itself.

Finally, there is the moment in which spirit achieves itself in intuition, *the ability for pure aesthetic concentration.* This moment is indeed the "unsayable" (or "mystic") part of Santayana's doctrine, for one can only describe what aesthetic concentration, properly speaking, is *not.* It is *not* a judgment or belief; it is *not* perceived as the result of organic "satisfac-tion" or "consummatory experience," though that may be its *cause.*[30] It is *not* an emotion, "aesthetic" or otherwise (thought emotions can be the objects of intuition, in which case they are not undergone). Spirit must be awake and focused so completely upon its object as pure appearance that these concerns do not enter in to distract it. It is a supreme instance of what Keats called "negative capability." At most, Santayana will describe this condition as one of play and "a return to innocence" (RS, 192/RB, 746). Elsewhere he says that "contradiction and torment are inexplicable" to spirit; it "runs and sparkles wherever it may, the free child of nature" (PSL, 51–52). In its detachment, "Anything is enough if it be pure" (PSL, 53). This purity is primarily a result of a tremendous ability to exclude the claims, concerns, demands, and attachments of the particular living psyche of the organism.

Spirit achieves catharsis in its aesthetic mode, a "disintoxication" of itself and a "disinfection" of the world (PSL, 30; RS, 200/RB 774; UR, 287). It is that moment in which, as Santayana describes it in *The Sense of Beauty,* "The sense of suffering disappears in the sense of life and the imagination overwhelms the understanding."[31] Here, for the sake of liberation, the philosophical imagination suspends both the moral and cognitive for the aesthetic mode. Indeed, Santayana sees in this act the very desire of the universe to seek "God." An "ultimate religion" based on this "would need to be more imaginative, more poetical than that of Spinoza, and the word God, if we still used it, would have to mean for us

30. Although Santayana did see some connection between his views and Dewey's notion of the consummatory. See Ap, 541.
31. *The Sense of Beauty* (New York: Scribner, 1896), 241–42; MIT ed., 244–45.

not the universe, but the good of the universe. There would not be a universe worshiped, but a universe praying; and the flame of the whole fire, the whole seminal and generative movement of nature, would be the love of God" (UR, 293). The sage, then, would be that very movement of nature toward "moments of unspeakable rapture . . . in which the soul would vanish as an object because, as an organ, it had found its perfect employment" (UR, 293). The sage attains liberation not for himself, since in the moment of attainment there is no self, but for nature, realizing nature's highest creativity in the production of spiritual insight, the creation of highest values from a valueless cosmos, like the creation of a Moorish garden in a desert wasteland.

Conclusion: The Sage as Aesthetic Construct

Strictly speaking, there is no "method" for aesthetic insight. As Augustine said of grace, it is not in our power to force it, and there is little reason for why it falls to some and not others. And yet, it is the one crucial thing for us. As far as I can tell, there is nothing in Santayana's writing that offers us a recipe or a guarantee for realizing the end once the conditions are met. The best we can do is to read, as I have tried to do here, the moments of his ontology as stages in a discipline of the heart and mind whereby the possibility of aesthetic insight is conceptually available: The doctrines are tools for spirit. But the transformation of the possibility into an actual moment of intuition is not mastered by concepts or dictated by the will. It is the happy conjunction of power and fortune; it is given to us or comes of its own accord, and either we have it or we do not.

This approach also offers an interesting way of reading Santayana's explicit works in aesthetics as central parts of his ontology rather than as mere discussions of a topic somewhat marginal to "serious" philosophy, for an understanding of the aesthetic is the clue to the mystery of Being. Santayana's "grammatology" of Being is not an essay upon the nature of what is "really real," *ontōs on*, nor is it the guide toward a true grammar that fits, glove to hand, onto the syntax of nature itself, as Galileo, for example, imagined mathematics to be the true language of nature. Santayana constructs a fictive grammatology in order to live a kind of life. His analysis of the "meanings of the word 'is'" is not determined by the final, correct insight, which is the *archē* for demonstrative science. It is the result of his rejection of nature and his embrace of the insubstantial world of essence. Santayana's categorial analysis of the word "I" disseminates its meanings from the cry in the heart for luminous freedom wrung from it by the disaster of matter. It discovers the shore of a world filled with beauty, empty of hope.

The dominating focus of this ontology, I have claimed, is a kind of life that is governed by the figure of the Santayanan sage, who is initially designed to appeal to us as a *literary figure*; that is, as an aesthetic construct. The sage is offered to us as an archetype; we read the doctrines in order to "read the sage," the fictive life of which they are expressions. Every philosophy, I have argued, operates with its own tacit or explicit way of imagining the sage in order to understand the philosophy. This is an aesthetic ideal that imposes upon a given philosophy its justification of method, its fundamental questions, its very comprehension of what counts or does not count as philosophy. As we read a philosophy we imagine ourselves into the role of this persona, the viewpoint from which the text makes sense. This is obvious when we have a dramatic character like the Socrates of Plato's dialogues; but the "image" of the Philosopher is present in Aristotle's omnicompetent knower, Augustine's confessional theologian, Descartes' solitary disembodied doubter, Kant's self-critical *Aufklärer*, Hegel's cunning dialectician of Spirit, Marx's suspicious critic, and Carnap's speaker of a pure logical language. An Austin or Wittgenstein has configured a hero in a story, even if the hero is the common, reasonable user of daily language, modestly but gradually snaring the dragon of philosophy. Rorty's postmodern raconteur is but one other *imago hominis sapientis*. Philosophy is read from a fictive life.

Santayana's sage is behind his writing as an aesthetic intuition of a certain kind of life. By *using* the sage in his writing, Santayana was able to investigate the tropes and stages that the sage had encountered and mastered, finally delivering the spirit into its possible liberation. Santayana's ontology emerges from the various moments that constitute the sage. Santayana's writing itself is offered as a means for the reader to emulate the disciplines of the sage. Reading is more a reenactment of the sage's "Passion" than a cool, legal evaluation of the "case" built up by his arguments. Intrinsic to the essences enjoyed by spirit are their cadences and aesthetic hues. Here style is not a gratuitous or affected irrelevant cloak for serious philosophy. In the rhythms and poise of the language, the life of the sage is to be found; for it was there Santayana achieved the sage for himself. Santayana found salvation not in a Platonic or Christian heaven, but in the empty beauty of the realm of spirit, in the worlds revealed by conjoining word with word.

This approach also allows us to read Santayana's other writings as continuations of his construction of the sage. Alexander Nehamas finds that Nietzsche, the human being and writer, succeeded in creating the author "Nietzsche," a fictive individual whom the reader has to construct as the "author" of the various books, much like Kierkegaard's pseudonymous authors. As Nietzsche transformed his life into literature, so Santayana's final disclosure of the sage may be found in his semifictional novel, *The Last Puritan*, and in his autobiography, *Persons and Places*. "Oliver Alden" and the "I" of the autobiography may be the ultimate personae of the philosopher "George Santayana," the moments in a real but nonexistent realm where an animal psyche was transformed at last into lyric spirit. In a letter, referring to his autobiography, Santayana commented that "reliving my life has been pleasanter than living it."[32]

Perhaps here, too, we must place one of Santayana's last and most neglected works, *The Idea of Christ in the Gospels*. Santayana begins that work by criticizing those who have attempted and would still attempt to write of the "historical Jesus." The figure of Jesus, he says, "is a product of inspiration"; "What is inspiration?" he asks:

> In a word, inspiration remakes the image of the world, or unmakes it, according to the mood of the soul. . . . It runs down into the very rudiments of mind: it marks the birth of spirit. . . . Inspiration is pictorial and prophetic. We find it at its height in the Hebrew prophets and the Gospels. . . . The influences and practices that tend to awaken inspiration are those that liberate and stimulate the inner man. . . .[33]

It is, of course, possible to criticize any persona behind a text, and it is possible to criticize the *sophos* behind Santayana's texts. The Santayanan sage is an "*immoraliste*"; if one's own sage is a *moraliste*, one will criticize him upon moral grounds. Silence is the response here, for an *immoraliste* can make no reply to the *moraliste* without thereby becoming a *moraliste*. If one's sage is an epistemologist of the modern variety who finds the

---

32. Letter to Thomas Munro, Dec. 10, 1944, in Cory, 354–55.
33. George Santayana, *The Idea of Christ in the Gospels* (New York: Scribner, 1946), 3, 6–7, 16.

duty to knowledge supreme, one can critique Santayana's epistemology—or for that matter, his philosophy of mind, analytical rigor, systematic coherence, and so on. Santayana repeatedly defended his "literary
psychology" as not being of the same nature as these other endeavors. If
one is a person who has a strong sense of the "weight" of our existential
involvement with the world, one can point out, as Merleau-Ponty did of
Husserl, that the result of the persistent effort to "bracket" the world in
the *epochē* simply reveals our irreducible being-in-the-world.[34] Here all
the Santayanan sage can say is, "But I have done it." There may also be a
place to argue that the aesthetic offers other, perhaps richer, modes and
so other ontologies, other sages. Such would be, in my view, the basis of
a Deweyan critique.[35] In any case, perhaps Santayana accomplished
something radically different from what contemporary academic philosophy aspires to. To read his texts from the "professional" standpoint may
obscure the very way in which they should be read; it may obscure what
is in fact most philosophical about them. Indeed, most texts in the history
of philosophy were not written from our contemporary standpoint at all.
To read them we may have to reimagine "the philosopher." Reflecting
upon Santayana's ideal of the sage opens the way toward a different reading of his texts, and perhaps others, even ours, as well.

34. See Maurice Merleau-Ponty's preface to *The Phenomenology of Perception*.
35. See my attempt to carry this out in "Santayana's Unbearable Lightness of Being: Aesthetics as
a Prelude to Ontology," chapter 9 in this volume.

FOURTEEN

BEAUTY AND THE LABYRINTH OF EVIL

Santayana and the Possibility of Naturalistic Mysticism

Among the thinkers of the past century who offer themselves to the
future for its reflection, Santayana must stand out as a singular
figure, one whose thought is dedicated to the overarching possibility of
the spiritual life undertaken without religious faith or metaphysical
dogma. Among the throngs that fill the philosophical bestiary of the
twentieth century, Santayana may be the one genuine contemplative
of note. The majority of doctrines dominant in the century have been
directed either toward the goal of action (Marxism, pragmatism,
existentialism) or the problem of knowledge, truth, and meaning (pragmaticism, positivism, analytic philosophy, phenomenology). Genuinely
contemplative philosophies cannot be classified with either one of these
categories, however much they may touch upon common themes. Given
that Santayana sought to find a basis for philosophy as a contemplative
life by grafting the classical doctrine of essence onto the modernist theory
of matter as power, his thought engages nearly the whole of the history

of the West, while ranging into the field of the systems of India as well. This may seem a puzzling bequest to the future from his century, so filled with violence and wreckage. If the true historical parameter of the century is measured by events, we might find that it could be dated from 1914 to 1991, from the onset of World War I to the exhausted collapse of the Soviet Union, a period in which the world was either preparing for war or actively engaged in it. But the violence of the century must include the rapid and constant reorganization of life forced upon the globe by technologies, some of whose impact is yet hardly discerned. It is possible to view Santayana against this backdrop as a piece of intellectual nostalgia, rather like a beautiful old church in a buzzing urban center that someone forgot to bulldoze to the ground.

I think such a response would be unfortunate because the spiritual life is a perennial concern for us, one that politics and technology cannot address, however successfully or intelligently managed they may be. The thought of Santayana offers, then, a permanent opportunity to explore the dimensions of the spiritual life without the confusions introduced by archaic physics or forgotten political aspirations. In the words of William James, "mystical classics have . . . neither birthday nor native land" and so have the opportunity to be as accessible or inaccessible as the contingent features of the world permit.[1] Santayana's writings may be read from this angle, and it is this approach I will take myself. Thus the problem I intend to explore does not try to address Santayana as a figure of the twentieth century or even as an "American" (and certainly not as a "pragmatist"!) of whatever stripe. Rather, I want to raise an issue internal to the prospect of the spiritual discipline, or *askēsis*, presented especially in Santayana's later philosophy, the problem of the relation of the spiritual and the moral lives. What, if anything, does the quest for a beatific vision have to do with the "problem of evil" in a naturalistic mysticism such as Santayana's? In this essay I will explore Santayana's vision of the spiritual life as a naturalistic contemplative discipline in relation to

---

1. William James, *The Varieties of Religious Experience* (Cambridge, MA: Harvard University Press, 1985), 332.

Platonism and Neoplatonism.[2] In response to Santayana's conclusion that the spiritual and moral lives are somewhat at variance with each other, I offer the example of Buddhism, which, though it reflects some of Santayana's fundamental premises, arrives at a different understanding of how these two lives are connected. In short I will try to show that a contemplative spirituality may acknowledge the existence of evil and develop a compassionate response to it without thereby surrendering the ideal of contemplative detachment. Santayana's ideal of the spiritual life is thus one, but not the only, possibility that is available, given the initial premises of his later system.

Santayana describes the quest of the spiritual life in terms of the radical separation of it from the natural world or "realm of matter," which forces the animal psyche to live in terms of "values" such as good and bad, which, in their extreme forms of judgment, may be described as "absolute good" and "evil." Instead, Santayana offers us an approach to the realm of essence that can be called a form of liberation insofar as spirit achieves its complete function without service to the alien needs of the psyche: intuition pure and simple. The question I wish to probe is the relation of the moral life to the spiritual, for Santayana certainly sees them not merely as divergent but in some ways as mutually inhibiting when not kept distinct. Morality, he claims, pushes spiritual life toward dogmatism, subverting it to the defense of local ideals instead of allowing

2. I find that my comments in this essay have unintentionally inserted themselves into a previous discussion carried on between Herman Saatkamp and my old teacher Paul Kuntz. (See *Overheard in Seville: Bulletin of the Santayana Society*, no. 3, 1985, and no. 10, 1992.) In his initial article, "Santayana's Neo-Platonism," Kuntz argued that Santayana's *Realms of Being* implied not only a spiritual ascent but an ontological order corresponding to it, one that was Christian as well as Neoplatonic. While acknowledging Santayana's use of the imagery of the spiritual ascent, Saatkamp did not find this to lead to any deep commitment to anything beyond a naturalism that accepts a plurality of goods, only one of which might be the "life of spirit." Kuntz's reply, "The Ascent of Spirit: Is Santayana's System a Naturalistic Neo-Platonic Hierarchy?" (1992), persisted with the original argument, focusing on a detailed exegesis of *Platonism and the Spiritual Life* (a key text for my essay as well). While I agree, as does Saatkamp, that Kuntz has commendably drawn attention to the Neoplatonic (and Indian) influences in Santayana's mature philosophy, which have tended to be neglected by those stressing Santayana's naturalism, I also agree with Saatkamp that Kuntz has pushed the argument a step too far and is in danger of ignoring the explicit role of contingency and plurality as the basis for any sort of life, spiritual or otherwise. In short, Kuntz tries to move Santayana's ideal of the spiritual life from being the expression of one of the many contingent values in nature (one that Santayana himself valued) to one everyone ought to adopt because nature herself recommends it, thereby transforming Santayana's ontology into a moralistic metaphysics. This move is explicitly rejected by Santayana. For an attempt to present a much more Aristotelian idea of a spiritual life, a practical rather than contemplative ideal grounded in Santayana's *The Life of Reason*, see the recent essay by yet another former teacher of mine, James Gouinlock's "Absolute Religion," *Overheard in Seville*, no. 12 (1998).

spirit to roam free and see things as they are without concern for their ulterior values for life. In retrieving the classical doctrine of essence, then, Santayana had to emphasize the rejection of the moral in the spiritual, lest his view be confounded with Platonism, a doctrine whose time had come—and gone, he thought—with the revolution in modern physics. The release of spirit into its own domain, into the play of essence, leaves behind all moral concerns, including the "problem of evil." While moral judgments may be made about the spiritual life an individual pursues, they are made from the moral angle, not the spiritual.

Santayana and Neoplatonism

There are two interesting essays where the issue of the relation of the moral and spiritual lives came to occupy Santayana, though they might be regarded as occasional pieces. Both were responses to bungled attempts to handle the topic of "Platonism"—or, more specifically, Neoplatonism—that was so close to Santayana's heart. One was the 1916 essay "Plotinus and the Nature of Evil," written in light of B.A.G. Fuller's *The Problem of Evil in Plotinus*. The second, *Platonism and the Spiritual Life*, was composed in 1926 and takes on Dean Inge's *The Platonic Tradition in English Religious Thought*.[3] I suspect that this monograph, which saw the light of day in 1927 along with *The Realm of Essence*, may also have been written in the afterglow of Santayana's reading of the Fifth *Ennead*, just published in MacKenna's translation.[4] Santayana paid the highest respect to the Plotinian system, which, unlike Plato's fundamentally political philosophy, he saw as truly oriented toward the spiritual life. In a letter from 1919, Santayana defends the philosophy of Plotinus to Robert Bridges in terms that come quite close to those of Santayana's own system:

> But it seems to me a very great system, very "good philosophy", and I am glad that the mystics in Oxford are taking him up, rather than

3. In fact it may have also been settling a score dating back to 1918, when Santayana had written in the margin of Inge's *The Philosophy of Plotinus*, "The motley eloquence of the pulpit, the lazy [line?] of a rhetorician and moralist who wants to talk about the world without studying it." Cited in John McCormick, *George Santayana: A Biography* (New York: Knopf, 1987), 268.

4. MacKenna's beautiful, if eccentric, multivolume translation of the *Enneads* began in 1917 with *Ennead* I (along with other extracts), and continued with a second volume in 1921 (consisting of *Enneads* III and II in that order), with a third in 1924 (*Ennead* IV). The final volume with the sixth *Ennead* was published in 1930. But my suspicion is as yet unverified.

pretending to find comfort in Hegel or in the meretricious psychology of Bergson. . . . Of course all those things he describes do not exist; of course he is not describing *this* world, he is describing *the other* world, that is, deciphering the good just beyond it or above it, which each actual thing suggests. Even this rendering of moral aspiration is arbitrary, because nature does not really aspire to anything, each living thing aspires to something different in divergent ways. But this arbitrary aspiration, which Plotinus reads into the world, sincerely expresses his own aspiration and that of his age. That is why I say he is a decidedly "good philosopher." It is the Byzantine architecture of the mind, just as good or better than the Gothic. It seems to me better than Christian theology in this respect, that it isn't mixed up with history, it isn't half Jewish, half worldly. It is the Greek side of Christian theology made pure; and that is the side which seems to be truly spiritual, truly sacrificial and penitentially joyful.[5]

It might help us to summarize the Plotinian analysis of the problem of evil as "nothing positive in itself, only the absence of Good," which has dominated the discussion of the topic in the West ever since St. Augustine appropriated it for use in Christian theology. The most famous place this occurs in the *Enneads* is in the Ninth Treatise of the Second Book, the essay directed against the Gnostics.[6] The Plotinian system, recall, finds the one true principle or *archē* of Being beyond Being itself, and so beyond Form, making it a simplicity that defies conceptual and linguistic understanding except as such understanding can turn itself toward its source and acknowledge its derivative status.[7] From this power, the world of Being "overflows," articulating itself into the world of Form and the

5. Santayana to Robert Bridges, Sept. 18, 1919, in *The Letters of George Santayana*, ed. Daniel Cory (New York: Scribner, 1955), 178. In this letter Santayana does comment on reading the first volume of McKenna's translation, just then published.

6. Recent scholarship has actually determined that this is but the last third of a much longer treatise, cut up and distributed throughout the *Enneads* by Plotinus' editor, Porphyry. The full treatise consists of *Enneads*, III.8, V.8, V.5, and II.9. When read together in proper sequence, the work ranks, in my view, as one of the greatest philosophical documents from antiquity. See the discussion by A. H. Armstrong at II.9 in his edition and translation of the *Enneads* (Loeb Classical Library; Cambridge: Harvard University Press, 1966).

7. The whole philosophy of Plotinus develops the logical consequences of Plato's sketchy and somewhat embarrassed treatment of the Good as "the Form of Forms" at *Republic*, 509c, which describes it as "transcending Being in dignity and power," a comment that provokes laughter from Glaucon and Adeimantus. As the *archē* of all Forms, Plotinus observed, the One cannot itself *be* a Form and so is *formless* and as the principle of Being cannot be said to "be" at all. Logos fails, though Plotinus is willing to describe the One as "limitless power" as well as pure simplicity. As "one" it is not at all a "numerical unity," something both conceptual and abstract.

Divine *Nous* that eternally thinks them and, in thinking them, can turn back toward their common source, understanding the Forms and itself in light of the One. But the activity of direct, contemplative insight into Form is also productive, generating another "overflow" into the mimetic order of the cosmos and the living, temporal soul that animates it. Action, time, body—all are degenerate modes of "contemplation" for Plotinus.[8] Beyond the rhythmic dance of nature, everlastingly turning about the One like dancers in a chorus, is the dim and weakened quasi-nothingness of matter, a mere reception of activity that cannot produce anything further itself. It is the termination of pure generative power into absolute impotence.

This is the context in which Plotinus faced the Gnostics, who held that the physical world was evil, produced by an arrogant and rebellious god in an act of cosmic hubris (possibly, some speculated, the very figure described in the Hebrew Genesis). By a saving act of intimate, esoteric knowledge—*gnōsis*—the soul could be delivered to its true home and cease to be afflicted by the body. Such a doctrine proceeds from a hard moral realism about the sorts of expectations one must face in our sojourn here in the realm of matter, from the fumbled attempts at order nature regularly produces and the daily ineptitudes of any given political or administrative system to the impressive catastrophes of the Black Death or mudslides that entomb twenty thousand people at once or similar human evils: Huns, Goths, Mongols, Nazis, the Japanese Imperial Army, and so on. I dwell on this because, in a certain sense (as Anthony Woodward has noted), Santayana's own view of nature bears at times rather close resemblance to the bleak view of the Gnostics.[9] Plotinus' response to this view was to say we shouldn't judge a city by looking only at its worst neighborhoods.[10] If the order of nature is confused,

---

8. "Contemplation" is the poor English word used for the Greek *theōrein* (θεωρεῖν). This word rejects any notion of the discursive process or muddled drifting, which our word "contemplation" drags in. It involves the idea of rapt, penetrating comprehension in which the truth, order, and beauty of something are fused together forever timelessly and made entirely lucid. See *Enneads*, III.8 and VI.9.

9. See Anthony Woodward, *Living in the Eternal* (Nashville: Vanderbilt University Press, 1988), 108–9, 111–13. What offsets his tendency toward the Gnostic view of the world, of course, is Santayana's equally hardheaded rejection of magic and supernaturalism, leaving him with a more realistic and occasionally genial expression of "natural piety" toward the Realm of Matter. Nevertheless, he did find idealism of any sort insufferably tender-minded.

10. *En.*, II.9.7.

it nevertheless leads us to recognize it as the image of the higher and more intelligible good, and, as a rippling reflection in water may turn us toward its source, so nature can direct us to go beyond itself. But the reflection is not "evil" for being a reflection, even if it is a troubled reflection. Disciplined reasoning, says Plotinus, allows us to place the goods and bads of the world in their proper place and rise above them to the genuine, higher goods.[11] More profoundly, Plotinus says that to hate the world is to remove oneself from the immanence of the divine, which is at the innermost center of our being. The genuine beauty of the world lures us to turn toward an inner and higher beauty that leaves the world and its imperfections behind. The emotion of contempt or hatred utterly fails to make this inward ascent. As Augustine would say, God is closer to us than we are to ourselves. *Pondus meum, amor meus*, he says: My love is my weight.[12] I stress this point because I believe it is crucial in Santayana's own response to "the problem of evil." Beauty is not a "solution" to the riddle of the existence of evil but a strategy that turns away from the problem itself. The response to evil, in other words, lies in the discovery of the spiritual life.

The Spiritual Life as Transcendent of the Problem of Evil

With this in the background, let us now turn to Santayana's 1916 essay "Plotinus and the Nature of Evil," ostensibly a review of Fuller's book on the topic. Fuller saw the problem of evil on the horns of a dilemma. The alternatives are either naturalism or mysticism. If one opts for naturalism, Fuller thought, then all values must be equal, for everything is equally "natural," the saint and the serial murderer and everyone in between.

---

11. A constant criticism in *Ennead*, II.9 is that the Gnostics are half-literate, irrational, pompous, and histrionic (the ancient world apparently had its fundamentalists). He says, "The rest of their teachings I leave to you to investigate by reading their books, and to observe throughout that the kind of philosophy which we pursue, besides all its other excellences, displays simplicity and straightforwardness of character along with clear thinking, and aims at dignity, not rash arrogance, and combines its confident boldness with reason and much safeguarding and caution and a great deal of circumspection: you are to use philosophy of this kind as a standard of comparison for the rest" II.9.14 (Armstrong trans.).

12. *Confessions*, XIII.9. The role of beauty in salvation is the key theme of *Ennead* I.6, one of the first and most influential of the *Enneads* read by Augustine. The idea of one's love being one's "weight" (or the natural place toward which one tends) is the guiding theme of Dante's *Commedia*: the souls exist in the manifested world of their genuine loves, from lowest to highest.

Each thing is perfect after its own unique kind. The only alternative, to Fuller at least, is mysticism, in which the *only* good is the highest reality and anything that separates itself from that good is automatically evil. The dilemma is summed up by Santayana as: "either all excellences are absolute and incomparable, or there is no excellence but one."[13]

With reference to the naturalist horn, Santayana argues that to say everything is equally a phenomenon of nature does not lead to pure moral relativism. Naturalism admits that the impulses that spring from the live creature may be premoral, but this is not the same as saying they are all equal, much less morally equal. Some are more in harmony with their environments than others, and insofar as they are out of harmony, may generate ideals naturally. As Santayana says, "Hence each nature ordinarily pronounces itself to be good, but imperfect, since it stumbles and creaks as it goes" (OS, 72). Moral values and ideals may have a natural origin without therefore being branded equal. As living interests become organized, so goods may be organized in a hierarchy of values. In short, as a naturalist it may be valuable to have a system of ethics more functional and in touch with the world than pure relativism allows, though this certainly does not prevent the naturalist from seeing that several systems are possible or may conflict with each other. This is truer when we consider values arising from nonhuman organisms. As Santayana puts it, "Had animals spoken, the Inquisition would have had a pretty work on its hands" (OS, 70).

This leaves the mystical horn of Fuller's dilemma. Santayana will not admit that the thesis that there is one supreme good means that everything else falls into some degree of evil, that the levels in the great chain of Being are but "so many stages of spiritual misery" (OS, 70). One overarching good does not exclude the possibility of subordinate goods. A good book may have good sentences and each sentence be composed of well-chosen words written out in perfectly formed letters. Each may be perfect after its kind and also involved in an overall order of higher and lower degrees of perfection. It is true, Santayana says, that Plotinus, believing as he did in the potency of form, reversed the true order of genesis—his mythology of the overflowing descent of creative power from beyond the Forms down through nature into the torpid murk of matter

---

13. *Obiter Scripta* (New York: Charles Scribner's Sons, 1936) 71. Hereafter cited as *OS*.

was an inversion of the truth. In nature, as we saw, there is a natural heterogeneity of goods. In this way, says Santayana, Plotinus "incidentally . . . missed the true explanation of the origin of evil, which lies in the natural conflict of many powers and many ideals" (OS, 75–76).[14] To thrive in nature we must adopt an organized economy of values so we can move in one direction at a time, but this does not mean we may not encounter someone else whose internal economy has set him at cross-purposes to ours. Platonism is basically a moral view that seeks to insist that its analysis of human values achieves a final, defining insight into the order of things as such, and this is merely presumptuous, according to Santayana. For such a person, he says, "His socratic wisdom in life will become Platonic folly in science" (OS, 76). Thus evil, for Santayana, is simply the partisan word for the inevitable clash of interests in a natural world that is inherently pluralistic in its aims and not governed by an overarching, coordinating good that redeems and saves all things.

Fuller's more fundamental problem lies behind the sophistic dilemma; it is a failure to understand mysticism as much as naturalism. The true mystic is not kept from a "hatred of finitude" simply by a mere inconsistency any more than the naturalist is kept from proclaiming the equality of every value. Pointing out to the mystic that he adores his supreme good only because he is separate from it does not lead at all to his condemnation of himself and everything else distinguished from that good as "evil." Actual mystics—not the "classroom idols" of Fuller's paradox—have been quite consistent with their principles when they felt "the tenderness and wonder which filled them in the presence of the creation" (OS, 77). Though it is true that the adoration of the mystic implies a separation from the source, this does not fill him or her with rage at the separation, but with humility and love. The problem, as seen by Plotinus, then, was not the existence of evil; "it was rather to rise above evil, to decipher a divine image in the worn and degraded lineaments of things and to save the soul from a temporal and sensuous life to which evil was native" (OS, 78). It may be that when evil cannot be erased,

14. Compare *Platonism and the Spiritual Life*, where he says, "Evil can arise only within each world when it becomes faithless to some Idea which it has begun to pursue, or is crossed in the pursuit of it either by some external enemy (if any) or by the inward contradiction and complexity of its impulses" (44). To judge the world as "evil" requires those very animal interests and concerns that are condemned in the act of judgment—"these feelings are part of the world which they condemn." Hence to turn from the moral world is to turn from such judgments altogether.

the natural impulse is to evade it as much as possible, but the root impulse of Platonism was a love of beauty, passing from lower to higher forms of it. The problem of evil, says Santayana, is for theologians and apologists for creator deities or pantheists wishing to assert that all is somehow good. But

> [i]t does not exist for the naturalist, because for him both good and evil are relative to finite interests necessarily at war in this crowded world. Nor does it exist for the Platonist, to whom it is obvious that the good is far away and that it was not the good that removed the good where it is absent. The problem of darkness does not exist for the man gazing at the stars. No doubt the darkness is there, fundamental, pervasive, and unconquerable except at the pin-points where the stars twinkle; but the problem is not why there is such darkness, but what is the light that breaks through it so remarkably; and granting this light, why we have eyes to see it and hearts to be gladdened by it. (OS, 86)

Even though Platonism is now in abeyance, being an ideal of values now out of fashion, it may be that "things come round in this world; the ruffians may be upon us some day when we least expect it and philosophy may have to retire again to the sanctuary." Santayana concludes with this enigmatic remark: "Even then we should search the books of Plotinus in vain for any solution to the artificial problem concerning the existence of evil; but if we searched them for a thread out of the natural labyrinth of evil, we might possibly find it" (OS, 86–87). Santayana indicates that there may be an important clue for us in the philosophy of Plotinus, something far different from a sophistical "solution" to the "problem of evil." Instead of a *solution*, there is an *escape*. But what is this "thread" out of the "natural labyrinth of evil"? And what is the relationship of Santayana's own later philosophy to this "escape"? Could Santayana's later philosophy be the naturalistic version of tracing the Plotinian thread out of the labyrinth, a version purged of Plotinus' moralistic metaphysics and with its myth of the descending emanation of the supernatural into nature inverted to become the ascent of spirit from the realm of matter?

Santayana's Ideal in Platonism and the Spiritual Life

I turn now to *Platonism and the Spiritual Life*, written a decade after Santayana's response to Fuller. Santayana scholars tend to neglect this monograph for some puzzling reason, since I find it one of the most lucid statements of his thought, something of an enchiridion to *Realms of Being*.[15] Coming as it did after *Scepticism and Animal Faith* and appearing simultaneously with *The Realm of Essence*, it offered at the time an important link between those opening works in Santayana's mature system and *The Realm of Spirit*, the concluding volume of the series, not destined to appear until some thirteen years and a war later. In other words, at the time of its appearance, *Platonism and the Spiritual Life* offered a crucial as well as succinct overview of the spiritual upshot of the trajectory for *Realms of Being*. As in the earlier essay on Plotinus, Santayana begins with a critique of a fumbled interpretation, this time by Dean Inge, who had described Platonism as "a firm belief in absolute and eternal values as the most real things in the universe."[16]

As we have seen, "value" for Santayana refers to something as it stands in contingent relationship to various human desires, and so does not express at all the eternal characters of Plato's *eidē*. Plato was willing to assert the eternal worth of the Forms for the soul because he thought the nature of the universe relatively fixed and eternal, a fact, Santayana says, that we now know not to be true. Secondly, Plato had conceived his Forms as causes, which for Santayana was a confession of faith in magic, since their power to make other things behave derived solely from their inward character of being. The true locus of casual power he identified with matter, conceived along the lines of a dynamic flux. However much he respected matter as the only source of existence, Santayana did not find in it any reassuring endorsement of an "absolute and eternal" set of values. On the contrary, contingency and conflict, waste and annihilation abound in nature. Given that death is the one "absolute" the live creature faces, the realm of matter might well have been that "labyrinth of evil" Santayana had spoken of earlier.[17] Nevertheless, natural piety insists that without matter neither animal psyche nor the embodiment of essence could exist. Thus the problem of the spiritual life is, How is it possible,

---

15. At least see John McCormick's rather dismissive remarks in his *George Santayana: A Biography*, 268. For *Platonism and the Spiritual Life* as an enchiridion, or "handbook," of Santayana's later philosophy, see my "Santayana's Sage: The Disciplines of Aesthetic Enlightenment," in this volume, chapter 13. By describing the work as an enchiridion, I am not only thinking of its similarity to the "handbooks" of Epictetus, Augustine, and Erasmus, but also of other short, major summaries of a philosopher's thought such as Spinoza's *Treatise on the Improvement of the Mind* or Leibniz's *Monadology*.

16. Quoted in *Platonism and the Spiritual Life* (New York: Charles Scribner's Sons, 1927), 2. Hereafter cited in the text as PSL.

17. In fact in this essay he describes it as "barbarous and in indefinite flux" (PSL, 33).

given that nature is not fixed and essences are impotent? The failure of Inge's effort to reassert the contemporary value of Platonism provoked Santayana to explore the permanent possibility of the spiritual life without it. The essay had in fact begun with this challenge: "One of these great things past is Platonism, and one of the great things always possible is the spiritual life" (PSL, 1).

Actually, Santayana does not see Plato as a genuine champion of the spiritual life at all. He quite correctly describes Plato as from first to last a political thinker. "To this descendent of Solon," says Santayana, "the universe could never be anything but a crystal case to hold the jewel of a Greek city" (PSL, 27).[18] His metaphysics, according to Santayana, was a sublimated and poetized mythology reflecting Greek morals. On the other hand, in Plotinus, for whom the political realm was a gesture and an afterthought, one finds a perfect expression of what the spiritual life is because it made the act of contemplation, the "flight of the alone to the Alone," the central theme of its system, to which, as we have noted, Santayana paid the highest of compliments.[19] As Santayana put it, the political world for Plotinus was a mere "barnyard" compared to the fortunes of the soul (PSL, 25).

Thus the spiritual life for Plotinus was not a "compensation" for frustrated political hopes, as it was for Plato. "Pure spiritual life cannot be something compensatory, a consolation for having missed more solid satisfactions," comments Santayana; "it should be rather the flower of all satisfactions, in which satisfaction becomes free from care, selfless, and wholly actual, and, in that inward sense, eternal" (PSL, 29). The underlying drive of Platonic spirituality, *erōs*, is replaced with the condition of what Santayana calls being "truly emancipated and enlightened" (PSL, 29). The spiritual life is the "disintoxication" from the moral life, the world of "values," not its sublimated fulfillment, according to Santayana. The function of pure intelligence becomes "to see such things as come its way under the form of eternity," which is to say as essences considered apart from their existence, truth, import, or history (PSL, 33).

18. For those who insist on thinking of Plato as primarily a metaphysician, some attention should be given to the likelihood that the tetrology beginning with *Timaeus* was broken off in mid-sentence in its second work, *Critias*, so that Plato could undertake his longest work, *Laws*.

19. *Enneads*, VI.9.11, the famous conclusion of the *Enneads*. Santayana says, "In the unclouded, synthetic, believing mind of Plotinus, this chastened mythology [i.e., Plato's] crystallized into *the most beautiful of systems*" (PSL, 23, italics added). This is no idle compliment.

Though spirituality arises from material conditions, including such moral virtues as "concentration of thought, indifference to fortune and reputation, warmth of temperament (because spirit cannot burn clear except at a high temperature)," nevertheless "when once aroused, it does not look back in that direction" (PSL, 38). It its purified state, spirit achieves "self-annihilation" (PSL, 40). The spiritual life for Santayana cannot be based on the ultimate fulfillment of the erotic desire of the good since it aims at the overcoming of all desire for the sake of liberation, that is, enlightenment.

Although Santayana wishes to speak of the life of spirit in this purely positive sense, in terms of liberation, he is willing to acknowledge two ways in which it can still maintain an orientation to the world of existence: one by bearing, as it were, the scars of its birth, and the other involving a selfless and somewhat icy tenderness as it looks down from its liberated heights. With regard to the first, Santayana gives a somewhat extraordinary and, I suspect, confessional description. He says:

> Were any world perfect . . . its spirit would view it with the same contemplative satisfaction with which it views any pure essence that spontaneously engages its attention. It would not, in respect to that perfect world, be harassed by remorse, as it must be in an imperfect world where it counts the cost of existence and considers the dreadful sufferings which plagued it like a nightmare, before something beautiful and good could appear for even a moment. I say *remorse* because such is the feeling that comes over me when I remember the travail which, at least in man, the spirit has had to endure in bringing its better life to birth: but the spirit itself has no guilt in the matter; it was caught in a vice; and it may accept and overlook that terrible gestation when at last it reaches the open and rewards itself with an hour of freedom and gladness. (PSL, 51)

As in the earlier essay on Plotinus, Santayana insists that the aim of spirit is not to rebuke the world for the darkness in it, but to gaze instead at the stars. The Gnostic who condemns the world as evil and who dwells upon that fact has merely transported the moral distractions of existence into the world of spirit, thereby spoiling its own natural radiance and joy with a halo of sadness and recrimination that could—and should—have been left behind.

The other response of spirit when it has achieved detachment is not blank indifference, but "joy" in anything when approached in "simplicity;" that is, without any "ulterior interest."

[I]n other words, purity comes of detaching the thing seen and loved from the world that besets and threatens it and attaching it to the spirit to which it is an eternal possession. But this thing eternally possessed by the spirit is not the thing as the world knows and prizes it; it is not the person, or nation, or religion as it asserts and flaunts itself, in a mortal anxiety to be dominant; it is only that thing in its eternal essence, out of which the stress and the doubt of existence have wholly passed. It is that thing dead, immortal, its soul restored, as Plotinus would have said, to the soul of the universe where, together with all other souls, it has always been contained in its purity and perfection. But the truth of it *there* is not the fact of it *here*; and therefore the world, though the spirit loves it far more truly and tenderly than it loves itself, is chilled and rebuked by that look of divine love, which, if it were heeded, would transmute its whole life and change it from what it so passionately and cruelly is, in time, into that which the spirit sees it to be in eternity. (PSL, 53–54)[20]

Thus the joy and tenderness with which spirit sees the world are due to spirit's ability to see the things of the world purely, as essences, and not as the mortal, suffering beings they are, caught up in the turbid flood of existence. Spirit apprehends things in the light of its own actuality: "awareness, intelligence, reconciliation" (PSL, 56). It welcomes the essences that come its way without hunger or desire or with the sense that better views are to be had elsewhere. As Dante's Piccarda says in her eternal place in the lowly lunar heaven, "There is no envy in these spheres" (PSL, 75).[21]

In this way, Santayana offers us a naturalistic mysticism, a "way out of the labyrinth of evil" that releases spirit to its free home, the infinite wilderness of essence where things may be selflessly possessed in their eternity and immediacy. Mysticism, Santayana observes, means silence because it involves "the negation of every human wish and idea" (PSL, 77). Names still carry "animal faith" with them, and so any discourse about "essence" may permit it to be overheard as a "temporal fact." "Silence is therefore imperative, if the mystic has any conscience" (PSL, 78).

---

20. Santayana's stress on the words "here" and "there" is an echo of Plotinian language, "here" being the world of nature and "there" (ἐκεῖ) being the divine world of *Nous* contemplating the Forms. Compare PSL, 64, and refer to the full text of the letter to Robert Bridges cited above.

21. *Paradiso*, III. This is the sphere of those who, though dedicated to a life of worship, have had to break their vows and return to worldly life; hence the significance of the mottled discoloration of the moon, which reflects their lives of "blended virtues." After speaking, Piccarda recedes, singing, "vanishing like a heavy thing downward in deep water" (123).

The only danger is that the mystic confuses his ecstasy for a higher reality or makes ecstasy itself his object. The first is a mistake in truth and the second in substitution of essence for the will, which must be renounced to be transcended. In renouncing words, Santayana says, we know them as symbols only; the straight but difficult way, in the words of San Juan de la Cruz, is "Nothing, Nothing, Nothing" (PSL, 81). Spirit is nothing and empties itself into nothing.

The discipline of the spiritual life is "disillusion," a term Santayana had used from the very beginning of his philosophical development.[22] Positively, this means that we experience the world as much as possible with the sense of "the ultimate in the immediate" (PSL, 83). Anxiety must be effectively banished, initially by all pragmatic means to achieve a temporary island of relative stability in the flux of existence, and ultimately by the concentration of spirit apart from the urgencies and anguishes of the animal host. Thus morality actually presents a serious danger to Santayana insofar as it may interject its "distractions" into the spiritual life—the heaven of Christianity, did it exist, might effectively *choke* the life of spirit with its perfect and pervasive moral industriousness. In other words, in a world where the Good and the Beautiful perfectly combine everywhere, it is far more likely that the Beautiful will be eclipsed by the Good and remain unseen for what it is. Romantic pantheism presents a similar problem, infected as it is with a subliminal need to moralize beauty. Wordsworth, for example, could not effectively free his spirit, struggling as it did "to wash the world white and clean, adopt it, and set it up for a respectable person" (PSL, 85). But, says Santayana, "The world is not respectable; it is mortal, tormented, confused, deluded forever; but it is shot through with beauty, with love, with glints of courage and laughter; and in these the spirit blooms timidly and struggles to the light among the thorns" (PSL, 85). Wordsworth's problem was that he could not banish the world and "Nothing is able to banish the world except contempt for the world, and this was not in him" (PSL, 85).

This, then, is Santayana's challenge: The condition of the spiritual life is to leave moral concerns behind; if the world is held in the light, it is the in cold light of the emptiness of essence under the sky of eternity.

---

22. See "A Religion of Disillusion," in *Interpretations of Poetry and Religion* (New York: Charles Scribner's Sons, 1900), and the much later, crucial essay "Absolute Religion," in *Obiter Scripta*.

But Santayana's discipline of liberation, like its Plotinian model, is a discipline of ascent. The irony, of course, is that Santayana has utterly rejected any Platonic metaphysics that would make this ascent one toward reality. His "ascent" is a flight that takes off from *terra firma* (or rather, given his view of matter, *terra infirma*) and must return to it. Indeed, it never really leaves the ground. It is more of a shift of attention away from the path before us toward the stars above. Like that of Plotinus, Santayana's *askēsis* requires perfection of inward concentration that ends in ecstatic union where simplicity of vision coincides perfectly with the simplicity of its object. But that is where Santayana's discussions leave us, both in the breviary of *Platonism and the Spiritual Life* and the conclusion of *The Realm of Spirit*.

The Descent of Spirit and Santayana's Dilemma

The trouble with the mystic ascent, however, is that the ladder is never really pulled up. There is the descent, the reawakening. This troubled Plotinus deeply. "Many times it has happened," he says: "lifted out of the body into myself, becoming external to all other things and self-encentered; beholding a marvelous beauty ... yet, there comes the moment of descent. ... I ask myself how it happens that I can now be descending."[23] For Santayana this is no more than the trough of the wave that we ride through until the next crest, and our moral concerns are those of keeping afloat and navigating the waters as best we may. The moral life is not abandoned at all, merely temporarily bracketed in precious moments of illumination. And it may be any kind of moral life, though Santayana recommends one that lives with piety toward the real natural harmonies that can exist between the rhythms of nature and our own bodies. Still, in the end, the moral life and the spiritual life have little to say to each other: The spiritual life offers itself to the moral life as a potentially welcome distraction; the moral life threatens to disturb the spiritual life, even while making it possible in the first place. The more the two are brought into harmony, it seems, the greater the danger that the spiritual life will become confused with the moral life—with "Platonism" being the unhappy result.

Is this a necessary conclusion? Or has Santayana presented us with something akin to Fuller's dilemma; that is, a false dilemma based upon

23. *Enneads*, IV.8.1. trans. Stephen MacKenna (London: Faber and Faber, Ltd., n.d.)

extremes that are artificial abstractions? First, Santayana does not claim that the spiritual life has an absolute demand upon all of us. There is a plurality of values for living beings, and what he has to say about the spiritual life only has bearing upon those for whom this has a positive value in the first place. Others may be perfectly happy wandering the "labyrinth" without concern for an escape. While his moral and political writings may speak to those individuals, Santayana recognizes that his ulterior philosophy of the spiritual life is not addressed to them at all. He is a contemplative speaking to contemplatives. In this dialogue, however, there may be a response that diverges from Santayana's own conclusions without violating the premises.

Second, there is some difficulty with the opposition between these two lives Santayana presents. There is something unsettling in the attempt to deal with the *reality* of evil (not the conceptual "problem of evil") by relegating it to the inherent plurality of values the natural world spawns and offering an aesthetic alternative that, from its own perspective, is value-neutral. Must an aesthetic attitude toward the world be forced to choose between the view that art's sole function is to serve morality or be limited to focus on pure form regardless of content? To use an example, Goya's *Third of May, 1808*, which shows Spanish patriots being executed by a French firing squad, or Picasso's *Guernica*, also a protest against the horrors of war, can both be viewed in the gallery in terms of their "pure form"; that is, in terms of their rhythm, balance, color, use of space, and so on. And one school of aesthetics would say this is really what constitutes them as "art," whatever their content may refer to. But a richer aesthetics would say that these works evoke through their aesthetic form the clarified *meaning* of the evils they portray, a clarification that may not have been lucidly present even to those who suffered the events directly. If one beheld a Greek tragedy while remaining oblivious to the moral content of the play, one would miss the meaning of the aesthetic experience.[24] The evocation of these meanings enables us to engage in a *contemplative response* to the world in all its aspects, including

---

24. The idea that art allows us to look at the "clarified meaning" of events that otherwise may remain dark is what I take to be the best understanding of the term *katharsis*, whatever Aristotle himself may have intended. Art, like tragedy, gives us emotional as well as intellectual clarification of meaning and value. The contrast between Santayana's formalist aesthetics and Dewey's aesthetics, which integrates form and content, is the theme of my essay "Santayana's Unbearable Lightness of Being," in this volume.

the moral. In other words, the aesthetic attitude can contemplate an "essence" as a *meaning* that has been purified or clarified via catharsis. And this may result in our ability to exist in the world itself with an enhanced understanding and vision of things. In other words, one of the aims of contemplative liberation may be to teach us a way of wisdom, an enlightened way of life that is thoroughly integrated, not tangential to, daily moral practice. The question that needs to be posed to Santayana is: Given the presuppositions of his ontology, can there be a method of liberation that offers a more inclusive response to the moral life and the nature of the existence of the natural world than the one Santayana himself offered? Can the spiritual life be directed toward a compassionate, mindful awareness of the world without thereby developing a moralism antithetical to the spiritual life?

The Buddhist Ideal of Compassionate Insight

The Buddhist tradition may offer an important example for Santayana's philosophy, sharing as it does a similar view of the physical world as a turbid flux of "dependent co-arising" or "inter-being" (*pratītya-samutpāda*), which is fundamentally "empty" (*śūnya*) and so pervaded with transitory instability, anxiety, and suffering (*dukkha*).[25] Buddhism does not take a Gnostic view of the world as inherently "evil," though at times it can dramatize its negative aspects rather excessively.[26] Nevertheless, the proper pragmatic Buddhist response is: If the world is like this, then what can we do about it? Like Santayana, Buddhist philosophy sees an intelligent or "awakened" (*bodhi*) response to the nature of existence that aims at liberation by clarity of insight (*prajñā*) into the fundamentals (or *dharmas*) and their behavior.[27] A great deal of attention is paid in Buddhist practice to training the mind to see beyond the apparent substantiality of ordinary experience and recognizing how objects and

25. Though *dukkha* can often carry the primary sense of "suffering," it can also mean "instability" and "impermanence." Thus the experience of happiness or joy, though certainly not "sorrowful" or painful at the time, is nevertheless *dukkha* when understood clearly.
26. The Buddha's famous "Fire Sermon" being one noted example of this tendency.
27. *Dharma* has a wide range of meanings (comparable to those of the Greek term *logos*): its core meaning is "that which upholds," and so is extended to "laws" or moral customs that uphold society, the laws of the universe, the basic elements of the universe, the elements of self, the expression of those laws in teachings, and specifically the teachings of the Buddha.

"self" arise functionally as products of change, desire, and inherited causal dispositions (*karma*).²⁸ With enough skill, this can effect the dissipation of desire born of illusion, the frantic "thirst" or "grasping" after things (*tṛṣṇā*) that gives rise to the existential "problem of evil," the reality of suffering. Not only does this dispel any false notion of the substantial self-identity of "objects," which are ways of designating events (even the elements or *dharmas* of the world are "empty," *śūnya*, said Nāgārjuna), but the self-identity of "essences," even of the nonexistential sort like Santayana's, suffers the same fate.²⁹ In other words, the critique of a Buddhist philosopher like Nāgārjuna would be that to assert the nonexistential identity of essences is still due to a degree of "attachment" or grasping, and when this is given up the essence is neither identical nor nonidentical and can be penetrated with an act of liberating insight (*prajñā*). When all things can be seen in their emptiness, their clear but momentary "suchness" (*tathātā*), then *nirvāṇa* and *saṃsāra* coincide.³⁰ Liberation is not a rejection of the world for the sake of some transcendent "there." Nirvāṇa is not a "place" (as if fire went "somewhere" when it was put out) but a "way"; not a "what" but a "how." *How* does one behold the world and respond to it when one has "passed through" the empty nature of desire?

"Form is emptiness, emptiness is form," says the Heart Sutra, but this insight does not terminate in pessimism, fatalism, skepticism, or nihilism.³¹ Rather, it leads to "tranquility" or the extinction of *dukkha* (i.e., "*nirvāṇa*"), which is also positively described at times as "bliss" (*ānanda*), a condition

28. This part of Buddhist teaching is called *Ahbidharma*.
29. Nagarjuna (ca. 150 CE) was one of the main philosophical exponents of the Mahayana school known as "the Middle Way," or *Mādhyamika*. By insisting on the emptiness of the *dharmas* (taken in whatever sense), Nagarjuna moved Buddhist philosophy from the dogmatic factionalism into which it had lapsed back to its original therapeutic mission. See Frederick Streng's fine study, *Emptiness: A Study in Religious Meaning*.
30. *Saṃsāra* is the "wheel" of existence of ordinary life lived in ignorance, and so subject to the demands of causality and grasping—the "Realm of Matter," in Santayana's terminology, as experienced by biological organisms. Santayana puts all morality into this sphere. By showing that *nirvāṇa*, the realm of liberated insight (Santayana's Realm of Spirit) is "empty" and so nowhere, it is nothing else than the world, but experienced in terms of its emptiness and so freed of its existential power. Indeed, the liberating nature of insight (*prajñā*) is that the world stands out far more clearly than before.
31. The Heart Sutra is a short but central Mahayana text containing a synopsis of the *prajñāpāramitā* teaching. "Form" (*rupa*) is actually more what we would call "substance" or even "body." See *Buddhist Texts Through the Ages*, ed. Edward Conze (New York: Harper and Row, 1954), 152–53 and Conze's commentary in *Buddhist Wisdom Books* (New York: Harper & Row, 1972).

that also involves the response of compassion (*karunā*) for all sentient beings, at least in the later Mahayana traditions stemming from the *Prajñāpāramitā* literature.[32] Buddhism does not seek to turn away from this world to another, better one. Rather, it is concerned with a careful way of "handling" this world without getting burned by it. In this approach contemplative insight and practical action are not opposed but mutually sustaining. The Buddha himself presented the Eightfold Path precisely as a "skillful way" of passing through this world, a moral discipline that was fundamentally connected with the spiritual life. The eight parts of the path are classified in three main groups. One consists of three virtues of right conduct: kindness and moderation in (1) speech, (2) actions, and (3) livelihood. Another includes three virtues of right mental discipline: (4) building habits of endeavor, (5) clarity of awareness, and (6) meditative concentration. The last has two virtues of right wisdom: (7) intelligent understanding and (8) "right thought." All work together, as the eight spokes of a wheel, to keep it moving smoothly.[33] But it is this last, "right thought," that I will briefly describe because it offers, I believe, a significant alternative to the severe antimoralism of Santayana's conception of the spiritual life while still accepting most of his analysis of the nature of existence. It shows us a "contemplative ethics of compassion" that does not fall into Santayana's conception of the moral life as a "distraction" to the spiritual life.

Right thought (*sammā sankappa*) is included with right understanding (*sammā ditthi*) as a necessary aspect of the nature of wisdom. "Right understanding" involves deep insight into the true nature of the world, especially with respect to the problem of suffering—the "labyrinth of evil," as Santayana would say. It is a strictly cognitive ability. "Right *thought*," however, is a discipline that works on meditative beholding suffering beings with compassion. It is not easy to say that this is a moral or aesthetic or emotional ability more than a "cognitive" one, since it also

32. These texts were the product of various thinkers in India between 200 BCE and 400 CE. They are critical of the earlier ideal of the enlightened sage (*arhat*), who simply rejects the world for his own salvation, and put forward the new ideal of the "awakened being of compassion," the *bodhisattva*, who turns toward the suffering beings of the world with enlightened understanding.

33. For a discussion of the Eightfold Path, see Walpola Rahula, *What the Buddha Taught* (New York: Grove Press, Inc, 1974), ch. 5. The Buddha presented the last two steps as the first two; Rahula defers discussion until the others have been examined. They do not form a series but, as I noted, a circle.

involves insight into the true nature of things. But it focuses upon those aspects of the world that help us attain compassionate awareness. It is an integral part of the nature of wisdom to cultivate benevolent selfless love (*mettā*) with respect to all beings and compassion (*karunā*) for all that are suffering. Buddhism believes that our daily actions, including those that are called "moral," spring from the sorts of beliefs we have that in turn generate desires which create the "objects" to which we become attached (including the "object" of the self). Attention to our basic beliefs and a clear understanding of how they constitute the objects of our world— and so of our lives—is a central concern for Buddhism. As Walpola Rahula says, "All thoughts of selfish desire, ill-will, hatred, and violence are the result of lack of wisdom—in all spheres of life, whether individual, social or political."[34] The way to overcome *dukkha* is to develop insights and daily habits that generate actions that do not lead to grasping, violence, and so to more suffering. All eight parts of the Eightfold Path cooperate and mutually sustain each other. Contemplation and practice work together to generate a life that is "liberated." And this may be contrasted to Santayana's philosophy, which tends to keep the spiritual and moral lives disjointed or, at best, irrelevant to each other.

The Buddhist discipline of right thought in particular might reveal a more functional connection between these two ends and so exhibit an alternative to Santayana's response to "the labyrinth of evil." Right understanding involves daily attentiveness to features of the world that might awaken the negative passions of grasping or hatred, beholding them instead with gentle but egoless benevolence attended by penetratingly clear understanding into their fundamental nature. It involves daily meditation practices that develop methods of beholding other beings so that feelings of benevolence and compassion are at the forefront of consciousness.[35] By contemplating others compassionately, one is not only more disposed to act in a compassionate manner toward them but in a way that evokes the ability of others to seek compassionate, liberated wisdom. For example, a great deal of obscurity of perception can arise from conscious or unconscious fears we may have toward things.

34. *What the Buddha Taught*, 2nd ed. (New York: Grove Press, 1974), 49.
35. *Mettā*, or benevolence, is the first of the four "*brahma-vihāras*" or "sacred houses" of *karunā* (compassion), *muditā* (sympathetic joy), and *upekṣā* (equanimity), these latter growing out of the cultivation of the first.

Beholding those things as "essences" not only allows us to see them more clearly but to transcend our fear of them. Compassion, or *karunā*, means seeing things as they truly are; this can only be done when the spirit is at peace. Another example is the meditation practice that seeks to cultivate enduring states of benevolent compassion by developing habits that focus on remembering acts of benevolence one has done or which have been done to one, gradually extending these thoughts outward toward recollection of acts of benevolence others have done to others and so on. By so doing, one comes to focus one's conscious thoughts regularly on being well disposed to others in the world.[36] As the Mahayana sages say, all beings are potentially the Buddha.[37] The path toward that goal of compassionate freedom lies in cultivating habits of "paying attention."[38]

To put these ideas into more Santayanan terms, the Realm of Essence may be constituted of an infinite number of essences, any of which may offer themselves to spirit as an object of contemplation. But some of those essences may be conducive toward leading a life of compassionate benevolence whereas others may be conducive toward quite the opposite sort of action. That is, there are a number of essences relating to aspects of compassion, and by disciplining ourselves to focus on these as they might be instantiated in the realm of existence, we can develop a mode of conduct that is at once "ethical" without involving "distraction" from the spiritual life. Indeed, by concentrating on such essences one might develop a mode of life that is even more highly conducive to the spiritual life than the one offered by Santayana himself, which suffers from a fluctuation between acting in the existential, moral life and intermittently escaping into the realm of spirit for its "hour of gladness." The sorts of essences spirit contemplates do not have equally neutral consequences for our existential psychic life, and the concern that essences might be contemplated is not merely a question for the animal psyche but for spirit as well. In particular, a life that is in harmony with spirit's ideal of liberation and persistently conducive to it should be preferred by both the

---

36. Compare Dante's purification before entering the Garden of Eden at the end of *Purgatorio*: He bathes in the river of Lethe to forget his sins and then in the river of Eunoë to remember all the good deeds he did and which were done to him. (*Purgatorio*, XXVIII, XXXI).

37. To explore how this is carried out in practice, see Sharon Salzberg's *Lovingkindness* (Boston: Shambhala Publications, 1995). Salzberg is an acclaimed American Buddhist teacher specializing in this particular form of meditation practice.

38. Sharon Salzberg, *Lovingkindness*, 192.

psyche and spirit over those lives in which the two do not sustain each other or, worse, in which spirit and psyche inhibit each other and are at best disconnected. In this sense, the Buddhist life of contemplative compassion offers a significant alternative to Santayana's conception of the spiritual life without fundamentally altering the premises from which Santayana's later philosophy sets out.[39]

I offer this as an example only—that we may see that there is more connection between the spiritual and the moral life than Santayana was willing to grant. Santayana thought of the moral life in Western terms, as a struggle of will, and so an effort reaching toward an end, rather than as a shadow that follows us because we have turned toward the light. In concluding, I will reaffirm that I think what Santayana has offered the future is an exemplary conception of philosophy in service to the spiritual life. His own rendition of this philosophy bears understandably the scars of its birth in the late nineteenth and early twentieth century, which saw the shattering of so many ideals and comforting illusions. No doubt it also bears the scars of its "terrible gestation" in Santayana's own life, which he only obliquely acknowledges. But I do not think that we need to dismiss the moral life from the spiritual or to condemn its presence in spirit as regrettable "remorse" tainting the otherwise happy intuition of essence. Compassion and benevolence are part of the wisdom of spirit, if handled properly. As the Japanese poet Issa said on the death of his child,

This world of dew
is only the world of dew—
and yet . . . oh yet. . . .[40]

39. In this sense, James Gouinlock's attempt to present a conception of the spiritual life based on the more Aristotelian views of Santayana's The Life of Reason—and those of Aristotle himself—does not present the strong counterexample to Santayana's later philosophy that Buddhism does, in my view, because it introduces a sense of naturalistic teleology that the later Santayana clearly abjures.

40. Kobayahsi Issa, The Spring of My Life, trans. Sam Hamill (Boston: Shambhala, 1977), 65.

FIFTEEN

THE SPIRITUALITY OF THE POSSIBLE
IN JOHN DEWEY'S *A COMMON FAITH*

The Question of Spirituality in Philosophy

It is more than an understatement to say that philosophy today is not associated with "spirituality." Professional philosophers disdain the topic. Some may try to approach it with a philosophical method, analytic or phenomenological, that is not itself inherently spiritual but cognitive. Those philosophers writing within a spiritual tradition—for example, people like Søren Kierkegaard, Gabriel Marcel, Martin Buber, or D. T. Suzuki—are segregated as "religious thinkers" or, like Emmanuel Levinas, seen as leading double lives. Otherwise the term "spirituality" suggests the range of New Age nostrums seeking to fill the void left by abandoned faiths and vapid materialism. It sounds even odder, at least to some, to hear the term "spirituality" connected with "American pragmatism."[1]

---

1. A moment's thought, however, brings to mind not only such obvious evidence to the contrary as William James's *Varieties of Religious Experience* but also the later thought of Santayana, Peirce's "evolutionary love," and, as shall be argued here, the Dewey of *A Common Faith*.

We should at least consider what philosophy loses by discounting or dismissing whatever is embraced in human existence or experience by this term. Many people place "spirituality" at the core of their lives as holding for them the deepest and most significant meanings of their existence. This phenomenon merits some attention from philosophy, insofar as it is concerned with human existence. After all, no one feels that way about epistemology. Yet when "spirituality" is removed from the philosophical vocabulary, "experience" tends to shrink ever toward that dry, narrow focus handled by "epistemology." Aside from epistemology, spirituality opens up the question as to whether we can experience nature and ourselves-in-nature as sacred. This may have serious ecological implications. As Eugenie Gatens-Robinson has said:

> The difficulty that many of us in the Western scientific culture have in understanding our moral and spiritual relationship with nature is clearly magnified by the poverty of our experience with nature. . . . [T]he ecological agenda of healing the earth cannot succeed as the deep separation is maintained between instrumental reason and the "reason" of emotion and spirit. . . . [I]t is not merely the loss of traditional modes of reasoning that has betrayed modern ecological consciousness. It is loss of access to the most basic perceptions, the perception of the sacred.[2]

A spirituality that can cultivate reverence for nature, while embracing science and taking up the responsible use of technology, may be indispensible for the future ecological welfare of the earth and the fate of many species besides ourselves. If spirituality has to do with the way we are capable of being related to something with reverence, a spirituality of nature may be essential in our being willing to care for it. Philosophy needs to be part of that impending issue as well as to maintain the widest and deepest awareness of "experience." In this sense, spirituality in philosophy may address the ways in which our embodied way of existence is oriented toward existence as a whole, "Nature."

What follows is an investigation in two parts. The first explores the significance of Dewey's little book *A Common Faith*. It argues for the importance of this neglected and disputed work for understanding

Dewey's whole philosophy, a point Dewey himself emphasized. I argue that it stresses the importance of a type of spirituality primarily oriented toward possibility rather than actuality. I think this orientation is a key to Dewey's philosophy as a whole. It may be a key to the person, John Dewey, himself. Thus the second part is a biographical exploration of the growth and development of Dewey himself in light of this "spirituality of possibility," providing, as it were, the existential decisions in his own life that lay behind the themes of *A Common Faith*. By raising the question of spirituality in Dewey, I also hope to restore a viable philosophical use of the term and at the same time present a richer understanding of Dewey's philosophy, one that is not adequately described by the terms "pragmatism" or "instrumentalism."

Part I: Spirituality in A Common Faith

DEWEY'S A COMMON FAITH: INCONSISTENT OR IRRELEVANT?

Dewey's own statement of the place of the religious in experience as put forth in *A Common Faith*, when not outright ignored, has generally been seen as inconsistent with or inconsequential to his general philosophical view. When it is discussed, it is often judged to be inadequate even by such discerning and sympathetic readers as John Herman Randall, Jr. and, more recently, Victor Kestenbaum.[3] Others, like Larry Hickman, interpret it as an application of Dewey's instrumentalism.[4] Russell Goodman notes that "Dewey's focus on a 'truly spiritual religion,' a religion of experience, is compatible with his constant emphasis on the reconstructive possibilities of human life."[5] Steven Rockefeller argues that, although Dewey quietly broke with Christianity after his move to Chicago in 1894, his Christian faith gradually evolved into a "moral faith"

---

3. See the highly critical account by John Herman Randall, Jr.—Dewey's student as well as colleague at Columbia—"The Religion of Shared Experience," in *Philosophy after Darwin*, ed. Beth J. Singer (New York: Columbia University Press, 1977), 241–67. For a more sympathetic and recent approach that nevertheless finds Dewey's position inadequate in the last analysis, see Victor Kestenbaum's *The Grace and Severity of the Ideal* (Chicago: University of Chicago Press, 2005), esp. the essay "Faith and the Unseen."
    4. See Larry Hickman, "Cultivating a Common Faith: Dewey's Religion," in *Pragmatism as Post-Postmodernism* (New York: Fordham University Press, 2007), 191–205.
    5. Russell Goodman, *American Philosophy and the Romantic Tradition* (Cambridge: Cambridge University Press, 1990), 94.

in democracy.[6] Michael Eldridge tries to explain the book as written for liberals who, having lost religion, still felt a need for something religious in their lives, but as of little importance for those who do not.[7] On the other hand, Douglas Anderson has suggestively drawn attention to the neglected "wild side" of Dewey, his "sensible mysticism."[8]

I believe the charges of inconsistency are deeply mistaken. But I do not think *A Common Faith* is merely an "application" of his instrumentalism, nor do I think that "the religious" can simply be handled as a "quality" of experience. While the book may be charged with brevity, it is by no means inconsequential to his philosophical outlook, not least Dewey's discussion of the idea of "the self as a whole" in terms of its orientation to "the Universe." This is something missed in purely contextualist readings. And while Kestenbaum is sensitively aware of precisely these odd expressions, he sees them as pushing Dewey's naturalism to the breaking point—all to the good, in his judgment. I also find Rockefeller's approach problematic because it tempts one to see Dewey simply as "switching religions," his "faith" having as its new object a set of "beliefs" about democracy.[9] Secular political ideals can be "religions," with full-blown dogmas. But Dewey did not have a "religion" of democracy in that sense or a naïve "faith" in the experimental method. One of the central points Dewey seeks to make in *A Common Faith* is that both "faith" and the religious attitude have nothing to do with "doctrines" of any sort. Contrary to Eldridge's claim, Dewey states explicitly that his lectures were addressed

---

6. See Steven Rockefeller, *John Dewey: Religious Faith and Democratic Humanism* (New York: Columbia University Press, 1991), 212ff. See also Robert B. Westbrook, *John Dewey and American Democracy* (Ithaca, NY: Cornell University Press, 1991), ch. 3. Rockefeller argues that Dewey, in his quest for "unity and freedom," should be seen as "the prophet of a new spiritual attitude and way of being—what one might call a distinctively American democratic form of spirituality" in which Dewey "envisioned the most thoroughgoing and radical unification of the ideal and the real of any American thinker" (4). What I argue here is that such a view is actually closer to what Dewey found in the traditional idealisms he ultimately rejected and that his own position involves a careful ontological and existential separation of the ideal from the actual while acknowledging at the same time their creative connection. Both modes are real, but not to be identified. See my review of Rockefeller in *Transactions of the Charles S. Peirce Society* 28, no. 4 (1992): 857–68.

7. Michael Eldridge, *Transforming Experience: John Dewey's Cultural Instrumentalism* (Nashville: Vanderbilt University Press, 1998).

8. See Douglas Anderson, "John Dewey's Sensible Mysticism," in *Philosophy Americana* (New York: Fordham University Press, 2006), 129–41.

9. Rockefeller provides an informative chapter on *A Common Faith* that looks at the contemporary debates on religion when Dewey's book was written. His basic position is that "Dewey's vision of the meaning and value of the democratic way of uniting the ideal and the actual culminates in his philosophy of the religious dimension of experience" (539).

to the *anti*religious naturalists and humanists who, he feared, had set up a new dualism, that between "Man vs. Nature," in place of the old. Dewey was trying to call attention to something important that many of his naturalist, liberal, humanist followers were missing. I find Anderson's indication of a Dewey who was "a wilder, richer, quasi-Emersonian figure" a more suggestive approach, and will try to flesh that out here.

I will argue that Dewey's talk of "the religious" does not so much designate a "quality" of experience as it has to do with an *attitude*, an orientation to possibility as a fundamental feature of existence. This idea lends some intelligibility to Dewey's talk about the relation of "the self as a whole" to Nature—"the Universe," as Dewey calls it—which is inclusive of both the actual and the possible. This is a crucial claim and affects our understanding of Dewey's mature thought. For Dewey there are two fundamental orientations in life: the first faces a universe in which ideals are fundamentally already *actual* in the heart of reality, secure and incontestable, and the second faces a universe in which the ideal as *possibility* is a genuine and pervasive feature, an invitation to risk and creativity. One might be called "the spirituality of the actual" and the other "the spirituality of the possible." Simply treating "the religious" as a quality of experience does not bring out this other, more important feature.

Such orientations affect the whole way the self approaches life and experience. It affects *how we live.* Dewey sees the first attitude as deeply fearful; it pursues a "quest for certainty," clings to dogmas and rituals of the past and faces the future blindly. The latter attitude is based upon the courage to take up action to realize beckoning ideals; it recognizes the possibility of failure or error. Even success comes with humility, knowing the ever-present possibility of tragic blindness that comes with our finitude. This view recognizes our embeddedness in nature but also the limits of whatever control we may have. Dewey calls this double acknowledgment "natural piety." Many people have identified the religious with the first of these two attitudes and connect it with some religion; therefore, in rejecting religion, they reject spirituality as well. This happens for many who reject a childhood faith in favor of a set of scientific beliefs about the world. What is a conflict between a set of religious beliefs and one of scientific beliefs is seen as a conflict between science and spirituality. Dewey thinks this is the result of accepting a false dilemma and carries with it an impoverishment of existence. Also, even though this decision sets one dogmatic view aside, it may foster another. In an extreme form "scientism" becomes another religion.

One problem that those raised in the Western religious traditions have is the identification of "spirituality" with "religion," understanding "religion" to mean a set of intellectually held beliefs and fixed moral commands. This is particularly true of the various forms of Christianity, which from early on in its history was defined by a series of intense, even violent, *theological* disputes. At the very beginning there was the clash between Paul, who thought Christianity could be for the gentiles, and James, who held it was only for Jews. The Trinitarian debate and the Monophysite controversy (over whether Christ had one or two natures) are further examples. In many cultures, however, the spiritual is reflected in a way of life that expresses reverence and affirms relationships. Joseph Campbell enjoyed telling the story of the philosopher who asked the Shinto priest what his "theology" was; the priest replied, "We don't have a 'theology.' We dance."[10] Among Native American peoples, ceremony and dancing are also fundamental ways of expressing *how* one is reverently connected to the whole domain of the sacred. The user of the calumet, or "peace pipe," in smoking it also offers it to the four surrounding sacred directions and to the earth below and sky above. This puts the individual at the center of sacred orientation to the world. The Navajo healing ceremonies aim at putting an individual back into healing harmony, or *hozho*, with all existence. One is reintegrated into the process of life, of "walking in beauty." Having this distinction between a theological religion and a spiritual practice in mind will be helpful in understanding Dewey's approach.

THREE CLAIMS: POSSIBILITY AS SUCH, THE SELF AS A WHOLE,
OPENNESS TO EXPERIENCE

I want to explore three related ideas. First, the "religious" in *A Common Faith* points to a dimension of existence or Nature that can be described as "possibility as such." The second idea is that this allows Dewey to speak of the orientation of "the whole self" (not just a contextual self) to "the Universe" or Nature insofar as it includes possibility as such. And, third,

10. Recounted in Stephen and Robin Larson, *A Fire in the Mind: A Life of Joseph Campbell* (New York: Anchor Books, 1991), 438.

this orientation establishes an attitude of openness to experience, a "creative faith," if you will, which is a dominant characteristic of Deweyan spirituality. Let me expand these claims.

POSSIBILITY AS SUCH

There is a spiritual *ground* to Dewey's outlook, an understanding of spirituality itself precisely as *openness to possibility*—not just to these or those possibilities in a given situation, but to "*possibility as such*," to the acceptance of a fundamental openness in existence. It is one thing to acknowledge specific immanent possibilities in a situation, such as the routes one may choose to get to a destination. But it is different to acknowledge that existence, Nature, itself exhibits a radical dimension of *possibility as such*, a "generic trait" of creative indeterminacy that permeates nature and experience.[11]

THE SELF AS A WHOLE

The acknowledgment of possibility as such reveals a new possibility for the *self as such*: The self *as a whole* is oriented toward existence *as a whole* in terms of whether it accepts or denies *possibility as such*. This affects the very possibility of the self itself: *How* the self grasps its own possibilities affects *what sort of self* it becomes. In other words, a self that simply sees various possibilities attached to this or that situation and does not see *possibility as such* sees itself as a contextual self; it does not grasp its own selfhood in relation to possibility as such. It cannot take an orientation to existence as a whole. It is ultimately decisive, for Dewey, whether one orients one's life toward the world as a domain that has *possibility as such*—as one that is capable of generating the ideals that give life meaning, but which are not themselves already definitively secure in some actualized, unassailable Platonic heaven—or whether one turns toward a

---

11. Victor Kestenbaum in "Faith and the Unseen" believes Dewey does go beyond seeing possibilities as simply contextual and grounded in actual situations, while also holding that this pushes beyond Dewey's naturalism and pragmatism. Kestenbaum's essay is worth close reading, but I think Dewey was fairly clear about seeing possibility as another dimension of Nature, which all too often is simply seen as a collection of actualities.

view of the world in which there is no *possibility as such*, one in which the world is at its core radically determinate.

Dewey indicates that to opt for the latter is an act of weakness or fear, resulting in various "quests for certainty," whether they fixate upon dogmatic faiths or something else. The former alternative, the acknowledgment of *possibility as such*, requires a courageous and complex orientation of the self to existence. This includes surrendering the comforting notion that the ends of our aspirations, those that give meaning to our lives, are guaranteed either in their existence or even in their final meaning, much less that they are ultimately within our control. Spirituality in this mode requires that we undertake a degree of existential risk and accept the immanent possibility of tragedy, for even with the best of intentions, the final meaning of our actions may betray us. This requires courage and resoluteness, but also humility, compassion and a certain "tragic wisdom" about our own finitude. This is what Dewey means by the phrase "natural piety." Lack of natural piety is expressed in what Dewey calls "aggressive atheism."

OPENNESS TO EXPERIENCE

Another central aspect of Dewey's spirituality is manifest in "openness to experience." By this is meant his refusal to allow formalistic or rationalistic views or methods to predetermine an understanding of the qualitative richness and creative openness of experience. One is disposed toward novelty, change, growth, diversity, and the future. This is part of the orientation of the "whole self" to *possibility as such*. This was a choice Dewey himself faced in his development; when Dewey rejected idealism it was for the sake of an openness to experience.[12] As I have said, the question is not just one of a cognitive ontological commitment, of whether one holds a "propositional attitude" to "the universe is open" or "the universe is closed." It is also an existential commitment that determines how a self will live its life.

---

12. In using the term "existential" I am trying to preserve the sense of a fundamental orientation toward the possibilities of life that itself establishes the conditions of the self one can be; I do not intend that this term be taken in the sense of positing some nonnatural "will" in human existence set over against "Being" or Nature, say, in the manner of Sartre. The whole point of Dewey's outlook is to avoid such notions and assert the "inhabitation" of Nature by human existence. His is an ecological ontology, or "eco-ontology" in my terminology.

In Dewey's orientation to the *possible as such* I believe one outcome was that he was able *as a philosopher* to limit the scope of knowledge within the larger domain of experience. In other words, it helped him overcome "the intellectualist fallacy."[13] This is perhaps Dewey's most radical thesis, and it certainly cuts against the grain of the Western tradition. Thus, I argue that Dewey's own spirituality, which is to be understood in terms of what he himself says about "the religious" in *A Common Faith*, is not only exhibited in such decisions as rejecting "religion" but ultimately in the fundamental orientation of his mature philosophy: seeing human existence as part of nature ("natural piety"), a view of nature as embracing the possible as well as the actual, the acknowledgment of the primacy of the noncognitive dimension of experience, and a fundamental attitude of openness to experience.

This idea of nature as including the possible makes *A Common Faith* no casual book in Dewey's corpus. I think it comes from the core of Dewey's being. Dewey's account of the religious dimension of experience is not just another instance of Dewey "fighting against dualisms," an "application" of his philosophy to the itinerant topic of "religion," much less a bone to his followers who were nostalgic for their lost religions. It is a statement of the basic existential decision that shaped his life and defined his spirituality. In other words, Dewey's concern for the ways in which experience transcends our formalisms, which is at the root of his philosophical development, expresses itself most consciously in his distinction between "religion" and "the religious," and this, in turn, gives us a way of understanding Dewey himself, philosopher and human being, *wholly.*

Let us then look at Dewey's distinction between "the religious" as a mode of experience and "religion" and see how the former is based on acknowledgment of the ideal as possible—opening up the acknowledgment of *possibility as such.* This in turn gives us a way of understanding Dewey's unusual (and controversial) claim about the religious as an orientation of "the whole self" in relation to Being as a whole (or "the Universe," in Dewey's terms). It will incidentally clarify what Dewey means by "God." Then I will take up the issue of "openness to experience" as a feature of Deweyan spirituality.

13. See, for example, *The Quest for Certainty* (LW, 4:232).

"RELIGION" VERSUS "THE RELIGIOUS"

In *A Common Faith*, John Dewey proposed a radical disjunction between the various *religions*, for which he had little use, and the *religious* dimension of experience, upon which he placed high value. Not only are we to distinguish between religion(s) and "the religious," but we are told that religion more often than not manages to kill religious experience rather than foster it. The aim of *A Common Faith*, emphasizes Dewey, is "the "emancipation of the religious from religion."[14] This was not a message Dewey delivered to those clinging to some form of religion. When Dewey gave the Terry Lectures at Yale in 1933, published the next year as *A Common Faith*, he was not addressing advocates of religion so much as those who in the name of humanism and science had thrown "the religious" out with religions.

> *A Common Faith* was not addressed to those who are content with traditions in which "metaphysical" is substantially identical with "supernatural." It was addressed to those who have abandoned supernaturalism, and who on that account are reproached by traditionalists for having turned their back upon everything religious. The book was an attempt to show all such persons that they still have within their experience all the elements, which give the religious attitude its value.[15]

In other words, Dewey was trying to defend the importance of spirituality in a naturalistic philosophy. His repeated concern is that naturalism or naturalistic humanism has lost "natural piety."[16] It is to *those people* above others that Dewey addressed his lectures. "I believe," says Dewey, "that many persons are so repelled from what exists as a religion by its

---

14. See LW, 9:19; see: 4, 8 (twice), 11, 23, 45, 56.

15. John Dewey, "Experience, Knowledge and Value: A Rejoinder," in *The Philosophy of John Dewey*, ed. Paul A. Schilpp (Greensboro, NC: Tudor Publishers, 1938), 597.

16. "It is the part of manliness to insist upon the capacity of mankind to strive to direct natural and social forces to humane ends. But unqualified absolutistic statements about the omnipotence of such endeavors reflect egoism rather than intelligent courage.... The essentially unreligious attitude is that which attributes human achievement and purpose to man in isolation from the world of physical nature and his fellows. Our successes are dependent upon the cooperation of nature. The sense of the dignity of human nature is as religious as the sense of awe and reverence when it rests upon a sense of human nature as a cooperating part of a larger whole. Natural piety is not of necessity either a fatalistic acquiescence in natural happenings or a romantic idealization of the world. It may rest upon a just sense of nature as the whole of which we are parts, while it also recognizes that we are parts that are marked by intelligence and purpose, having the capacity to strive by their aid to bring conditions into greater consonance with what is humanly desirable" (LW, 9:18).

intellectual and moral implications, that they are not even aware of attitudes in themselves that if they came to fruition would be genuinely religious." He adds:

> To be somewhat more explicit, a religion . . . always signifies a special body of beliefs and practices having some kind of institutional organization, loose or tight. In contrast, the adjective "religious" denotes nothing in the way of a specifiable entity, either institutional or as a system of beliefs. It does not denote anything to which one can specifically point as one can point to this and that historic religion or existing church. For it does not denote anything that can exist by itself or that can be organized into a particular and distinctive form of existence. It denotes attitudes that may be taken toward every object and every proposed end or ideal. (LW, 9:8)

The religious is not a specific type of experience, one that can be distinguished from scientific or moral experiences, for example. It is not a "specifiable entity." Note that Dewey characterizes it as an attitude toward *every object and every proposed end or ideal.* It is a general orientation, a way that the self is disposed.

Although Dewey goes on to speak of "the religious" as "a quality of experience," he does so when he is explicitly trying to state it is not a special type of experience but something that can characterize experiences of all sorts. It may seem to be quite similar to his characterization of the aesthetic in *Art as Experience,* but I believe there is a significant difference. "The religious" is not a context-specific quality, one characterizing "*an* experience," but is an "adjustment in life and its conditions," a "reorientation" (LW, 9:11). It can be described in terms of "adaptation," as long as this is not taken as some *particular* adjustment to a *specific* circumstance—especially insofar as this might be a passive accommodation to things beyond our control. But neither should it be confused with an active response to specific situations, for here is where the danger of hubris begins in the foolish notion that we can triumph over nature all on our own. What Dewey is at pains to emphasize is that the religious is an "adjustment" of our *whole being* to *Nature as a whole,* which he calls "the Universe."

> Now both these processes [adaptation and accommodation] are often called by the more general name of adjustment. But there are also changes in ourselves in relation to the world in which we live that are

much more inclusive and deep seated. They relate not to this and that want in relation to this and that condition of our surroundings, but pertain to our being in its entirety. Because of their scope, this modification of ourselves is enduring. It lasts through any amount of vicissitude of circumstances, internal and external. There is a composing and harmonizing of the various elements of our being such that, in spite of changes in the special conditions that surround us, these conditions are also arranged, settled, in relation to us. This attitude includes a note of submission. But it is voluntary, not externally imposed. . . . And in calling it voluntary, it is not meant that it depends upon a particular resolve or volition. It is a change *of* will conceived as the organic plenitude of our being, rather than any special change *in* will. (LW, 9:12–13)

This is an extraordinary and important statement, for most of Dewey's readers would deny that the phrases "our being in its entirety" or "organic plenitude of our being" could be meaningfully uttered by Dewey: Is not experience (and so the self) a piecemeal affair of plural contexts and "reconstructions"? What meaning can be given to an act that is "voluntary" but not any particular act of will? Indeed, one of Dewey's best readers, John Herman Randall, Jr., regarded the "individualism" expressed in this passage as the glaring inconsistency in Dewey's otherwise sensible naturalistic, democratic "religion of shared experience."[17] This passage and others have been appealed to by less sympathetic readers, such as Richard Bernstein and Richard Rorty, who claim that Dewey's mature philosophical naturalism was riven by an inconsistent propensity to "idealism," a charge I have challenged elsewhere.[18]

An important third point follows: The religious is our *imaginative way of being in the world and the world's availability as the possible or ideal.* More specifically, Dewey says that "the religious" arises when imagination "intervenes" or "enters profoundly" into life so that it "completely interpenetrates all elements of our being" (LW, 9:13–14).

---

17. "There is a rather surprising individualism in the Terry lectures," writes Randall, adding, "and one can only rub one's eyes" (Randall, 263). Randall believes that the question of "natural piety" and "spirituality" should be separated (246) and that Santayana, in *Reason in Religion,* was far more successful. It will be part of my argument that this individualism is a crucial aspect of Dewey's philosophy and that natural piety and spirituality, as defined here, can be integrated successfully.

18. See my *John Dewey's Theory of Art, Experience, and Nature: The Horizons of Feeling* (Albany: State University of New York Press, 1987).

The connection between imagination and the harmonizing of the self is closer than is usually thought. The idea of a whole, whether of the whole personal being or of the world, is an imaginative, not a literal, idea. . . . Neither observation, thought, nor practical activity can attain that complete unification of the self which is called a whole. The *whole* self is an ideal, an imaginative projection. Hence the idea of a thoroughgoing and deep-seated harmonizing of the self with the Universe (as a name for the totality of conditions with which the self is connected) operates only through imagination—which is one reason why this composing of the self is not voluntary in the sense of an act of special volition or resolution. An "adjustment" possesses the will rather than is its express product. . . . The self is always directed toward something beyond itself and so its own unification depends upon the idea of the integration of the shifting scenes of the world into that imaginative totality we call the Universe. (LW, 9:14)

This similarly remarkable passage deserves careful pondering: Neither thought *nor practical activity* can bring about the harmonization of the self with the universe—this cannot be "produced" instrumentally; and though this may be accomplished through "the imagination," this is not any *specific voluntary act of will.* The "adjustment" *possesses* the will. This transcends any particular "problematic situation" for Dewey, and so is not a matter of *conscious* volition any more than it is instrumentally produced. Rather it has to do with that dimension of experience upon which our specific cognitive acts and inquiries are based. It springs from the deepest levels of the self and involves the way one faces existence and lives, "walking in beauty to old age," as the Navajo would say.

Likewise, imagination is clearly not the personal, conscious power of creation, much less the more traditional "faculty" of fancy. It also is something far deeper. Imagination is the access to the dimension of ultimate possibility. This is not merely awareness of the various possibilities of the self contextually taken, but acknowledgment of the dimension of possibility itself such that it transforms the meaning of *any* present experience. One may abstractly assert that there are possibilities "in" a situation, whether or not we grasp them. But if they are not acknowledged or understood, they cannot direct conduct. Beyond awareness of various possibilities in any given situation there is the potential acknowledgment of the dimension of the possible—the awareness of the pervasive presence of possibility—that can change our comportment to existence as such, but only if we are aware of it. This is why Dewey says that it comes upon us or not at all. The "whole self" realizes that the "Universe," Nature, existence, is not constituted of *things* or actualities with various possibilities, but involves possibility as a constitutive dimension, one that is disclosed by imagination. Indeed, imagination is just this interplay between the actual and the possible. The spiritual lies in the way we exist in possibility as well as the way in which possibility exists for us.

THE SELF AND CREATIVE INDIVIDUALITY

Acknowledgment of possibility as the source of the ideal has two results: We must accept that a possible ideal is not actual and so falls into the domain of the precarious, and we must acknowledge that the possible transcends ultimate human control, which brings an element of humility and natural piety in recognition of our finitude, a sense of grace if we attain the ideal, and the persistence of the *question* of self-knowledge necessary to avoid hubris. The way in which we are open to this dimension has more to do with the awareness of the "qualitative horizon" of experience than with any conscious thought or action.[19] The question for the "self as a whole" is whether or not it acknowledges *possibility as such* as a fundamental way of Nature. This is why the issue transcends any given situation. What Dewey is trying to express, I believe, is an orientation that affects the way the self becomes actualized in experience, how a life is actually lived, and the sort of person one actually becomes.

In this sense, individuality is a legitimate fundamental concern for Deweyan spirituality, contrary to what Randall maintains. To miss the ultimate importance of the individual as a creative center of existence is to miss a *great deal* of what Dewey was all about. *Individualism, Old and New* is concerned with the loss of genuine individualism in modern society—the "lost individual." *Art as Experience* looks at the potential integrated individuality of experience that makes it *an experience.* The question of creative individuality as a metaphysical approach to the question of time is expressed in one of Dewey's most important essays, "Time and Individuality." It is the key theme in "Creative Democracy—The Task Before Us." In spite of Randall's fear that this moment in Dewey's

---

19. See the important essay "Qualitative Thought," LW, 5:243–62.

thought reflected a lapse into his Protestant heritage, it can be shown that individuality was a consistent and persistent theme in Dewey's work.[20] Individuality for Dewey is the creative response to existence and it is absolutely vital to everything Dewey has to say about ethics, art, education, democracy—and faith.

Ideals come through the imagination, but in order to affect creative action, they must be recognized as possibilities whose truth is in the making, and not be treated as realized actualities whose existence simply "justifies" our actions or lives insofar as they conform to a fixed standard. "The authority of an ideal over choice and conduct is the authority of an ideal, not of a fact, of a truth guaranteed to intellect, not of the status of one who propounds the truth," adds Dewey (LW, 9:15). He goes on to say that moral faith "has been bolstered by all sorts of arguments intended to prove that its object is not ideal. . . . It is argued that the ideal is already the final reality at the heart of things that exist" and that failure to acknowledge this is a moral weakness. But the contrary is the case, asserts Dewey: "They have failed to see that in converting moral realities into matters of intellectual assent they have evinced lack of *moral* faith. Faith that something should be in existence as far as lies in our power is changed into the intellectual belief that it is already in existence" (LW, 9:15–16). Thus the orientation of "the whole self" must be to see the possible as *authentically contingent* and that the possibilities of the present are not available except through "imagination." A failure to see a possibility means that it cannot be operative as a guiding ideal of intelligence. What any given awareness of a possibility offers to imagination, then, is not just the finite possibility itself, but the reality of *possibility as such* as a "generic trait" of existence, and it is this that the "will," the possibility of the self itself, ultimately turns toward or away from. Courage and fear lie at the roots of this turning.

Those possibilities have religious potential when they seem to offer an integration of values (and so the possibility of a meaningful existence, the possibility of being of a "self"):

> The religious is "morality touched by emotion" only when the ends of moral conviction arouse emotions that are not only intense but are

---

20. See Randall, 265. The ultimate significance of individuality for Dewey is evident to any careful reading of his texts, for individuality is ultimately the creative response to existence from the physical on up to the personal forms of being. See his extremely important essay "Time and Individuality" (LW, 14).

actuated and supported by ends so inclusive that they unify the self. The inclusiveness of the end in relation to both self and the "universe" to which an inclusive self is related is indispensable. . . . The religious attitude signifies something that is bound through imagination to a *general* attitude. This comprehensive attitude, moreover, is much broader than anything indicated by "moral" in its usual sense. (LW, 9:16–17)

By retaining the ideal in the mode of possibility, we lose the assurance that the ideal will prevail or even turn out in existence what it seemed in imagination. This is the tragic dimension of existence—which is why Dewey stresses the lesson of hubris and the need for self-knowledge as crucial for a life of wisdom. To recall, Dewey says, "The outcome, given our best endeavor is not with us." If "fear created the gods" when so little of nature was understood or under control, adds Dewey, the rise of technological mastery has not eliminated the fundamental reality of the precarious as a "generic trait" of nature. It is "part of manliness to insist upon the capacity of mankind to strive to direct natural and social forces to humane ends," says Dewey, "But unqualified absolutistic statements about the omnipotence of such endeavors reflect egoism rather than intelligent courage" (LW, 9:18). We must not lose the awareness of our ultimate dependence on conditions beyond our control.

The question is what form this awareness takes: fear or courage. "Fear never gave stable perspective to the life of anyone," Dewey comments astutely. Many lives are ultimately lived within this fear. Fear may make us seek absolutes in religion, science, or politics, but the essential feature is refusal to open one's existence to the precious, the possible, and the need for courage to exist as such. This does not mean that one should adopt some opposite Promethean outlook, which expresses hubris in its own way: "The essentially unreligious attitude is that which attributes human achievement and purpose to man in isolation from the world of physical nature and his fellows" (LW, 9:18). The proper alternative is "natural piety," which avoids fatalistic pessimism or false illusions of mastery. It acknowledges our role and our capacities, but recognizes that we are parts of a larger whole. It calls forth the need for both courage and humility in our character—and this is as much needed in intellectual inquiry as anywhere. Even "faith" in inquiry, says Dewey, cannot cling to dogmas about method any more than to dogmas about a priori truths. Inquiry is both genuine exploration and authentic self-questioning, a use of intelligence to organize and understand the world while being aware that at any given moment our assumptions may be wrong, even tragically wrong.[21]

Dewey rejects in the strongest way the notion that faith must be bound up with the assent to some belief or doctrine about the universe, including beliefs about ourselves: The question of truth is entirely a function of inquiry over time and the fallible instrumentalities we use to ascertain it. That any truth is open to change or even rejection is one of the basic existential commitments to undertaking the path of inquiry itself. Nor does Dewey admit any sort of self-evident truth to mystical or ecstatic experiences, while nevertheless acknowledging their significance. What is left for faith, then? A faith that is genuinely religious, says Dewey, can be described as "the unification of the self through allegiance to inclusive ideal ends, which imagination presents to us and to which the human will responds as worthy of controlling our desires and choices" (LW, 9:23). The content of various religions has not given us facts so much as presented ideals to the imagination. Whether or not Jesus or the Buddha lived or said the things attributed to them, their religious significance lies in the ideals they present as possibilities for our existence. Such ideals are not merely present in the religions of the world, but they pervade all aspects of culture. And it is as ideals that these symbols exercise a claim upon us, for how we respond to them affects who we become.

"GOD" AS CREATIVE POSSIBILITY

Dewey applies this to the question of the meaning of the word "God." Instead of using it to refer to a being, even the highest being, let it stand, he says, for "the unity of all ideal ends arousing us to desire and actions" (LW, 9:29).[22] To place God in the realm of the possible, in other words, is a fundamental act of courage—or, better, a refusal of fear and of hubris. To assert the ideal as possible is not to deny it reality, for "the reality of

21. See the concluding chapter of *The Quest for Certainty*, especially where Dewey says, "At the best, all our endeavors look to the future and never attain certainty. The lesson of probability holds for all forms of activity as truly as for the experimental operations of science, and even more poignantly and tragically" (LW, 4:245).

22. One might compare Dewey's concept of God with Paul Tillich's idea of "ultimate concern." See Paul Tillich, *The Dynamics of Faith* (New York: Harper and Row, 1957), ch.1, and John Herman Randall, Jr.'s essay "The Ontology of Paul Tillich," in *Philosophy after Darwin*, ed. Beth J. Singer (New York: Columbia University Press, 1985), 121ff.

ideal ends as ideals is vouched for by their undeniable power in action" (LW, 9:30). Nature includes both the actual and the possible. Thus a genuine ideal is the one that actually inspires and guides conduct— throughout life. It becomes the way we appropriate the meaning of our existence in the universe, and so the creative basis for understanding the meaning of our particular actions and choices.

While Dewey insists that the ideal not be identified with some realized actuality, he is equally insistent that the ideal not be severed from actual existence: "What I have tried to show is that the ideal itself has its roots in natural conditions; it emerges when the imagination idealizes existence by laying hold of the possibilities offered to thought and action" (LW, 9:33). It is easy to misunderstand Dewey's claim, for it may sound like a weak effort to save the ideal from nonexistence, that somehow "ideals" and possibilities are already "contained" in the actual and lie ready-to-hand, waiting only for an act of will to "imagine" them. This would be tempting to those who want, in the end, a universe of actuality rather than one of possibility. It also reveals a hubris of the imagination, as if it were some technique "in control" of the domain of the possible. In Dewey's effort to deny some sort of actualized Platonic realm of ideals, he may be equally misunderstood to say, with Aristotle, there is nothing new under the sun, that all possibilities are ready-to-hand potentialities. What in fact Dewey is saying is that because the ideal *is* rooted in existence it has the *power* to *transform* it. It is, so to speak, the "revolutionary" or creative power of the present; it determines how the present will be directed and so what meaning the present will have. A given situation whose possibilities for creative integration and realization are not grasped is one that succumbs to meaningless chance or routine habit. This is even truer of a whole life. One of the most fundamental problems of freedom is that possibilities are not seen at all; this is especially evident in the nature of social possibilities, such as women and men not seeing certain roles as available for them.

> The aims and ideals that move us are generated through imagination. But they are not made out of imaginary stuff. They are made out of the hard stuff of the world of physical and social experience. . . . The new vision does not arise out of nothing, but emerges through seeing, in terms of possibilities, that is, of imagination, old things in new relations serving a new end which the new end aids in creating. (LW, 9:33–34)

And it is "this *active* relation between ideal and actual to which I would give the name 'God'" (LW, 9:34). Whatever disadvantages the term "God" may have, Dewey insists on the need that, in our "distracted age," this point be brought out "with all clearness and force"; i.e., that possibilities for ideals to be actualized are real and that "there are forces at work that threaten and sap existent goods as well as prevent their expansion" (LW, 9:35). The failure to realize them is first of all a failure of imagination, failing to understand existence in terms of the possible, as simply actual instead. It is the reality of possibility at the heart of actuality that is the creative moment that turns a whole life in one direction or another. Whether one calls such a creative union "God" or not is not important, but, says Dewey, "such a working union of the ideal with the actual seems to me to be identical with the force that has in fact been attached to the conception of God in all the religions that have a spiritual content; and a clear idea of that function seems to me urgently needed at the present time" (LW, 9:35).

One reason for the urgency, says Dewey, is that the "aggressive" or "militant atheism" of modern times has actually something in common with the supernaturalism that it loudly rejects.

What I have in mind especially is the exclusive preoccupation of both militant atheism and supernaturalism with man in isolation. For in spite of supernaturalism's reference to something beyond nature, it conceives of this earth as the moral centre of the universe and of man as the apex of the whole scheme of things. It regards the drama of sin and redemption enacted within the isolated and lonely soul of man as the one thing of ultimate importance. Apart from man, nature is held either accursed or negligible. Militant atheism is also affected by lack of natural piety. The ties binding man to nature that poets have always celebrated are passed over lightly. The attitude taken is often that of man living in an indifferent and hostile world and issuing blasts of defiance. A religious attitude, however, needs a sense of the connection of man, in the way of both dependence and support, with the enveloping world that the imagination feels is a universe. Use of the words "God" or "divine" to convey the union of actual with ideal may protect man from a sense of isolation and from consequent despair or defiance. (LW, 9:36)

This is why I have urged that *A Common Faith* is directed more to the "aggressive atheist" than to the proponents of supernatural religions or, as Eldridge thinks, to liberals who still miss something religious in their lives. Dewey is not concerned that some vestigial, yet evanescent senti-ment from the age of belief be preserved, something that may have been felt as needed in his day but less and less as time goes on. Dewey is con-cerned that the old dualism that erected the supernatural through the identification of the real and ideal, a dualism that cut the nerve of creative growth and suppressed the religious quality of existence, might be repeated with a new form of atheistic dualism that equally suppresses the creative power of imagination and reduces life to the pain, vanity and nonsense of the immediate alone. "Were the naturalistic foundations and bearings of religion grasped," he concludes, "the religious element in life would emerge from the throes of the crisis in religion. Religion would then be found to have its natural place in every aspect of human experience that is concerned with estimate of possibilities. . . . All that is significant in human experience falls within this frame" (LW, 9:38–39).

This statement, especially the last sentence, signifies the centrality of this concern within Dewey's own general philosophical project. The problem of the "religious" is for him another way of addressing the prob-lem of experience itself as a whole. This is a claim that comes from the core of Dewey's being and is not a tangential remark that may or may not be vaguely consistent with his naturalism. In the next section, I will try to discern some moments that illustrate how and why this concern is reflected in Dewey's orientation as a philosopher and human being.

Part II: John Dewey's Spirituality

A LIFE ORIENTED TOWARD POSSIBILITY

Let us look, then, at some indications of the way in which Dewey's own spirituality manifested itself in the orientation of his "whole self" toward the Universe in terms of *possibility as such.* How did Dewey accept a life that acknowledged openness to possibility rather than retreat into a closed doctrine or some halfway compromise? That Dewey was raised by an evangelical mother and struggled with her religious temperament is often commented upon, but how Dewey interpreted or understood the struggle is not, except insofar as testifying to his desire to "overcome dualisms" even at a young age. What I believe was at issue—and gradu-ally made itself articulate to Dewey—was the way in which a religion that cultivated a sense of fear and sin was at odds with a spirituality that could be genuinely open to experience. In Dewey's youth, there were three things that helped turn him in the latter direction: a mentor (H. A. P. Torrey), a book (James Marsh's edition of Coleridge's *Aids to Reflection*), and an experience, which Dewey described many years later as "mystical." Later, as a young man, there were two further key figures, again a mentor and a text: George Sylvester Morris and the writings of Ralph Waldo Emerson. While in Dewey's view, Torrey and Marsh both ultimately remained caught in the conflict between their religious sensibility and the religion of Christianity, and so failed to achieve their full potentialities, Morris and Emerson represented individuals who were not so bound. While Dewey came to reject Morris's idealism without losing his esteem for Morris as a person, Emerson remained an important intellectual figure for him. It is Emerson's ultimate faith in the possibility of experience to embody the ideal that makes him, in Dewey's eyes, an archetypal philosopher, "the philosopher of democracy." When Dewey spoke on the centennial of Emerson's birth in 1903, he described him as being "the one citizen of the New World fit to have his name uttered in the same breath with that of Plato" (MW, 3:191). This was said at a crucial point in Dewey's own career, one that would lead him to become himself in the next four decades "the philosopher of democracy." Thus, after examining the early influences that opened up the "possibility of possibility" to Dewey, I will conclude with examining Dewey's assessment of Emerson as a paradigm philosopher, the philosopher of democracy, and what bearing this has on Dewey's own spirituality.

DEWEY'S REORIENTATION IN RELIGION

Let us begin with Dewey's early religious "choice," his rejection of his mother's strict form of evangelical Congregationalism. There are two well-known short accounts that Dewey gives in two autobiographical essays: the brief intellectual history he wrote in 1930, "From Absolutism to Experimentalism," and the more extended semi-autobiography coauthored with his daughter Jane, published in 1938 as part of the Library of Living Philosophers volume on him. Lucina Rich was not only much younger than her husband, she was also "more intense" and "stricter" than Archibald, whom Dewey called "easygoing." Though raised a Universalist, she became a Congregationalist as a result of revival meetings she attended as a young woman.[23] We hear of Lucina Rich Dewey persistently asking young John, "Are you right with Jesus?" and whether he had "prayed to God for forgiveness"—phrases that sum up the Protestant interpretation of spirituality as introspective self-criticism governed by a sense of a perpetual disposition to sin.[24] This had perhaps an added weight for John Dewey, who had been given the same name as his deceased older brother, John Archibald. The older brother was scalded to death as an infant, the guilt for which probably lay heavily upon Lucina's own conscience.[25] (John Dewey had no middle name, the blank further attesting to the dead brother.) Dewey remarks, "I was brought up in a conventionally evangelical atmosphere of the more 'liberal' sort; and the struggles that later arose between acceptance of that faith and the discarding of traditional and institutional creeds came from personal experiences and not from the effects of philosophical teaching" (LW, 5:149–50). In other words, the response to evangelical Christianity was based more on Dewey's own temperament and character than on an intellectual conflict with science. Dewey later comments upon "the sense of divisions and separations that were . . . borne in upon me as a consequence of a heritage of New England culture"; the divisions of "self from the world, of soul from the body, of nature from God," which Dewey felt as "a painful oppression—or rather, they were an inward laceration" (LW, 5:153). It is significant, I think, that two of the three divisions deal with spiritual concerns. Dewey's struggle was not an intellectual one between scientific theories and theological doctrines; it was deeper. It was about a worldview that young Dewey refused from the core of his being.

But what really was this refusal? One major form of the Protestant experience, that stemming from Luther and Calvin, has to begin with an awareness of sin and a fear of pride. One must constantly look inward to interpret the state of one's soul, but even that is unsure. To be in sin is to act from love of self rather than love of God—and since the Fall, all mankind is in a state of sin. It is impossible for us to transcend selfish motivation on our own. But God has chosen some for grace—not for any merit on their own parts, for mankind can do nothing to atone for

23. See discussions in "Biography of John Dewey" in Schilpp, 6, and Rockefeller, 35–39.
24. See George Dykhuizen, *The Life and Mind of John Dewey*, 7, and Rockefeller, 37.
25. See the account in Rockefeller, 36.

sin—but in order to manifest His glory. But, can one know if one is in a state of grace? By scrutinizing one's motives? Yet no matter how altruistic and selfless an act may seem, still at the root one may find, as Kant says, "the dear self." Such quandaries had led, after all, to Jonathan Edwards's *Treatise on the Religious Affections.* Grace can only exist as a pure act of inward faith in a predetermined set of beliefs and love of God and this is incapable of being proved by any outward act. It was just this sense of the futility of "works" to alleviate his sense of sin that consumed young Luther as a monk. Life is lived in fear of God and distrust of self, which, oddly, often result in rigid dogmatism. Thus there is in this type of Lutheran or Calvinist Protestantism also a disposition toward the judgmental and formal. Absolute values and the order of reality are absolutely determined before Creation. There is nothing we can do, and we cannot even know the state of our own souls; there is only the question of accepting God's will.

Though Dewey turned from this orientation, it is important to note that we still hear its voice at times in Dewey's private moments, that is, in his poetry, where his internal struggle is often itself the theme. One motif running through many poems is Dewey pleading with his stern conscience that drives him to the point of exhaustion and despair or upbraids him for standing back in order to enjoy the beauty of life's presence. For example,

> Comrade conscience, cease thy talk
> Your part but talk as mine was strife
> While I do take the flowered walk
> And dally with sweet soft things alluring
> Rested mayhap, I'll resume thy hard life
> Of search, stern comrade, for things enduring.[26]

Even more forceful is the following:

> Not now thy scourging rod—
> Thy staff, instead, oh God;—
> Something to support and stay,
> A guide along the ling'ring way.

---

26. *The Poems of John Dewey,* ed. ann Boydston (Carbondale: S. Illinois University Press, 1977), no. 43. "To Conscience," 29.

Thy wrathful rod withold
E'en though my sins be infinite, untold,
Since to punish thou hast eternity,
Now for a little space let be, let be.
Spare thy just avenging wrath
Walk with me a grassy path
Beside still waters for a little hour . . .[27]

And elsewhere, he says "Great God, I thee implore. . . . A little space in which to move . . . A little time in which to love. . . ."[28] The Puritan voice may have been overcome in Dewey's mind, but it had not been stilled. It spoke, but was refused.

Dewey's earliest essay on religion, "The Place of Religious Emotion" (1886), presents clearly and forcefully a protest against the religious upbringing he had been given by his mother. He says, "There are two unhealthy developments of emotion. . . . One is deadness or apathy of feeling. The other is undue or unregulated stimulation. It is as certain as anything can be, that without a spontaneous and active interest in things that are lovely and of good report, there will be no sincere devotion, no earnest service" (EW, 1:90). The sign of unhealthy religious emotion is, says Dewey quoting Martineau, "keenly watching the spiritual weather in the mind, gauging the affections, refining the temperature, describing the clouds, but spell-bound in the personal atmosphere and never carried out into the light of lights" (EW, 1:91). "Religious feeling," Dewey adds in his own words, "is unhealthy when it is watched and analyzed to see if it exists, if it is right, if it is growing"—the very thing his mother's question had asked.

When Dewey rejected his childhood religion, he was rejecting a whole conception of life based upon fear and a sense of the dependence of human existence upon an arbitrary will that could not be changed.[29] But he was also rejecting the life of endless inward self-scrutinizing. Thus, in turning from his mother's religion, Dewey was not just rejecting "divisions" but a life based on "fear and trembling." The antithesis of such an attitude would be to look outward toward the emotional, creative, and

27. Ibid., no. 136.
28. Ibid., 8.
29. For studies of Calvin and Calvinism, see H. O. Taylor, *Thought and Expression in the Sixteenth Century*; Perry Miller, *Jonathan Edwards*; and Herbert Schneider, *The Puritan Mind*.

practical world of "works," a faith not in doctrine or dogma but in life's possibilities. And though his desire for wholeness at first led him to embrace a form of absolute idealism, it also afterward led him away from it—toward a worldview that acknowledged consciously the reality of possibility and contingency. But at this early stage, before his encounter with idealism, we can see three influences that helped redirect his life: his teacher H. A. P. Torrey, James Marsh's edition of Coleridge's *Aids to Reflection*, and the "mystical experience" Dewey had as a young man in Oil City, Pennsylvania.

Dewey expressed particular fondness and indebtedness to his college mentor, H. A. P. Torrey. Dewey comments in both autobiographical essays on the liberal atmosphere of the University of Vermont—"liberal" as "in the Congregational type" where "the emphasis on evolution aroused little, if any visible resentment" (LW, 5:148).[30] Dewey had been given a vision of the idea of organic unity in his exposure to Thomas Huxley's *Elements of Physiology and Hygiene*. But Torrey himself awakened Dewey's mind to the possibility of thinking. Like other seniors, he took capstone courses from Torrey, including one on Butler's *Analogy of Religion*, which Dewey remembered for its "cold logic and acute analysis" (LW, 5:150). Philosophically, Torrey was something of an intellectual chimera: liberal Christianity combined with Scottish intuitionism and German idealism via Coleridge and Marsh. Dewey remembered him as "a man of a genuinely sensitive and cultivated mind" and also as a victim of his environment and timidity. Dewey says that "in a more congenial atmosphere than that of New England in those days, he would have achieved something significant. He was, however, constitutionally timid, and never really let his mind go"; Dewey saw this as the indication of "an inner conflict that prevented his native capacity from coming to full fruition" (LW, 5: 148). This is a close echo to Dewey's own inner conflicts.

Later, three years after his graduation, Torrey spent a year privately mentoring Dewey in philosophy, and it was here Dewey saw him "let his mind go more freely than in the classroom" and reveal a potentiality he had not seen before (LW, 5:149). Thus, in the end, while being an inspiration, Torrey was also a walking lesson in how unresolved internal conflicts and a certain intellectual fear can lead to intellectual and

30. Schilpp, 10.

experientially dead "solutions." If Lucina Dewey's Christianity represented one form of life based on fear, Torrey's timidity and his unconsummated thought represented another. I think it would be easy to underestimate the impact such an experience might have on a shy young man beginning to discover he could think for himself. In the words of *A Common Faith*, Torrey lacked moral faith.[31]

Torrey introduced Dewey to one book in particular that spoke to him at this crucial stage in his life: Coleridge's *Aids to Reflection*. The book was locally famous because James Marsh, who had prepared the American edition with a renowned introductory essay, had been President of the University of Vermont in Dewey's home town of Burlington. This was an important book that had helped inaugurate Transcendentalism in America.[32] Marsh himself remained something of a hero to Dewey, even in his later years. Herbert Schneider recalled how difficult it was to get Dewey to reminisce, but "Finally, at some birthday dinner we gave for him, we bought him a copy of Marsh's 1829 edition of Coleridge's *Aids to Reflection* and asked him whether this recalled anything to his mind. Then he opened up and said, 'Yes, I remember very well that this was our spiritual emancipation in Vermont. Coleridge's idea of the spirit came to us as a real relief because we could be both liberal and pious; and this . . . book, especially Marsh's edition, was my first Bible.'"[33] (Note: not his *second* but his *first* Bible.) Schneider reaffirmed this later in an interview, recalling Dewey as saying, "All I can do on religion is to say again what I learned from Coleridge way back in my childhood, and this *A Common Faith* is, as far as I am concerned, just a restatement of my early faith that I got at the University of Vermont through Marsh and Coleridge."[34]

Coleridge places the whole emphasis of the spiritual life on reflective experience and action over doctrine. Dewey wrote an insightful essay commemorating the hundredth anniversary of Marsh's edition. Of Marsh himself, Dewey says, "Were I to attempt to select a single passage that might serve as an illuminating text of what he thought and taught, it would be, I think, the following: The thinking man 'has and can have but

31. See Rockefeller, 53ff.

32. See Rockefeller, 12, and Octavius Brooks Frothingham, *Transcendentalism in New England* (1876).

33. *Dialogue on John Dewey* (New York: Horizon Press, Inc., 1959), 7.

34. Stephen Rockefeller, *John Dewey*, 56–57. See discussion on 57–60.

one system in which his philosophy becomes religious and his religion philosophical'" (LW, 5:183). Stephen Rockefeller notes, regarding this passage, that Marsh's edition "encouraged his faith in intelligence and philosophical quest. It assured him that he could be both 'liberal and pious.'"[35] This remains something of an understatement, for it suggests the sort of compromise that had been reached by Torrey—and which Dewey also rejected. What Dewey found in Coleridge (and Marsh's interpretation of him) was an unequivocal statement of faith in the possibility of one's own experience to be the source of redemptive existence: *that* was the source of true religion. In his commemorative essay, Dewey says that Marsh, following Coleridge, was concerned with "the re-awakening of a truly spiritual religion which had been obscured and depressed under the prevalent philosophies of Locke and the Scottish school" (LW, 5:182). It was, in other words, a spirituality that avoided doctrinalism for what Dewey calls "moral faith."

As Coleridge himself says in the *Aids*, "To restore a commonplace truth to its first uncommon lustre," he says, "you need only translate it into action. But to do that you must have reflected on its truth."[36] Reflection is quite different from the introspective self-criticism suggested by Lucina's "being right with Jesus." Reflection is taking a truth beyond analytical reasoning into the synthetic world of imagination; in the case of the moral life, when prudence ceases merely to follow established moral rules and becomes a spiritual organ of the moral life, it is "holy prudence," a power that gives the individual a faith in his or her own creative powers in relation to the world. Coleridge says that "the most frequent impediment to men's turning the mind inward upon themselves is that they are afraid of what they shall find there."[37] For Coleridge, this meant in particular a willingness to go beyond the conventional, unthinking acceptance of words and instead to treat them with an "experimentative faith" because "if they are not things, they are living powers."[38] The practical lesson from Coleridge is not some "rational" reconciliation of Christian doctrine with liberalism (as with poor Torrey),

---

35. See Rockefeller, 57.
36. Samuel Taylor Coleridge, *Aids to Reflection*, ed. James Marsh (Burlington: University of Vermont Press, 1829), Aphorism III.
37. Ibid., Aphorism XIX.
38. Ibid., preface, 64–65.

but a liberation of the conscience to have faith in itself in relation to the world as illumined by a spiritual imagination. As James Garrison says, "Spirituality for Samuel T. Coleridge was the living principle of unity and the source of all creative synthesis." It is "the hidden meaning of all method and art"—the creative imagination—that integrates otherwise fragmentary experience.[39] Imagination, in its primary sense, is beyond volition and control and involves the inward openness to the creative roots of all experience. This appeal to the "deep self" becomes the basis of the spiritual life in *Aids to Reflection*. As we have seen, the fundamental problem of *A Common Faith* is described precisely in terms of "imagination"—how the "Universe" is imagined and how the self is imagined in relation to it.

In his essay on Marsh, Dewey himself notes Coleridge's "radicalism" in his attack on doctrinal "bibliolatry." For Coleridge (and Marsh), "Faith was a state of will and affections, not merely an intellectual assent to doctrinal and historical propositions"; "knowledge of spiritual truth is always more than theoretical and intellectual. It was the product of activity as well as its cause. It had to be lived in order to be known" (LW, 5:181, 196). Here the Protestant conscience becomes the servant of emotionalized experience and aestheticized nature, its discipline transformed into a method for wisdom. Where Dewey eventually parts from Coleridge, as Garrison says, is where Coleridge affirms the identification of the ideal with the real by appealing to figures like Schelling, Plotinus, and Plato.[40]

In light of this, it is of more than passing interest that Dewey in 1929 ultimately passed a judgment upon Marsh very similar to that he would upon Torrey the next year. Dewey is at pains in his essay to show Marsh's radicalism, for with the passage of time Marsh had come to appear as a conservative. And yet, Dewey notes, "Marsh shrank from controversy; he deprecated becoming involved in it" (LW, 5:182). While Marsh yearned for a truly spiritual Christianity rather than "a mere body of doctrines," he was afraid of being confused with "unbelieving critics." "The situation in which he thus found himself accounts, I think," says Dewey, "for the air of apologetic timidity which surrounds the expression

---

39. James Garrison, "Dewey, Coleridge, and Spirituality as Poetic Unity" (unpublished essay), 1.
40. Garrison continues with a fascinating comparison of Coleridge's methodology with Dewey's instrumentalism, relying primarily upon Coleridge's *The Friend*.

of his deepest thoughts" (LW, 5:184). As with Torrey, this was partly due to the times but also to "his modest distrust of himself." Dewey notes—again like his assesment of Torrey—that Marsh had a genuinely philosophical mind, but reined it in because of his desire to conform to Christianity. "He never developed the independence in thought which matched his philosophic powers" (LW, 5:184). While Marsh may have helped inaugurate Transcendentalism, Dewey notes that "he never had that detached position which marked Emerson . . . and accordingly did not reach an unimpeded development of his own powers" (LW, 5:184; see 196). In the language of *A Common Faith,* Marsh and Torrey both suffered from allowing "a religion" to constrict a genuinely religious sensibility whereas Emerson did not. Dewey concludes, "Religion was to him the supreme worth, yet his conception of what constitutes religion was a virtual condemnation of a large part of what passed in his time and still passes for religion"; Marsh "wished to use scholarship and philosophy to awaken his fellow countrymen to a sense of the possibilities that were theirs by right as men, and to quicken them to realize these possibilities in themselves" (LW, 5:196). It is important to note here that Emerson is selected as an example of one who succeeded in escaping the constrictions of "religion."

Dewey's assessments of Torrey and Marsh may help us to understand the so-called mystic experience that Dewey referred to in his 1942 interview with Max Eastman and which has received curious, amused, or awkward acknowledgment in the literature. The fact that Dewey chose to remember the experience in his eighties itself is significant. It happened when Dewey was a young high school teacher in Oil City, barely in his twenties. Eastman reports, "One evening while he sat reading he had what he calls a 'mystic experience.' It was an answer to that question which still worried him: whether he still meant business when he prayed. It was not a very dramatic mystic experience. There was no vision, not even a definable emotion—just a supremely blissful feeling that his worries were over." Eastman quotes Dewey's own effort to put this experience into words: "'What the hell are you worrying about, anyway? Everything that's here is here, and you can just lie back on it.'" Dewey added, "I've never had *any* doubts since then, nor any beliefs. To me faith means not worrying. I claim I've got religion and I got it that night in Oil City."⁴¹ He likened this faith to the "poetic pantheism" (Eastman's words) of Wordsworth, "whom he was reading at that time," and of Whitman.

This last comment is perhaps the telltale part of the story, for it acknowledges the deep connection Dewey had to the romantic poets in general. Ideals must be presented in imagination, says Dewey. The romantic poets certainly shaped Dewey's imagination, and a comment needs to be made about them. Wordsworth's and Coleridge's *Lyrical Ballads* was a revolutionary volume when it appeared in 1798. It violated all the standards of English classicism embodied in the work of Alexander Pope—the use of wit and reason for the end of edification. This is found in Wordsworth's poems about "common subjects" speaking rustic English and in Coleridge's use of the supernatural in his contribution, *The Rime of the Ancient Mariner*. The break with the poetry of the preceding age was also sharply put forth in Wordsworth's accompanying essay, which declared that the aim of poetry is to heal the dualism generated in modern times between man and nature which had resulted in the atrophy of natural human feeling. Later, in the autobiographical epic poem *The Prelude*, Wordsworth would tell how his early childhood experiences growing up in the country led him to experience the world as sacred, beginning with the intertwining of the music of his nurse's lullabies with the sounds of the stream beside his home. Whitman's *Leaves of Grass*, which first appeared in 1855, likewise asserted a rough solidarity with the beauty of ordinary, "low" subjects, especially "the common people," whom Whitman described in his introduction as "unrhymed poetry." Whitman also defiantly asserted that the "Americans of all nations at any time upon the earth have probably the fullest poetical nature."⁴² "The greatest poet hardly knows pettiness or triviality," said Whitman, "If he breathes into anything that was before thought small it dilates with the grandeur and life of the universe."⁴³ If ever there was a poet who would have agreed with the voice of Dewey's mystical experience, it is Walt Whitman. Whatever the origin of that experience, the result was

41. Eastman, "John Dewey," *Atlantic Monthly* 168 (1941), 673.
42. Walt Whitman, *Walt Whitman's Leaves of Grass: First (1855) Edition*, ed. Malcolm Cowley (New York: Viking, 1959), introduction, 6.
43. Ibid., 9.

exactly the sort of organization of the whole self" that Dewey speaks of in *A Common Faith*, and the possibility of that orientation is to be found in Marsh, Coleridge and the Romantics. It involves acknowledgment that above and beyond the conscious intellect is a fecund, creative source for experience, meaning, and reason.

A former student of Dewey's, Earl Peckham, recalls one class in which he asked Dewey, "Doesn't emotion play a part in the thought process?" Peckham says, "His stare fixed on me. I was embarrassed. He was silent— then he walked slowly over to the window and looked into the night, for the better part of two minutes. Then he looked back and fixed his stare on me . . . and said in a very slow and almost inaudible voice . . . 'Knowledge is a small cup of water floating on a sea of emotion.'"[44]

This story summarizes one of the most important revolutions Dewey achieved: the recognition of emotion, aesthetic quality, and imagination as essential aspects of the meaningful way we experience the world and of our intelligent conduct in it. Dewey's refusal to treat all forms of experience as instances of "knowing" and his acknowledgement of radical indeterminacy affect every aspect of his thought. To take such a step would be a major decision for a philosopher, and that is how Dewey experienced it. Dewey had two positive examples, one a teacher and the other a thinker who came to exemplify for him the sort of faith in experience and independence of mind he found ultimately lacking in Torrey and Marsh. The teacher was George Sylvester Morris and the thinker was Ralph Waldo Emerson.

DEWEY'S PHILOSOPHICAL DECISION

In "From Absolutism to Experimentalism," Dewey makes a revealing comment that has attracted little notice: "I imagine that my development has been controlled largely by a struggle between a native inclination toward the schematic and formally logical, and those incidents of personal experience that compelled me to take account of actual material" (LW, 5:150). Dewey further states that the "emphasis upon the concrete, empirical, and 'practical' in my later writings" was contrary to his "natural tendencies," and this is what has made thinking and writing for him "hard work" in contrast to his early period, when they were

44. Robert Bruce Williams, *John Dewey: Recollections* (Washington D.C.: The University Press of America, 1982), 127.

"comparatively easy" (LW, 5:150–51). Dewey's mature work is often criticized for vagueness and a lack of formal rigor, as if Dewey had a natural tendency to the one and an aversion to the latter. But what he says in this passage is the opposite—that his natural tendency was toward the formal and rigorous, but that it was "personal experience" and "actual material" that "compelled" him to turn from his natural bent. That Dewey did not instinctively shy away from formalism and in fact inclined toward it is borne out in his first book, *Psychology*, which is a systematic tapestry. Dewey's often-criticized manner of writing is not the result of a character trait, one that philosophers generally attempt to correct, but of a philosophical *decision*. The question to ask is, Why did he make it?

His decision to turn from the "logical and schematically formal" and to emphasize the "concrete, empirical and practical" precisely came about in an effort *to correct* what he saw as a philosophical flaw in his character. That is, it was the temptation to the formal that was the flaw he found in himself *as a philosopher*. He says that his tendency in that direction "was a protest and protection against something in myself which, in the pressure of the weight of actual experiences, I knew to be a weakness." It would have been easy, he says, "to give way to the dialectic development of a theme" but "the pressure of concrete experiences was, however, sufficiently heavy, so that a sense of intellectual honesty prevented a surrender to that course" (LW, 5:150–51). Whatever the flaws of his style, born of the "struggle" in himself, Dewey says that he remains wary of "a tendency of other thinkers and writers to achieve a specious lucidity and simplicity by the mere process of ignoring considerations which a greater respect for concrete materials of experience would have forced upon them" (LW, 5:151). It is not clear what Dewey means exactly by "concrete materials of experience" or the "protest and protection against something in myself" that a formal philosophy offered by contrast. But the question, as it posed itself to Dewey, was one of intellectual courage—avoiding the easy, but "specious" line of schematic, formal thought for the more difficult engagement with a world that did not conform so well to that desire.[45]

I believe this is Dewey's own confession of his yearning, his personal "quest for certainty." The ideal of certainty offers a temptation to turn

---

45. I think the more extensive answer Dewey himself gives is the first chapter—the original especially—of *Experience and Nature*. See "Dewey's Denotative Method," chapter 2 in this volume.

that ideal into an object of belief, an actuality, and to ignore precisely what counts against it, what Dewey calls "the precarious" and noncognitive or qualitative dimensions of existence. Because nature has such traits that are so resistant to knowledge or logical articulation, philosophers who have given in to this weakness, who have failed the test, ignore, dismiss or degrade them to lower levels of being. The challenge that Dewey felt to call forth his integrity as a philosopher, that oriented his "whole self" to "the Universe," was an existential moment for him to acknowledge the dimension of "possibility as such," as I have called it.

I suggest this confessional statement connects with those other deep experiences mentioned: the rejection of Congregationalism, the promises and compromises of Torrey and Marsh, the mystical experience. The temptations to a false certainty or superficial compromises to maintain doctrinal commitments were rejected by Dewey as a philosopher as they had been in his religious emancipation. What this meant was to live by a faith in the possibility—not the actuality—of the ideal without disregarding the radical contingency of the world and the limitations of our best knowledge and intelligence at any given time.

To call such an event a decision or an existential moment in Dewey's life makes it sound too punctual; in fact it applies to the long development of Dewey's early philosophy, from his first effort to substitute empirical psychology for Hegel's dialectic through his Chicago years as an "experimental idealist."[46] When Dewey did ultimately abandon idealism as a viable solution, it was precisely because he saw it as incapable of attending to the empirical matters at issue, among which was the need to make ideals genuine guides to action because they were not preexistent actualities. Dewey's refusal of formalism, as an act of intellectual courage as well as honesty, I believe, is one of the most significant aspects of his own orientation, that is, spirituality, and certainly is *the* determining feature of his mature thought as a whole, even in—especially in—*Logic: the Theory of Inquiry.*[47]

---

46. See Dewey's first essays, such as "The New Psychology" (EW, 1). By 1894 Dewey calls himself an experimental idealist in his *Ethics: A Handbook* (EW, 4:264). For a discussion of Dewey's idealist phase see "The Aesthetics of Reality" (chapter 1 this volume) and chapter 2 of my *John Dewey's Theory of Art, Experience, and Nature.*

47. The preceding discussion gives a particular significance to Dewey's struggle with logic throughout his career; this is Dewey trying to come to peace with his formal and schematic side in an intellectually satisfying—and honest—way.

FROM "ABSOLUTIST" TO "EXPERIMENTALIST": MORRIS AND IDEALISM

Dewey's regard for George Sylvester Morris is widely recognized in the biographies. He never describes Morris with the qualifications he has for Torrey or Marsh. What comes across is the passion and vitality with which Morris engaged philosophy. Through Morris, Dewey was exposed to and embraced absolute idealism, especially as represented in the work of Thomas Hill Green. Yet within a year of Morris's death, Dewey had begun to criticize Green's version of idealism—and then Morris's own—precisely on the question of treating ideals as actualities rather than as possibilties so they could be effective in action. Ever since its publication in 1890, Dewey had been struggling to assimilate William James's *Principles of Psychology*. Yet for a time Dewey moved closer to Hegel, though still keeping the dialectic at arm's length.[48] With his move to Chicago in 1894, psychology once again seemed to offer an alternative, now in the form of pedagogical psychology, the psychology of how humans actually learn, to the Hegelian method of displaying the absolute as the ultimate presupposition and condition of anything else being known, or being at all. It is at this point that Dewey actually begins to criticize and improve upon James's theory of emotion and account of learning and to develop his own "circuit of coordination" to replace the "reflex arc concept." During this time, Dewey becomes very quiet about "idealism."

When Dewey actually "abandoned" idealism is a matter of dispute. In his autobiographical essay "From Absolutism to Experimentalism" he refers vaguely to a fifteen-year period of "drifting" away from Hegelianism, and this is where he ends the tale of his development. In 1903, with the publication of *Studies in Logical Theory*, Dewey might still have been seen as the head of "the Chicago School" of idealism, though Dewey's own essays, which were highly critical of Lötze, were later reprinted in the "instrumentalist" text, *Essays in Empirical Logic*.[49] Certainly by 1905, with

48. For criticisms of Green see "The Philosophy of Thomas Hill Green" (EW, 3:14–35) and "Self-Realization as the Moral Ideal" (EW, 4:42–53). For Dewey's move toward Hegel, see "The Present Position in Logical Theory" (EW, 3:125–41, esp. 138).
49. Dewey does not give a particular date for his abandonment of idealism; he refers vaguely to a period of "drifting" in the 1890s. With Dewey's leaving Chicago in 1904 and his arrival at Columbia in 1905, there is a noticeable change, an attack not only on idealism but on all forms of philosophy that identify the real with the known. I would place the division in 1905 with the essay "The Postulate of Immediate Empiricism." But see Dewey's 1906 presidential address to the APA, "Beliefs and Existences," as well as the piece he wrote the next year, "Experience and Objective Idealism." These essays seem to be about as public a rejection of idealism as one could ask for.

his move to Columbia, Dewey aligned himself with the radical empiricism of James and others, opposing both idealists and realists. At the end of that year, in his Presidential Address to the American Philosophical Association, he made this explicit.[50] The next year he published a sweeping critique of idealism from Plato on.[51]

The year before Dewey left Chicago, in 1903, he gave a paper commemorating the centennial of Emerson's birth. We have already seen that Dewey regarded Emerson as an example of one who did not make halfway compromises in the manner of Torrey or Marsh. But in his 1903 essay Dewey goes much further, presenting Emerson as "the philosopher of democracy" for reasons that would, in the next five decades of Dewey's career, apply even more to Dewey himself. Dewey's commemorative essay for the celebration of his eightieth birthday, "Creative Democracy—The Task Before Us," when read in conjunction with the essay on Emerson, makes the latter quite prophetic of Dewey himself. It is perhaps a coincidence that in 1903, as Dewey was on the verge of rejecting idealism, he should happen to write on Emerson. But it is precisely here that I believe Emerson becomes significant in understanding Dewey, especially in terms of his spirituality; that is, in terms of the "orientation" of his whole self.

ANTITHETICAL ARCHETYPES: HERBERT SPENCER
AND RALPH WALDO EMERSON

In his reflection upon the meaning of Emerson as an American philosopher, Dewey was also conjuring up an archetype of the philosopher he wanted to be. In addition, it allowed him to formulate more consciously the sort of philosopher he did *not* want to be. The following year after his essay on Emerson, Dewey published an excoriating critique of Herbert Spencer, who represents for Dewey the very antithesis of what a philosopher should be, an opposing antitype to Emerson's archetype. Read together, the two essays are something of a moral diptych: Good Philosopher and Bad Philosopher, as Darnell Rucker has noted.[52]

50. "Beliefs and Existences," in MW, 3:83ff. Also published in *The Influence of Darwin on Philosophy and Other Essays in Contemporary Thought* (New York: Holt, 1910).

51. "Experience and Objective Idealism," in MW, 3:128ff., and in *The Influence of Darwin on Philosophy.*

52. Darnell Rucker, introduction, MW, 3:xx.

The essay on Spencer gives us a portrait of one who has succumbed to the "schematic and formal" temptation completely; that is, a portrait of the sort of thinker Dewey might have been. Using Henry James's assessment of Emile Zola, whom Dewey found similar to Spencer, Dewey comments on the way in which both men's work is testimony to "sitting down to achieve a preconceived idea—an idea, moreover, of a synthetic and deductive rendering of all that is in the Universe" (MW, 3:194). From beginning to end, Dewey finds Spencer's work "detached . . . a rounded out and closed interpretation of the Universe." Unlike the systems of genuine thinkers like Aristotle or Hegel, whose thought has a unity because of "the unity of the *development* of a single mind," Spencer's "was a system in conception, not merely in issue" (MW, 3:195). Like Zola's work, the whole was as if willed into being from the start. Dewey then delivers what, in his view, must be the harshest judgment of all: In the place of genuine experience, with all its "qualities of individual contact and career," with its "accidents of circumstance, and corresponding emotional entanglements," Spencer substituted "experience by imitation," in which all these elements have been "shut out" (MW, 3:195). Philosophy by its nature must aim at *some* abstraction and seek the general. But Spencer's system has from the beginning decisively excluded *all* concrete material. The result, says Dewey, is a system that is "awful in its augustness" and "a piece of intellectual audacity of the most commanding sort" (MW, 3:196). It did not grow because it never was alive. Moreover, Spencer thought in a vacuum: personally remote, ignorant of ancient and modern languages and literature, and "devoid of historical sense." Dewey comments, "Certainly the world may wait long for another example of a man who dares to conceive and has the courage and energy to execute a system of philosophy, in almost total ignorance of the entire history of thought" (MW, 3:197). It is not the lack of knowledge that appalls Dewey so much as the absence of any *interest* in history or awareness how it affects thought. Spencer has no sense of the vitality and moving life of ideas, "of discovery, experimentation, and struggle" (MW, 3:197).

Let us turn, then, to Dewey's contrasting essay on Emerson. To defend the claim that Emerson is more than an essayist and is a philsopher, one might expect some excuse to be made at the start for the rhapsodic, unrigorous nature of his writing. But Dewey did not choose this route and took a surprisingly more forceful approach: As noted, he thought Emerson is "the one citizen of the New World fit to have his name uttered in the same breath with that of Plato." He who dismisses Emerson as a philosopher "but writes down his own incapacity to follow a logic that is finely wrought" (MW, 3:184). These are quite extraordinary claims: Emerson is a *paradigm philosopher*, not someone who might "possibly be considered a philosopher" in some generously open-minded moment. Dewey then quotes from Emerson's "Intellect": "We want in every man a long logic; we cannot pardon the absence of it, but it must not be spoken. Logic is the procession or proportionate unfolding of the intuition; but its virtue is as silent method; the moment it would appear as propositions and have a separate value, it is worthless." This is an insight that goes to the heart of the problem of philosophy for Dewey because "The desire for an articulate, not for a silent, logic is intrinsic with philosophy" (MW, 3:185). Emersonian (and Deweyan) logic is an art that emerges from experience and develops it. But experience precedes logic and is a noncognitive condition for it. This will be the central claim of one of Dewey's most radical essays, "The Postulate of Immediate Empiricism," which appeared with his move to Columbia in 1905. It is also the developing theme of his "instrumentalism," leading up to the long and important introduction to *Essays in Experimental Logic* (1916), to *Experience and Nature* itself, to the crucial, difficult essay "Qualitative Thought" (1930) and, at last, to *Logic: The Theory of Inquiry* (1938). In Dewey's language, conscious reasoning is ultimately dependent upon the unconscious body of intelligent habits that constitute the prereflective, qualitative "feel" and sense of the world. And this is what is ignored by all philosophies that presume to turn the world entirely into an object of knowledge and to assert that what is "real" is at heart "rational." Dewey's name for this is "the philosopher's fallacy."

And yet, Dewey affirms, "Emerson's whole work [is] a hymn to intelligence, a paean to the all-creating, all-disturbing power of thought" (MW, 3:187). This is an expression of faith, "the faith of the thinker," not of a creed or dogma. But whereas most philosophers make their "distinctions and classifications" true because of some system—and the example of Spencer should be remembered here—Emerson tested them against life. The great figures of the past, not just philosophers, but poets and all "representative men," are important above all for indicating to us our own power to make experience meaningful, whatever they may have said or done. The potential richness of our own experience should carry the weight of meaning for existence. This was the thought that Emerson set forth in *Nature* and it is what marks Dewey's faith in turning from his temperamental refuge of form and system to experience itself. "Against creed and system, convention and institution, Emerson stands for restoring to the common man that which in the name of religion, of philosophy, of art and of morality, has been embezzled from the common store and appropriated to sectarian and class use" (MW, 3:190). This is why Emerson is "the Philosopher of Democracy" for Dewey. The democratic philosopher restores to our daily experience recognition of its power to produce all that is of value and meaning. (And this will be the driving, central insight of Dewey's own *Art as Experience.*) If philosophy must inevitably be concerned with articulating meanings in a rational order, this does not deny that a fundamental aesthetic and poetic insight is primary. The two, reason and intuition, philosopher and poet, are not ultimately opposed, insists Dewey—indeed, those who assert they are Dewey calls "sophists" and not "philosophers" (MW, 3:186).

If Plato ultimately gave rise to the philosophy that separated poetry and philosophy, though he himself combined them, and became the archetype of "the philosopher of dualism" and "the philosopher of aristocracy," Emerson embodies a different archetype: the philosopher of democracy. This is not because of his individualism or because of any specific doctrine, including "Transcendentalism." It is because of his faith in experience. "For thousands of earth's children, Emerson has taken away the barriers that shut out the sun and has secured the unimpeded, cheerful circulation of the light of heaven, and the wholesome air of day" (MW, 3:191). Of course this sums up the central aim of Dewey's mature philosophy. Dewey had expressed such thoughts before this with respect to the aims of education, as in the famous statement "My Pedagogic Creed" (1897). But it is in the context of his essay on Emerson that such aims become defining of the democratic philosopher as such.

The key for democratic philosophy is not some theory of equality or even of representative government. It is the philosophical acknowledgment of the meaning of the world that lies beyond and that gives rise to intelligence itself. In *Art as Experience,* Dewey praises Keats because he knew that "reason at its height cannot attain complete grasp and a self-contained assurance. It must fall back upon imagination—upon the embodiment of ideas in emotionally charged sense" (LW, 10:40). Quoting Keats's famous lines "Beauty is truth, truth beauty—that is all / Ye know on earth and all ye need to know," Dewey states that "truth" is not mere "correctness" but "the wisdom by which men live." Because we live "in a world of surmise, of mystery, of uncertainties," says Dewey, "'Reasoning' must fail man . . ." But instead of turning to revelation, "the insight of imagination must suffice." True wisdom lies in accepting what Keats called "negative capability" and "half-knowledge." Dewey concludes, "Ultimately there are but two philosophies. One of them accepts life and experience in all its uncertainty, mystery, doubt, and half-knowledge and turns that experience upon itself to deepen and intensify its own qualities—to imagination and art" (LW, 10:41). This is, in effect, a statement of Dewey's own philosophical allegiance. It is also a statement of the faith that is expressed in the book published the same year as *Art as Experience*; that is, *A Common Faith*.

CODA: SPIRITUALITY AS WONDER—DEWEY ON CLAUDE MCKAY

It is said that when Santayana was asked what he thought about *A Common Faith* his response was, "Very common indeed." Though I have dealt with the term "faith," perhaps something needs to be said about the word "common." For Dewey, it does not mean "ordinary, insignificant, uninteresting." It refers to the inherent capacity of experience to generate and embody those values and meanings that fulfill human existence.

In 1948 Claude McKay, a Jamaican poet of the Harlem Renaissance, was in poverty and failing health. He had met Dewey years earlier and spent an evening with him and the Italian-born journalist and IWW activist Carlo Tresca discussing Trotsky over a bottle of wine.[53] He asked Dewey to write an introduction to a final collection of his poems. Dewey agreed. It would be one of the last pieces Dewey wrote. Dewey obviously liked the poems, especially those dealing with McKay's childhood in Jamaica. Of those he said,

> Were I to single out one line from the poems to convey what comes nearest to telling what the poems mean to me I think it would be from 'North and South,' reading
> *And wonder to life's commonplaces clings.*
> I realize that the eyes of insensitive readers may linger on 'commonplaces' and less lightly [sic] over the wonder that clings to them.

53. Wayne Cooper, *Claude McKay* (Baton Rouge: Louisiana State University Press, 1987), 365.

But that wonder which never fails or falters in the case of Claude McKay's vision is that in which commonplaces are identical with what is common in the life of all men since it cannot be escaped and yet is capable of being expressed only by one who has like McKay the eyes of a poet and the voice of a singer. (LW, 17:58)

It is indicative of Dewey's spirituality that he also acknowledged the power of McKay's poem "Baptism," which expressed bitterness over the racism he had experienced in life. Dewey recognized that "the poem is deeply dyed with hate, but with a hate that is clean, never mean or spiteful." Dewey's spirituality did not believe that our differences would be automatically resolved, but he believed that by knowing where we were, and by having faith in the capacity of human experience to grow, we could find, eventually, a way for making our lives ways of "walking to old age in beauty," as the Navajo prayer says: *Sa'a naghai bik'e hozho.*

SIXTEEN

EROS AND SPIRIT

Toward a Humanistic Philosophy of Culture

"Philosophy and Civilization" is one of Dewey's most important—and most neglected—essays. It is unsettling to anyone who wants to think of Dewey primarily as a "pragmatist," since Dewey says the aim of philosophy should be to deal with the meaning of culture and not "inquiry" or "truth." He says, "Meaning is wider in scope as well as more precious in value than is truthm and philosophy is occupied with meaning rather than with truth" (LW, 3:4). Truths are one kind of meaning, but they are only an "island" lying in "the ocean of meanings to which truth and falsity are irrelevant. We do not inquire whether Greek civilization was true or false, but we are immensely concerned to penetrate its meaning," he adds, and continues, "In philosophy we are dealing with something comparable to the meaning of Athenian civilization or of a drama or a lyric" (LW, 3:5). He concludes by saying:

> As long as we worship science and are afraid of philosophy we shall have no great science. . . . As far as any plea is implicit in what has been said, it is, then, a plea for the casting off of that intellectual

timidity which hampers the wings of imagination, a plea for speculative audacity, for more faith in ideas, sloughing off a cowardly reliance
upon those partial ideas to which we are wont to give the name of facts.
(LW, 3:10)

Many "Deweyans" given that quotation without its source would
repudiate it. The dominance of scientism, the worship of science, is such
a pervasive phenomenon in Anglophone philosophical culture that to
question it seems almost to be an attack on philosophy itself. Nevertheless,
my concern here will be to follow Dewey's advice and articulate elements
of a philosophy of civilization. I speak more within the humanist than the
pragmatist tradition. I think that to characterize American philosophy
primarily as "pragmatism" is a disservice to its pluralism. Even to characterize James, Peirce, and Dewey essentially as "pragmatists" is narrowing.
Aristotle was a logician, but we do not call his thought "logicism"; logic
was only an organon for philosophy, not philosophy itself. So, too, should
we regard the "pragmatism" of James, Peirce, or Dewey as an organon of
their thought and try to describe their philosophical positions in a more
holistic way. After all, Dewey called his own position "naturalistic humanism" or "cultural naturalism," not "instrumentalism." Thus my objective
will be to expand the critical horizon beyond pragmatism to humanism,
beyond science to culture.

I will sketch a philosophy of culture drawing on Royce, Peirce, Dewey,
and Mead and locate the role of philosophy within it. I draw upon the
American tradition; I do not intend to advocate "Americanism." I am
mindful of a warning that Dewey delivers (also in "Philosophy and
Civilization"): "A deliberate striving for an American Philosophy as such
would be only another evidence of emptiness and impotency" (LW, 3:9).
I propose to understand cultures as "spiritual ecologies" that sustain that
basic need for meaning that I have called "the Human Eros." A cultural
or spiritual ecology is structured around key modes of forming the
identity of self and world. The narrative mode I call "Mythos," while
those core meanings and values that determine the dominant patterns
of cultural self-understanding I call "Tropes," which are embodied in
Mythoi, symbols, and the spectrum of cultural practices. They function
as dominant modes of cultural self-interpretation. I turn to Royce's
profound theory of interpretation developed in the second part of
The Problem of Christianity, which itself creatively appropriates aspects
of Peirce's semiotic. His ideas of a "community of memory" and a

"community of hope" are important. More attention, however, needs to be given to the problems of the "community of the present," especially in terms of what Royce called our "moral burden" of finitude. Of concern are ways in which cultures transmit patterns of suffering, prejudice, and hate as part of their self-identities. Here I think Dewey and Mead's model of communication as "taking the role of the other" is significant, especially as it may help generate a "community of interpretation" through imagination. I suggest a way of broadening Peirce's concept of abduction to a general semiotic function, a creative search for interpretants. Imagination is taken to mean the disclosure of possibilities. Interpretation is engagement of possibility. The real purpose of philosophy, says Royce, is interpretation, especially interpretation of a culture in light of its possibilities for a genuine community. Not only is philosophy a discipline that should be concerned with culture, requiring imagination as much as reason, but it should ask its practitioners to search for those meanings that may best fulfill the Human Eros. When Eros engages culture as education (itself the dialogue of death and life, of past and future generations), it transforms into care, the selfless giving by the past in the present to the future; that is, Eros becomes *agapē*. In light of this, I conclude with some thoughts on the potential agapic orientation of philosophical hermeneutics. That is, the "spirit" in which we undertake the practice of philosophy, especially in its cultural role, is important for the way philosophy understands itself and the world it seeks to address and create.

The Human Eros

Human existence, I maintain, is driven by a desire, an Eros, to experience life with a sense of meaning and value. Insofar as this arises from our being, we can, with Marcel, call this an "ontological need" for human fulfillment. This is also a biological need, as necessary to our physical existence as air, water, and food. If this need is not fulfilled, we either experience depression or die; otherwise Eros becomes destructive, seeking to annihilate the self or the world that has denied it meaning. This dark face or persona of Eros we may call "Eris," the Greek personification of Strife. Human beings may die with their humanity fully intact; their deaths may even affirm their humanity. But to destroy an individual's or a people's sense of meaningful, value-imbued existence is to undertake the destruction of human *being*. What can destroy our humanity as such, our existence as human beings? History is rich with ingenious examples of ways in which an individual's humanity is taken away and the identity of whole peoples is pushed to the threshold of insignificance. Viktor Frankl articulated this issue in his account of trying to help his fellow concentration camp prisoners live from day to day with a sense of meaning under conditions that were meant to strip away their humanity. He saw that our primary need is to experience meaning and value in our lives, and his form of psychotherapy, based on the search for meaning, was his response.[1]

My second thesis is that culture functions as a spiritual ecology for the Human Eros. Eros weaves about us an environment of meaning and value, of symbols, stories, and customs—that is to say, a world of spirit—by which it sustains itself and meets our ontological need. A spiritual ecology creates an "oikos," a home within which human existence may dwell. Cultures are not just technologies of adaptation; they are ways of consummating Eros itself. It is through culture, then, that human existence inhabits the earth, transforming it into a "home" or world. Different cultures attest to the variety of worlds in which the Human Eros has creatively adapted itself. One basic aim of philosophy should be the study of spiritual ecologies, of how they constitute their worlds, of human inhabitation. That is, philosophy should not *initially* approach cultures with the question "Are these beliefs true?" but instead with "How are these meanings lived?" This philosophical anthropology involves *tropology* (the study of tropes), *symbology* (the study of symbols), and *mythology* (the study of Mythoi). The overall study of how cultures establish homes or spiritual environments of meaning for human existence can be termed "philosophical ecology."

At the outset, a humanistic philosophical ecology must engage in reflection upon Eros itself, undertaking a study of the different personae

---

1. Viktor Frankl, *Man's Seach for Meaning*, 3rd edition (New York: Simon & Schuster, 1984). "Man's search for meaning is the primary motivation in his life and not a 'secondary rationalization' of instinctual drives. This meaning is unique and specific in that it must and can be fulfilled by him alone; only then does it achieve a significance which will satisfy his own *will* to meaning" (105). The work of Ernest Becker: *The Denial of Death* (New York: Free Press, 1973), *Escape from Evil* (New York: Free Press, 1985), and *The Birth and Death of Meaning* (New York: Free Press, 1971); and the work of Rollo May: *Love and Will* (New York: Norton, 1969), *The Courage to Create* (New York: Norton, 1975), and *The Cry for Myth* (New York, Norton, 1991), are also pertinent contributions to this thesis. See also "The Human Eros," chapter 5 in this volume.

of Eros in culture. A study of Eris would involve exploring the ways in which Eros is denied to individuals, classes, or whole peoples.[2] Other faces of Eros relevant for a philosophy of culture would be (1) modes of generating and sustaining orders of meaning (Cosmogenic Eros), (2) the irruption of a transformational presence, often an Other, that lays a claim upon our lives[3] (Epiphantic Eros), (3) creative action (Poietic Eros), and (4) self-giving care for the other (Agapic Eros).

COSMOGENIC EROS

This is the drive toward the creation and maintenance of orderly worlds of meaning and value that constitute a world for inhabitation. Hesiod's *Theogony* makes Eros, "most beautiful of the gods," among the first gods to emerge from Chaos. Eros was a condition for further creation that culminates in the proportioned, balanced cosmos perfected and ruled by Zeus. This type of Eros is manifest in the establishment and development of basic forms that constitute cultural order, which can range from rituals and ceremonies to laws to a native language itself. For example, the care for and development of the English language that we see in writers, poets, and teachers, for example, serves Cosmogenic Eros. It is a force in the psychogenesis of each of us. At birth we are in a state very much like that of Hesiod's Chaos, a storm of organic needs and blind powers that step-by-step grow into an articulate and self-governed conscious human being. We *experience* the genesis of a living cosmos in ourselves. This can become the basis of an ongoing desire for learning, inquiry, and creation. Here is the origin of truth in Aristotle's claim that all human beings have a natural desire to comprehend. Life here has a cosmogenic orientation.

EPIPHANTIC EROS

Whereas the cosmogenic world seeks to *establish order*, epiphantic Eros is *transformative of self and world*. It bursts into our world, shatters and reconstitutes it by its undeniable claim on us; it is a disclosure whose

---

2. See *Facing Evil*, ed. Paul Woodruff and Harry A. Wilmer (Chicago: Open Court, 1988).

3. While romantic love is a dominant example, so would be the irruption of beauty, a religious manifestation of the divine (for example, the "voice of God" telling Moses to return to Egypt), the encounter with a discipline of knowledge, creation or action that changes one's life, and so on.

radiance opens our own being up entirely so that the self undergoes transformation. The invasion of beauty changes us. As Aristophanes in the
Symposium says, there is an incompleteness and vulnerability in our existence as an individual ego; what was thought to be a complete self is
shown to have a missing Other. Epiphantic Eros destabilizes our world by
opening us up beyond ourselves to the power of embodied beauty in the
Other so that the self is no longer what it is without the affirmation of
the Other. To say "I" is also to say "Thou." In taking this step, the ego risks
itself, for it beseeches affirmation from the Other as well. This is the familiar form of Eros whose power is the theme of much poetry and literature.

POIETIC EROS

The third persona of Eros, Creative or Poietic Eros, is both *transformative
and orderly*. It undertakes a self-creative task of living through the light of
an adopted ideal and is manifest in various forms of creative living: art,
social reform, science—in short, anything that guides a life creatively. In
the *Symposium*, Diotima tells Socrates that we are all pregnant: we give
birth to the deeds of our lives. It is the variously refracted light of the
Beautiful that draws us on. The self is also transformed by giving itself to
an ideal task, but transformation here is generative of new order and
meaning. To the extent that a culture goes beyond merely providing a
world of ordered meaning, serving Cosmogenic Eros, and nourishing
Poietic Eros, it takes a creative and transformative orientation to its own
order, for ideals open up possibilities and inspire individual commitment
and action so that an individual life becomes interpreted by the ideals to
which it has given itself.

AGAPIC EROS

The act of self-giving opens up the possibility of *agapē*. It may seem contradictory to speak of "Agapic Eros,"[4] but Paul Tillich observes:

> The so-called "types" of love are actually "qualities of love," lying within
> each other and driven into conflict only in their distorted forms.

---

4. Theologians such as Anders Nygren like to contrast the "selfish" love of Eros with the altruistic
love of Christian *agapē*.

No love is real without a unity of *eros* and *agape*. *Agape* without *eros* is obedience to a moral law, without warmth, without longing, without reunion. *Eros* without *agape* is chaotic desire, denying the validity of the claim of the other one as an independent self, able to love and be loved. Love as the unity of *eros* and *agape* is an implication of faith.[5]

Agapic Eros exhibits a steadfast, unconditional love and care for the Other as such, and so it becomes a radical affirmation of the Other, a bestowal of absolute value, a gift by Eros to Eros. This may be limited to one or a few individuals but in its widest forms becomes a love of humanity that seems to come from a transhuman power. As such, it is the love that "bears all things, believes all things, hopes all things, endures all things" (1 Cor. 13:7). Nominally it begins with any love that renders care for the well-being of another. Infants encounter this in the love given by parents, although there is a long journey in psychological growth before it can be given. But it can expand from family to group to humankind. Though there is not self-effacement, there is selfless giving. Teaching, in its deeper aspects, exhibits this sort of giving to the young and to those in ages beyond. *Agapē* as a force in civilization is a progressive transcendence of the finite barriers that mark off a "we group" from a "they group." This is the moral of Jesus's parable of the Good Samaritan in answer to the lawyer's question, "Who is my neighbor?" (Luke 10:29–37).

Such is a sketch of how a philosophy of culture might begin to treat the primary subject of Eros itself in terms of the spiritual ecologies whereby human existence inhabits the world. It is meaning more than truth that is at issue. In that light, we may now turn to some basic ways in which cultures establish and sustain their ecologies of meaning.

"Mythos" and Other Terms for Philosophical Anthropology

MYTHOS

One primary way in which we gain a sense of a meaningful self and world is through stories; the world is narratively given to us, since we are *told*

---

5. Paul Tillich, *Dynamics of Faith* (New York: Harper and Row, 1957), 114–15. See Douglas Morgan, *Love: Plato, The Bible, and Freud* (Englewood Cliffs, NJ: Prentice Hall, 1964).

the stories of the world, our family, and ourselves before we tell them. Not only from infancy on do we learn the world through stories, but there are also special, highly important stories that we repeatedly use to define who we are and explain why we value or believe what we do. There are stories we are commonly told as children to help us understand the culture group, the "we" with whom we are to identify. There are personal stories that we treat as constitutive of the meaning of who we are as individuals—stories that constitute the "I." The formation of a sense of identity and world through story can apply to the individual, a group, a culture or a whole civilization. "Mythos" is the term I have proposed to denote such constitutive core narratives. Mythos does not mean a "false story" but one that serves this end of *determining the meaning of a self, a group or the world.*

For example, in attempting to explain to someone "who we Americans are," any number of "mythic" stories could be used: the discovery of the New World, the Plymouth Colony, the Revolution, and so on. How these stories are told affects the sense of meaning of the identity of the self and culture. Philosophers pass on the "story of philosophy" in the same way, using certain figures in determining its core meaning.[6] Not long ago, Anglo-American philosophers told the story of "philosophy" so that Heidegger was "not a philosopher." We have certain Mythoi that we use to tell others and ourselves to reveal who we are. Mythoi can have degrees of importance. They may be bland stories about where one grew up or extremely personal, even painful accounts of transformative events in one's life. The more important Mythoi are those that constitute the inner core identity both of world and self. When these are threatened, Eros very quickly can transform into Eris. If, for example, one learned that she had been adopted or that one's beloved father was an officer in a death camp, it could cause a crisis in self-identity and the meaning of one's world. Likewise, when the idealized meanings of people who have come to have mythic importance for a culture, such as Thomas Jefferson or Martin Luther King, Jr., are critically questioned or drastically modified a crisis

---

6. The ways in which philosophy mythically constructs its own past while remaining oblivious to its own mythic creation would be an illuminating study, especially as different traditions focus on different mythic philosophers: Nietzsche, Wittgenstein, Heidegger, etc.

in meaning can follow. The intensity of emotion such challenges provoke indicates the depth at which some sense of the meaning of self and world is at issue. The information is not received as an interesting new fact but as a threat. The sensitivity of the meaning of these figures and the Mythoi that surround them testify to their symbolic importance in sustaining a way of inhabiting the world. The point is that Mythoi serve the Human Eros in all its personae, and one area of a philosophy of culture would be "Philosophical Mythology" undertaken in this sense.

TROPES

Cultural symbol systems tend to be organized around core ideas and values; these are central in defining the cultural self and world and may be embodied in a variety of ways, but especially in Mythoi. These generic, central, cultural themes, ideas, and values may be called "Tropes." For example, "Virtue/Excellence" (ἀρετή) and "Reason/Proportion" (λόγος) are key tropes in classical Greek culture; "God" (elohim, YHWH), "Covenant" (berit), and "Law/Teaching" (Torah) are key tropes in the Hebrew world. Greek and Hebrew culture embody these tropes again and again in a variety of ways to reaffirm the meaning of their worlds and their own self-understanding. In American culture, "Freedom" is one such trope, and it would be embodied in Mythoi like the ones mentioned as well as in symbolic images, movies, advertisements and so on.

SYMBOL AND AVATAR

Tropes have a deep, archetypal and general character that allows them to be variously evoked. The range of types that tropes may adopt as vehicles of expression are a kind of symbol: tropic symbols. A trope may be evoked through a number of such symbolic types. A deep cultural trope (e.g., Freedom) is rendered determinate by a range of forms that constitute a symbolic syntax. Different cultures may share the trope of "the Hero," but the range of determinate forms that trope takes on will vary greatly from culture to culture (e.g., Odysseus, Moses, Rama). Symbols themselves must be concretely embodied to function as living incarnations of cultural meaning.[7] Such concrete embodiments or incarnations can be called "*avatars.*" Tropic symbols mediate the trope and its avatars. Thus "Freedom" is a trope of American culture; "The Cowboy" is one of the ways the trope is symbolized. But "The Cowboy" remains an abstract type until it is brought to life in a Mythos that gives it concrete embodiment and becomes an avatar, such as John Wayne's portrayal of Hondo Lane in *Hondo!* or of Tom Doniphon in *The Man Who Shot Liberty Valance.* Avatars vivify the symbol as an object of attention for cultural self-understanding. A range of symbols grounded in the same trope allows for a deep sense of world meaning to be experienced by the members of the culture.

CONSTELLATIONS

Some tropes are closely related, inhabiting proximate regions or clusters of mutual cultural reference. These relations may be harmonious but may also have tension or conflict. Such clusters of tropes can be called "*constellations.*" For example, the trope of "Freedom" in American culture is closely related to that of "Individualism" as well as to that of "Equality under the Law." The tension and ambiguities in their relationships are often the subject of much cultural self-interpretation. Indeed, one of the cultural functions of art and philosophy is to explore just such tensive relationships. The celebration of freedom as being "free of the law" leads to the hero avatars of the "rugged individualist" who doesn't play by the rules (e.g., Harrison Ford as Indiana Jones or, once again, John Wayne's characters) or who is set outside of the law (such as the namesake hero of *Shane*) or is an outlaw in fact (e.g., Paul Newman's character of Luke in *Cool Hand Luke*). Avatars of freedom as "rule of law" show up iconically in images of "the Founding Fathers," the Constitutional Convention or the Constitution itself, in police dramas, or in heroic

---

7. With Peirce, I take a symbol to be a general way of interpretation—that is, a way of organizing the world through a meaningful set of responses or habits that have a rulelike aspect. But symbols, like habits, are best understood when they are creative or developing and not when they have been degraded to the level of automatic responses. In *Metaphor and Reality* (Bloomington: Indiana University Press, 1962), Philip Wheelwright has argued for the "tensive" nature of vital symbols in contrast to "steno signals" that operate at the level of automatic responses. Art and religion cultivate vital symbols because they invoke the attention and cooperation of the beholder and so come to enliven his or her experience with meaning.

defenders of the law (c.g., Gary Cooper in *High Noon*) or justice (like Gregory Peck as Atticus Finch in *To Kill a Mockingbird*). The tension between individualism, freedom, and rule of law evokes creative and reflective endeavors in making sense of this tropic constellation of Individuality-Freedom-Law.

For example: John Ford's movie *The Man Who Shot Liberty Valance* is a complex exploration of all these core tropes of American culture, their relationships, and their tensions. John Wayne's character, Tom Doniphon, and Lee Marvin's character, Liberty Valance, are both "individualists," but Doniphon has a code of morals, embodying the harmonious relation of Individuality and Freedom, whereas Liberty Valance does not, and so he represents the danger of "Freedom Outside the Law." Jimmy Stewart as Ransom Stoddard, the "dude" lawyer from the East, represents the Rule of Law. At first, he is distanced from the trope of Individualism, but ultimately is strongly connected with it.[8] The movie mythically embodies a range of American tropes ("Progress" and "The Frontier"). Its central Mythos is the passing of the West, interpreted as the passing of lawless individualism, in which manliness could flourish, for the tamed world of safety under the law. Wayne's character is the willing sacrifice by letting Ransom take the credit for killing Valance as well as breaking the "code of the West" by which he has lived.[9]

Sophocles' *Antigone* explores a similar conflict in Greek culture, the relation of "polis" and "piety," with the connected tropic virtues, or lack thereof, in Self-Knowledge (Creon, who commits *hubris*) and Self-Control (Antigone, whose impulsiveness ends her life before she can be rescued). The Book of Job is an agonized attempt, or series of attempts, to reconcile the tropes of "God" and "Justice," which had been brought together into a constellation through the interpretation of the Mythos of the Exodus by the prophets, God ceasing to be merely a tribal god of power to become a universal one of goodness. Likewise the Hindu Bhagavad Gita is an

---

8. Ford's own recognition of the "mythic" quality of the story is reflected, for example, in the names "Liberty Valance" (which echoes the word "violence") and "Ransom Stoddard" ("Ransom" playing on Stewart's character as a willing sacrifice; "Stoddard," an old Puritan name, reflects his high moral code). The "neutrality" of Wayne's character's name puts him in between the tension embodied in the relation of Liberty Valance and Ransom Stoddard. But throughout, the movie clearly indicates that it is telling a Great American Mythos.

9. The code of the West is that a man fights his own battles and does so without committing murder by stealth. In shooting Valance, Doniphon breaks the code by which he has lived—in order to save the Mythos that good will prevail over evil.

extended effort to explore and harmonize the tension between the moral code of society, to perform one's *dharma*, or inherited duty, and so risk acquiring *karma*, and to achieve spiritual liberation, *mokṣa*, through renunciation.[10] Chinese culture had to negotiate a tensive relationship between the Confucian trope of achieving The Way (*Dao*) through Social Ritual (*li*) and education and the Daoist trope of achieving the Way through Spontaneity (*zuran*).

Thus, a philosophy of culture would involve a study of Mythoi, tropes, constellations of tropes, symbols, and avatars. It would discern patterns of cultural interpretation that could, in turn, thereby become the object of critical reflection. The point, though, is that philosophy would not occupy some neutral, mythic-free standpoint. Philosophy embodies Mythoi or it would not be significant. The question is how *consciously* this is done. Positivism, for example, embodied the Mythos of Scientific Progress and narrated the role of the philosopher as a logical technician in service to that end; it did this dogmatically and resisted fervently alternative concepts of philosophy, rejecting even recognizing them as "philosophy" since they threatened its own Mythos.

The Community of Interpretation

Cultures as spiritual ecologies are living systems. For understanding the dynamics of meaning in a community as a living process, Josiah Royce's *The Problem of Christianity* is important, not least for its application of the semiotic of Charles Peirce.[11] Royce makes a number of important claims. The first set has to do with his understanding of the community: (1) the community is a "time process," involving a "community of memory" and a "community of hope"; (2) the community is a community of interpretation, semiotically construed; and (3) the present moment is a

---

10. The hero, Arjuna, though fighting in a "just war," will be engaged in fighting those to whom he owes reverence and honor—relatives and teachers—and even in fulfilling his *dharma* as warrior, threatens the whole order of society—for war leads to orphans and widows, loose morals, and the mixing up of the *varnas* or fundamental divisions of society; i.e., the castes. See Bhagavad Gita, First Teaching.

11. Josiah Royce, *The Problem of Christianity* (Chicago: University of Chicago Press, 1968, introduction by John Smith; originally published 1914). Hereafter cited in the text as PC.

moment of decision.[12] Royce adds to these: (4) insistence upon the radical temporalism of Peirce's semiotic; that is, the *formal* nature of the sign relation (object-sign-interpretant) is an *inherently temporal process*; and (5) the claim that philosophy is interpretation. Interpretation, says Royce, "takes us at once into the very heart of philosophy," and indeed "Interpretation is . . . the main business of philosophy" (PC, 274, 297).[13] Finally, (6) Royce connects interpretation with the ontology of human existence in terms of our inherent communal being, the inescapability of our "moral burden"—which today would be called "finitude"—and the possibility of atonement as commitment or "loyalty" to a redemptive ideal of an integrated humanity, "the Beloved Community." His analysis of these themes as they bear on "the problem of Christianity" in the first part of the book leads to a general theory of "the community of interpretation," and it is to that I now turn.

However irreducible our individuality may be, it exists within a living community that is itself the inheritor of a shared past, just as the individual self at any given moment is the inheritor of a personal history: "A self is, by its very essence, a being with a past" (PC, 244). So is a community, whose "conscious history, real or ideal, is part of its very essence" (PC, 243). The past is not simply the causal condition of the present, but is appropriated as *a remembered history that is owned*. It is adopted as Mythos and functions as one interpretive horizon constituting the present. The other interpretive horizon is that of the future, not just as

12. The analysis of the finite community of the present is the least developed part of Royce's position, but I believe an important supplement can be made by using the model of communication developed by John Dewey and George Herbert Mead, emphasizing the idea of "taking the role of the other." The role of imagination becomes crucial here. The fundamental problem for interpretation and communication is the disclosure of possibility. Imagination is precisely this—the disclosure of possibilities. I suggest an enlargement of Peirce's concept of abduction as a general semiotic principle, the imaginative search for possible interpretants.

13. This challenges the dominant conception of philosophy insofar as the "problem of knowledge" has commanded the center stage for so long. (And, even here, isn't it odd that all the attention we devote to "the problem of knowledge" is exclusively concerned with *knowledge of objects*? What about *knowledge of the Other*, knowledge as an *I-Thou* rather than *I-It* relation: intimate, concrete, emotional, personal knowledge, as in "Adam knew Eve"? See the classic discussion in Martin Buber's *I and Thou*, 2nd ed., trans. Ronald Gregor Smith [New York: Scribner, 1958]).The investigation of the implications for these epistemologies would involve a comparison and contrast of the Greek idea of *epistēmē* with that of the Hebrew idea of *da'at*. For the latter, see Hosea 6:6, wherein Hosea says on God's behalf, "For I desire steadfast love and not sacrifice, the knowledge [*da'at*] of God, rather than burnt offerings." That Anglo-American philosophy's paradigm of knowledge is of impersonal rather than personal knowledge speaks volumes about its unquestioned presuppositions.

what may be but what is *anticipated* or foreseen in some degree; it is present as the horizon of possibility and hope appropriated as *"our hope."*[14] Individuals who appropriate a common history *as theirs* belong to "a community of memory." Royce uses the example of the Maoris, who express kinship by naming the canoe in which their tribal ancestor arrived, *"I* came over in the canoe Tai-Nui" (PC, 246).

Insofar as individuals appropriate *as theirs* an anticipated future, they can be said to belong to a "community of expectation" or "a community of hope" (PC, 248). In my terminology, the primary ways in which the community of memory or the community of hope are appropriated are through Mythoi. Royce stresses the act of ownership with respect to both horizons: a certain history is *mine* and a certain hope or desire is *mine*; if you share them, they are *ours* and that makes us a *we*. Royce holds that the self can be "ideally extended" (PC, 252–53; see 264ff.). It is not necessarily the *actual* history or the future that constitutes a community; it is the past-as-interpreted and the future-as-interpreted that are the basis for our personal and communal identities. This capacity of the self to extend its identity in time determines the self it is: "The present self, the fleeting individual of to-day, is a mere gesticulation of a self. The genuine person lives in the far-off past and future as well as in the present. It is, then, the ideally extended self that is worthy to belong to a significant community" (PC, 255). "The time-process, and the ideal extensions of the self in this time-process, lie at the basis of the whole theory of the community" (PC, 268). This is crucial for understanding the function of philosophy, which must undertake to ponder the meaning of cultural history and to articulate what might be a common hope, an ideal that ultimately for Royce is to interpret the present finite community in terms of the ideal, universal "Beloved Community" (PC, 267ff.).

Thus a community is deeply constituted in the present by its *mythic* memory of the past and the *mythic* hope of the future, and these together provide a basis for understanding the present as a *communal present* that carries with it disclosure of possibilities. That is, the horizons of memory and hope are mediated by cultural tropes, symbols, avatars, and Mythoi so as to determine what possibilities we see and what they mean. Not only do Mythoi function to maintain the sense of identity in the community,

---

14. The idea of "Jerusalem" as a national hope or "Roma" as a national destiny may be examples.

but so do the repeated embodiments or avatars of key tropic symbols in the culture. Avatars of tropic symbols appear in Mythoi that serve to disclose the trope; this gives them their deep significance and power to command attention. Avatars by virtue of their concreteness have the ability actually or existentially to remind a community or reinforce its awareness of what makes it a community—what gives structure to the world that is an ecology for the Human Eros. They focus conscious attention upon the Mythos, symbol and trope. This is especially evident in communities engaged in war or undergoing crisis.[15]

Royce says little about the "community of the present," which for him seems to be essentially one of cooperation, given his example of two men rowing a boat (PC, 327ff.; see 263ff.). But it is exactly here that certain questions may be posed. Cultural Mythoi serve to provide a collective sense of the "we" of a community, but also thereby to mark out those who are "not us," that is, "They." These are deep boundaries and we cannot just "will" our self-identity to transcend them to embrace a universal humanity.[16] Royce sees our failure to overcome a limited concept of community as an indication of our "moral burden," that is, sin. In fact, we cannot overcome finitude on our own. Royce is willing to see our capacity for self-transcending love (or loyalty) as a form of grace (PC, 269).

Aside from the problem of how we may "extend the self," there is also a problem with the appropriation of the "moral burden" of the past. This involves an inheritance of pain, resentment, prejudice, and vengeance. The stories of old sufferings and injustices perpetrated on "us" by "them" in the past are transmitted to newer generations and constitute part of the community of memory: "You did this to my people." In our desire to grow up and be members of a community, which the Human Eros needs, we become vehicles for perpetuation of ignorant prejudice, bigotry, resentment, and active hate as well. In struggling to become a member of a community in the present, I inherit the We/They structures of the past.

---

15. See the studies by Garry Wills on the mythic, constitutive power of the Declaration of Independence and Lincoln's Gettysburg Address: *Inventing America* (Garden City, NY: Doubleday, 1978) and *Lincoln at Gettysburg* (New York: Simon & Schuster, 1992).

16. Jesus's complex use of parables to get people to see the Other as Us illustrates the difficulty; to illustrate the law of the Torah to "love thy neighbor," he tells a story in which a Samaritan—a contemptible outcast, a pollution to the purity of the law—is in fact the one who embodies the Law in his concern for the other, an unknown person belonging to a culture that despises him. Similarly, at John 8, Jesus breaks down the "otherness" of the woman taken in adultery.

This is what could legitimately be called our original sin, for it is there waiting for us when we are born. But I think it is better to call this transmission of suffering "karmic inheritance." It is one of the problems to be addressed by a philosophy of culture. Insofar as the disclosure of possibilities in the present is conditioned by the community of memory, it is subject to the limitations of the structure of the past as well.

Royce applied Peirce's triadic analysis of the semiotic process to the problem of cultural interpretation. The problem of meaning is not just one of passing from concept to percept. "Each of us," says Royce, "in every new effort to communicate with our fellow-men, stands, like the traveler crossing the boundary of a new country, in the presence of a largely strange world of perceptions and of conceptions" (PC, 283). And this is true, too, for self-understanding; we are constantly haunted by the risk of misunderstanding. "In our inner life it not infrequently happens that we have—like the traveler, or like Hamlet in the ghost-scene, or like Macbeth when there comes the knocking on the gate—to pass a boundary, to cross into some new realm, not merely of experience, but of desire, of hope, or of resolve" (PC, 285). This is not a question of determining whether our old ideas "work" or not, for "our situation is rather this: that *both* our ideas and our experiences . . . both our ideas with their 'leadings' and our intuitions are in the process of dramatic transformation. At such times we need to know, like Nebuchadnezzar, both our dream and its interpretation" (PC, 285). Interpretation is an ordered triadic relation; Royce illustrates this with the example of an Egyptian text (the object), the Egyptologist translating it into English (the sign) and the "possible English reader" (the interpretant), (PC, 286).[17] In Peirce's terms these would be object, sign (or representamen), and interpretant, an irreducible semiotic structure, with the interpretant itself becoming a sign calling for a further interpretant and so on. This applies to the process of self-interpretation, as Peirce showed in his 1868 critique of Descartes, "Questions Concerning Certain Faculties Claimed for Man."

17. The translator is a "sign" in Peirce's sense of trying to get a reader of English to stand in the same relation to the object, the hieroglyphics, as he himself does. See CP 2:227–33, 274. The Egyptian text itself functions as a sign for an Interpretant (one who can read hieroglyphics) with regard to an object, e.g., a prayer to a god. The English translation might be an object in the text of a scholar (sign) using it to argue for a theory of Egyptian religion (interpretant), and so on. Peirce does not equate interpreters with interpretants; they are one class of interpretants. Royce, with his emphasis upon the issue of community, does not get involved with this further distinction.

While the triadic sign-structure is often taken formally, Royce firmly grasps the irreducible temporality of Peirce's object-sign-interpretant relation. In fact, he sees this semiotic structure as perhaps the fundamental nature of time itself, the present "presenting" itself as a sign for a possible interpretant, a possible meaning, with reference to the past (see PC, 288). *The semiotic triad is an irreducible temporal relationship.* Moreover, interpretation is fundamentally a *social* temporal process (PC, 290). The temporal structure of the semiotic self is what might be called an existential ontology: The past-as-interpreted is that which I cannot change; the future is where I may yet act; and so the present is the moment of decision whereby I choose which future shall stand as the meaning of myself (PC 293, see 160ff.). This is an existential ontology of a social rather than individual kind, since this meaning is ultimately determined by the *community.* Over against the "sterile" world of conception and the "desolate wilderness of perceptions where neither God nor man exists," interpretation "seeks an object which is essentially spiritual. . . . [I]nterpretation seeks a city out of sight, the homeland where, perchance, we learn to understand one another" (PC, 291). Interpretation presupposes that we "acknowledge the being and inner life of our fellow men," reveals how "selves and communities may exist," and "touches the heart of reality"; "it is the process in which you engage whenever you take counsel with a friend, or look in the eyes of one beloved, or serve the cause of your life" (PC, 294–95). This last is an absolutely crucial point: The ultimate *hope* of interpretation is where the Other, grasped now partially and through a glass darkly, stands before us, and we to her, face to face. Thus the ultimate ideal hope of interpretation is love; for Royce, this requires grace, which he describes as the ability to "fall in love with the universe" (PC, 270). Thus the present is *existentially* encountered as a process of social semiosis engaging the ontological modalities of actuality *and* possibility, facticity *and* creative freedom.

Semiosis reveals another significant aspect of human ontology: its inherently social nature. Royce says, "I can only be saved by the community" (PC, 357). In other words, the *meaning* of my "self" only arises and exists within a community of interpretation, even if I come to rebel against it. In realizing my own unique individuality, I do so by my "will to interpret"; my future self will be the interpretant of the present one and its history, and the meaning of my actions will be signs calling for an interpretant. Because of its capacity to disclose relations, interpretation can establish continuity, which in the human context means overcoming alienation to some degree; in interpreting each other we seek a community wherein we shall have truly understood each other. "Whatever else men need, they need communities of interpretation" (PC, 318). The primary function of philosophy, the humanities, and the arts is to interpret the community so that past, present, and future have depth of meaning and it has greater self-understanding (PC, 333ff.). Royce points to the prophet Amos: There was a conflict between the need for justice and a religion that had become focused on Temple ritual. Amos speaks on behalf of the "idea of God who, as he declared, delights not in sacrifices but in righteousness" (PC, 307). Out of cultural strife, interpretation holds out the hope of redemptive understanding. It can reveal the possibilities of a culture for moral growth and deeper values and meanings, thereby extending it as a home for the Human Eros. The problem of the community of the present is to discern those possibilities: That is a problem of *social* imagination. Royce has little to say about this, but I think Dewey's and Mead's model of communication may be of help and may also suggest a way in which the "we/they" dichotomy may be overcome.

Imagining the Other and Creative Understanding

In *Experience and Nature*, Dewey analyzes meaning in terms of the communicative process. George Herbert Mead developed these ideas in the lectures published as *Mind, Self, and Society*.[18] Dewey observes that with the emergence of communication human beings can be *guided* by symbolic intelligence and no longer just pushed along by organic and physical forces (LW, 1:132). Communication as a *process* is at the heart of meaning for both thinkers. Language may be analyzed as a formal, structural system; it is nevertheless essential to affirm that its temporal, dialogical dimension is primary. This is a dimension, moreover, in which a *hearer* is required as much as any speaker. In other words, "dialogical

---

18. *Mind, Self and Society*, ed. Charles Morris (Chicago: University of Chicago Press, 1934), hereafter cited in the text as MSS. The theory really should be called the "Dewey-Mead Theory of Meaning" insofar as both men were mutually influential, Dewey both working out the basic model of learning behavior (in "The Reflex Arc Concept in Psychology," 1896) and then expanding it to social interaction mediated by symbols or gestures. Mead made numerous refinements and developments of this general thesis.

space" precedes "logical space," and part of this space is the receptive, interpretive disposition without which speech is impossible.[19]

The key idea used by both Dewey and Mead is that of "taking the role of the other."[20] Initially this requires that one be able to respond to a sign or gesture in the same way that the other does, and so the gesture becomes a "significant symbol" (see MSS, 65–75). This also is the genesis of our "self" insofar as we may come to see ourselves from the standpoint of others. Mead says, "We are more or less unconsciously seeing ourselves as others see us. We are unconsciously addressing ourselves as others address us" (MSS, 68). To use Dewey's own homely example of one person asking another to bring him a flower, the one making the request must first imaginatively take the standpoint of the person whom he will address in order to assess how his signs or gestures are *likely* to be interpreted. He must imagine how he would act were someone to make the same gesture. He tests his responses to a possible range of gestures or symbols and this allows him to select those that are most likely to represent his intended meaning. If you are playing with a small child, you must try to imagine what it is like to be a small child so that gestures meant as play do not frighten the child instead. Thus, the responses of the other are interpreted as indicating communication, misunderstanding, or complete failure. By taking the role of the other, both sympathy and self-criticism become possible.

Note that this process is compatible with Peirce's understanding of semiosis. In fact, Peirce's triadic analysis of meaning is actually very illuminating precisely at this point. The "sign" is the gesture that I will use to communicate my intention; the intended meaning is the object (such as the desire to play catch). And I take on the role of the Other in a moment of pure imaginative abduction to function as the interpretant of the sign I am contemplating using. Formulated as a problem, the question is, "Which sign would most likely convey my desire to play catch?" or "Does this sign put the other in the same relation to my intention as I stand myself?" In trying to take the child's point of view I can search

19. It is more than odd how in all the decades philosophy has devoted to theories of meaning, theories of listening have been almost completely ignored.

20. A point minimized by Charles Morris; see *Signs, Language, and Behavior* (New York: Prentice Hall, 1946), 45. Dewey is careful to emphasize the importance of listening (and apparently was himself quite a good listener). Receptivity is of course a key theme in hermeneutics, especially in Gadamer.

abductively, experimenting in imagination with what likely interpretations would result from certain gestures or actions on my part, and so
I select that which most accurately and effectively expresses my meaning.
It may be that, taking on in imagination what I think a young child might
experience, the gestures or signs I had thought would express my intention in fact might easily indicate something else. This works equally well
in looking at the process of artistic creation: The artist takes on the role of
a possible interpretant in order to assess the meaning of the gestures in
paint or music and whether they effectively express the aesthetic object
that is being created.[21] This is clearly a semiotic process though the signs
involved are often nonlinguistic. In this way I can be the interpretant of
myself in generating an expressive act. That I project abductively a hypothetical self—that of the potential interpretant of my gesture—accounts
for how I may be *surprised* when, instead of being correctly understood,
clearly I am not. In this way cooperative behavior and the "conversation
of gestures" may arise.

So far we still have only a condition for communication; genuine communication involves something more, which Dewey and Mead neglect
and Royce does not. Insofar as *one* person only is taking the standpoint of
the other, we may have simply a situation which aims at manipulative
control. Even if we both take the role of the other, if an "I-It" relationship
holds there is only mutual manipulation, not genuine communication.
But when the other *also* takes the "standpoint of the other," a mutual,
shared, participatory dialogical space is established, which makes it possible for *both* members to try to see *themselves* from the standpoint of the
other, *and it is thereby possible for each to grasp that they are both doing
this.* When the person with whom I am attempting to communicate
grasps not only the meaning indicated by my gestures, but *the fact that I
am trying to communicate*, the situation *may* cease to be one of manipulation on my part. Not only may the Other become a "Thou" to my "I" (and
my "I" changes in being genuinely related to a "Thou"), but both become
a "We." At most Dewey vaguely indicates this with his stress on "participation." Communication emerges when both are imaginatively taking
on the role of the other while aware that *the other realizes this as well.*

21. See Mead, in MSS, 147f.

The dialogical space becomes a mutual exploration of possibilities. We can call this "mutual imaginative alterity."[22]

The imaginative leap to the Other and our combined recognition of the fact in communication becomes a mutual "will-to-interpret," a "community of interpretation" (PC, 314ff.). We both wish to understand and be understood. We can only do this together, each "I" depending on each "Thou." The "We" comes about when each member is not just "taking the role of the other," but is "taking on the role of the conversation" as a teleological process. The goal is to overcome "my narrowness and your estrangement," that is to say, alienation (PC, 314). Our loyalty to the process of communication, in Roycean language, is also a loyalty to this ideal, however vague, and this operates as a shared imaginative standpoint, a shared interpretant. The acts of mutual interpretation are thoroughly triadic, as Royce insists (PC, 315–17). What I am emphasizing is the mutual commitment—call it "loyalty"—to a creative process of communication in which we acknowledge each other's participation.[23] Thus, while the Dewey-Mead model of communication significantly enriches the concept of interpretation, Royce's idea of a community of interpretation significantly points to something beyond the ideal of cooperation.

22. I hazard that it is through the elementary play of gestures between adult and infant that we come gradually to grasp the idea of possibility as such. Language, as a system, is itself a cultural mode of *existence* that allows us to explore possibilities of meaning and action. But it is important to note that "Language" is only theoretically a "system"; it *develops in each of us* in the play of gestures that leads us from infancy into self-awareness. This *is language itself*, however formally or systematically it may be analyzed. This is an ontological, not a psychological, claim: *Language originates in our learning language.* One of the dangers of formal logic has been the illusion that the "essence" of language or reason is a static, thoroughly rule-governed, narrationless system. I am proposing not only that the dialogical nature of communication is at the heart of meaning, but that its genesis in every human as the dialogue of parent and infant is as well. See the profound study by Daniel Stern, *The Interpersonal World of the Infant* (New York: Basic Books, 1985), esp. 173–74, which discusses an extended study involving dialogue between a parent and infant at bedtime. Stern draws the following conclusion: "Language, then, provides a new way of being related to others (who may be present or absent) by sharing personal world knowledge with them, coming together in the domain of verbal relatedness.... But language is not primarily another means of individuation, nor is it primarily another means for creating togetherness. It is rather the means for achieving the next developmental level of relatedness, in which existential life issues will be played out. The advent of language ultimately brings about the ability to narrate one's own life story with the potential that holds for changing how one views oneself. The making of narrative is not the same as any other kind of thinking or talking. It appears to involve a different mode of thought from problem solving or pure description. It involves thinking in terms of persons who act as agents with intentions and goals that unfold in some causal sequence with a beginning, middle, and end."

23. This standpoint is somewhat different from Mead's notion of the "generalized other," which is the internalized organization of the whole community, or at least those involved in the same process (MSS, 154).

In taking the role of the Other, the possibility for a community of interpretation comes to be.

Teleology and Imagination

There is a transactional model of teleology—let us call it "conversational teleology"—that is an alternative to the Aristotelian model of a predetermined, fixed end and that does not revert to a mechanist, cybernetic model. Look at the structure of conversation. Conversations are neither predetermined nor purely random; they operate within contexts of meaningful possibilities. At any given moment, certain possible responses and not others can make sense in varying degrees with very different meanings that will interpret the unfolding sense of the conversation and affect what possibilities will make sense in the immediate future. Order *emerges* from the process, but it will be unpredictable. Retrospectively, at any moment a coherent narrative of the development can be given. When misunderstandings occur, the participants usually begin by retracing the path of the dialogue to find the point at which they diverged. The transactional or conversational model offers a creative, developmental, evolutionary concept of order.

Chess offers an example. When the pieces are set up there are billions of possible games (purely random series of moves do not count as a game). The range of White's initial moves is limited to the knights and pawns, as is Black's first response. Not all openings are equally reasonable, nor are all the possible replies. As the game progresses new possibilities and patterns of meaning open up. Chess (and other games) are just a highly formalized adaptation of the human experience of conversational teleology. What this model illustrates, however, has metaphysical importance: There is a highly intelligible way of thinking of teleology as an interactive process without fixed ends that exhibits meaningful order at each stage with creative possibilities for further meaning. The telos is the contextual development of the process in a meaningful way. Such a model of "conversational teleology" can be applied to a general "ecological semiotics." Ecosystems as a whole, their developments, and the behavior of their various populations can be understood this way. Organisms, species, and populations can be regarded as being in conversation with the environment and each other.

Creativity is a function of disclosure of possibilities that are capable of developing long-term patterns of growth. In the case of human beings, we can designate the disclosure of possibility as the nature of imagination itself. In this sense imagination is essential for intelligence and reason because they depend on disclosure of possibilities. Instead of contrasting reason with imagination, we need to contrast a limited disclosure of possibilities to that of a rich disclosure: Imagination is a search for meaning. Once again, Peirce's idea of abduction is of importance. Peirce described abduction primarily as a capacity for "the operation of adopting an explanatory hypothesis" that would make sense out of puzzling aspects of the world. That is, he treats it as a phase of inquiry. But it is also at work in ordinary perception. He says, for example, that "the abductive faculty, whereby we divine the secrets of nature, is, as we may say, a shading off, a gradation of that which in its higher perfection we call perception."[24] Ordinary perception involves a degree of abductive inference insofar as we cognize or interpret something *as* being what we take it to be. But abduction does not have to be limited to cognitive inquiry. Douglas Anderson has shown that abduction can be equally well applied to the artistic process (including God as creator). Science aims at "reasonable ideas" that stand in an "analogical" relationship to their objects, as a map corresponds with a given territory; art aims at "reasonable feelings" that are "about" a new quality that is "essentially metaphorical in character."[25] A metaphor "is what it represents . . . by virtue of a similarity which it creates" (CPCSP, 73). Though the artist deals with feelings more than with ideas, she still "hypothesizes" possible ways of producing something that, according to Anderson, "tentatively settles the artist's unsettled feeling" that marked the urge to create (CPCSP, 64). In this way, "artistic abduction is a semiotic process, as is scientific inquiry" (CPCSP, 65).

This recognition of the role of abduction in artistic creativity points to a broader, more fundamental interpretive function: abduction as the semiotic process of the search for the interpretant. Abduction is part of the way we make sense of the world. The forms it takes in science or art

24. *The Essential Peirce*, Vol. 2, ed. The Peirce Edition Project (Indianapolis: Indiana University Press, 1998), 224 (Sixth Harvard Lecture, 1903); see also the Seventh Harvard Lecture, "Pragmatism as the Logic of Abduction," 226ff.
25. Douglas R. Anderson, *Creativity and the Philosophy of C. S. Peirce* (The Hague: Martinus Nijhoff, 1986), 6off., 68; see 113. Hereafter cited in text as CPCSP.

can be viewed as refined developments of this basic semiotic function: the projection of possible interpretants to make sense of signs. First of all, abduction is the ability to treat something *as if it were a sign*, a possible meaning that "calls" for an interpretant. The first abductive leap is to interpret something, anything, *as* a sign; once we learn to do this, it rapidly becomes a generalized habit.[26] Then it is an *imaginative search* to discern possible meanings of a sign by experimenting with alternative interpretants. It is an effort to discover the "difference that makes a difference," in Gregory Bateson's phrase.[27] Our basic perception is an interpretation of the world, taking things *as something*; it is largely unreflective because the interpretive habits that come into play are so fixed and automatic. Ecological psychologist J. J. Gibson uses the term "affordance" to describe the ways in which an environment fits the needs of a species.[28] Thus at a very basic level animals are seeking "the difference that makes a difference" that signifies an affordance. Every time we are brought up short by something not being what it seemed, we see the effect of a tacit abductive habit being suddenly frustrated. When experience becomes routine, we lose awareness of alternative possibilities of meaning. This is why both scientists and artists develop techniques for reengaging the "surprise of the world," that is, to cease taking the ordinary interpretive

26. One very dramatic instance of this is the well-known story Helen Keller, blind and deaf, tells in her autobiography, *The Story of My Life*, of the day she realized that the movements of her teacher's fingers were letters spelling out the word "w-a-t-e-r"; that is, she realized what *language* was.

27. Gregory Bateson, *Mind and Nature* (New York: Dutton, 1979), 99; *Steps to an Ecology of Mind* (New York: Ballantine Books, 1972), 271–72. Bateson explains this essentially in cybernetic terms (see "Cybernetic Explanation" in *Steps*). This is what for him constitutes a "bit" of information; it is essentially the exclusion of other meaningful possibilities (such as the color of a stoplight being green rather than red or yellow). I am not making the claim that Peirce's semiotic can or should be reduced to a cybernetic model. Quite the contrary. The cybernetic model seems to collapse into a series of dyadic relationships (Bateson's metaphors are mostly mechanistic—he was vastly impressed by James Watts's invention of a steam engine with a "governor," a mechanism for homeostatic self-regulation, and James Clerk Maxwell's mathematical analysis of it sixty years later. See *Mind and Nature*, 103ff.) What I mean to indicate is that in "taking" something *as a sign*, the interpretant is *designating a difference that "makes a difference"*; i.e., a possible determination of meaning, a "hypothesis," if you will, as to the nature and function of something *as a sign*. In a foreign country, I see an unfamiliar road sign and guess at its meaning, or perhaps there is a sign by the road that may or may not be a "road sign," and that would be the first question of what the "difference that made a difference" was.

28. James J. Gibson, *An Ecological Approach to Visual Perception* (Boston: Houghton Mifflin, 1980), 132. An "affordance" is a "fit" between organism and environment, but the affordance must be identified as such by the organism, and this would be by detecting the "difference that makes a difference."

habits we have developed as final or ultimate. Thus both scientific and artistic abduction rely on a more basic semiotic imagination.

Cultures are transmitted dispositions of interpretation; they provide ranges of common interpretants. A rattlesnake in the Southwest will mean different things to a Christian or a Pueblo Indian: To one it may be a symbol of evil, to the other a blessing promising rain; for both the response may be instantaneous and emotional. To a herpetologist, it may rationally signify something about the desert ecosystem. The snake is a sign in all three approaches, but the difference in the interpretant determines a difference in the meaning the sign carries. So in an individual's experience, the more possible interpretants one may project for the snake, the more the range of alternative meanings opens up. To grasp these meanings one develops more complex responses to the possible meanings of the world. Abduction depends to a great extent upon cultural symbol systems as ready-to-hand interpretations of the world. The more the creative exploration of possibilities is developed, the more complex and reflective our responses may be and the more diversely we may be able to interpret a present situation.

Imagination is not simply an individual process, but a social and cultural one. Abduction can be understood as a process of social imagination in terms of the dialogue of a community of interpretation (especially a community of inquiry) that develops along the lines of a conversational teleology. Creative cultural interaction may disclose more meaningful ways of development. This is where Royce's view of philosophy as cultural interpretation becomes highly relevant. Philosophy as a practice of cultural interpretation is inherently abductive and so imaginative; it is the search for meaning consciously undertaken. Reflecting on the past as a community of memory, oriented toward the future as a community of hope and engaged with the dialogic space of the community of the present—this I take to be the nature of philosophy as cultural humanism.

From Eros to Agapē

Royce emphasized the inherently temporal nature of Peirce's analysis of semiosis, that the present takes the past and addresses itself to a future interpretant to give meaning to present action. I have characterized culture as a task of Eros, the creation of a spiritual ecology within which human existence may experience meaning and value. Cultures provide worlds that pass on to new generations structured ways of making sense of existence, relying not merely on formal systems of symbols but upon what I have called Mythoi and tropes. These are ways in which individuals and groups come to have a cosmos of common reference, a world, and a sense of self-identity. I noted that in generating the sense of "we" there is also the generation of "they," a division that easily may threaten Eros and transform it into Eris, becoming fear, suspicion and hate. Royce's application of Peirce's semiotic to the problem of community as a time process provides a model of cultural process in which the abductive search for meaning is central. The Dewey-Mead model of communication enhances our understanding of the dynamics of the community of the present as an opening dialogic space through imagination, establishing a mutual alterity that gives rise to a community of interpretation. In this way the Other can become a Thou and we become a "We." From this comes a generative, creative order, a "conversational teleology." Here, Peirce's idea of abduction might be broadened to be a general semiotic function, the search for the interpretant. Royce sees the central mission of philosophy to be interpretation, and this aims at establishing a community of interpretation operating by its own ideal, which Royce calls "the Beloved Community" and which in my terminology would be characterized as a world in which the Human Eros is sustained and nourished. In other words, philosophy is a humanistic endeavor to take the past and address it to a future so that the present may be illumined by meaningful ideals, lures for Eros. Humanistic philosophy does not operate in a neutral void. It accepts its role of cultural interpretation that searches for the fulfillment of Eros through the development of meaningful order. When the community of interpretation understands itself in light of the Beloved Community we discern how Eros is transformed into *agapē*.

While culture may be analyzed structurally in a synchronic way, ontologically it is temporal: culture is a process of transmission through time. To be a learner and a teacher is fundamental to our human being. We have language and culture because we were taught as infants; language comes to each of us, every member of the species, as a *learning of language*. That is an ontological claim. To say "mother tongue" is to glimpse this truth. At some point when we are infants, gestures, cries, objects cease being mere responses or stimuli and become symbols. The first lesson in semiotics we learn is reading facial expressions. We gradually learn to "play the game" of taking the role of the other and realizing the other is doing the same. The "acquisition of language," so marginalized as a "psychological question" by philosophers of language, is in fact *how language exists*—in each of us and down through the centuries. The being of language arises in being learned and taught. As we become fluent members of the culture, we can in turn pass it on. The function of culture as transmission has a deeper dimension; it is ultimately a dialogue between death and life. As Dewey observes at the beginning of *Democracy and Education*, all the members of any community are fated to die, and if they died all at once, their culture would be extinguished. But because they do not, culture can be passed on through time. Education exists because of death. Teaching is not just one career option among many. *It goes to the root of what we are.*

Cultures are inherited patterns for the possibility of meaning. While they transmit these possibilities as a gift to the future generations, cultures nonetheless bear the burden of finitude, for the possibilities of one culture may not translate meaningfully into those of another. Indeed, here one is very much like Royce's individual at a boundary in need of interpretation. Moreover, to be raised as fluent in one culture is thereby not to be raised in others. Finitude is also present in the way cultures build upon the "We-They" dichotomy. By articulating constellations of tropes through Mythoi and symbols, cultures weave spiritual ecologies for the Human Eros. But these ecologies may be mysterious or threatening to each other. When a spiritual ecology is threatened, Eros itself easily becomes Eris, and the cooperative forces that had gone to create a world of reasonableness and meaning become violent, hate-filled and destructive beyond measure.

A further burden of culture, in addition to the danger of being a prisoner of its own history in terms of the limits of its interpretive range and its divisions of the world into "we" and "they," is that, in ordering its world, it imposes suffering more upon some than upon other members of the community. The fulfillment of Eros for some comes by its denial to others. The privileged Eros often develops ways in which to make the suffering of others invisible or seeks to justify visible suffering through Mythoi. The idea in Hinduism of an individual being fated to belong to a certain caste or *jati* (occupational subcaste), is an example: better to do one's own dharma badly than do someone else's dharma well, says the Bhagavad Gita.

Finally there is the finitude of "karmic inheritance" that lies in the community of memory. Cultural memory is often filled with the sufferings or injustices of the past and these aspects of culture are transmitted to new generations along with everything else. As Royce says, we can extend our sense of self to identify with past events; so we may come to hate "them" as our ancestors hated "them." The victims of history have no hope for direct redemption—we cannot undo the history of slavery or the Native American genocide, and nothing the living can do will erase what happened and give those victims new life. But to be forgotten is the final violence done to victims of history; our memory is the only redemption they will have. So here is the paradox of the community of memory: One must remember pain and suffering, but in doing so one may perpetuate pain and suffering. To generate more pain and pass along karmic history is not a redemption of the past either. However much one may idealize a "Beloved Community," the problem of our existence is finitude and tragic ignorance. Thus I think the communities of interpretation, like philosophers, who are mindful transmitters of culture, must remember the victims of history from a standpoint of compassionate insight and in the light of tragic wisdom that teaches us our own finitude. It is only by insight into the nature and manner of transmission of suffering in all its forms that a community may find release from those forces. Here the memory of the suffering of history is of immense value as long as it is done for the end of greater compassion and love.

The problem of the community of the present is to engage these issues, to take up the burden of the past and carry its meaning toward some better world in which the blindness and hate of the past are no more. The concern for this future is self-transcending; in passing along the meaning of culture we are giving to a future that we shall not have. To be able to give in the spirit of other-oriented creative care is the transformation of Eros into *agapē*. Thus, the standpoint of philosophy as interpretation is to seek those interpretants that remember and release us from the pain of the past, foster insight and compassion, admonish with tragic wisdom, and above all undertake the ontological task of establishing what we do as a gift to the future in the name of love.

Terminology for a Philosophical Anthropology

The Human Eros: The fundamental desire in human existence is to experience the world (including oneself in it) with an embodied sense of

meaning and value. To negate this negates human *being*. Four faces of
Eros are as follows:

Cosmogenic Eros: The desire to generate and inhabit ordered worlds
of meaning.

Epiphantic Eros: Eros that is self-transformative through encounter
with an Other.

Poietic Eros: Eros that is creative of new meaning.

Agapic Eros: Eros that is creative of meaning for others.

Eris: Eros denied turns into a destructive power that rages against
what denies meaning to one's being or, when turned inward, becomes
the negation of oneself.

Spiritual ecology: The symbolic environment or "world" that a cultural symbol system creates for a particular dwelling of the Human Eros.
It is culture considered as a way of sustaining an aesthetics of human
existence. A particular cultural world may be designated as an "oikos," or
"home," for the Human Eros.

Inhabitation: The fulfillment of the Human Eros is through culture-
in-nature, so that a vital ecology of meaning, an oikos, is maintained.

Oikos: The inclusive term for a "home" or pervasive way of inhabitation; that is, a "way of life," a *world*, a spiritual environment of meaning
and value inhabited by the Human Eros; for example, "the Greek world,"
"the World of Hinduism." In syncretic civilizations, different worlds
may coexist, so that the "Hindu world" and the "Jain world" may be
part of "the world of India." Worlds may be transhistorical and trans-
national, "the World of Judaism." Worlds are interconnected through
Mythoi.

Trope: An archetypal core meaning or value that a culture uses to
understand itself and, therefore, needs exemplification. A trope avails
itself of any number of *tropic types* or various intermediary forms that
become recurrent cultural themes at a certain generic level; e.g., The
Cowboy, The Rebel, The Patriot, etc. may all be types relating to the trope
of Freedom. Tropic types are a general language of tropes that must be
further specified.

Avatar: A vital embodiment, incarnation, or enactment of a trope or
tropic type that renews the Human Eros in terms of locating a significant
part of the spiritual ecology. It is one way a trope can be concretely

embodied and so function as regenerative of meaning. There may be degrees of symbolic exemplification and degrees of the importance of the tropes exemplified. The trope of "Freedom" may be embodied in a movie character, an advertisement, the Statue of Liberty, the Constitution, etc. All these are avatars. If The Cowboy is a type of the trope of Freedom, then John Ford's movie *The Man Who Shot Liberty Valance* is an avatar, as is John Wayne's character, Tom Doniphon.

Constellation: A closely related web or cluster of tropes that have a high degree of *relevance* toward each other. These are groups of interconnected core meanings; e.g., in Greek culture: *aretē*, hubris, *dikē*, self-control, measure, proportion, etc.; in American culture: individualism, freedom, economic "happiness," progress, etc. The dominant constellations that characterize a culture's way of expressing itself for the sake of fulfilling the Human Eros can be characterized as a *cultural persona*.

Mythos: A symbolic structure that provides a key element in creating and preserving a sense of self and world, the meanings that define existence. Cultures have Mythoi, but so do groups within a culture and particular individuals. A Mythos is not a "myth" (a false story) but an *important* story or symbolic structure. It conveys a fundamental sense of existential truth, a truth in the sense in which a personal story about one's past is regarded as "existentially true" and not just as factually true. Tribal myths and rituals are archaic forms of Mythoi—there is something of the sacred in their presence. The structure may be narrative but need not be. The structure of a temple may also be a Mythos. Philosophical systems are Mythoi.

Sign: An element of a semiotic system that yields itself to a variety of syntactical relationships so that the system can selectively be adapted to a variety of contexts to make sense of them. Specifically, a "sign" is a semiotic relationship wherein one element (often itself called "the sign") stands for some object to some possible or actual interpretant. Relationality is essential to a sign (C. S. Peirce). Signs may become progressively rich and become symbols just as symbols may become gradually emptied of incarnate meaning and function as "signs" in the sense of being mere indicators of their meaning, e.g., names and other denotative functions, connotative functions, directive and practical functions, etc.

Symbol: A type of sign with habits as interpretants (Peirce, CP 2.295) standing in a relationship to its object or referent (what it is "about"). Symbols must have a degree of detachment from their referents, but this "symbolic space" can range from extreme externality (in which the symbol functions purely denotatively) to extreme internality (in which the symbol and its meaning become almost indiscernibly fused). The more "external" the meaning is, the less important is the material medium of the symbol itself; it needs only to be correctly identified. The more "internal" the meaning is, the more important the materiality of the symbol becomes, so as to "house" the meaning (e.g., a work of art is "about" itself). Susanne K. Langer's "discursive/presentational" distinction of symbols should be thought of as extremes of a continuum, not as a dichotomy, and symbols themselves may move back and forth upon it. Symbols constitute the worlds of meaning inhabited by human beings and so are modes of our being. Cultures are dynamic systems of such worlds.

Community of interpretation: The dynamic, shared form in which culture exists as a process of meaning ("spirit") and in which we come to have a self at all.

> **Community of memory:** The past-as-interpreted for determining who "we" are; that is, the mythic past.
>
> **Community of hope:** The future-as-interpreted for determining who "we" are; that is, the mythic future.
>
> **Community of the present:** A disclosure of possibilities for cooperative action; the meaningful possibilities of the present as opportunities for existential decision; that is, the mythic present.
>
> **Moral burden:** The finitude of any "we" in a community of the present that demarcates itself from a "them."

Conversational teleology: A form of open-ended teleology that exhibits rational growth: At any given instant in the process of interpretation a range of meaningful possibilities is present in varying degrees of coherence and creativeness. As certain of these possibilities are selected, further ranges of possibilities are disclosed, and so on. Prospectively the outcome is not strictly predictable, but retrospectively a meaningful, coherent history is revealed.

Bibliographic Essay on Resources for Native American Thought

The literature concerning Native North American worldviews and religious attitudes is immense and overwhelming. The purpose of this analytical bibliography is to highlight those titles which may be of use to those who wish to incorporate Native American ideas into their existing courses on American philosophy or who wish to begin the long, fascinating exploration of this field on their own. I will not pretend that I have a command of this literature. My primary aim is simply to help others get started as best I can. Thus I have generally tried to identify works that are accessible to the amateur and that are or recently were in print.

General Surveys

The most important recent survey of Native American thought is *American Indian Thought: Philosophical Essays*, ed. Anne Waters (Oxford: Blackwell, 2004), which not only has many essays by Native Americans but is edited by a Native American philosopher. Leonard Harris, Soctt L. Pratt, and Anne Waters have edited an anthology of American philosophy that includes Native American material, *American Philosophies: An Anthology* (Wiley-Blackwell, 2001). Hartley Burr Alexander wrote two important volumes for the "Mythology of All Races" series that survey North American and Latin American mythologies (Volumes X and XI). Though dated, these still offer one of the best resources for gaining some sense of the diversity encompassed by the rubric "American Indian worldviews." His later interpretive work, *The World's Rim*, examines a range of Native North American rituals as offering insights into a philosophical outlook. It was his contention that human understanding proceeded from the lived body and articulated itself symbolically outward. Unfortunately, this work, in paperback for many years, has fallen out of print. For mythology, see John Bierhorst's *The Mythology of North America* (Oxford, 2002), the most comprehensive survey now available. For regional and symbolic analysis, see Ake Hultkrantz's *The Religions of the American Indians* (University of California Press, 1967), a lucid analysis by an important anthropologist, ranging from Mayan to Woodlands cultures and addressing such important topical issues as shamanism. Two other books can be mentioned as providing helpful overviews. Denise and John Carmody's *Native American Religions* (Paulist Press, 1993) is likewise a useful survey, embracing South as well as Meso- and North America, with an extensive bibliography. The book is intended as a school text (study questions are included) and has something of a religious orientation. See also Sam D. Gill's *Native American Religions* (Wadsworth, 1982). Two important essays by Marilyn Holly can be recommended: "A Chorus of Powers" (in *The Mystical Chorus*; Millennium Books [Australia], 1995) is a very helpful overview of Native American beliefs. This easily could be incorporated as a basic text for any survey of American philosophy that wished to use some native material. Also see Holly's article "The Incorporation of American Indian Philosophy into Undergraduate Philosophy Courses," *Teaching Philosophy* 15:4 (1992), 349–64. The anthology edited by Dennis and Barbara Tedlock, *Teachings from the American Earth* (Liveright, 1975), is an excellent collection of primary and interpretive essays focusing on general concepts, such as the Hopi concept of time or Ojibwa ways of categorizing persons, or shamanistic practices of curing and obtaining visions. This work is intended as a sourcebook for anthropologists more than philosophers. On a more popular level, the collection *I Become Part of It*, edited by D. M. Dooling and Paul Jordon-Smith (HarperCollins, 1992), presents an appealing, highly readable array of traditional myths and contemporary essays by both Native American and non-Native American writers. The materials come from *Parabola*, a journal of myth and tradition. In many respects, the materials gathered here indicate the living vitality of Native American culture. While the Tedlock and Tedlock book might function better as an upper-level or reference text, the Dooling and Jordon-Smith book would perhaps be better for lower-level courses. *The Portable North American Indian Reader*, ed. Frederick W. Turner (Penguin, 1972), attempts the impossible in one fat little volume, embracing writings from traditional and contemporary Native American cultures, and is best treated as a good, if dated, "sampler." Joseph Epes Brown's collection of essays, *The*

Spiritual Legacy of the American Indian (Crossroad, 1993), is also an excellent candidate for use as a text in a survey of American philosophy. Brown, inspired by John Neihardt's classic *Black Elk Speaks*, sought out and worked with the Lakota holy man Black Elk in the 1940s to help him transcribe *The Sacred Pipe*. His essays included in this slim volume are sensitive and insightful, though they tend to focus on Plains Indian culture. The title essay, "The Spiritual Legacy of the American Indian," has also been independently published as a pamphlet by Pendle Hill. Should a single, limited text be wanted for a course, this monograph alone would make a good choice. Unfortunately, the fact that there are two books in print with the same title by the same author can make textbook-ordering chancy. One of the most handy general reference sources is *Atlas of the North American Indian* (Facts on File, 1985) by Carl Waldman.

Pan-Indianism

Vine Deloria Jr.'s *God Is Red*, Second Edition (Fulcrum, 1993) offers a special problem. This is one of the few attempts made by a Native American writer to define a native theological outlook. The book has, furthermore, been extensively revised since its first appearance in the 1970s. It contains many valuable contrasts between what Deloria considers to be Native American and Judeo-Christian spirituality, such as the contrast between a religion based on the idea of sacred space and one based on the idea of sacred time. Unfortunately, in my view, the book achieves these dramatic contrasts by caricaturing "Western" as well as "pan-Indian" themes. Pan-Indianism is a sensitive topic. Many Native Americans are attempting to discern a common identity. This is especially important to those who have lost much of their own tribal traditions, including, perhaps, even their original language. The danger lies in reading the experience of other native peoples either through the eyes of a particular regional culture or, worse, appropriating the romanticized view of "Indians" offered by the Rousseauian vein of Western culture. *God Is Red* falls into the first camp. The attempt, however, to define "pan-Indianism" is a philosophical issue, and Deloria often has highly provocative insights. (For example, he notes that the Judeo-Christian tradition, based on a historical sense of time and a sacred text, has sought to control the interpretation of history by texts rather than to control sacred places; it is typical of Deloria that in making this comment, true enough in itself, he ignores the history of attempts to control the Holy Land.) The book is further marred by its eccentric scholarship (the works of Immanuel Velikovsky are defended) and its shrill, cranky tone. See the review by J. Douglas Rabb, *Transactions of the Charles S. Peirce Society*, Summer 1995, Vol. XXXI, No. 3, pp. 681–96. *Indian from the Inside* (Lakehead University, 1993) by Dennis J. McPherson and Douglas Rabb is a far more successful attempt, relying here on the worldview of the Ojibwa for its insights into what constitutes an "Indian" philosophy. Scott L. Pratt's *Native Pragmatism: Rethinking the Roots of American Philosophy* (Indiana University Press, 2002) argues for the influence of Iroquois ideas on colonial American intellectual figures and so, eventually, on pragmatists. While I find the claims tenuous, the subject matter is worth exploring.

Regional Studies

Perhaps more appropriate than attempts to make hasty claims about pan-Indian culture would be to gain a sense of the cultural outlooks dominant in some of the specific Native North American lifeways. Ten major regional divisions are commonly discerned among Native North American cultures: Arctic, Subarctic (Eastern and Western), Northeast Woodlands, Southeast, Plains, Southwest, Great Basin, Plateau, California, and Northwest Coast. Common geography and cultural contact led to a similarity in lifeways, though even here highly important differences can be detected, as for example the settled, communal, agricultural lives of the Pueblo Indians and the once semi-nomadic, isolated, herding lives of the Navajos. I cannot include studies for each of these major areas here but will instead focus on a selected few that I have found helpful in gaining a deeper sense of the worldview shared over a limited region. For the Northeast Woodlands, I recommend Elisabeth Tooker's *Native North American Spirituality of the Eastern Woodlands* (Paulist Press, 1979). This book examines cosmology, visionary dreams, and ceremonies, focusing on Winnebago, Iroquois, Menominee, Delaware, and Fox tribes, among others. (Unfortunately, Tooker takes a rather idiosyncratic reading of the central idea of *orenda* or sacred power; see the discussion by Marilyn Holly in "A Chorus of Powers," cited above.) There is a companion volume, *Native Meso-American Spirituality*, by the noted Aztec scholar Leon Portilla, in the same series ("Classics of Western Spirituality"). See also the major study by Thomas V. Overholt and

J. Baird Callicott, *Clothed-in-Fur and Other Tales: An Introduction to an Ojibwa World View* (University Press of America, 1982). Arthur Parker's *Seneca Myths and Folktales* (1923; University of Nebraska Press, 1989) has valuable discussions as well as an impressive collection of Seneca-Iroquois myths. Basil Johnston's *Ojibway Heritage* (University of Nebraska Press, 1976) is a fine account of this Algonquian tribe's mythology. Hamilton Tyler's *Pueblo Gods and Myths* (University of Oklahoma Press, 1964) is a very good survey of Pueblo religion and worldviews. Alfonso Ortiz's *The Tewa World* (University of Chicago Press, 1969) is a classic in structuralist anthropology written by a Tewa. Frank Waters and a Hopi, Oswald White Bear Fredericks, co-authored *The Book of the Hopi* (Viking, 1963), a tribal telling of the creation story, myths, rituals, and history of the Hopi as understood by themselves today. *Zuni* (University of Nebraska Press, 1979) is an important collection of writings by Frank Hamilton Cushing, edited by Jesse Green. Cushing lived among the Zuni in the 1880s, was initiated into the Bowpriesthood, and wrote extensively on these people. The most important philosophical exposition of Navajo worldview I have found is *The Main Stalk: A Synthesis of Navajo Philosophy* by John R. Farella (University of Arizona, 1984). See also Trudy Griffin-Pierce, *Earth Is My Mother, Sky Is My Father: Space, Time and Astronomy in Navajo Sandpainting* (University of New Mexico, 1992). *The Navaho* by Clyde Kluckhohn (Harvard University Press, 1948) is an introductory cultural survey of this tribe. The culture of the once nomadic and semi-nomadic peoples of the Plains has received extensive treatment. Perhaps the most famous account is *Black Elk Speaks* (1923; University of Nebraska, 1979) by John Neihardt and Black Elk. Some contemporary criticism has qualified the romantic emphasis of this book, but it remains a powerful visionary work. *Lame Deer: Seeker of Visions* (Simon and Schuster, 1972) by John (Fire) Lame Deer and Richard Erdoes is more contemporary. A brief rendition of Lakota mythology can be found in *The Sons of the Wind* (HarperCollins, 1992), edited by D. M. Dooling. *The Sacred Pipe* (University of Oklahoma Press, 1953) by Joseph Epes Brown and Black Elk is a good account of major Lakota ceremonies and their religious significance. A major in-depth study is James Walker's *Lakota Belief and Ritual* (University of Nebraska, 1991). I highly recommend the important study by Howard Harrod, *Renewing the World: Plains Indian Religion and Mortality* (University of Arizona Press, 1987). A recent attempt to expand this culture's worldview philosophically is Robert Bunge's *An American*

Urphilosophie, unfortunately now out of print. Mention should be made here of Vine Deloria Jr.'s own attempt to articulate the philosophical implications of the Plains worldview, *The Metaphysics of Existence* (Harper & Row, 1979). For non-Siouan peoples, see George Grinnell's classic studies *Pawnee Hero Stories and Folk-Tales* (University of Nebraska Press, 1961) and *The Cheyenne Indians* (University of Nebraska Press, 1972). There are several other major cultural regions: Californian, Northwest, Subarctic, and Southeastern. Much space cannot be devoted to these here, though some attention to the rich Northwest fishing cultures or the Five Civilized Tribes of the Southeast would be recommended to gain further sense of the immense diversity embraced by the term "Native North American." For the Southeast, see James Mooney's study *History, Myths and Sacred Formulas of the Cherokees* (Bright Mountain Books, 1992), a reprint of an important nineteenth-century study. A recent survey and discussion of Southeastern myths is *Native American Legends* (August House, 1987), edited by George E. Langford. A more contemporary, interpretive account can be found in Marilou Awiakta's *Selu: Seeking the Corn-Mother's Wisdom* (Fulcrum, 1993), a mythic/poetic reflection by a Cherokee writer. For the Northwest and central Northwest, see Ella Clark's *Indian Legends from the Northern Rockies* (University of Oklahoma, 1966) and *Indian Legends of the Pacific Northwest* (University of Oklahoma, 1953). A good rendition of the Raven cycle is *The Raven Steals the Light* by Bill Reid and Robert Bringhurst (Douglas & MacIntyre, 1984), a collection of Haida myths.

Anthologies of Myths

The term "myth" covers a range of stories, sacred to profane, which at times can seem completely opaque to someone outside the culture or which can suddenly illuminate a whole dimension of human understanding. *American Indian Myths and Legends*, ed. Richard Erdoes and Alfonso Ortiz (Pantheon, 1984), is one of the best. Alice Marriott and Carol Rachlin have two less cumbersome collections with informative notes: *Plains Indian Mythology* (Meridian, 1985) and *American Indian Mythology* (Thomas Y. Crowell, 1968). Two other fine collections of myths are *The Red Swan* (University of New Mexico Press, 1976), edited by John Bierhorst, and *Voices of the Winds* (Facts on File, 1989), edited by Margot Edmonds and Ella Clark. A small but rich collection can be found in *The Story-Telling Stone* (Dell, 1965) by Susan Feldman. A good collection of

Coyote stories is Barry Lopez's *Giving Birth to Thunder, Sleeping with His Daughter: Coyote Builds North America* (Dell, 1977).

Autobiographies

In addition to the classic *Black Elk Speaks*, several important autobiographies and coauthored autobiographies can be mentioned. Charles Eastman's *The Soul of an Indian* (University of Nebraska, 1911) is a brief, eloquent account of a Lakota. More recent accounts are *Lame Deer: Seeker of Visions*, mentioned above, and *Fools Crow* (University of Nebraska Press, 1979) by Thomas Mails. Another famous classic is *Black Hawk* (University of Illinois Press, 1990), edited by Donald Jackson, which first appeared in 1833 and relates the life of the great Sauk leader. *Sun Chief* (Yale, 1942), edited by Leo Simmons, is the story of a Hopi. *Hosteen Klah* (University of Oklahoma, 1964) by Franc Johnson Newcomb is the story of a Navajo sandpainter and healer. Two books by Native American women are also noteworthy: Wilma Mankiller's *Mankiller* (St. Martin's Press, 1993) and Mary Crow Dog's *Lakota Woman* (Harper, 1990). Mankiller was chief of the Cherokee.

Approaches to Myth

Joseph Campbell and Mircea Eliade have both written valuable interpretive guides to the subject of myth. Campbell's *Myths to Live By* (Penguin, 1972) consists of highly readable essays on various topics, including the importance of myth today. Eliade's many books often repeat his basic insights. I have found *Myth and Reality* (Harper, 1961) and *The Sacred and the Profane* (Harcourt Brace Jovanovich, 1959) both immensely helpful. Campbell's interviews with Bill Moyers, printed as *The Power of Myth* (Doubleday, 1988), are also recommended. Paul Radin's *Primitive Man as a Philosopher* (D. Appelton, 1927; Dover, n.d.), though dated, is still a helpful book. Radin himself did much work with the Ojibwa. An interesting approach that listens to multiple "voices" (mythic, historical, personal) is found in Kiowa writer N. Scott Momaday's *The Way to Rainy Mountain* (University of New Mexico Press, 1976); his collection of outstanding essays, *The Man Made of Words* (St. Martin's Press, 1998), is to be recommended also.

Index

AMERICAN PHILOSOPHY

Douglas R. Anderson and Jude Jones, series editors

Kenneth Laine Ketner, ed., *Peirce and Contemporary Thought: Philosophical Inquiries.*

Max H. Fisch, ed., *Classic American Philosophers: Peirce, James, Royce, Santayana, Dewey, Whitehead, second edition.* Introduction by Nathan Houser.

John E. Smith, *Experience and God, second edition.*

Vincent G. Potter, *Peirce's Philosophical Perspectives.* Edited by Vincent Colapietro.

Richard E. Hart and Douglas R. Anderson, eds., *Philosophy in Experience: American Philosophy in Transition.*

Vincent G. Potter, *Charles S. Peirce: On Norms and Ideals, second edition.* Introduction by Stanley M. Harrison.

Vincent M. Colapietro, ed., *Reason, Experience, and God: John E. Smith in Dialogue.* Introduction by Merold Westphal.

Robert J. O'Connell, S.J., *William James on the Courage to Believe, second edition.*

Elizabeth M. Kraus, *The Metaphysics of Experience: A Companion to Whitehead's "Process and Reality," second edition.* Introduction by Robert C. Neville.

Kenneth Westphal, ed., *Pragmatism, Reason, and Norms: A Realistic Assessment—Essays in Critical Appreciation of Frederick L. Will.*

Beth J. Singer, *Pragmatism, Rights, and Democracy.*

Eugene Fontinell, *Self, God, and Immorality: A Jamesian Investigation.*

Roger Ward, *Conversion in American Philosophy: Exploring the Practice of Transformation.*

Michael Epperson, *Quantum Mechanics and the Philosophy of Alfred North Whitehead.*

Kory Sorrell, *Representative Practices: Peirce, Pragmatism, and Feminist Epistemology.*

Naoko Saito, *The Gleam of Light: Moral Perfectionism and Education in Dewey and Emerson.*

Josiah Royce, *The Basic Writings of Josiah Royce.*

Douglas R. Anderson, *Philosophy Americana: Making Philosophy at Home in American Culture.*

James Campbell and Richard E. Hart, eds., *Experience as Philosophy: On the World of John J. McDermott.*

John J. McDermott, *The Drama of Possibility: Experience as Philosophy of Culture.* Edited by Douglas R. Anderson.

Larry A. Hickman, *Pragmatism as Post-Postmodernism: Lessons from John Dewey.*

Larry A. Hickman, Stefan Neubert, and Kersten Reich, eds., *John Dewey Between Pragmatism and Constructivism.*

Dwayne A. Tunstall, *Yes, But Not Quite: Encountering Josiah Royce's Ethico-Religious Insight.*

Josiah Royce, *Race Questions, Provincialism, and Other American Problems*, expanded edition. Edited by Scott L. Pratt and Shannon Sullivan.

Lara Trout, *The Politics of Survival: Peirce, Affectivity, and Social Criticism.*

John R. Shook and James A. Good, *John Dewey's Philosophy of Spirit, with the 1897 Lecture on Hegel.*

Josiah Warren, *The Practical Anarchist: Writings of Josiah Warren.* Edited and with an Introduction by Crispin Sartwell.

Naoko Saito and Paul Standish, eds., *Stanley Cavell and the Education of Grownups.*

Douglas R. Anderson and Carl R. Hausman, *Conversations on Peirce: Reals and Ideals.*

Rick Anthony Furtak, Jonathan Ellsworth, and James D. Reid, eds., *Thoreau's Importance for Philosophy.*

James M. Albrecht, *Reconstructing Individualism: A Pragmatic Tradition from Emerson to Ellison.*

Mathew A. Foust, *Loyalty to Loyalty: Josiah Royce and the Genuine Moral Life.*

Cornelis de Waal and Krysztof Piotr Skowroński (eds.), *The Normative Thought of Charles S. Peirce.*

Dwayne A. Tunstall, *Doing Philosophy Personally: Thinking about Metaphysics, Theism, and Antiblack Racism.*

Erin McKenna, *Pets, People, and Pragmatism.*

Sami Pihlström, *Pragmatic Pluralism and the Problem of God.*

Thomas M. Alexander, *The Human Eros: Eco-ontology and the Aesthetics of Existence.*

1398434